FOREIGN EXCHANGE FUTURES
A Guide to International Currency Trading

ALLAN M. LOOSIGIAN

FOREIGN EXCHANGE FUTURES
A GUIDE TO INTERNATIONAL CURRENCY TRADING

DOW JONES-IRWIN
Homewood, Illinois 60430

© DOW JONES-IRWIN, 1981

All rights reserved. No part of this publication may be reproduced, stored in a retrieval system, or transmitted, in any form or by any means, electronic, mechanical, photocopying, recording, or otherwise, without the prior written permission of the publisher.

This publication is designed to provide accurate and authoritative information in regard to the subject matter covered. It is sold with the understanding that the publisher is not engaged in rendering legal, accounting, or other professional service. If legal advice or other expert assistance is required, the services of a competent professional person should be sought.

From a Declaration of Principles jointly adopted by a Committee of the American Bar Association and a Committee of Publishers.

ISBN 0-87094-271-9
Library of Congress Catalog Card No. 81–68091
Printed in the United States of America

34567890K87654

Foreword

THE FOREIGN EXCHANGE MARKET grew during the decade of the 1970s into the largest financial market in the world. It also became much more complex. The institution of floating exchange rates signaled the inability of governments to retain their historical control over the marketplace and introduced a different set of rules.

The public needs to know more about this new market. Changing currency values affect everyone who works for, or invests in, a multinational corporation, purchases a foreign-made product, or simply travels abroad. Yet why and how these values change remains a mystery to most people outside the small community of foreign exchange dealers. Allan Loosigian herewith attempts, and to a great extent succeeds, in clarifying this mystery.

This book undertakes to explain the role of currency futures within the broader context of foreign exchange. It provides a theoretical and practical analysis of the use of currency futures for the management of foreign exchange risk as well as trading vehicles for speculation.

Fabian M. Tapia
Senior Vice President
Deak-Perera International
Banking Corporation

Preface

PEOPLE WHO LIVE in New York City are wise not to own an automobile, but if they move to California that's the first thing they should buy. Or so I was told before making such a move some 10 years ago. I also was advised that a European car would provide greater value for my money than an American model, so I took time out during a short vacation abroad to look for a suitable vehicle to take with me to the West Coast. My prudent intention to pick up a no-frills economy model was quickly forgotten, however, when a friend I was visiting in Germany told me that his neighbor had a slightly used Mercedes touring coupe he wanted to sell. We went next door, and my friend's neighbor pulled open his garage door to reveal the most beautiful automobile I had ever seen.

A bargain was quickly struck. The owner was asking 28,000 Deutsche marks. I responded with a bid of 20,000, and we shook hands on 24,000. I agreed to cable the funds back to Germany upon my arrival in California, at which time he would put the car aboard a freighter bound for San Francisco. Our deal was made in August 1969 when the exchange rate was 3.7 Deutsche marks to $1, and I silently congratulated myself for "stealing" what surely would become a classic automobile for the foreign currency equivalent of about $6,500. But by the time I reached the West Coast, the Deutsche mark had been revalued—"marked up," to succumb to an irresistible pun—by 10 percent. That meant that the price in dollars of the DM 24,000 I had agreed to pay for my bargain-basement classic car had risen by nearly $650—which was roughly equivalent in those days to the price of a respectable used VW Beetle, the no-frills utility car I had intended to buy in the first place. Such was my costly initiation into the world of foreign exchange dealing.

Instructive though that experience may have been to me personally, it would hardly qualify as a graduate-level case study in international finance. Still, the difference between my 1969 monetary mishap and present-day foreign exchange losses is mainly one of degree. In 1977, Exxon Corporation had to write off against its worldwide earnings a loss of nearly $250 million from adverse foreign exchange fluctuations. Other multinational companies have suffered sizable if somewhat less staggering losses from foreign exchange. The largest bank failure in U.S. history—the 1974 collapse of the Franklin National Bank—occurred as a result of unsuccessful and unauthorized trading in foreign exchange.

Reports on the price action of the world's major currencies have been upgraded from an inside page of the financial press to prime-time television news coverage. Correspondents interview finance ministers, gathered to grapple with the latest international monetary crisis, in a melodramatic manner that somehow manages to combine the fanfare of a film premiere with the solemnity of a wake. In academe, economics professors devise incredibly complex plans—the more scholarly they are, it seems, the more tedious as well—that propose to save the world by reforming or replacing its monetary system.

Here is yet another book dealing with many of the same topics. In its defense, as well as my own, it doesn't purport to resolve the great monetary issues of the day. That's better left to politicians who would become statesmen and to professors in search of tenure. Though it must address itself to matters of international organization (and, I hope, cooperation) as well as with the theory of foreign exchange, the emphasis of this book is on practice—that of individuals and companies which do business in the international marketplace and seek to limit the exchange risk to which they are normally exposed when they spend, earn, or invest money outside their own country. We also examine the other aspect—critics would say the dark side—of foreign exchange trading: How venturesome persons who may or may not be involved in international trade seek to make speculative profits by correctly forecasting movements in the exchange rates between various currencies. As the title indicates, the focus of this book is on how these goals are pursued via the organized futures markets for foreign currencies, rather than by the interbank forward market in foreign exchange.

Part One of the book surveys the development of foreign exchange dealings from their origins in antiquity to the present day. It draws the distinction between immediate, or spot, and forward rates and describes the mechanics and mathematics of futures trading in foreign currencies. Part Two provides a theoretical and practical analysis of the factors affecting a country's exchange rate vis-à-vis other currencies, particularly its balance of payments, relative inflation rate, and the policies of the central bank and treasury. This part also examines the effects of market psychology, rumor and conjecture on exchange rates, as well as the various techniques that have proven useful in forecasting exchange rates. Part Three focuses on the day-to-day management of exchange rate risk by companies and individuals active in the international arena. It starts with the yardsticks and methods of measuring such risk and then examines the various strategies to hedge against the risk. A closing chapter is devoted to foreign exchange speculation, namely, who should engage in it and how.

I want to repeat the caveat contained in the introduction to my earlier book, *Interest Rate Futures,* to which this is intended as a companion volume: Price change always entails risk. Futures trading, whatever the underlying commodity or purpose, is a risky enterprise under the most favorable circumstances. Exchange rates under the present flexible rate system are in themselves highly volatile. Marry the two, as currency futures do, and you have the potential for inordinate financial loss. So, caution is the most emphatic byword. Futures trading, even for hedging purposes, is likely to prove more detrimental if undertaken haphazardly than not hedging at all. This warning isn't meant to discourage beginning hedgers or speculators, but is simply to stress the importance of careful study and preparation before entering the marketplace.

A final note: No single writer is likely to fill the void in the field of foreign exchange left by the death in 1973 of Paul Einzig. But possibly the best mark of respect by those of us who learned the subject from his many invaluable works would be to follow his example. This book is an attempt to do so.

A.M.L.
Stamford, Connecticut

Acknowledgments

AMONG THE MANY MEMBERS of the foreign exchange fraternity who have aided me in the preparation of this book, I am especially grateful to: Anthony Apuzzo of the U.S. Tobacco Company and Raymond Ruzek of Emery Air Freight for their insights into the management of corporate foreign exchange exposure; Nan Sedergren of the Chicago Board of Trade for her analysis of Class B arbitrage; Leo Melamed of the Dellsher Investment Company and the Chicago Mercantile Exchange for his account of the circumstances leading to the establishment of the International Monetary Market; and David Rossman of the Berliner Handels–und Frankfurter Bank for reading and commenting on various parts of the manuscript in their early stages, and for his ideas regarding econometric modeling approaches to exchange rate forecasting.

Above all, I am greatly indebted to Everett Groseclose of Dow Jones & Company, without whose encouragement and support this volume and the preceding one dealing with interest rate futures might never have seen the light of day.

A.M.L.

Contents

PART ONE: FOREIGN EXCHANGE

1. **The origins and uses of foreign exchange**   3

   The international role. How foreign exchange developed. Theories of foreign exchange. The gold standard. The impact of World War I. Currencies and business.

2. **Creation and demise of the Bretton Woods system**   17

   The issues at Bretton Woods. How the system worked. The role of the U.S. dollar. The beginning of the end. From dollar shortage to dollar glut. Doubts and criticisms. The system starts to come undone. Changing relationships.

3. **The world of floating exchange rates**   33

   The Smithsonian agreement. The float versus fixed-rate debate. The speculation factor. The Laffer-Mundell critique. The European snake. The IMF role fades. The foreign exchange market. Reducing exchange risk. The birth of the IMM.

4. **Spot and forward exchange markets**   51

   The competitive market. The role of arbitrage. Spot market theory. The forward market. Interest rates and foreign exchange. Quoting margins, not prices. Impact of speculation. Pricing and invoicing questions.

5. **The mathematics and mechanics of currency futures trading**   69

   How the futures market differs. From the investor's viewpoint. Prices and values. Margin requirements. The delivery mechanism. Nuts and bolts of trading. Phil Plunger and Dan Decimal.

PART TWO: DETERMINANTS OF FOREIGN EXCHANGE

6. **The balance of payments and how it affects currency values**   89

   The balance of payments. A bevy of balances. The various balances. The adjustment process. The elasticity factor. Liquidity and forward pricing. Four track records. Source materials. Plunger's yen for profit.

7. **Inflation and purchasing power parity** 117

Prices and exchange rates. The nature of inflation. Economic growth versus inflation control. Effects on exchange rates. Transmitting inflation. Focus on OECD nations. Plunger is pound-ed.

8. **Exchange rates and government policy** 139

Econometric modeling. Some general observations. Effect of money-supply growth. The multicountry model. Effect of interest rates. Five case examples. Interest rate parities. Three exchange rates. Central bank intervention. Four intervention strategies. How strategies are picked. Intervention techniques. What makes them so smart?

9. **Expectations, news and rumors: The effects of market psychology** 163

The Eurocurrency market. Significance of Eurocurrency. An important formula. A simulation. A second simulation. Real world is different. Up and down with the pound. Buy the rumor, etc. Attitudes and conventions.

10. **Is forecasting futile?** 181

Tough predictions. Three approaches. Interpretations of forecasting. Who the forecasters are. Forecasters' track records. Value of charting. Basic econometric modeling.

PART THREE: THE FUTURES MARKET FOR FOREIGN EXCHANGE

11. **Futures trading versus the interbank forward market** 209

The differences. How the futures market evolved. Efficiency and lags. Types of arbitrage. Banks' role. Champagne or beer profits?

12. **Foreign exchange exposure—what it is and how it's measured** 225

Three classifications. Translation and transaction risk. Bookkeeping treatments. Translating income. Economic risk. The reporting system. Monitoring economic risk. Time frames and predictions.

13. **Hedging foreign exchange exposure: Options, strategies, and tactics** 243

Fluctuation insurance. Risks and strategies. Hedging with futures. The bratwurst hedge. Translation hedging. Other kinds of hedges. Management tactics. Weighing the alternatives. What does hedging cost? Other considerations.

14. **International money management** 261

Methodology and objectives. Intercurrency transfers. Effect of flexible rates. Reluctant forecasters. Selecting risk-control strategies. More complex strategies. To hedge or not. Tax considerations. Hedging translation exposure. Futures hedge methodology. *FASB 8* controversy. Debating the merits.

15 Speculating in foreign exchange   **281**

The 1976 peso plunge.   The saga of Mr. X.   The trading plan.   Planning with prices.   Technical analysis.   Putting a plan into action.   Spreading approaches.

Appendix A   296

Appendix B   299

Appendix C   305

Index   309

PART ONE

FOREIGN EXCHANGE

Chapter 1

The origins and uses of foreign exchange

AMONG THE POWERS conferred by the Constitution on the Congress of the United States is that of ". . . coin[ing] Money, regulat[ing] the Value thereof, and of foreign Coin. . . ."[1] Whether or not the Founding Fathers deliberately gave the currency clause precedence of place over the power to raise an army and declare war, they were certainly aware of the important role money plays in preserving the national security and well-being.

Just as the quality and size of a country's armed forces determine its stature in the military sphere, the value of its money in relation to other currencies is a measure of its economic power. At times these two vehicles of power thrive together, but equally often one is nurtured at the expense of the other. That's why a guidebook on foreign exchange trading such as this should be as concerned with the distribution of power among the major trading nations as with payments balances, inflation rates and related statistical series. But whether we choose to regard money simply as a means of payment or in the strategic sense as an index of national economic power, it is appropriate to begin such a study by making a distinction

---
[1]Article I, section 8.

between the domestic and international roles of the same currency and by showing how the two, while usually compatible, have been known to work at cross-purposes. Moving from the individual country to the community of nations, the principal theme of our study is the way in which various currencies relate to one another in the world marketplace. These relationships, to oversimplify a bit, collectively comprise the international monetary system.

The international role

It isn't necessary to have a master's degree in economics to be able to distinguish between the several roles of money as a medium of exchange, unit of value, and store of wealth. If we aren't to be restricted to a system of barter, we need money to put a price on goods and services, buy and sell them, and try to stretch what little is left over until our next paycheck.

Money has basically the same uses internationally, except that some adjustments have to be made to get it out of one country and into another in a form that is spendable. It is well and good for Levi Strauss & Co. to sell jeans by the carload to fashion-minded people in Europe, Asia, and elsewhere throughout the world. But when it comes time for the company to replenish its inventory of denim, write paychecks for its workers, and send dividends to the stockholders, the francs, lira, yen, or whatever other currencies the jeans were sold for are of no immediate use at corporate headquarters back in San Francisco. To be spendable at home they must be converted into U.S. dollars in the foreign exchange market. Foreign exchange is the currency of any country other than your own. In Japan, for example, the U.S. dollar is foreign exchange, while in the U.S. the Japanese yen is foreign exchange. For people in Japan and in the United States—or any two countries for that matter—to do business with one another, there has to be a mechanism in place to allow yen to be exchanged for dollars, and vice versa. Otherwise, unless a U.S. company that sells its goods in Japan has reason to spend its yen receipts in that country, they would be about as much use to it as czarist rubles or Confederate dollars.

Until such time—which would appear at this stage to be remote, to say the least—that an effective world government makes some form of international money a workable concept, the national currencies of the major trading nations likely will continue to perform that role collectively, undergoing a mutation each time goods, services, or capital flow from one country to another. Buyers and sellers tend to do business with one another when it's mutually advantageous to do so. These advantages, which usually are what the buyer considers to be the optimum combination of price, quality, and speed of delivery, are sought whether the transaction occurs within or across a country's borders. Bulk goods, for example, enjoy a substantial cost advantage when they're produced in a country where the going wage for unskilled labor is the equivalent of 10 cents an hour. But with luxury or high-fashion items, where cachet and snob appeal are the primary attractions, a high price doesn't seem to be a deterrent. On the contrary, it may even provide a greater inducement to buy.[2]

Opportunities for trade arise wherever such differentials are to be found. Simple barter—I'll trade you 4 chickens for 2 cooking pots and 10 handsful of corn—was the original means of exchange when people first discovered the economic advantages to be gained from work specialization and commerce. The limitations of this cumbersome method soon became apparent, however, especially where goods had to be transported over long distances to a common site to be swapped. To make life easier for everyone, gold and silver—which already were prized for their intrinsic value by the beginning of recorded history—became widely accepted mediums of exchange (i.e., money), first as bullion and later in coins.

How foreign exchange developed

The history of foreign exchange began when the coins minted by one sovereign were first offered in payment within the realm of another, raising the question of precisely how much they were worth in terms of sovereign 2's coinage. It was no coincidence, therefore, that goldsmiths were the first bankers and moneychangers from antiquity through the Middle Ages. In fact, for centuries after paper money became accepted legal tender within the commercially developing countries of Europe, metal coins continued to serve as the principal means of exchange between them because of the difficulties encountered in determining the comparative value of notes issued by a foreign entity. The gold or silver content of coins at least could be measured.

Foreign coins were in widespread circulation throughout the Roman Empire, especially in those provinces neighboring their country of origin. When the occupying legions marched into a newly conquered province, official moneychangers called *argentarii* followed in their train, setting up shop to exchange Roman coins for those of that province. The argentarii did double duty as bullion dealers, a logical service since most foreign coins would be accepted only on the basis of their metallic content rather than at their face value. Consequently, the profession of moneychanger required a high degree of skill in weighing and assaying coins to determine their metallic worth. It was not until coins came to be quoted and accepted on the basis of their face value that we can begin to speak of a foreign exchange market in the sense that we know it today.

---

[2]The illustration of the exported Levis cited above appears to fall into this category. Only American-made jeans, it seems, suitably fit the tastes and figures of their worldwide clientele

As with the early reluctance to accept paper money in international dealings, during unsettled times all coins became suspect and dealing reverted to the practice of weighing and assaying for bullion content. The problem of debased coinage became acute during the declining years of the Roman Empire when the later emperors—not unlike some modern statesmen—deliberately depreciated the currency to serve their own personal or political ends, and Roman coins weren't accepted at their face value outside the empire. At the high mark of its development, however, the Roman age could boast a system of foreign exchange to rival that of a much later period. Residents of one country could buy from, or sell to, those of another. There were commercial channels to make capital transfers of various kinds between countries and even opportunities to engage in rudimentary forms of speculation and arbitrage between domestic and foreign currencies. As occurred in all spheres of learning and accomplishment, the demise of the classical world and the onset of the Dark Ages brought a prolonged hiatus in the development of foreign exchange practices and even a regression to the earlier stages of barter and bullion transfer. When the advancement of commercial activity had resumed by the 11th century, its center shifted to the northern Italian city-states, which had assumed the leadership of international trade, hence of foreign exchange dealings, in the early Middle Ages. The word *banker* is itself derived from the outdoor benches (*banca*) upon which money changers in Genoa, Venice, and other centers conducted their business.

By the 13th century, bills of exchange had superseded gold and silver coins as the principal medium of foreign exchange. These instruments usually related to a particular commercial transaction and were drawn on a party in the trading partner's country (drawee), who was obliged to redeem the bill in his own currency. Not only was it easier, faster, and more economical to deliver such instruments by courier than to dispatch a shipment of coin and bullion under heavy guard, but there was substantially less risk of loss by theft because the bills in their earliest form were usually nonnegotiable.

The use of bills of exchange was spurred by a loophole in the medieval usury laws of the Church, which overlooked a domestic loan disguised as a foreign transaction, and the interest on it concealed as a fictitious exchange rate. This masquerade was carried so far that facilities were created at provincial trade fairs where the bogus bills supposedly were payable, when in fact they were simply returned to the maker for redemption in their original currency at face value plus the agreed interest charge.

Just as money changing and bullion dealing were related businesses during the earlier period, physical trade and foreign exchange transactions had become so intertwined by the 16th century that it was difficult to draw a dividing line between merchants and bankers. Thus emerged an elite fraternity of businessmen who called themselves, reasonably enough, merchant bankers.

Theories of foreign exchange

The development of a formalized theory of foreign exchange didn't gain momentum until the late 17th century. Previously, whatever academic work had been pursued was undertaken primarily by ecclesiastical scholars preoccupied with the ethics of foreign exchange, such as disguised usury and related problems. By the advent of the French Revolution, however, secular economists had taken up the subject, treating such topics as the terms of trade, comparative price levels, quantity of money, and relative interest rates—issues that practitioners and students of foreign exchange have dealt with to the present.[3]

By the end of the 17th century it was generally accepted by both scholars and dealers that the net balance of a country's exports to and imports from its trading partners was a controlling factor in determining its exchange rate. Demand for a country's currency by persons and companies throughout the rest of the world, to whom it comprises foreign exchange, is a function of their desire to buy its goods, employ its services, and to travel and invest there. Conversely, the supply of its currency in the hands of the rest of the world is the result of a country's purchases of goods and services abroad (imports) and its expenditure of capital there, whether for investment or for such nonproductive purposes as maintaining its own or an ally's armed forces. In brief, and overly simplified, an increase in foreign demand for a country's goods and services, and a heightened desire to invest or otherwise commit funds there, will, other things remaining equal, cause its currency to appreciate relative to other currencies. If the demand increases by, say, 5 percent, while the controlling elements on the supply side remain constant (which in fact they seldom do), the value of that currency in the foreign exchange markets would appreciate by a like amount.[4] Another country's currency is likely to weaken—that is, to depreciate—when there is a surfeit of it awash throughout the world, brought about by its citizens' heavy purchases of foreign goods and services. Whichever of the two—exports or imports— is greater, determines whether a nation is running a trade surplus or deficit, which is a major element in its overall balance of payments.

Early students of international economics also were aware that exchange rates are affected by the relative quantities of money and general price levels among a group of trading countries. To reiterate, the ability of a country to sell its goods and services and to attract funds from abroad, as compared with its citizens' inclination to buy things and otherwise to spend their money there, is determined by its competitive standing in the world. If its costs of industrial production, particularly its wage levels, are comparatively high, it is likely that a country's goods will be overpriced in the world market

---

[3]Many of these topics are considered at length in Part Two.

[4]For a mathematical expression of this relationship, see Formula 2 in Appendix B, Foreign Exchange Calculations.

and its business firms will not succeed in achieving a high level of exports. At the same time, foreign-made goods will seem inordinately cheap to its residents, encouraging more imports and thereby throwing that country's trade balance into deficit. When the country uses up its monetary reserves and exhausts the other means of temporary relief available to it, its exchange rate is likely to decline. Preferably, a country's wage and price levels would be significantly below those of its trading partners, making its goods highly competitive overseas and discouraging its citizens from buying what appears to them overly expensive goods abroad. The consequent boost in exports and limitation of imports produces a trade surplus that serves to drive the currency-exchange rate higher.

These two concepts—respectively, the balance of payments theory and the purchasing power parity theory—have preoccupied students of international money for the past 300 years. At first they debated which of the two theories was the "correct" one. After 200 or so years of deliberation, they agreed that the theories complement rather than contradict each other.

One conclusion that all schools of thought came to share by the beginning of the 19th century was that—in keeping with the philosophy expressed in the U.S. Constitution quoted at the beginning of this chapter—the state should become directly involved with the economy and with foreign exchange matters. These early forms of government intervention included banning the export of bullion and coins (or at least exacting a fee to export), imposing import restrictions (including high import duties), prohibiting foreign exchange transactions at unfavorable rates, raising or lowering the exchange rate, and entering into official foreign exchange transactions. Though the ultimate purpose of these measures was to retain the bullion and coin that was already in the country and to attract more, the idea of achieving this result by maintaining favorable exchange rates became so fixed in the minds of the politicians and bureaucrats of the time that the means eventually became an end unto itself.

The gold standard

Though it began amidst the turbulence of the French Revolution and the Napoleonic wars, the 19th century following the Battle of Waterloo offered the greater part of the world the longest period of peace and stability it has enjoyed in modern times. It ended only with the outbreak of World War I in 1914. In many facets of life the period was hailed as the golden age of European civilization. That term quite literally applies to what could be called an international monetary system when the major trading nations adopted the gold standard. Even today, some 65 years later, a passing reference to the pre-1914 gold standard evokes in some people a nostalgic yearning for a return to some sort of monetary Camelot.

The gold standard was neither legislated into existence, per se, nor created through administrative fiat. Rather, it evolved over the better part of a century, starting in Great Britain where it was centered and attained its purest form. Like that of most European countries, the British monetary system developed through the Middle Ages on a bimetallic basis, with gold and silver coins circulating side by side. As the operation of Gresham's famous law—"bad money drives out good"—threatened to force one or the other metal out of circulation as the price ratio between them changed, Britain stopped the coinage of silver altogether in 1798 (with the exception of the shilling, a token coin with a face value higher than its metallic content). Free coinage of gold bullion commenced in 1816, and in 1823 Britain established full convertibility of paper money into coins—the famous gold sovereigns.

The gold standard system among countries was based on two key elements: full backing of the participating currencies by gold reserves and the commitment by the respective governments involved to convert their paper money into gold and back into notes freely in unlimited amounts and at fixed prices. The latter were called "gold parities," and their maintenance fixed the exchange rates of the various currencies to one another. If, for example, Great Britain set the price of gold at five pounds sterling per ounce, the United States decided upon a price of $25 an ounce, France pegged its franc at 50 to the ounce, and these parities were maintained, the exchange rates among the three currencies would remain fixed as follows:

$$1 \text{ oz. gold} = £5 = \$25 = FF50$$

therefore

$$£1 = \$5 = FF10$$

or

$$FF1 = \$0.50 = 2 \text{ shillings } (£\tfrac{1}{10})$$

and

$$\$1 = FF2 = 4 \text{ shillings } (£\tfrac{1}{5})[5]$$

Anchored to the common denominator of gold in this fashion, the currencies of those countries that adhered to the gold standard could fluctuate in price among themselves only by the minor variations—the so-called gold points. Gold points consisted of the cost of shipping gold from one country to another, plus insurance charges and loss of interest for the duration of shipment.

In addition to imparting stability—critics of the system would say rigidity—to the exchange rates of its adherents, the gold standard imposed an often-harsh discipline on these nations' domestic economies. According to the rules of the gold standard game, countries that experienced an inflow

---

[5]These rates are hypothetical, chosen arbitrarily for simplicity of illustration.

of gold (as might result from a trade surplus) were expected to issue more currency commensurate with their increased reserves. A country's inflated money supply led to higher prices and wages and in turn to increased imports and reduced exports, thereby causing gold to flow out of the country. Those countries that were running trade deficits, and thereby losing gold, adjusted by contracting their money supplies. This deflation set off the contrary process of reducing prices and wages, lifting exports, cutting back imports, and bringing gold back into the country. Through these supposedly automatic adjustments, the system kept its equilibrium.

With the benefit of hindsight, one can make a convincing case for labeling this system the *pound sterling standard*. Gold served as a measure of value and common denominator, to be sure, but in practice it was sterling in which much of the world's trade was financed and settled. The bill of exchange drawn on London became such a convenient means of financing commerce that it was adopted by many of the other important trading nations. In fact, only three countries—Britain, the U.S., and the Netherlands—adhered to a pure gold standard in the sense that they tolerated the free and unlimited export of gold. Other countries, which purportedly fixed their currencies to gold, in practice resorted to various devices to hinder, if not stop outright, their loss of gold reserves. By doing so, they maintained what was deprecatingly described as a "limping gold standard" that allowed them to avoid some of the more severe consequences—deflation, especially—of the rules of the game.

By the turn of the 20th century other countries with a continuing need for pounds to make their international settlements found it convenient to hold that currency, fully convertible into gold as it was guaranteed by the British government to be, as part of their official reserves. Thus, as the golden epoch neared its end, the pound already was established as an international trading currency, and its use by other countries as a reserve currency had begun.

The ascendancy of sterling as the international trading and reserve currency made London the leading foreign exchange center of the period, with Paris and New York also emerging as important markets. Other major developments in the field during the years prior to World War I were an increasingly active market in foreign bank notes, greater use of mail and telegraphic foreign exchange transfers, and a growing participation by banks and their customers in forward transactions. Also during this period came the first attempts to formulate a theory of forward exchange rates.

The impact of World War I

The primary objectives of official foreign exchange policy during the halcyon years of the international gold standard were those of fostering the stability of exchange rates, discouraging by all available means their depreciation, and of retaining as much freedom in foreign exchange dealings as was consistent with the desired stability. In pursuing these objectives, the emphasis in policy shifted from preserving an existing reserve of coin and bullion to maintaining stable exchange rates. In the process, countries paid closer attention to the amount of specie held in official reserves than what was in circulation.

The financial dislocations that occurred during World War I impaired the ability of the belligerent governments to stick to the rules of the international gold standard, and their attempts to restore the system to its earlier form after the war were unsuccessful. To finance their conduct of the war, the combatant powers printed paper money far in excess of their gold reserves. After the war they were unable to accumulate sufficient fresh reserves to reinstate the full backing and free convertibility into gold upon which the prewar system was based.

The gold that the belligerents spent to fight the war flowed mostly to those neutral countries that sold them food, raw materials, and arms. Though the U.S., the foremost of these neutral suppliers, kept the dollar pegged to gold, it also abandoned the old rules of the game. If it had followed them, the United States would have had to inflate its money supply and raise prices. Its refusal to do so increased the gold flow to America, since prices of its goods remained substantially below those of the warring European powers.

The years immediately following the armistice witnessed wide fluctuations in leading exchange rates as the European nations struggled to repair and restore their war-shattered economies. The nearly unanimous desire of those politicians and officials responsible for the management of their countries' monetary affairs was to return the greatly depreciated currencies to their prewar gold parities as quickly as possible. Their wishes turned out to be politically indefensible to the extent that the degree of deflation necessary to restore the earlier parities would have fostered intolerably high unemployment. The essential change in the earlier system was that the various national treasuries and central banks would be entitled to count gold-backed foreign currency as part of their official reserves as well as the metal itself. With the addition of fully convertible foreign currency to bullion reserves, participating countries were prepared to return to the prewar rules of the game, increasing their money supplies as reserves came in, and contracting money supplies as reserves left.

The nations that subscribed to the new gold exchange standard enjoyed varying degrees of success in reinstating their former parities. In the end, their attempts were doomed to failure by the onset of the Great Depression. In the meantime, the worst monetary fate befell the war's principal loser, Germany. Her obligation under the Treaty of Versailles to make huge reparations payments—in cash and in goods—to the winners fueled a hyperinflation that drastically reduced the value of her currency, wiped out the life savings of an entire generation, and left millions destitute. The old mark had become practically worthless by 1923 as prices rose by the hour, wages were paid twice daily, and mothers sent their children pushing wheelbarrows filled with paper money to the corner bakery for loaves of bread. Finally, the thoroughly discredited currency was replaced; existing marks were exchanged for new reichsmarks at a rate of 1 trillion to 1! The trauma brought on by this experience has remained embedded in the national psyche of the German people to the present day, provoking adamant opposition to any government policy that smacks of inflation.

As one of the victorious Allies, Great Britain was set on reasserting her leadership in international trade and on reinstating the pound as the premier transaction and reserve currency. Winston Churchill was chancellor of the exchequer when the pound once again became fully convertible in 1925. Chiefly at his insistence—"so as to be able to look the dollar in the eye," he said—sterling was pegged at its prewar parity level. Leading British economists, John Maynard Keynes among them, protested that putting the pound at what was under the circumstances an unrealistically high level would impede exports, stifle the overall economy, and contribute to greater unemployment. Although Churchill's chauvinistic view carried the day, the economists' dire forecast proved correct. The British economy stagnated for six years.

The return to the prewar parity overvalued the pound by 10 percent or more under the conditions that prevailed in England and elsewhere in the 1920s.[6] The British government's dogged defense of that artificial level subjected the country to severe economic strains. The problem of an overvalued pound was compounded by an undervalued French franc, which gave France's goods a great competitive advantage in world trade and prompted a large, one-way flow of gold from England to France. The French, too, refused to follow the rules that called for them to inflate their money supply in response to the gold flows from Britain. Thus, the forces of adjustment that were supposed to make the system work weren't allowed to operate as they were intended.

The British government bowed to the inevitable in 1931 when it severed the costly and untenable tie between sterling and gold. The pound was allowed to float—that is, to respond to market forces without the government's intervention to maintain any particular exchange rate. As soon as official support was withdrawn, the pound depreciated by 30 percent.

The monetary ball then bounced into the opposite court. As the exchange rates of the pound and the Commonwealth currencies linked to it depreciated, currencies that were kept at their existing parities became overvalued by comparison. Those countries took their turn at beginning the cycle of reserve losses, deflation, and unemployment that had forced

---

[6]Thus, a shirt that cost 20 French francs in France might be priced at 1 pound and 2 shillings in England at a time when the pound/franc exchange rate was 20 to 1. Instead of devaluing the pound by 10 percent, the British government chose to pursue a deflationary policy designed to depress the price of shirts (among other goods and services) to £1.

Britain off gold. Countries, such as France, that held sterling as part of their official reserves suffered heavy losses in their foreign exchange accounts when the pound plunged 30 percent after being allowed to float. Understandably, these countries felt betrayed, and vowed never again to be left holding a mixed currency bag. They agreed among themselves to form a gold bloc, accepting that metal alone in payment of international obligations. The gold bloc countries counted on the United States joining them, but when President Roosevelt took the United States off gold and devalued the dollar in 1934, they found themselves out of step with the rest of the world and paying dearly for the privilege. After enduring another two years of declining industrial production as a consequence of overvalued exchange rates, France and the other gold bloc countries also succumbed in 1936. But their dogged defense of unrealistic gold parities for so long continued to have a debilitating effect on their economies up to and beyond the outbreak of World War II.

Much of the academic debate as well as practical policy decisions that took place between the two world wars revolved about the issue of whether fixed or flexible exchange rates best served the interests of individual countries and of the international monetary system. The issue was a primary concern of the delegates to the Bretton Woods conference, who gathered in 1944 to shape the post-World War II monetary order. Now, some 35 years later, after both approaches have been tried and to some extent found wanting, scholars and practitioners continue to debate the merits of each.

Currencies and business

Scaling down abruptly to the personal level, anyone who proposes to deal in futures contracts or the actual currencies, should begin with the arithmetic of foreign exchange and gain a clear insight about how, quantitatively, currency fluctuations affect companies that do business in the world market. After all, numbers are what international business—and the foreign exchange game in particular—are all about, and it's high time that the reader learn how to keep score.

As was noted, one of the purportedly positive features of a fixed-rate system, such as the international gold standard, is that pegging the values of the various currencies to the common denominator of gold also pegs them to one another. It may well be that one of the reasons for using the word *standard* in this context is that everyone involved with a fixed-rate system knows where they stand. To continue our illustration with the hypothetical rates cited on page 9, so long as the price of gold in both U.S. dollars and French francs was kept at their official parity levels, the French franc would remain fixed—apart from minor deviations within the gold points—at 50 cents. If, back in 1875, a New York importer was quoted a price of 200 francs per case of French champagne, he could be assured that the dollar cost to him for the vintages of '79, '82, '87, and beyond would be $100 for as long as the franc price remained constant. There must have been something quite comforting about this certainty. But when the cost of sustaining such stability becomes too great for a country to bear (as occurred in Britain in 1931, the United States in 1934, and France in 1936) and its exchange rate is left free to move about daily, or even hourly, the situation becomes more complicated. If the champagne importer (or his son) were still in business in New York in 1936, he would be confronted with the uncertainty of just how much the 1938 vintage, say, would cost in dollars by the time that year was bottled and ready to be shipped.

If it isn't clear by this point that an exchange rate is simply the price of the principal unit of one country's currency quoted in terms of another country's currency, there is rough sledding ahead. See Figure 1–1. It may not be quite so obvious that the same exchange rate can be expressed in reverse—that is, as the number of monetary units (or fraction thereof) of the first country exchangeable for one unit of the second country's currency. To illustrate, if one French franc is quoted by the direct method at FF1 = $0.25, the indirect reciprocal quotation must be U.S. $1 = FF4. Algebraically, if

$$FF1 = \$0.25$$

then

$$FF4 = \$1$$

The two methods of expressing the same relationship can cause some confusion at first sight, so care should be taken to be certain which method is being used. The direct method is employed throughout this book for quoting both spot and futures market exchange rates.[7]

It follows, therefore, that an increase in the exchange rate of the U.S. dollar from four to five francs is equivalent to the franc declining from $0.25 to $0.20. A statement, therefore, that a particular exchange rate rose or fell is in itself incomplete and possibly misleading until it is specified which currency is being expressed in terms of the other.

A specific exchange rate—whichever way it is expressed—in itself says nothing about the relative strength or desirability of the two currencies being quoted. A franc/dollar exchange rate of 4 to 1 does not imply that the dollar is four times stronger or more valuable than the franc any more than it has a greater value than four quarter-dollar coins. By the same token, the dollar is not half as valuable as the British pound at a £1 = $2 exchange rate. Such ratios merely reflect the basic denominations of the respective

---

[7]The Wall Street Journal, New York Times, and other leading newspapers print daily quotations of principal foreign currencies versus the U.S. dollar as both the exchange value of one dollar and the fractional dollar value of one unit of the foreign currency.

Figure 1–1
Foreign exchange rates

```
                    Foreign Exchange

                    Thursday, May 28, 1981
         The New York foreign exchange selling rates below
         apply to trading among banks in amounts of $1 million
         and more, as quoted at 3 p.m. Eastern time by Bankers
         Trust Co. Retail transactions provide fewer units of
         foreign currency per dollar.
                                                    Currency
                              U.S. $ equiv.        per U.S. $
         Country               Thurs     Wed      Thurs     Wed
         Argentina (Peso)
           Financial          .000307   .000307   3250.00  3250.00
         Australia (Dollar)   1.1390    1.1386     .8779    .8783
         Austria (Schilling)   .0609     .0606    16.42    16.49
         Belgium (Franc)
           Commercial rate    .02643    .02631    37.83    38.01
           Financial rate     .02579    .02573    38.76    38.86
         Brazil (Cruzeiro)    .0118     .0118     84.47    84.47
         Britain (Pound)     2.0695    2.0700      .4832    .4831
           30-Day Forward    2.0806    2.0807      .4806    .4831
           90-Day Forward    2.1012    2.1029      .4759    .4755
           180-Day Forward   2.1160    2.1190      .4726    .4719
         Canada (Dollar)      .8326     .8314    1.2010   1.2028
           30-Day Forward     .8316     .8311    1.2025   1.2033
           90-Day Forward     .8310     .8312    1.2033   1.2031
           180-Day Forward    .8307     .8306    1.2038   1.2039
         China (Yuan)         .5750     .5750    1.7392   1.7392
         Colombia (Peso)      .0187     .0187    53.41    53.41
         Denmark (Krone)      .1369     .1362     7.3062   7.3445
         Ecuador (Sucre)      .0329     .0329    30.35    30.35
         Finland (Markka)     .2310     .2301     4.3289   4.3466
         France (Franc)       .1813     .1802     5.5150   5.55
           30-Day Forward     .1807     .1795     5.5350   5.5725
           90-Day Forward     .1804     .1795     5.5425   5.5725
           180-Day Forward    .1803     .1795     5.5450   5.5700
         Greece (Drachma)     .01768    .01761   56.56    56.79
         Hong Kong (Dollar)   .1826     .1826     5.4770   5.4760
         India (Rupee)        .1182     .1181     8.46     8.47
         Indonesia (Rupiah)   .001589   .001589  629.00   629.00
         Ireland (Pound)     1.5701    1.6043      .6369    .6233
         Israel (Shekel)      .0993     .0993    10.07    10.07
         Italy (Lira)         .000864   .000866 1158.00  1155.00
         Japan (Yen)          .004466   .004458  223.90   224.30
           30-Day Forward     .004510 z          221.75   z
           90-Day Forward     .004586 z          218.05   z
           180-Day Forward    .004679 z          213.70   z
         Lebanon (Pound)      .2356     .2354     4.2450   4.2475
         Malaysia (Ringgit)   .4254     .4255     2.3510   2.35
         Mexico (Peso)        .0414     .0414    24.18    24.17
         Netherlands (Guilder).3873     .3858     2.5820   2.5920
         New Zealand (Dollar) .8734     .8748     1.1449   1.1431
         Norway (Krone)       .1754     .1749     5.7018   5.7169
         Pakistan (Rupee)     .1013     .1013     9.87     9.87
         Peru (Sol)           .0024     .0024   409.01   409.01
         Philippines (Peso)   .1283     .1283     7.7950   7.7950
         Portugal (Escudo)    .0163     .0162    61.22    61.47
         Saudi Arabia (Riyal) .2949     .2948     3.3905   3.3910
         Singapore (Dollar)   .4625     .4634     2.1620   2.1580
         South Africa (Rand) 1.1790    1.1760      .8487    .8503
         South Korea (Won)    .001464   .001464 683.10   683.10
         Spain (Peseta)       .01087    .01085   92.03    92.13
         Sweden (Krona)       .2034     .2026     4.9154   4.9351
         Switzerland (Franc)  .4810     .4797     2.0790   2.0845
           30-Day Forward     .4844     .4833     2.0642   2.0691
           90-Day Forward     .4909     .4900     2.0372   2.0410
           180-Day Forward    .4974     .4971     2.0104   2.0115
         Taiwan (Dollar)      .0274     .0274    36.47    36.47
         Thailand (Baht)      .0482     .0482    20.72    20.72
         Uruguay (New Peso)
           Financial          .0942     .0942    10.61    10.61
         Venezuela (Bolivar)  .2330     .2330     4.2915   4.2915
         West German (Mark)   .4305     .4287     2.3230   2.3325
           30-Day Forward     .4328   z          2.3105   z
           90-Day Forward     .4366   z          2.2902   z
           180-Day Forward    .4403   z          2.2710   z

         SDR                 1.16423   1.16724   .859999  .856720
         Special Drawing Rights are based on exchange rates
         for the U.S., West German, British, French and Japanese
         currencies. Source: International Monetary Fund.
```

Source: *The Wall Street Journal*, May 28, 1981.

currencies as they have evolved. Much more important questions—ones that will occupy center stage throughout this book—are: In what direction, and to what extent, are the exchange rates with which we are concerned likely to change? These two questions define exchange rate risk.

Should our friends at Levi Strauss & Co. succeed in selling 10,000 pairs of jeans to a Paris department store for 50 francs a pair, it is a not inconsiderable matter of $25,000 to them whether the franc/dollar exchange rate is 4 to 1 (FF 500,000 = U.S. $125,000) or 5 to 1 (FF 500,000 = $100,000) at the time they're paid in francs. If L.S. & Co. contracts to deliver and take payment for the jeans a year after the sales agreement is reached, it has no way of knowing, like our champagne importer, what the dollar equivalent of 500,000 francs will be one year later. It is to resolve this type of uncertainty that forward and futures transactions in foreign exchange are initiated.

It should also be clear at this point how a depreciated currency makes a country's goods more competitive in the world marketplace. If Levi Strauss & Co. decides that it must charge the Parisian department store the French franc equivalent of $10 a pair to clear a profit on its jeans, the store's buyers will not be totally indifferent (even after making allowance for the aforementioned enthusiasm abroad for American jeans) about whether their cost in francs is FF 40 or FF 50 when, let us say, the going price for French-made jeans in Paris is FF 25 a pair. The lower the dollar/franc exchange rate drops—at FF 2 to $1, a $10 pair of jeans would only cost FF 20—the greater the inclination of the French consumer will be to favor the American import over the domestic product.

The concepts behind this simple example prompted the careful study of the balance of payments and purchasing power parity theories over the past 300 years and were uppermost in the minds of the planners at Bretton Woods when they debated the relative merits of fixed and flexible exchange rates.

Chapter 2

Creation and demise of the Bretton Woods system

DURING THE YEARS following World War I, each of the former belligerent countries tended to pursue a go-it-alone economic policy. In contrast, even as World War II still raged in Europe and the Pacific, the member states of the Anglo-American coalition determined that it would be in their individual as well as collective interest to extend their alliance into various forms of peacetime cooperation. The principal expression of this cooperative spirit was the establishment of the United Nations. In the economic sphere, representatives of the Western alliance met at Bretton Woods, New Hampshire, in the summer of 1944 to forge a postwar monetary order. The conference site was adopted as the popular name for the system they devised, which governed the official management of foreign exchange rates for the next 27 years.

People who are not involved with foreign exchange either in theory or in practice are inclined to regard the subject as an arcane science, best left to academic economists and international bankers. "Parity points," "crawling pegs," "snakes in tunnels" and the like don't hold much meaning for anyone other than those specialists and, perhaps, reptile fanciers. But when the jargon is translated into everyday English, the fundamental concepts do not seem quite so forbidding. At the risk of oversimplifying the elements and relationships involved, an analogy may be drawn between the international payments mechanism and the flow of money within a local community. A family must have money to live. In most instances, it earns what it needs by selling to the other members of its community some product or service, even if, in the case of unskilled labor, it is sheer brawn. If our community is a model for the world, where each household is a separate country, such sales would represent exports. The proceeds from these sales are in turn used to buy the necessities of life—food, clothing, fuel, and so forth—from other community residents. These purchases are comparable in our model to the imports of a country. On both the local and international levels, an economic unit is in balance when its income is equal to its expenditures. If a household or country earns more than it needs to spend, a surplus accumulates which can be put aside for the inevitable rainy day. One kind of rainy day is at hand when the household finds itself spending more than it earns.

Countries and families that are unable to earn enough to live on have three alternatives. First, they can work for less pay, offering their output to their neighbors at bargain prices. As a temporary expedient, they can subsist on the savings they've been able to put aside during better days. These savings, or reserves, may be deposited in a bank or buried in the back yard—or, in the case of a country, in Fort Knox or a comparable stronghold. If neither of these alternatives is sufficient to keep the household going, it is time to call on the aid of a sympathetic banker who will lend enough to tide the family over until better days arrive. But such emergency loans provide only a temporary reprieve from reality. The alternatives of cheaper or harder work, or both, must be faced up to sooner or later, while the family or country goes through the painful adjustment of learning to live within its means. Furthermore, the loan eventually must be repaid.

The issues at Bretton Woods

It was noted in Chapter 1 that a principal result of a depreciating currency is a lower price for a country's goods and services abroad. In terms of our model, such a devaluation is the equivalent of a wage cut that brings more work and thus increases total income. An economic system, whether it encompasses a village or the world, is in equilibrium when all its members can continue through such adjustments to earn enough to cover their needs. If some families or countries consistently operate at a surplus and accumulate excessive reserves, while the less fortunate units continue to incur deficits after they use up their reserves, the system falls into disequilibrium and eventually ceases to function. The haves have more liquidity—money—than they need, while the have-nots don't have enough.

The delegates to the Bretton Woods conference had to deal with these complex issues, not in terms of a model community but under real-world conditions, including that of a single major country—the United States—emerging from the war with its economy intact. Specifically, they were assembled to make decisions concerning the fixing and, when necessary, the alteration of exchange rates, the composition and creation of new international reserves, and the generation of sufficient liquidity to serve the needs of the participating countries. Some critical observers have contended with the benefit of hindsight that the system the Bretton Woods' planners devised managed to function for as long and as well as it did in spite of, rather than due to, the accords they reached there. Wherever the credit should lie, the fact nevertheless remains that while their creation remained in operation the physical damage wrought by the war in Europe and Asia was repaired, and world trade grew at an unprecedented rate that has not been matched since then.

The major issue confronting the conference was that of reconciling the contending positions taken by the British and American delegations. John Maynard Keynes, the principal spokesman for Great Britain, doubtless recalled his country's ill-fated attempt to return to the gold standard during 1925–31, a policy which he and other economists opposed at the time. He proposed a system of international credits, or overdraft privileges, which he called "bancor," to be made available to countries having such trouble making ends meet that they were incurring balance-of-payments deficits. Keynes's proposed credits in effect would have amounted to gifts in that they would be covered by grants from countries that had accrued a surplus—of which the United States was then the only one among the belligerent countries—and would be forgiven if the recipient countries were unable to repay them within a stated period.

The United States rejected this open-ended claim on its largess. While acknowledging its desire and responsibility to help its Allies—and, as it turned out, its former enemies—to get back on their feet after the war, it declined to issue a blank check underwriting their payments deficits in perpetuity. Instead of endorsing Keynes's bancor proposal, the Americans—like the British themselves in 1925—advocated a return to the tried-and-true medium of payment between nations: gold. In place of unlimited overdraft privileges to relieve countries with payments problems, the White plan (so-named for its principal author at the U.S. Treasury Department) supported the establishment of a currency pool in which all participating countries would deposit their own currencies as well as gold under a quota system, and from which countries in trouble could borrow.

Today, some 35 years after the event, the differences between the British and American positions at the Bretton Woods conference do not appear as striking as the similarities. There was for example, agreement that the freely fluctuating exchange rates that preceded and again followed the short-lived attempt to return to the gold standard between the two world wars were a destabilizing influence and as such were inimical to the growth of world trade. Yet it was also agreed that a country's struggling through thick and thin to defend rigid exchange parities pegged to gold was equally undesirable. Accordingly, a middle ground between the extremes of totally unmanaged currencies and a fixed-rate system was sought and, when reached, was described in terms of "fixed bands" and "adjustable pegs"—the sort of jargon that is the bane of students of foreign exchange, and which will be translated presently into ordinary English.

In the second instance, there was agreement among the conference delegates that the world's existing gold reserves—of which three quarters were then held by the United States—were insufficient to supply the liquidity needed to finance the postwar recovery of Europe and Asia. They also conceded Keynes's assertion that some type of aid to countries beset with temporary payments difficulties was preferable to putting them through the sort of painful price and income adjustments Britain underwent during the ultimately unsuccessful defense of sterling's gold parity from 1925 to 1931. The International Monetary Fund (IMF) was established as the mutual assistance currency pool that was proposed in the White plan, to which all of the countries party to the Bretton Woods Articles of Agreement would make prorated deposits of gold and currency. The subscribing members would then have the right to draw on the fund when they fell short on reserves.

Third, the signatory nations concurred that a revival of the every-man-for-himself attitudes that prevailed during the 1920s and 1930s would be harmful to them all. In an effort to avoid resorting to the exchange controls, competitive devaluations and discriminatory tariffs that disrupted their trade relationships during the Great Depression, they agreed to use the International Monetary Fund as a forum for international consultation and cooperation as well as an emergency source of credit.

The IMF Articles of Agreement were signed at Bretton Woods in July 1944, and ratified by the respective member governments by the end of 1945. Washington, D.C., was chosen as the seat of the fund and its affiliated organizations, the International Bank for Reconstruction and Development (the World Bank) and the General Agreement on Trade and Tariffs (GATT). The first meeting of the fund's board of governors was held in Savannah, Georgia, in March 1946.

How the system worked

Such were the circumstances of the creation of an international monetary system that incorporated a gold-exchange standard similar to the one in existence between the wars with an emergency currency fund and a mechanism of adjustable exchange parities. The purpose of the latter was to provide countries experiencing payments difficulties a means of improving their position by revising their exchange rates with the concurrence of their trading partners.

The IMF members hoped that the adjustable peg system would provide them with the best of both monetary worlds: exchange rate stability and flexibility. The intent was for each country to designate a par value for its currency, and then take the necessary steps to maintain its exchange rate within a stipulated range above and below this parity rate. The device of expressing the value of a particular currency in terms of an official gold price was retained, but in the IMF system the U.S. dollar was the only currency that was convertible into gold by statute. The other currencies were linked with gold via the dollar, which meant that their value could be reduced by raising their theoretical gold price and increased by lowering it.

Table 2–1
Official IMF par values in U.S. dollars, 1951

British pound	2.8000
Canadian dollar	1.0169
Deutsche mark	.2380
Dutch guilder	.2632
French franc	.2857
Japanese yen	.00277
Mexican peso	.1156
Swiss franc	.2286

Source: *International Financial Statistics,* May 1976.

Once the official parity of a currency was established, the rules of the IMF game provided for the free play of market forces within a range of 1 percent above and below that par value. The expectation was that this 2 percent range, called a "band," would allow a country sufficient latitude to adjust to changes in competitive standing, relative rates of inflation, and the other factors that determine exchange rates in an uncontrolled market environment. But if commercial buying or selling pressures threatened to drive the exchange rate through the upper or lower parity levels, the government was expected to exert contrary pressure: selling its own currency to keep the rate below the upper limit or buying it to keep the parity floor intact. In many instances countries established intervention points closer to their official parity rates than the 1 percent premium or discount permitted by the IMF rules. A common intervention band during the early postwar years was ¾ percent on either side of parity.

A detailed discussion of the mechanics of official intervention in the foreign exchange market is reserved for Chapter 8. It should suffice to note at this stage that dollars are the currency customarily used by most central banks to carry out their support operations. Since, for example, the parity rate of the Italian lira in 1951 was $.00160 (625 lira to the dollar) IMF rules

Figure 2–1
IMF parity, official and effective British pound intervention limits

2.8280	Official upper limit: + 1 percent of parity
2.8210	Effective upper limit: + .75 percent of parity
↓	Bank of England sells pounds, buys dollars
2.8000	Official dollar: pound parity Bank of England sells dollars, buys pounds
↑	
2.7790	Effective lower limit: − .75 percent of parity
2.7720	Official lower limit: − 1 percent of parity

required the Bank of Italy to exchange dollars for lira if the latter threatened to fall below the $.00158 (631 lira) lower support point, and to execute the reverse transaction if the lira was about to rise above the $.00162 (619 lira) upper level. The former operation—propping the lira up—could be sustained for as long as the Bank of Italy had dollars to sell for lira. If Italy ran out of dollar reserves, the bank would be obliged to buy—that is, borrow—dollars from the IMF or some other source, or else discontinue its lira support operations. If, to take another example, the Dutch guilder was subject to heavy buying pressure in the foreign exchange market, the Netherlands central bank was expected to sell guilders before the dollar/guilder rate rallied above $.265, the upper intervention point for the guilder. In contrast to the Bank of Italy, which would lose dollar reserves by buying lira, the Netherlands bank would gain them as it accumulated dollar balances in return for the guilders it sold.

A downward movement in an exchange rate, such as the decline in the lira to its lower intervention point, was referred to as a "depreciation." The converse, such as the rise in the guilder rate, would be called an "appreciation." Both fluctuations resulted from the interplay of market forces within the fixed IMF band. When these forces, bullish or bearish, built up to the point where the central bank of a particular country wasn't able any longer to contain its exchange rate within the official band, the situation fell into what the IMF articles described as a "fundamental disequilibrium." Such a condition required a more radical remedy than central bank intervention: an official change in that currency's price in terms of gold and the U.S. dollar—its parity—and therefore an adjustment in its exchange rate against all other currencies whose parities remained constant. A downward change in parity was designated a devaluation; its converse, an increase in parity, was a revaluation. A country such as Italy that suffered from repeated trade deficits and chronic shortages of monetary reserves was considered in a state of fundamental disequilibrium, and was permitted under the rules of the IMF—albeit grudgingly—to devalue its currency by as much as 10 percent. In the case of the lira example cited above, that would mean a reduction in parity from $.00160 to $.00146. At the devalued rate a new band would be established between $.00144 and $.00148. The opposite parity adjustment—revaluation—didn't become an issue until the 1960s, when the unthinkable occurred and the U.S. dollar became the currency subjected to heavy selling pressures.

The role of the U.S. dollar

The dollar and gold together comprised the keystone of the Bretton Woods system. Given the dollar's replacement of the British pound as the system's principal reserve and transaction currency, and adding the innovation of the adjustable peg, this arrangement was similar to the gold exchange standard that prevailed for a short time 20 years before.[1] Gold remained the ultimate means of payment, at least so far as official international transactions were concerned. However, the dollar—which the U.S. government was committed to convert freely into gold by buying from and selling the metal to other governments and their central banks at $35 an ounce—became a secondary reserve which soon overshadowed gold in practical importance. Other IMF member countries were on a derivative gold standard inasmuch as the content of their currencies was defined by their dollar parities although the currencies themselves weren't convertible into gold.

It is important in this regard to distinguish between the two senses of the word *convertible*. As was just noted, the U.S. dollar was the only currency under the IMF system convertible by statute into gold at the demand of other countries. No other country, not even Great Britain, was required to do this. Currency convertibility, on the other hand, refers to the exchange of one currency for another, free of any sort of controls or restrictions. Due to the problems and dislocations that were associated with postwar reconstruction, the major European currencies did not regain full convertibility in the latter sense until 1958.

Because of the special role of the dollar in the IMF system, and the demand by all other countries for American goods with which to achieve their reconstruction, the dollar became the world's money and the United States in effect became its money manager. During the heyday of the pure gold standard the major gold fields that were discovered in California and Australia, and later in South Africa, supplied the additional liquidity needed to keep pace with the expansion of world trade. There were no comparable gold discoveries to supplement existing liquidity 50 years later, and with nearly three quarters of the world's monetary gold stock held by the United

---

[1]Though yielding the premier position to the dollar, the pound remained an important reserve currency, particularly throughout the British Commonwealth and other countries that were part of Britain's former empire.

States, other countries were glad to accept the American dollar—"good as gold" as it was then regarded—as a substitute reserve. Indeed, they had no real alternative.

The beginning of the end

As was noted at the beginning of this chapter, a country's reserves, plus whatever it could borrow from the IMF or some other source, limited the extent to which it was able to incur deficits in its balance of payments. Being the provider of international liquidity as the issuer of the world's principal reserve currency, the United States wasn't subject to the same limitations as the other countries were. As long as everyone else had confidence in the value of the dollar—and throughout the 1950s there wasn't any reason to feel otherwise—the United States had the exclusive privilege of funding its deficits by sending more dollars abroad rather than adjusting by the conventional means of contracting its money supply, reducing prices and income, and bringing its international accounts back into balance by exporting more and importing less. In monetary jargon, the dollar was asymmetrical—that is, an exception to the rules the other nations were required to observe, which placed the burden of keeping the system in equilibrium on the less-favored countries. A further cause of asymmetry was the fact that while the deficit nations were expected to adjust their exchange rates, reduce price and income levels, and use up their reserves, countries that accumulated surpluses were under no such compulsion to participate in the adjustment process. To the contrary, there was a feeling that countries compiling repeated surpluses were hard-working and virtuous, and therefore deserved to be rewarded with growing reserves, while deficit countries were profligate and slightly sinful because they were living beyond their means.

The first recourse under the Bretton Woods system, then, was for a country's central bank to intervene in the private market to maintain its exchange rate within the parity points while the government tried to stimulate a balance-of-payments surplus. Lacking such a current surplus, the monetary authority—be it central bank or government treasury—was obliged to dip further into the country's gold and foreign exchange reserves to make up any deficit as the attempts to turn its unfavorable trade or capital position around took on an increased sense of urgency. If that country was unable to get its act together before its reserves-plus-borrowings ran out, its final resort was to devalue its currency as permitted by the rules of the IMF. The hope was that such a (presumably) one-time measure could attain for it the competitive advantage in the world markets that would otherwise require a protracted period of deflation, price and wage reduction, and almost certain unemployment. The only country that was exempt from these rules of monetary behavior was the United States, which, as noted earlier was in the unique position of being able to finance its deficits by creating more dollars, which to the rest of the world were supposed to be as good as gold. This arrangement was satisfactory to the other members of the IMF system as long as the United States demonstrated to those countries that the dollar reserves they were accumulating in growing amounts would in fact retain their golden luster.

One constraint on this adjustment process was the stigma attached to devaluation as a means of redressing a country's unfavorable balance of payments position: A country that devalued its currency was considered guilty of financial mismanagement and of cheating its foreign creditors—which, in a sense, was true, since the creditors would be repaid a lesser amount than they lent in terms of their own currencies after a devaluation.

To afford countries in payments distress a way of getting their houses in order before suffering the disgrace of devaluation, and in the interest of overall exchange rate stability, the IMF made available to them the resources of the currency pool to which the founding members had subscribed when the fund was established. Under IMF rules a country deemed to be experiencing a temporary, as opposed to a fundamental, disequilibrium in its payments position was entitled to draw from the fund, in a prearranged series of steps, foreign exchange—usually dollars—with which it could continue to support its beleaguered currency in the open market after its own reserves were exhausted.[2] This relief came with conditions attached, of course. Borrowing countries became subject to the oversight of the IMF staff in devising and executing policies to remedy the payments imbalance that prompted the loan.

During its most effective period, the 1950s and 1960s, the IMF staff was accorded high marks for its performance, especially in providing financial and technical assistance to improve a country's monetary and trade relationships with the rest of the world. There were, however, critics who believed that the fund was committed to administering a system that was inherently unsound. They cited, among other shortcomings, the vague distinction between temporary and fundamental disequilibrium, and the failure of the Bretton Woods' planners to anticipate the disruptive effects that large-scale movements of capital—"hot money"—from country to country would have on central banks' attempts to keep exchange rates within their parity points.

From dollar shortage to dollar glut

Though there was no precise date marking their division, the chronology of the Bretton Woods era falls into two successive periods. The decade

---

[2]Unfortunately, the IMF Articles of Agreement didn't spell out the difference between temporary and fundamental disequilibrium. The former presumably included such short-lived disruptions as crop failure, bad weather, and labor disputes that would be corrected in due course, while the latter were factors that had become ingrained in a nation's economy and therefore required some overt act of policy to remove.

of the 1950s was regarded as one of dollar shortage, when the primary concern of all other countries than the United States was that of acquiring enough liquidity to finance their postwar reconstruction. Following the return of the major European countries to full currency convertibility in 1958, the system moved increasingly into a condition of dollar glut as the nations' dollar reserves accumulated to the point where they were uncomfortable holding the dollars they had and were loathe to accept more.

As was mentioned earlier, the system tolerated and even encouraged the continuation of American payments deficits as a source of liquidity for a reserve-deficient world. The assumption always remained, however, that such deficits were the result of U.S. indulgence, really a disguised form of foreign aid that could be terminated at will. So confident were U.S. economic policymakers that their country's financial, technological, and productive leadership were beyond challenge that they made substantial currency devaluations by the major European countries a condition for the continuation of the Marshall Plan. They reasoned that unless the other currencies depreciated to a more competitive level vis-à-vis the dollar, the billions allotted to the Marshall Plan would be misspent because the recipient countries would in any case be unable to revive their export industries. The Americans considered their probable loss of export trade as a result of the devaluations a worthwhile price to pay to help rebuild a strong, anti-communist Europe as their first line of defense in the escalating cold war. Accordingly, Belgium lowered its parity by 12 percent, Germany by 20 percent, and Britain, Sweden, and Holland by 30 percent—devaluations that far exceeded the 10 percent adjustments envisioned in the IMF Articles of Agreement as appropriate to correct a fundamental disequilibrium. As was the intent, these sharp devaluations turned the trade advantage against the United States and toward Europe to the extent that the 1949–1958 period came to be known as one of "beneficial disequilibrium." The prevailing feeling was that it was proper for the United States to give back some of the economic gains it had accrued during the war while Europe had been turned into a battlefield. Some international economists have argued with the benefit of hindsight that the 1949 round of devaluations was excessive, that their purpose of restoring equilibrium could have been accomplished by devaluations that were within the IMF's 10 percent guidelines.

Whatever the merit of that argument, the fact is that beginning in 1950 and for every year thereafter, with the exception of 1957, 1968 and 1969, the U.S. balance of payments moved into a steadily larger deficit position. During the years of beneficial disequilibrium, most observers took these deficits to be part of America's contribution to Western security. It was only after it became evident at some point in the mid-1960s that these deficits were not strictly voluntary that concern began to be expressed on both sides of the Atlantic.

Compared with the two decades that followed, the 1950s were relatively tranquil years for the foreign exchange markets. Hampered as they were by numerous restrictions, the markets were responsive to and indicative of bona fide supply and demand to only a limited degree. A number of countries maintained a two-tier structure of exchange rates, quoting separate rates for commercial and investment transactions. France devalued her franc twice, by 5 percent in 1957 and 15 percent the following year, to keep her products competitive in the export market and to discourage increased imports from entering her domestic market. The British pound also came under severe selling pressure during the 1957 Suez invasion, but the $2.80 parity established in 1949 was successfully defended by Bank of England exchange market support.

The return of the European countries to full currency convertibility in 1958 was a watershed event that marked the end of the dollar shortage and the beginning of what became known in its extreme state as a dollar glut. There is a certain irony in the fact that the removal of the remaining currency controls in Europe precipitated an increasing outflow of gold from the United States, which in turn caused that country to rely more heavily on capital controls and other devices inconsistent with the free market mechanism. Prior to 1958 less than 10 percent of the total U.S. deficits resulted in a loss of gold; that figure grew to over 60 percent during the decade that followed.

Doubts and criticisms

Though most other countries continued to express their confidence that the United States could turn its payments situation around at will, France—no doubt mindful of its unhappy experience with its sterling reserves in 1931—disputed its obligation to hold as part of its monetary reserve a currency about which she professed to harbor serious doubts. In a critique of the dollar's role as a reserve currency, which was generally considered to be motivated as much by political as by economic considerations, President De Gaulle's principal monetary advisor, Jacques Rueff, advocated as a means of increasing the world's liquidity a doubling or even tripling of the dollar price of gold. The Americans, to whom such a move would have represented a 50 percent to 67 percent devaluation of the dollar, dismissed the Rueff plan as just another De Gaulle challenge to their leadership of the Western alliance, and spoke caustically about the ingratitude of some people whom they had helped to put back on their feet after the war at great cost to themselves.

There were also, however, doubts expressed on the American side of the Atlantic concerning the long-term viability of a system that was fueled by a continuing U.S. payments deficit. In his influential book, *Gold and the Dollar Crisis*, Robert Triffin of Yale University argued that there was an inherent defect in an international monetary order based upon a reserve currency, the dollar, which was convertible into gold at a fixed price.[3] Triffin's thesis was that as more dollars poured out of the United States to

---

[3]Robert Triffin, *Gold and the Dollar Crisis* (New Haven: Yale University Press, 1960).

satisfy a growing worldwide demand for liquidity—money with which to trade, consume, and invest—its increasing inability to honor the commitment to convert all of these dollar claims into gold on demand was sure to undermine confidence in the dollar and end its usefulness as a reserve currency. Should the United States take whatever action was necessary to reduce or eliminate its payments deficits on the other hand, that reduction would be drawn from the reserves of its trading partners, thereby cutting back on the world's liquidity supply. Triffin proposed to resolve this contradiction by replacing the gold-dollar combination with a new reserve vehicle similar to Keynes's bancor concept rejected at the Bretton Woods conference. He further advocated a change in the adjustment process to allow exchange rates to float,—that is, to respond freely to supply and demand rather than to remain pegged at a particular level by central bank intervention in the foreign exchange market.

President Kennedy's administration was the first that had to deal with the adverse effect of trade deficits and capital outflows on U.S. gold reserves and the impaired standing of the dollar abroad. The first gold crisis erupted even before he took office, triggered by speculation that it was his intent to devalue the dollar by raising the price of gold as the French advocated. His advisors believed, however, that capital export controls of various kinds would reverse the outflow of gold and restore the dollar's health, thereby sparing the United States the humiliation of devaluing "the almighty dollar" under duress. For political and strategic reasons, it was unacceptable for the free world's reserve currency to be discounted, despite the well-reasoned arguments of Triffin and other academics. The gold crisis was resolved temporarily by the creation of a two-tier market that retained the $35 gold price for official transactions and introduced a free market price for private dealings. A gold pool was established by the United States and Western European countries to regulate the private market along the lines of central bank intervention in the foreign exchange market.

The system starts to come undone

It could no longer be glossed over by the time of the Johnson administration that U.S. deficits were not being deliberately generated for the good of the rest of the world. The Interest Equalization Tax, closing the U.S. capital market to foreign borrowers, was extended in scope and duration. So-called voluntary guidelines that limited U.S. business investment abroad became mandatory as the government attempted to stop the alarming loss of reserves through the exercise of more comprehensive controls. The administration's misguided attempt to prosecute the Vietnam War and advance the president's Great Society social programs without containing the resulting inflation by raising taxes persuaded observers that there was something chronically wrong with the dollar which capital controls in themselves could not cure.

The irony of imposing such controls as the Interest Equalization Tax and Office of Foreign Direct Investment regulations was that they actually further undermined rather than alleviated the payments situation. Excluded from the U.S. capital market for funds to invest abroad, American as well as other businessmen discovered the great pool of dollars that had been deposited in foreign banks as a result of U.S. payments deficits—a previously untapped reservoir of capital that became known as the Eurodollar market. Disregarded at first by the governments and central banks of the countries in which it developed, and not subject to the banking regulations governing domestic credit markets, the Eurodollar market mushroomed in size and importance because it offered advantageous terms to both borrowers and lenders. And due to a minimal degree of national supervision, it also became a conduit through which enormous sums could be shifted from country to country with a speed and facility undreamt of scarcely 10 years earlier. These characteristics made the Eurodollar market an ideal source of borrowed capital with which speculators could launch "bear raids"—selling attacks—on both the pound and dollar during the 1960s to force the devaluations that central bank intervention and capital controls were intended to prevent.

The attention of the bear raiders was first focused on the British pound, as selling pressures brought it to the brink of a devaluation in 1964. That speculative assault was beaten back by extensive buying of the pound by the Bank of England. It was during that 1964 siege, however, that the expression "gnomes of Zurich" was coined by British politicians who thought Swiss bankers made plausible scapegoats for the plight of the pound and the sorry state of the economy in general. But the selling was by no means confined to Switzerland nor, for that matter, to bankers. Multinational corporations increasingly assumed the role of speculators in foreign exchange, not so much to make a killing by forcing a devaluation of the pound, but to protect themselves against the loss in asset values that would accrue if a devaluation in fact occurred. Regardless of the motivation behind it, however, the effect of the selling was to exert heavy pressure on the $2.80 parity rate and to drain British reserves in the Bank of England's efforts to support that rate.

These pressures subsided when the bank's determination to defend the pound became evident, but resumed and grew to huge proportions in a fresh wave of selling in November 1967. This time, however, the government was unable to summon the resources required to repulse the speculative attack, and the pound was devalued 14 percent to $2.40.[4] It was generally agreed after the fact that the step should have been taken years

---

[4]The Bank of England lost $250 million of reserves in one day alone, November 17, 1967, the Friday before the devaluation was announced.

sooner, sparing Britain a decade of struggle and the loss of billions in reserves to defend a parity that, according to the judgment of the market place, was unrealistic.

The strong currency countries found themselves in the reverse predicament—a less dire problem, to be sure—as dollars and other currencies flowed to them in an effort by their owners to preserve their existing value. Germany, for example, was as reluctant to let the Deutsche mark appreciate as Britain was to see the pound decline. German export industries in particular were opposed to a rising mark because it would reduce their competitive price advantage in world markets. Moreover, the conversion of foreign exchange into marks increased the German money supply, rekindling the inflation phobia that stemmed from the hyperinflation in Germany 45 years earlier.

While Britain exhausted her reserves in buying pounds to support her exchange rate, Germany was obliged to sell marks to buy dollars, thereby swelling its reserves to embarrassing levels.[5] Unwilling to absorb additional dollars and unable to halt the inflow through restrictions on the import of capital—foreign currency holders were willing to pay a negative interest rate to own marks—Germany raised the parity of the mark in September 1969 from $0.25 to $0.27, an 8 percent revaluation. That such a deliberate upward revision in parity was never considered in the IMF articles was a telling sign that the Bretton Woods system was coming undone.

Changing relationships

As significant as the devaluation of the pound and revaluation of the mark were, the central problem remained the condition of the dollar. Although the appreciation of the mark should have made the dollar's position less precarious, heavy dollar sales continued, keeping other currencies at their upper intervention levels and forcing those countries to accumulate still more dollar reserves. The volume of dollars held by foreign central banks by 1969 had far surpassed the value of the U.S. monetary gold stock, making full dollar convertibility impossible if every official holder chose to exercise its right to exchange dollars for gold. As unhappy as they were with this situation, the other IMF members, with the exception of France, concurred that it would not be in their interest to precipitate a crisis through wholesale conversions into gold.

Each side pointed an accusing finger at the other. The United States maintained that the European countries and Japan weren't doing their fair share to bring international payments flows back into balance. They should, American officials argued, follow Germany's example and revalue

---

[5]The Bundesbank—German central bank—purchased $400 million on March 15, 1968, and $850 million on November 18–19, 1968, just two instances among many of the daily influx of dollars.

their currencies. Failing that, they were exhorted to inflate their economies, which would accomplish the same result, making their goods more expensive in the world market and give the United States a better chance to compete. The Japanese and Europeans would have none of it. They were adamant that the Americans had brought this upon themselves by their own extravagance, and that it was their responsibility to get their economic house in order after two decades of self-indulgence.

Wherever the responsibility lay—and there was enough to go around—the dispute really arose out of the changing political and strategic relationships between the nations in the late 1960s. The United States realized that it no longer could afford to maintain its perceived leadership role at the expense of its own economic interest, especially since its allies supposedly were capable of fending for themselves. Believing themselves able to stand on their own, the Japanese and Europeans became highly critical of the United States abusing its privilege of liability financing in the pursuit of policies abhorrent to them, such as the prosecution of the Vietnam War, in itself a major cause of the offending deficits.

Into this impasse came a new Republican administration in early 1969. Since the other nations resisted repeated American requests to revalue, and threatened to nullify any unilateral devaluation by the United States with devaluations of their own, it resorted to a policy of benign neglect as the only means available to it to resolve the situation. The U.S. Treasury Department and the Federal Reserve System were instructed to cease their intervention in the foreign exchange market to support the dollar, leaving it to the other central banks to buy dollars if they wished to prevent their currencies from appreciating in relation to it. But as they tried to do just that, they again began piling up unwanted dollars. The flow of dollars into Germany in particular became so massive through 1970 and 1971 that on May 5, 1971, after the Bundesbank was compelled to purchase $1 billion within 40 minutes, the foreign exchange market in that country was closed. When it reopened, the mark was left free to float upward, which meant that the Bundesbank declined any longer to buy dollars and sell marks. Experiencing the same buying pressures, though not to as great a degree, Holland also allowed the guilder to float, and Austria and Switzerland revalued by 5 percent and 7 percent respectively.

The summer months that followed saw the foreign exchange markets in a highly nervous state. The August release of the latest U.S. balance-of-payments statistics disclosed an explosion in the current deficit from an already shocking $10 billion to an incredible $30 billion. As if that wasn't enough to throw the market into turmoil, a report issued at about the same time by a congressional Joint Economic Subcommittee caused additional consternation; it said that because of the ballooning balance-of-payments deficit, the United States might have no choice but to devalue unilaterally and suspend gold convertibility of the dollar. During the week of August 9–13, more than $3.5 billion fled into European currencies. Over the following weekend, as part of the President's new economic policy, the United States announced it was repudiating its promise to exchange dollars for gold on demand, and that the dollar would be left to find its own level in the foreign exchange markets. Convertibility had ceased and the peg was pulled. Though there were sporadic attempts to repair or modify the system during the years that followed, by "slamming shut the gold window" the United States unilaterally jettisoned the Bretton Woods agreement—thereby leaving itself open to charges of breach of trust—because it couldn't any longer afford to adhere to the bargain struck in 1944.

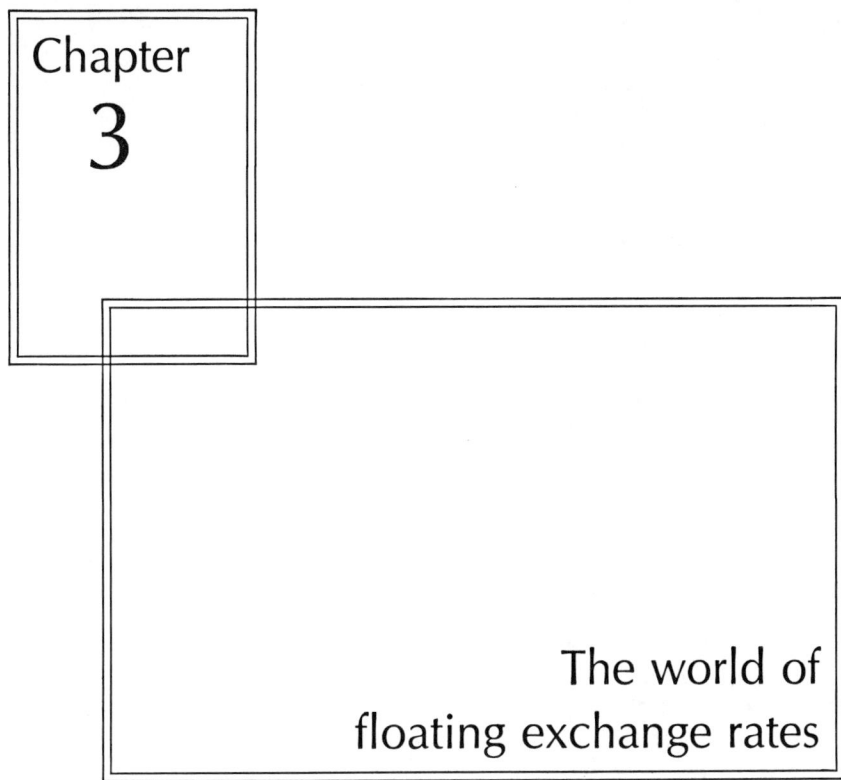

Chapter 3

The world of floating exchange rates

THE UNITED STATES unilateral abrogation of the dollar's convertibility into gold dealt a fatal blow to the dollar exchange standard. The Bretton Woods system lingered in intensive care for over a year before dying, however, while the world's finance ministers and IMF experts struggled to revive it through emergency treatment they referred to as "reforms." Even then, it was never accorded a proper burial because its mourners clung to the hope—as some of them still do—that it might someday be resurrected.

The Japanese and Europeans reacted to the bombshell announcement from Washington with consternation and outrage.[1] Knowing that a devalued dollar would jeopardize their export sales as well as reduce the nominal value of their official reserves, they charged the United States with violating their trust. American officials conceded that a multilateral res-

---

[1] I happened to be in Paris when the news broke, and judging from the newspaper headlines and my own conversations with local bankers and other businessmen, one might have thought the U.S action was the economic equivalent, 30 years later, of the sneak attack on Pearl Harbor.

olution of the currency crisis would have been preferable to their August 15 fait accompli, but claimed the latter action was taken only as a last resort, after numerous attempts to negotiate a mutually agreeable settlement had failed. Then they invited their disgruntled IMF partners to help pick up the pieces of the monetary system they had just toppled and to put together a workable replacement.

The Smithsonian agreement

As their colleagues in the banks' trading departments intervened in the exchange markets to hold their respective currencies as close to their by then defunct IMF parities as they were able, central bankers and treasury officials from the major economic powers met in an atmosphere of ill feeling to resolve the major differences between the United States and the other countries. Their attempt to put Humpty Dumpty together again culminated in the Smithsonian agreement of December 1971, which provided for:

1. A general realignment of exchange rates—chiefly an 8.5 percent devaluation of the dollar against other major currencies.
2. An increase in the official dollar price of gold (the means by which the devaluation of the dollar was accomplished) from $35 to $38 an ounce.
3. The expansion of intervention bands from plus or minus 1 percent of parity to plus or minus 2¼ percent.
4. A formal, albeit grudging, acceptance by the other countries of the continued nonconvertibility of the dollar into gold.

Table 3–1
Smithsonian parities in U.S. dollars, December, 1971

British pound	2.6057
Canadian dollar	1.0022
Deutsche mark	.3059
Dutch guilder	.3073
French franc	.1914
Japanese yen	.00324
Mexican peso	.0800
Swiss franc	.2554

Source: *International Financial Statistics*, May 1976.

The Smithsonian agreement embodied the prevailing hope that the long overdue dollar devaluation and wider fluctuation bands were all that was needed to put the Bretton Woods system back into operation. A cheaper dollar, so the reasoning went, would make American goods more competitive in world markets, improve U.S. trade and payments balances, and thereby restore the entire system's earlier viability. But apart from the official rhetoric they dutifully provided for public consumption, many conference delegates retained private reservations about the persisting surfeit of dollars throughout the world and their lack of gold convertibility. Few if any of them were heard to echo the hyperbole of the President when he hailed the Smithsonian accord as "the greatest monetary agreement in history."

The guarded optimism proved short-lived and, even at that, unjustified. Despite the dollar devaluation of nearly 9 percent, U.S. trade and balance-of-payments reports continued to make dismal reading. Even at its depreciated level, confidence in the dollar continued to slip away. The monetary policy that should logically follow a currency devaluation is one of contraction, to prevent higher prices from negating the desired results of increased exports and reduced imports. Yet the administration did precisely the opposite, pursuing highly expansionary policies which, though masked by wage and price controls, aggravated the country's payments deficit and pushed the dollar down to its lower intervention limit—that is, forced other rates to their upper (expanded) limits.

As before, the renewed weakness in the dollar affected all of the major trading nations. The principal strong currency countries, Germany and Switzerland, were once again inundated with unwanted dollars that were being dumped in favor of Deutsche marks and Swiss francs. A dispute over which measures were most appropriate to curb the inflation that accompanied these dollars provoked a parliamentary crisis in Switzerland before the decision was reached to unpeg the Swiss franc, a drastic step indeed by a country which had so rigorously practiced as well as preached the virtues of maintaining a stable currency. Beset by contrary pressures—wholesale selling of the lira—Italy resorted to dual exchange rates for commercial and financial transactions in its attempt to slow the massive outflow of capital.

The dollar was officially devalued for the second time in February 1973 as the United States tried to bring its value down to a level foreign exchange traders considered realistic. But continued selling on the premise that it would drop still further kept the market in turmoil. Unable to absorb the massive selling of dollars, this time compounded by similar speculative pressure on the British pound, the markets again were closed on March 1. When they were reopened several weeks later, any further attempts to hold exchange rates within official limits were abandoned. In foreign exchange jargon, rates were (ostensibly) free to float wherever the forces of supply and demand drove them. The Bretton Woods system had endured for more than a quarter century. "The greatest monetary agreement in history" reached at the Smithsonian had lasted 14 months.

The float versus fixed-rate debate

As was noted in Chapter 2, Robert Triffin and other academic writers had urged that floating exchange rates replace fixed parities well before the deficiencies of the latter became generally apparent. They maintained that a floating rate system would free a country's monetary officials—treasury secretaries, finance ministers, and central bankers—from having to choose between the often conflicting national goals of high employment, economic growth, and a stable price level at home on the one hand, and a strong currency and positive payments balances abroad on the other. Faced with the need to reconcile domestic policy decisions with exchange rate and balance-of-payments considerations, officials were reluctant to apply the prescribed action because it was politically troublesome: contracting the money supply and thereby depressing the overall economy for the sake of making a country's products and services more competitive in the world market. The same end could be achieved without provoking a recession, the academic economists argued, by abolishing fixed parities (and bands) and allowing exchange rates to float where they may in response to market forces without central bank intervention.

All that was appealing in theory, replied those business people and government officials who prided themselves on their realism, but the old system had performed admirably for over 25 years and there was nothing wrong with it that a few technical adjustments would not soon correct. The practitioners warned the scholars that their proposed abandonment of fixed parities would make the conduct of international business too uncertain and would therefore risk retarding the continued growth of world trade. As it turned out, both sides of the debate were equally right—or wrong, depending upon the bias of the party making the assessment.

Ever since the early methods of barter gave way to transactions involving money in its various forms, national currencies have been the yardsticks by which prices of the same goods can be compared from country to country. The purchasing power parity theory[2] was a formal expression of the recognition that a country's general price level, therefore its inflation rate, was a principal determinant of its currency's value in relation to the currencies of other countries, meaning its exchange rate. For any number of exchange rates to remain stable over an extended period, therefore, price levels in those countries must rise and fall together, and at the same rate. For that condition to prevail, each country must logically share the same living standard, income level, consumption tastes, productivity, interest rates, and so forth. It's a most unlikely prospect. It is equally unlikely, given the disparity of these factors in the real world, that central banks would be capable of executing monetary policies in their respective countries that would induce such harmony.

The Bretton Woods system of gold and dollar reserves, adjustable pegs, and IMF drawing rights was essentially an institutional mechanism by which countries could adjust to continuing changes in this disparity or, to resort once again to jargon, to bring the system back into equilibrium. But it

---

[2] See Chapter 7 for a discussion of the purchasing power parity theory.

would be far better, claimed the exponents of floating, to make the required adjustments through free market changes in exchange rates, as would be the case with any other prices. If flexible exchange rates could reconcile varying rates of inflation throughout the world, the argument ran, monetary authorities would have far greater latitude in applying monetary policy to their domestic economic and political requirements without undue concern over the international consequences of that policy.

The second argument frequently advanced in favor of a floating system is that, since traders' expectations regarding current and future economic conditions play an important role in determining exchange rates, fixing rates to specific parities interferes with the proper translation of these expectations in the exchange rate pricing mechanism. The market's disregard or inaccurate appraisal of these expectations would tend to aggravate the dislocations that signaled the imminent breakdown of the Bretton Woods system.[3]

The fundamental economic factors that affect a currency's exchange rate after it has been allowed to float include:

1. The size and rate of increase or decrease in a country's money supply and its prevailing monetary policy.
2. The size and trend of a country's trade and payments balances.
3. Its rate of economic growth, as measured by gross national product and other important indicators.
4. The level and changes in key long- and short-term interest rates, as compared with similar rates in other countries.
5. The general perception by the rest of the world of a currency as strong or weak on the basis of the foregoing factors, and the effect of rumors relating to such factors.
6. Dependency on outside energy sources, especially foreign oil.
7. The extent of central bank intervention in the foreign exchange market.

Identifying and listing these factors (though not necessarily in the order of their importance) is just the first step in analyzing them. The major effort—the art, if you will—lies in assessing their relative weight, which is in itself subject to continuing change, and in making some reliable judgments about the ways in which they interact to determine present and projected exchange rates. That is the essence of the task of the foreign exchange forecaster, and is the thrust of Part Two of this book.

The brief, undistinguished record of the Smithsonian agreement made it clear, if any clarification was needed, that pursuit of conflicting economic goals was at the root of foreign exchange instability. Some countries incurred price increases of 15 percent to 20 percent annually as a consequence of pursuing inflationary policies to promote economic growth, hold down

---

[3]The importance of expectations and market psychology in shaping exchange rates is treated in Chapter 9.

unemployment, and achieve other admittedly commendable goals. Other countries somehow managed to accomplish these objectives while holding their money supplies and price levels relatively constant. But the central bankers of these two kinds of countries couldn't mesh easily on the foreign exchange front, and when they tried their countries had to give up much control over monetary policy for the sake of exchange stability.

Even when the exchange markets were closed in March 1973 and, after they reopened, fixed parities were abandoned, most observers thought that floating rates were merely a temporary expedient that would be discarded as soon as the immediate crisis passed and the monetary wisemen succeeded in putting the old system back into working order. That they have thus far—nearly a decade later—found it impossible or inadvisable to do so has invested the present floating rate system with a greater sense of permanence than was originally accorded to it. Meanwhile, the debate over the relative merits and disadvantages of fixed and floating rates continues.

The speculation factor

One of the most frequently raised objections to floating exchange rates is that they encourage currency speculation, which in turn causes further instability and, in a vicious circle, more speculation. Critics of floating rates argue that firms doing an international business face much greater financial risks than they did under the old system, and at best incur higher hedging costs in their attempts to protect themselves against exchange rate losses. The extent to which floating exchange rates provoke disruptive speculation or merely reflect the economic instability prevalent in today's world hasn't been determined empirically. Like most chicken-or-egg propositions, it would appear likely that each in turn exacerbates the other.

There is no doubt that speculation plays an important role in the foreign exchange market, as it does in other financial markets. The controversy arises over whether speculation has a stabilizing or destabilizing effect on exchange rates. Even under a floating rate system, central bank intervention can in itself exaggerate or hamper rate movements. Despite the foregoing arguments in favor of floating, governments in fact can rarely bring themselves to tolerate a "clean float"—one in which the central bank abstains completely from intervening in the exchange markets. The alternative is a so-called managed, or dirty, float, in which the central bank continues to intervene on an irregular basis to keep its currency's rate at or near what it considers a desirable level.

The early predictions that the uncertainty engendered by floating exchange rates would seriously impair international trade haven't been realized. Many of the American business persons and government officials who initially were opposed to floating have come to regard it with favor and have perhaps themselves benefitted by the increase in U.S. exports that has resulted from a depreciated dollar. Moreover, they've learned that the operating problems of doing business under a floating rate regime aren't as great as they had at first feared.

The Laffer-Mundell critique

Ironically, just at the time that an initially skeptical business community had begun to feel comfortable with floating rates, questions concerning their long-term efficacy were raised from within the same academic community where they were first advocated. In a jointly developed critique of the floating rate system, Arthur Laffer of the University of Southern California and Robert Mundell of Columbia University, have argued that flexible exchange rates are the principal cause of the steadily escalating inflation rate throughout the 1970s. Their conclusion is that the situation cannot be corrected until some kind of fixed-rate system is reintroduced. The Laffer-Mundell theoretical model is based on the distinction between real and nominal prices. Real prices represent the intrinsic value of goods in relation to one another, whereas nominal prices are the same values expressed in money terms. Laffer and Mundell assert that a country cannot eliminate or reduce a payments deficit by devaluing its currency because, while nominal prices will fall as a result of the devaluation, real prices will not. They believe that, to the contrary, devaluation serves only to speed up a country's inflation rate because nominal prices eventually will rise to equal comparable prices in other countries. They also claim that the so-called ratchet effect, which makes prices flexible going up but rigid coming down, is responsible for inflation spreading from one country to another. Thus worldwide inflation becomes the chief result of the monetary adjustment process as it occurs under a floating rate system.

Whereas the proponents of floating rates argue that their primary benefit is the freedom they offer from balance-of-payments and reserve constraints in the shaping of monetary policy, Laffer and Mundell contend that this is a spurious advantage. They maintain that the suppression of inflation is more critical than policy independence at this juncture, and that can be accomplished only by monetary integration through fixed exchange rates. They want, in effect, to reaffirm the Smithsonian agreement and to restore the dollar to its former role as the world's key currency—but not, this time, convertible into gold.[4]

In their rebuttal of the Laffer-Mundell interpretation, the pro-floaters adhere to the conventional monetarist view that inflation is the consequence of a country increasing its money supply at a faster rate than its output,

---

[4]See Jude Wanniski, "The Case for Fixed Exchange Rates," and Arthur B. Laffer, "Global Monetary Growth and Inflation," in *The Currency Carousel: A New Era in Monetary Affairs*, ed. Thomas G. Evans, Princeton, N.J.: (Dow Jones Books, 1977).

thereby creating the classic too-much-money-chasing-too-few-goods situation. They contend that it was excessive monetary expansion and not currency devaluations that set off the worldwide inflation of the 1960s and 1970s, with the United States earning the lion's share of blame. The United States was able to "export" its inflation to its trading partners, so this line of reasoning runs, because such countries as Germany, Switzerland, and Japan were required under the rules of the IMF game to inflate their own currencies to supply the marks, francs, and yen that banks, corporations, and speculators were rushing to buy in exchange for the increasingly suspect dollar. It was fixed and not floating rates that was, according to this view, the "engine of inflation." The floaters also challenged Laffer and Mundell's assertion that, once reinstated as the world's money manager, the United States would mend its profligate ways and exercise the monetary restraint necessary to make their proposal tenable.

The pro- and anti-floaters at least can agree that in practice the choice is not between the extremes of rigid parities and a perfectly clean float. Rather, the realistic policy alternatives are those of adjustable pegs which provide for periodic devaluations and revaluations, and flexible rates managed to a greater or lesser degree by central bank intervention. One might in fact conclude that in practical terms, the fixed versus floating debate has been much ado about form rather than substance. As one analyst has observed, " . . . the choice is not between permanently fixed and fluctuating rates but between temporary stability subject to the shock of sharp change and a more or less even fluctuation."[5] If he were offered the privilege of amending his remarks with the benefit of hindsight, however, the analyst might have added that the experience of recent years has given us reason to expect less rather than more even rate fluctuation.

The European snake

In any event, the post-Smithsonian monetary system does not match the textbook model of a floating rate system. Most IMF member countries, especially the developing ones, have kept their currencies pegged to the U.S. dollar, British pound, or French franc. Of greater import to international trade and capital flows is the joint currency float instituted in 1972 by the European Economic Community. Forming what is popularly if not affectionately known as the European "snake," the member countries of the Common Market have undertaken through foreign exchange market intervention by their respective central banks to keep their exchange rates within a 2.25 percent maximum range between the strongest and weakest currency.

---

[5]Frank Graham, "Achilles Heel," quoted in T. D. Willett, *Floating Exchange Rates and International Monetary Reform*, Washington, D.C.: (American Enterprise Institute, 1977).

Figure 3–1
The EEC snake and the French franc: Deviations from the dollar par values of March 1973

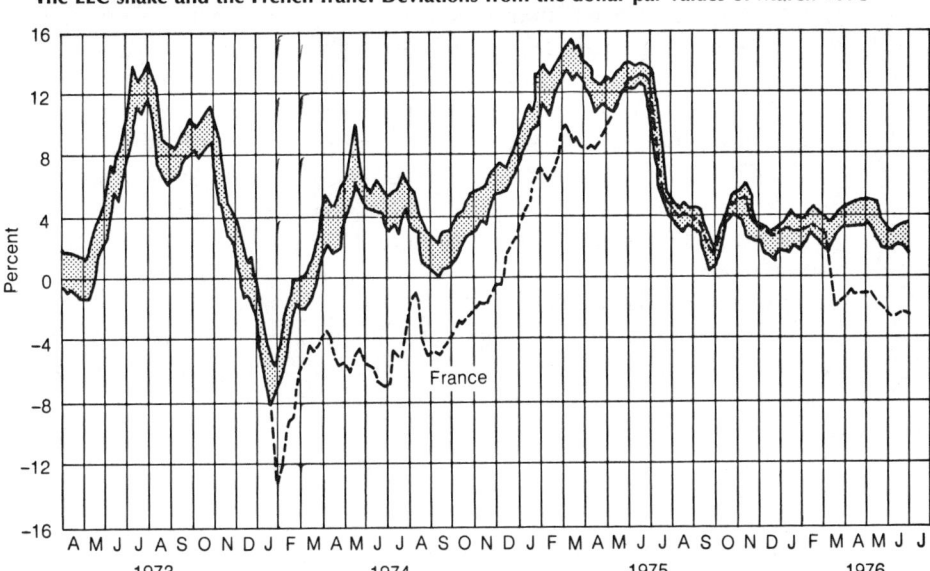

Source: OECD, Economic Outlook, July 1976, p. 66.

They further agreed to float jointly against other currencies—the dollar in particular—within a wider band, leaving the snake free to wriggle about inside this tunnel.

The snake agreement has implications that extend beyond the borders of Europe. What amounts to a regional attempt to coordinate and ultimately integrate national economic policies provides a working model for those who, like Laffer and Mundell, would apply the system on a worldwide scale. But despite the Common Market's natural geographic and economic cohesion, the snake has been subject to the same kind of disruptive forces that undermined the Bretton Woods and Smithsonian agreements. The strong-currency countries reluctantly tolerated inflation as the price for holding their exchange rates beneath the snake's upper limits. The weak-currency countries expended reserves in their attempts to hold their rates above the lower limits. The monetary and political costs of remaining in the snake were sometimes more than some members were able or willing to pay. Britain and Denmark participated in the joint float for a short time, but soon found it necessary to drop out. France withdrew, rejoined, and then left a second time. Italy discontinued its support of the lira in January 1972, a decision which threw the entire burden of keeping the snake relationships intact onto the surplus countries. During the same period, the existing members were unable to reach agreement on the terms under which Switzerland might join the snake. The Swiss wanted to enter with their franc set at a low exchange rate to encourage a high level of exports to the other members. The other countries wanted the Swiss franc to be priced high enough to stimulate their own exports to Switzerland, but not so high as to increase the average of all their currencies vis-à-vis the rest of the world, in particular the United States and Japan. Unable to arrive at a satisfactory compromise, the Swiss finally dropped their bid for membership.

By mid-1973, the worst fears concerning floating rates had not been realized. International corporations had acquired greater expertise in hedging their exposed foreign exchange positions. Stimulated by improved U.S. trade figures, a modest recovery in the dollar brought relative tranquility to the foreign exchange markets. Though the dollar was no longer the official benchmark of a fixed-parity system, it remained the world's principal transaction and reserve currency, and so its improved standing gave weary traders a sorely needed respite from recurring currency crises. Even then, the belief persisted that the float was merely a stopgap expedient that would sooner or later end with a return to some modified form of fixed-rate system.

The IMF role fades

The months following the collapse of the Smithsonian agreement saw a marked decline in the influence and stature of the International Monetary Fund. Still, the IMF remained officially committed to a restoration of the Bretton Woods system or something closely resembling it. It was hoped that some progress toward this end could be realized at the September 1973 annual IMF meeting in Nairobi, Kenya. But the conference closed without its delegates arriving at any decisions of consequence, and the IMF remained an organization in search of a system to administer.

In October 1973 the hostility in the Middle East flared into another Arab-Israeli war. The embargo on Mideast oil and subsequent tripling of its price had a vast impact on the international monetary system, which continues to be felt. In the first instance, the burden of higher oil prices fell unevenly on various importing countries. Second, international capital flows were drastically altered with the funneling of immense oil payments into members of the Organization of Petroleum Exporting Countries. There were no immediate indications about how and where the OPEC countries would invest their swelling surpluses, and how their investment decisions would affect currency values among the oil-importing nations.[6] Finally, the uncertainty over the lasting monetary effects of the oil situation meant that any possible return to a fixed-parity system was deferred indefinitely.

Among the major economic powers, Japan was, as the country most dependent on imported oil, hardest hit by the 300 percent price increase.

---

[6]According to estimates by the U.S. Treasury Department, gross revenues of the OPEC countries rose nearly fourfold between 1973 and 1974, from about $25 billion to about $95 billion.

In January 1974 the Bank of Japan failed to act when the yen fell against the dollar, thereby accepting a de facto devaluation of its currency. It was but one example of how central banks chose to respond—in this case, by not doing anything—to the increase in the world price of oil.

Contrary to the initial expectation that the oil price increase would be highly inflationary, it turned out to be the immediate cause of the most severe recession to envelop the world since the Great Depression of the 1930s. Gross national product in seven major OECD countries slowed about one-half percentage point during the second half of 1974 and nearly 5 percentage points in the first half of 1975.[7] Industrial production declined for seven consecutive quarters in the United States and six consecutive quarters in the OECD countries as a group, with drops in total output of 13 percent and 11 percent respectively. The bottom of the recession appeared to have been reached in most countries by mid-1975, although unemployment figures did not show any significant improvement until the end of that year. According to most indicators, the recession had run its course by the first quarter of 1976, and the world's monetary experts accordingly turned their attention from promoting economic recovery back to the increasingly insidious problem of inflation.

Finance officials pursued diverse policies that they believed suited their countries' interests. In Germany they continued to give first priority to subduing inflation, but at times overestimated the policy independence that floating rates supposedly afforded them. As was noted above, the primary responsibility for keeping the snake intact fell to them as the strongest-currency country in the joint float, while several of their partners in the snake were at the same time experiencing downward pressures on their currencies.

England also appeared to exaggerate the freedom from balance-of-payments considerations that a floating pound allowed her. Tolerating what many considered a ruinous inflation rate, the Bank of England was more often than not compelled to engage in "dirty floating" to prevent the pound from falling to the $1.50 level that was estimated by foreign exchange traders to be its true value in the absence of official support. The United States had, of course, long enjoyed an unusual degree of monetary and fiscal freedom as a consequence of the dollar's special role in the Bretton Woods system. Even with the advent of the currency float, the use by other countries of the dollar to stabilize their own exchange rates automatically benefited the U.S. position because it created a demand for dollars that otherwise would not have existed.

Monetary bureaucrats and their political superiors continued to confer and issue hopeful communiques. IMF delegates were pushed further out of the limelight when heads of government and their finance ministers held

---

[7]Organization for Economic Cooperation and Development, a quasi-official Paris-based body dedicated to the advancement of the goals indicated by its title.

an economic summit meeting at Rambouillet, France, in November 1975. The fixed versus floating debate reached the highest level as the host French government advocated a return to fixed parities and dollar-gold convertibility while the Americans resisted any changes in the status quo. The Rambouillet meeting concluded with the scarcely profound revelation that the surest means of securing exchange rate stability was to achieve economic stability. But the leaders and their advisors had no fresh insights about how that might be attained.

At its January 1976 meeting in Jamaica, the IMF's Committee of 20—a consultive group of finance ministers who were attempting to make headway on the issue of monetary reform—addressed the awkward problem of how to acknowledge the existing reality of floating exchange rates without compromising their avowed intent to restore some type of fixed-rate system. The committee's best effort was to propose that the major trading nations endeavor to hold their currencies within a relatively narrow band—something on the order of a worldwide snake—for a six-month trial, at the end of which they would formalize the then-existing exchange rates as the system's new fixed parities.

Though the grounds for his enthusiasm were not readily apparent to most observers, the U.S. Treasury secretary William Simon hailed the Jamaica conference as "a new Bretton Woods"—a rave review doubtlessly inspired by the "greatest monetary agreement in history" assessment made by his former Chief Executive at the conclusion of the Smithsonian meeting four years earlier. *The Wall Street Journal*'s editorial writers, among the staunchest of fixed-rate advocates, endorsed the secretary's paean. But, having seen such hyperbole come to naught in the past, the *Journal* qualified its approval with the caveat that "our analysis will be clearly proven wrong if over the next several months the dollar plunges sharply or climbs rapidly against European currencies."[8]

The *Journal* was right to hedge its opinion. Scarcely had the Jamaica conferees dispersed to their own countries when the exchange markets were once again beset by crisis. The Italian government suffered a no-confidence vote in parliament, subjecting the lira to renewed selling pressures, which in turn disrupted the entire European snake. The lira-dollar rate plunged from 686 to 733 within days, forcing the caretaker government to close the foreign exchange market in Italy. This drastic step gave the fixed-rate people fresh ammunition with which to attack the floating rate system on the grounds that it was working no better than the parity system had.

England was, like Italy, seriously affected by the world recession and escalating oil prices. This was the period before her North Sea oil deposits had begun to flow to the refineries. As her trade and payments deficits grew ever more calamitous, speculation threatened to depress the pound below $2. The Bank of England, after a strenuous effort to support it at that psychologically critical level, finally bowed to the selling pressure and

---

[8]"A New Bretton Woods?" *The Wall Street Journal,* Jan. 14, 1976, p. 12.

the pound plummeted, pushing increasing amounts of "nervous money" into the stronger currencies.

It was not merely an academic debate over abstract theories that was at stake here, but export sales, jobs, and ultimately standards of living. The suspicion spread throughout the rest of Europe that Italy and England were deliberately pushing their currencies lower to gain unfair trade advantages over the countries that were struggling to abide by the conditions of the joint float. Ill-feeling replaced the cooperative spirit engendered by the recent economic summit meetings, and the anti-floaters had still more grist for their mill. Plans were put forth for yet another hybrid approach. This time it was a renewed call for a system of crawling pegs, a compromise between fixed and floating rates to the extent that official par values would be recognized, but revised frequently enough to avoid such major rate changes as had occurred when Italy and England withdrew their support of the lira and pound. The irony of the situation was that just as the IMF had reluctantly sanctioned floating rates the system was again in danger of coming undone.

The foreign exchange market

With the British pound plunging from $2.43 to $1.67 between March 1975 and September 1976, to take the most extreme example, the question was repeatedly asked whether this extreme volatility was an honest reflection of such fundamental economic factors as trade balances, relative price levels and comparative interest rates, or whether it was fomented by speculation. Or, expressed another way, if speculation were a major force in the foreign exchange market, should it be commended as a stabilizing factor or condemned as a disruptive one?

Being the highly specialized field that it is, the foreign exchange market does not attract the broad participation of private investors and nonbank financial institutions that, say, the stock market does. Even the trading departments of large commercial banks impose strict limits on the size of the open speculative positions their foreign exchange traders are permitted to assume. Multinational corporations and import/export firms probably are more active as principals in the foreign exchange market than are their commercial bank intermediaries. But it is difficult to determine how much of their trading arises strictly from a need to hedge conventional business operations and how much from a desire to profit from currency fluctuations. Many corporate foreign exchange transactions probably contain an element of both.

Whether the increase in exchange rate volatility since the advent of the float era is a symptom or a cause of international economic instability, the fact remains that companies which enter the foreign exchange market in conjunction with their regular business operations are exposed to a higher degree of financial risk now than under the official parity system. In its most basic sense, exchange rate risk is the possibility that a currency's value may appreciate or depreciate in terms of other currencies—that is, the exchange rate is liable to change—at any time in the future. Within the perspective of an individual firm, it can be defined as the increased variability in consolidated earnings, including those of its foreign affiliates, due to currency fluctuations in the countries where the business operates.

Reverting to the example cited in Chapter 1, it should be clear that the proceeds in dollars of the sale for French francs of American jeans to a Parisian department store will be determined by the dollar/franc exchange rate at the time the transaction is consummated. Obviously, the greater the variability in the dollar/franc rate, the greater the uncertainty in projecting the dollar receipts from a number of such sales spread over a period of time. Table 3–1 is a summary of how the hypothetical quarterly earnings per share of the jeans firm, Levi Strauss & Co., for example, might be affected by converting the same number of French francs into U.S. dollars at irregular intervals under the former fixed-parity system, under a floating system where no attempt is made to limit exchange rate risk and under floating rates with exchange risk management.

Table 3–1
Hypothetical quarterly earnings per share under different foreign exchange assumptions

Quarter	Scenario I (Fixed exchange rates)	Scenario II (Floating exchange rates, no risk management)	Scenario III (Floating exchange rates, with risk management)
1	$.51	$.48	$.50
2	.52	.55	.505
3	.50	.47	.515
4	.51	.53	.52

In Scenario I, under the conditions prevailing before August 15, 1971, quarterly per-share earnings might have remained on a relatively stable plateau, rising or falling by variations of a cent or two.

Scenario II depicts the same worldwide operational earnings flow translated into dollars under the current floating rate regime, showing 12 percent to 15 percent sharper swings in quarterly results.

In Scenario III, the corporation is assumed to have undertaken a program of active exchange risk management, which brings quarterly earnings per share more into line with the moderate pattern of Scenario I than the more erratic fluctuations observed under the assumptions of Scenario II.

Reducing exchange risk

A multinational company reduces or at least diversifies its foreign exchange risk by the very fact that it does business in a number of countries, assuming that the rate movements of the several currencies involved tend to cancel each other out. A more activist approach to risk management begins with forecasts of possible exchange rate changes and projections of the actual amounts involved in terms of the company's domestic currency if the rate forecasts prove correct. The alternate methods of measuring foreign exchange risk exposure overlap sufficiently to allow their joint consideration. They are the cash flow approach and the balance sheet approach. Both begin with the company's listing its asset/liability and income items according to their currency denomination—dollars, francs, pounds, marks, and the like—and then grouping them into exposed and unexposed categories according to whether each foreign currency is considered stronger or weaker than the domestic currency.

The amount and degree of exchange risk are two distinct considerations. While a multinational company can determine the amount it has at risk in a particular currency by its decision to do business or not within that country, the degree of exchange risk is largely influenced by political and economic factors over which the company has little or no control. The fact that these factors are uncontrollable as well as unpredictable makes it highly desirable for an international company to engage in some sort of covering or hedging program. One common technique is to vary the leads and lags in making and receiving foreign currency payments, with a view toward paying off liabilities denominated in strong currencies and obtaining receipts due in weak currencies as quickly as possible.

The other principal means of covering such risk is to enter into a forward exchange contract, the purpose of which is to fix the exchange rate as of a future date when receipt of a particular currency is expected or payment of it is due. The organized exchange markets for such futures contracts and their use for covering risk (as well as for speculative objectives) are the main subjects of this book.

It was observed in Chapter 1 that forward dealings in foreign exchange grew out of a loophole in the ecclesiastical anti-usury laws of the Middle Ages. Interestingly enough, and perhaps not a pure coincidence, commodity futures contracts were first regularly traded at the same medieval trade fairs where these feigned forward exchange transactions took place. Futures markets in agricultural commodities reached their modern state of development in the United States and England during the second half of the 19th century. Futures contracts evolved to alleviate pricing problems associated in the first instance with growing, processing, financing, and distributing grain and cotton.[9] Firms engaged in the production and marketing of these and other commodities looked to the related futures markets to hedge against the price risk implicit in the handling of such products. Just as a multinational corporation would obtain forward cover to hedge an exposed position in, say, lira or yen, it might if it happened to be in a food-related business, cover in a like manner its exposure in coffee, cocoa, sugar, or wheat.

[9] See Allan M. Loosigian, *Interest Rate Futures,* Princeton, N.J.: (Dow Jones Books, 1980), pp. 4–11.

Though the rationale and techniques of forward price hedging were similar with respect to foreign exchange and agricultural commodities, each futures market evolved spontaneously around its related immediate or spot—for "on the spot"—market.[10] In the case of grain they developed as an integral part of the terminal markets in Chicago, Kansas City, and Minneapolis. Cotton futures exchanges flourished in the import/export centers of New York, New Orleans, and Liverpool, England. Similarly, forward dealings in foreign exchange were conducted chiefly by the same international network of commercial banks in London, New York, Paris, Amsterdam, Frankfurt, Zurich, and Vienna that handled the actual currencies.

It was not until after the first dollar devaluation and the initial resort to floating exchange rates that the two parallel markets—forward exchange and commodity futures—converged with the establishment in May 1972 of the International Monetary Market affiliate of the Chicago Mercantile Exchange. The simultaneously competitive and complementary relationships between the IMM and other financial futures exchanges which have since been established and the so-called interbank forward market will be discussed at some length in Chapter 11. It will suffice at this point to understand that both markets[11] provide contractual arrangements with which businesses can manage their foreign exchange risk exposure. Both markets also are arenas for speculative currency trading. As is the case with the multinational corporations that deal in the interbank market, it is sometimes difficult to discern where hedge transactions on the IMM leave off and where speculation begins. Deep thinkers might retort that any financial commitment made under conditions of uncertainty contains a greater or lesser element of speculation.

The birth of the IMM

The Chicago Mercantile Exchange (CME) has been regarded historically as the junior commodity exchange in that city, a successor organization to the old Butter and Egg Board established in 1874—25 years after the Chicago Board of Trade. During the 1960s, seeking new ways in which to compete more effectively with its intracity rival exchange, the CME was successful in introducing a number of livestock related futures contracts, including those for frozen pork bellies, live hogs, and live cattle. By the end of the decade, the exchange leadership was eager to expand its contract list even farther beyond the traditional agricultural and natural resource commodities traded there and elsewhere.

The CME chairman, Leo Melamed, a tough and highly successful trader in his own right (and a lawyer as well), had long entertained the idea of

---

[10]Also referred to as the cash market, presumably for "cash and carry."

[11]To avoid confusion, the IMM and other exchanges will henceforth be referred to as the futures market in foreign exchange and the interbank system as the forward market.

applying the concept of futures trading to financial instruments, particularly foreign currencies. Melamed realized, however, that as long as the Bretton Woods structure with its relatively narrow parity bands remained intact, there was little justification in creating a futures exchange to duplicate the existing interbank forward market in foreign exchange. Only in the event the IMF system ceased to function and exchange rates became more volatile than before, he reasoned, would the idea of exchange traded currency futures contracts become feasible.

By 1970, the idea of an organized currency futures market had gained support from a prestigious quarter in the person of Milton Friedman of the University of Chicago. Having made his reputation by his readiness to put his economic theories to the test of the marketplace—in fact, that *was* in large part his reputation—Friedman had a hunch in 1967 that money could be made by selling the British pound short. When the professor called not one but three major Chicago banks to place a sell order, he was politely but firmly turned away by each, a rejection that cost him a possible $40,000 in profits when the pound was devalued from $2.80 to $2.40.

When Leo Melamed and his fellow CME directors learned of Milton Friedman's belief that the remaining days of the Bretton Woods system were numbered, and Friedman was in turn apprised of their interest in organizing a currency exchange of the sort he may profitably have used at the time of the 1967 British pound devaluation, the pork belly traders and the future Nobel Prize winner established an innovative and somewhat disestablishment alliance. Melamed later acknowledged that "the International Monetary Market would not have been conceived were it not for the help and inspiration provided by Dr. Friedman. It was [he] who gave us the courage to believe we were onto something big and worthwhile."[12]

Armed with Friedman's endorsement, Melamed and the chief economist of the CME, Mark J. Powers, took to the road to enlist additional support in banking and government circles in the United States and abroad. On the whole, they encountered hostility, ridicule, and indifference. Interbank foreign exchange traders were generally appalled at the thought of admitting into their (would-be) exclusive ranks a "bunch of crapshooters in pork bellies." They, of course, did not shoot craps, but rather made reasoned politico-economic judgments. In Washington, U.S. Treasury Department and Federal Reserve Board officials were at best lukewarm to the CME proposal. The predictable reaction in Europe was that if such a marketplace did in fact come into being, it belonged there.

Melamed and Powers decided to move ahead with their plans in spite of their less-than-avid reception by the foreign exchange establishment. Should the projected currency contracts prove successful, they reasoned, they would pave the way for an array of financial instrument futures on U.S.

---

[12] Edgar Shook, "Playing the Global Money Game—Chicago Style," *Chicago Sunday Sun-Times*, February 24, 1974, pp. 8–13.

Treasury obligations, money market instruments, coins, and precious metals. They believed that this potential family of financial contracts would fare better within a separate organizational entity, and accordingly decided to establish an adjunct exchange to the CME—the International Monetary Market.

The IMM was in a real sense born amid the wreckage of the Bretton Woods system. As plans for the currency contracts proceeded, the foreign exchange markets experienced more frequent and severe crises, which culminated in August 1971 in the administration's abrogation of the U.S. commitment to redeem its dollars in gold and the first of two dollar devaluations. In January 1972, a month after the hasty patchwork of the Smithsonian agreement, the IMM obtained its Illinois state charter. On May 15 the new exchange opened its doors—it was actually allotted a corner of the CME floor—for trading in seven currency contracts. By late June, four of those currencies—the British pound, Deutsche mark, Japanese yen, and Canadian dollar—had been set afloat by their respective central banks.

The time for foreign currency futures had indeed arrived, but success by no means came with a rush. The first few years saw the fledgling exchange struggle for acceptance by the foreign exchange establishment and by the financial community at large. By 1976, the critical mass in trading volume was reached and surpassed. "The rest," says Leo Melamed with undisguised satisfaction, "is history."

Chapter 4

Spot and forward exchange markets

WHILE THE WORLD'S MONETARY STATESMEN appear to feel more at home in French chateaux (Rambouillet), Caribbean beach resorts (Jamaica), and African game preserves (Nairobi), the negotiations that determine the day-to-day behavior of exchange rates take place in the drab, cluttered, and invariably noisy back offices of banks in the major financial capitals. This chapter departs from the historical narrative and looks over the shoulders of the traders who populate these offices. Envision them punching buttons on their telephone consoles, scanning the chattering Telex machines, and peering at electronic quotation boards, all the while making rapid, almost instinctive, calculations as they buy and sell the equivalent of millions of dollars of foreign currencies during the course of a working day.

Technical descriptions of how the foreign exchange markets work invariably resort to higher mathematics to make their point, and probably evoke the same bewilderment from most readers as might a formula to produce, say, rocket propellant.[1] Leaving such abstract theory to those among the initiated who can appreciate it, the treatment that follows strives to cover the basic concepts in terms that will be familiar to anyone who took an introductory economics course in college.

Foreign exchange is so named because two parties agree to trade national currencies (though not necessarily their own) at a specified price or rate. Each commits to pay to the other a certain amount of currency by a certain date—within a day or two if it is an immediate or spot transaction, or in three, six, or more months in the case of a forward or futures transaction. One occasionally hears the charge that such exchanges are inherently bad in that they are often undertaken by speculators for their personal—and undeserved—gain, and somehow serve to disrupt the world economy. To the contrary, without the means to exchange currencies, residents of different countries would be reduced to a barter system in their economic dealings, and the overall level of prosperity would suffer as a result.

It is the amount that each party to the transaction pays to his or her counterpart that determines the exchange rate for that particular deal. If, for example, a trader at Germany's Commerzbank contracts to wire his opposite number at New York's Citibank 1 million Deutsche marks in exchange for $500,000 (Commerzbank is selling marks to buy dollars and Citibank is buying marks and selling dollars), the ratio from the German bank's perspective is:

$$DM\ 1 = \$0.50 \qquad \text{(Equation 4–1)}$$

and

$$\$1 = DM\ 2 \qquad \text{(Equation 4–2)}$$

is the reciprocal rate from Citibank's standpoint. However the quotation is expressed, two marks are changing hands for each dollar.[2]

Banks don't swap paper currency in transactions of this magnitude. Rather, the transfer is made in book entry form, the only physical evidence of which is an exchange of Telex messages between the two banks confirming the deal their traders made with one another. Settlement of a so-called spot or immediate transaction is actually made on the second

---

[1] As an example to satisfy the curious reader,

$$K = j - 1$$
$$S_{i,j}(t) = \prod_{K=i} S_{k,k+1}(t)$$

denotes a trilateral equilibrium condition among three spot or immediate exchange rates. Additional examples can be found in Appendix B.

[2] For the sake of continuity as well as simplicity, the dollar/mark rate (Equation 4–1) will be used for illustrative purposes throughout this chapter. Naturally, the same relationships apply to any combination of currencies.

business day, or "value date," following the day of the trade. This interval gives Citibank time in the example cited above to effect the transfer of a $500,000 credit to an account designated by Commerzbank, which in turn deposits its DM 1 million to Citibank's account. If the two banks that are parties to a trade do not happen to maintain accounts with each other, the transfers are made to their respective correspondents. Banks sometimes agree to a cash settlement, where the trade is done and payment is made on the same day, or on next-day terms, as is the custom with U.S. dollar/Canadian dollar transactions. But, because of the difference in trading hours over several time zones (traders in Western Europe are returning from lunch as the New York market is opening), two-day settlement is the normal practice for transoceanic trades.

Rather than trying to profit by riding out a major currency swing—say, buying DM 1 million at $0.50 ($500,000) with hopes of selling them some time later at $0.60 ($600,000)—dealers usually favor turning over large sums of foreign exchange quickly, each time for a small price difference on the order of two- or three-hundredths of a cent. Whether tiny or large, it is the spread between these traders' buying and selling rates that makes profits for their banks. If the rates should move in their favor while engaging in these quick in-and-out trades, so much the better. Should they move in an adverse direction—down when the trader is "long," up when he is "short"—that's part of the game as well.[3] Traders are paid to score more pluses than minuses. If they don't produce profits on balance, others who covet their jobs will replace them soon enough.

When quoting his dealing rates to his counterparts within the bank network, therefore, a trader will state two prices, a buying price (bid), which he is prepared to pay for a particular currency, and a selling price (offer), at which he will sell the same currency to other traders. The difference between the bid and offer is the spread, out of which the trader's profits, if any, are derived. In the example of the Deutsche mark/dollar transaction cited above, the Commerzbank trader's quotation might be

$$DM\ 1 = \$0.4999 - .5001 \qquad (Equation\ 4-3)$$

Since the professionals in the foreign exchange market are assumed to be familiar with the preceding digits, the quotation would be noted in their particular shorthand as 99–01. If that happened to be the prevailing quotation when Citibank's trader inquired as to Commerzbank's $/DM rate, he'd understand that he could expect to pay $500,100 for DM 1 million if he were a prospective buyer, and receive $499,900 if he were a seller. If Commerzbank's man could buy and sell marks all day at those rates, he would make a gross profit of about DM 400 ($200) on each DM 1 million

---

[3]As in dealing with stocks, a foreign exchange trader who buys a certain currency is said to be "long" that currency or to have taken a long position in it. When the trader sells without having owned it, i.e., a short sale, he or she is therefore "short" the currency or has a short position in it.

turnover. Since he might expect to turn over the equivalent of DM 20–40 million in various currencies during a trading day, what might at first glance appear to be an insignificant profit on each trade would amount to a handsome profit for the bank.

The competitive market

The trading banks aren't the only ones dealing in these narrow price margins. These banks' corporate customers do, too, which gives the market a highly competitive character. If, for instance, our friends at Levi Strauss & Co., having enjoyed a superb sales season in Germany, have on deposit there a balance of DM 20 million that they wish to convert into dollars and bring home, it is of little importance to them whether they make the conversion through Commerzbank, Citibank, or the Bank of America. They will place the business in most cases where they can get the best rate. If Commerzbank is quoting $/DM at $0.4999–5001, for example, while Citibank's quote is $0.5001–5003, L.S & Co. can earn an additional $4,000 on the exchange by making the switch through Citibank. Corporations can and do shop for the most favorable rate, and dealers soon become aware when a competitor is quoting a better rate (a better rate for a prospective buyer is not the same as a better rate for a prospective seller). To embellish upon the example just cited, Commerzbank, to make its quote more competitive, might raise it by two points (.0002), or Citibank could lower its by the same amount, depending upon the tendency of the market at that particular moment. If there is no definite trend, the former might raise its quote a point and the latter could lower its own by as much, putting each at $0.5000–.50002.[4]

A trader's quotation can be as much influenced by the overall trading philosophy of his or her bank as by current market conditions. Senior management may at some banks tolerate a certain amount of "aggressive trading"—one should not say "speculate," because banks are not supposed to do that—while others instruct their traders to assume as little risk as possible. Whatever the specific guidelines happen to be, a dealer will generally manage a position in the trading account with an eye for profit while buying from and selling to corporate customers and other participants in the interbank foreign exchange markets. As is the case with other kinds of trading, the dealer is constantly engaged in such tactical operations as going long on some currencies and selling others short, laying off excessive

---

[4]It is not necessary when revising a quotation to maintain the same spread, in this illustration .0002. Dealers can and do respond to changes in market conditions by making their spreads wider or narrower. Generally, the more narrow a spread is, the more competitive the quote is considered to be, because prospective buyers and sellers are both being offered a better rate.

positions with other dealers, and employing certain averaging techniques that are geared to a rising or falling market.

Competitive market-making keeps quotations closely in line, not only within individual financial centers, such as New York, London, or Frankfurt, but also among the various markets. *Spatial arbitrage* works to reduce any rate discrepancies that may arise between these centers until there is no longer any advantage—other than those that occur because of government-imposed restrictions—to be gained from buying a certain currency in one city and selling it in another. It is just as easy, given the sophisticated state of modern communications technology, to shop for the best quotation throughout North America, Europe, and, as far as time differences permit, the Far East, as it is to call the local banker across town.

The role of arbitrage

An arbitrage is considered a nearly riskless transaction because the purchase and sale are made at practically the same time. Therefore, if for some reason the dollar/mark rate were quoted at $0.4997–99 in New York and $0.5001–03 in Frankfurt, a trader sitting in Hong Kong or anywhere else could buy marks for dollars in New York and simultaneously convert them back into dollars in Frankfurt until the cows came home, turning a sure $400 profit for each $1 million lot for the cost of sending Telex wires between cities. Such opportunities to coin money seldom arise, and when they do, don't last for very long. Foreign exchange traders are a sharp-eyed lot, or else they would not be in that business. As more traders spot the discrepancy—perhaps that is another reason why it is called the spot market—they'll climb aboard the bandwagon, buying marks in New York and selling them in Frankfurt. The inevitable result, as anyone who has taken Economics 101 already knows, will be that the New York rate will rise and the Frankfurt rate will sink until the two rates become, if not identical, close enough so that the arbitrage operation no longer will bring in enough profit to cover the cost of sending Telex messages.

A similar process—this one with the faintly risqué label of *triangular arbitrage*—serves to keep all of the principal exchange rates so closely in line with one another that there are no prolonged opportunities to profit by selling one currency to buy a second, using that one to buy a third currency, and so on. Disregarding the dealer spread for the moment, we saw in Chapter 1 that if

$$DM\ 1 = \$0.50$$

and

$$£1 = \$2$$

then

£1 = DM 4

This triangular relationship must prevail, because supposing that the mark suddenly plunges to $0.40 while retaining its value versus the pound, it would once again be a case of coining money to buy for dollars all the marks one could possibly get his hands on at $0.40, convert them into pounds at the £1 = DM 4 rate and then change the pounds back into dollars at £1 = $2. If, on the other hand, the mark soared to $0.60 while remaining unchanged against the pound, the obvious move would be to sell marks for dollars, buy pounds at the £1 = $2 rate, and convert the pounds back into marks.[5] Like the spatial arbitrage, these transactions will of themselves bring the cross rates back into line. But under actual trading conditions, arbitrageurs would set to work long before the cross rates, also referred to as indirect parities, opened to such a wide gap.

Spot market theory

Turning briefly to the theoretical side of the spot market mechanism,[6] the immediate demand for a country's currency by foreigners—foreign exchange from their point of view—is determined by:

1. The extent of their demand for that country's goods and services.
2. The size of transfer payments (gifts, pensions, and so on) by them to residents of that country.
3. Their desire to invest in that country's stocks, bonds, real estate and the like.
4. The desire by foreign individuals, banks, and official government agencies to increase their holdings of that currency.

The reciprocals of these items determine the supply of that currency in the foreign exchange market. Because it is an exchange transaction, the fact that one currency is being supplied means that another is in demand, and vice versa.

Figure 4–1 is a conventional demand schedule for Deutsche marks in terms of dollars. The line slopes down and to the right, indicating that the demand for marks by dollar holders to purchase German products, services, and securities and to make pension, royalty, and other types of payments varies in inverse relation to the dollar/mark exchange rate. It is a graphic display of the fundamental concept that as a country's currency depreciates in relation to others, its goods and services become more competitively

---

[5]It would be possible in the first situation to coin money by exchanging, say, $1 million for DM 2.5 million at $0.40, converting the marks into £625,000, which could be used to buy $1,250,000 at the £1 = $2 rate. Readers may test their grasp of the concept by performing a similar calculation for the second situation where $/DM rises.

[6]Lest the reader raise hopes of being let off so lightly, be warned that this discussion is but a forerunner of a more extensive analysis to be undertaken in Part Two of this book.

priced, and therefore in greater demand in the world marketplace.

The upward sloping schedule in Figure 4–2 shows the other side of the relationship, namely that as the dollar/mark exchange rate appreciates, more marks are offered for exchange into dollars. This is a logical development in that as the mark appreciates, goods priced in dollars become more of a bargain in the eyes of mark holders, who therefore have an incentive to convert more of their marks into dollars. Figure 4–3 superimposes one schedule atop the other to establish at their point of intersection what the deep thinkers term the *equilibrium dollar/mark exchange rate*, or in our symbolic shorthand, $/DM. They say that the equilibrium rate is the price at which the market is "cleared," meaning that the supply of and demand for marks in dollars are in balance. Equilibrium exchange rates are determined for each pair of currencies in the same manner.

The same relationships are presented in numerical form in Table 4–1, where possible equilibrium exchange rates are listed in column A in mark terms (DM/$) and in column D in dollar terms ($/DM) as they are determined by various quantities of dollars demanded and marks supplied. Consistent with conventional price theory, $/DM rises as the number of marks required to satisfy the demand for a constant number of dollars declines, and DM/$ increases if the dollar demand rises faster than the mark supply.

The supply-and-demand forces that establish the equilibrium exchange rate are not constant—the schedules in Figures 4–1 and 4–2 move around the landscape—so that equilibrium is not achieved at any given rate for very long. In strictly theoretical terms, that is what proved to be the undoing of the fixed-parity system. Figure 4–4 shows how shifting supply-demand schedules bring about the rate fluctuations that are characteristic of a floating rate system. The extent to which central banks tolerate a clean float or

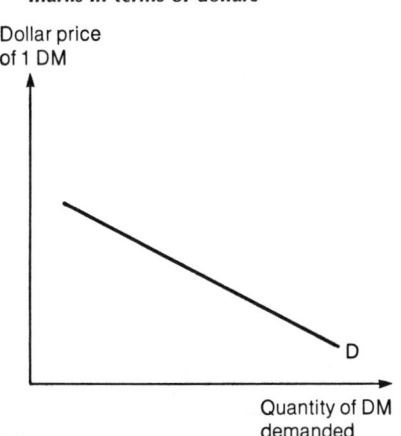

Figure 4–1
Demand schedule for Deutsche marks in terms of dollars

Figure 4–2
Supply schedule of Deutsche marks in terms of dollars

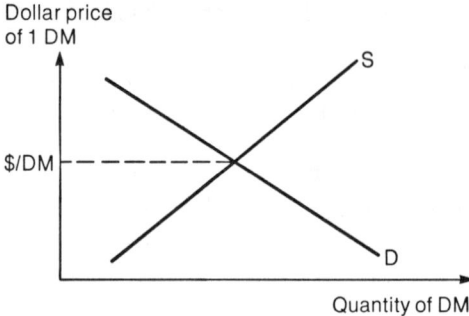

Figure 4–3
Equilibrium dollar/mark exchange rate

engage in dirty floating through systematic market intervention determines in large part how far exchange rates actually move.

Figure 4–4A (left) depicts three separate supply-and-demand schedules plotted on the same axes as were the previous diagrams. The supply-demand lines have been removed from Figure 4–4B to highlight with greater clarity the intersection points, which determine the equilibrium exchange rates for the three schedules. Also, the element of time replaces the quantity of DM supplied and demanded along the horizontal axis to demonstrate how a particular rate, in this case $/DM, varies with continual changes in the factors that determine it. It is the introduction of the dimension of time that provides the cue for us to proceed in our discussion from the spot to the forward market for foreign exchange.

The forward market

Although the immediate or spot value of a currency is the basis upon which all exchange rates are computed, it is the forward or future exchange

Table 4–1
Dollar/mark supply-demand schedules and resulting exchange rates

(A) Mark/dollar exchange rate (DM/$)	(B) Quantity of dollars demanded	(C) Quantity of marks supplied	(D) Dollar/mark exchange rate ($/DM)
5.00	1,000	5,000	.20
4.00	2,000	8,000	.25
3.00	3,000	9,000	.33
2.00	4,000	8,000	.50
1.50	6,000	9,000	.67
1.00	10,000	10,000	1.00

Source: Adapted from H. Robert Heller, *International Monetary Economics* (Englewood Cliffs, N.J.: Prentice-Hall, 1974), p. 32

Figure 4-4

A. Shifts in supply and demand schedules

B. Dollar/mark rate fluctuations

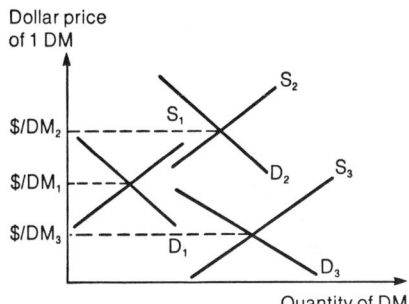
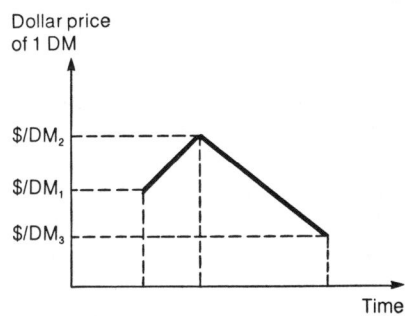

rate that is the more significant for the purposes of pricing and financing merchandise in world trade. An international transaction of any size usually requires a lead time of up to six months or longer from inception to fruition. It is the forward rate that spans the particular period in question to the time, for example, when merchandise is invoiced, payment is due for an overseas plant, or a dividend from a foreign subsidiary is scheduled to be remitted to the parent company.

A forward exchange transaction is not an outright purchase or sale along the lines of the trades described earlier in this chapter. Rather, it is a contractual commitment to buy or sell a specified quantity of foreign exchange at a specified future date (maturity of the contract) and for a specified price (forward exchange rate). All of these terms are set when the contract is agreed to. The conditions of the contract must be honored on the maturity date regardless of what the spot rate for that currency happens to be at that time.

Most major foreign exchange market-makers deal in both spot and forward markets. They find it useful on occasion to operate simultaneously in both markets in carrying out the same or a related transaction. Rather than buying or selling a certain currency outright, dealer banks may buy one maturity, either spot or forward, and sell another maturity of the same currency. Such an operation is conceptually similar to a geographic arbitrage between, say, Frankfurt and New York, except that in this case the rate differentials arise rather from time differences than those of space. Such dealings are known as "swaps," and are tantamount to concurrent lending (the currency being sold) and borrowing (the one being purchased) operations because the original transactions are slated to be reversed within a specified period.

If a trader buys, say, DM 1 million for spot value and sells the same amount forward for delivery in three months, he is materially reducing if not entirely eliminating his exchange risk with regard to that position. That is because he has arranged to sell the marks at an established price at the same time that he purchases them. By so doing he is fulfilling his role as a market-maker—prepared to take the other side of a prospective purchase or sale—without subjecting himself to inordinate risk. Since he will most likely unwind the swap by selling the spot marks and buying back the forward contract before its maturity date, the trader is primarily concerned not with the absolute exchange rates on either side of the swap but with the point difference between them. The trader's gross profit on the completed transaction is determined by the change in the differential between the spot and forward rates during the period he carries the position in his book.[7]

Forward rates of various maturities can be greater or less than the applicable spot rate. If they are greater, forwards are said to be at a "premium" over the spot rate. If they are less, they're at a "discount." To illustrate, in Table 4–2, suppose that three-month forward Deutsche marks are priced at a premium to spot like this:

Table 4–2
Three-month forward DM at premium to spot

	Bid	Offer
Spot DM	$0.4999	0.5001
3-mos. DM	$0.5049	0.5053
3-mos. premium	50	52

If forwards were quoted below the spot rate, the discount might be something on the order of this:

Table 4–3
Three-month forward DM at discount to spot

	Bid	Offer
Spot DM	$0.4999	0.5001
3-mos. DM	$0.4948	0.4952
3-mos. discount	51	49

The key to success in dealing with forward exchange—and therefore with currency futures—is to understand the factors that determine the size of a forward differential, and why it takes the form of a premium or a discount.

In the case of a premium forward structure, fewer forward marks are required to buy a certain number of dollars than spot marks would be. If forward marks happened to be at a discount to spot, more would be required. And if 3-month marks are at a premium over spot, it is more than likely that longer maturities (six, nine, and 12 months) would be quoted at increasingly

---

[7]If the trader bought spot DM 1 million at 0.5000 and simultaneously sold the same amount of six-month forward DM at 0.5100, and three months later unwound the two positions by selling spot at 0.5040 (+$4,000) and buying back what is by that time three-month forward DM at 0.5120 (−$2,000) his gross profit would have been $2,000.

higher premiums. Discounts would likewise probably grow wider with time if a discount forward structure were in effect. The forward structure of the dollar/Deutsche mark rate ($/DM), which has typically been quoted at a premium in recent years, might appear as:

Table 4–4
Spot and forward rates, three months to one year

	Bid	Offer
Spot DM	$0.4999	0.5001
3-mos. DM	0.5049	0.5053
6-mos. DM	0.5100	0.5102
9-mos. DM	0.5150	0.5153
1-yr. DM	0.5201	0.5205

According to Table 4–4, forward Deutsche marks priced in dollars are quoted at an approximate $0.0050 premium for each three-month interval for the year following the spot date. This sequence is called "the term structure of forward rates," an expression that should be familiar to investors in fixed-income securities (bills, notes, and bonds) and traders in interest rate futures contracts. Forward dealings in foreign exchange and investing in the national securities of various countries are such closely related activities that this differential between spot and forward rates—whether it be a premium or discount—is known as the "implied interest rate." How the difference in yield on comparable investments available at a given time in two different countries determines the extent of the premium or discount in their forward exchange rates is accordingly called the "interest rate parity theory."

Interest rates and foreign exchange

Having just taken in DM 20 million from fashion-conscious jeans buyers in Germany, the corporate treasurer at Levi Strauss & Co. gazes out of his office window over San Francisco Bay and ponders the pleasing question of how best to invest the funds for the three months until the company begins to accumulate inventory for the next selling season. His principal alternatives are to:

A. Leave the funds in Deutsche marks for the time being and invest them for 90 days in the German money market.
B. Convert the marks immediately into dollars and invest the funds in 90-day U.S. Treasury bills or comparable money market securities.

Assuming that both alternatives comprise what are for all practical purposes riskless investments, he will most likely select the one which provides the higher rate of return.

But there is already a potential risk implicit in the situation—exchange rate risk. If the treasurer decides to take up alternative A, he must accept the possibility that the dollar/mark rate will move against him during the 90-day investment period. An adverse rate fluctuation might not only erase the ostensible yield advantage of putting the funds into a mark-denominated investment, but could conceivably result in the conversion at the end of 90 days of fewer dollars than if he had let the funds remain idle during that time. The practical resolution of this dilemma is to hedge—that is, sell forward DM 20 million for three-month delivery at the same time that the funds are invested in the German money market.[8] In this fashion, the Levi Strauss & Co. treasurer can fix at the outset the precise number of dollars he is due to receive when his mark investment matures. There exists a link between the three-month forward dollar/mark rate and the German—U.S. 90-day interest differential, therefore, because the amount of forward premium the L.S. & Co. treasurer must pay above the spot $/DM rate will determine whether a given interest rate differential justifies the choice of alternative A.

The treasurer's calculation of his projected hedge operation would be something along the following lines:

Figure 4–5 shows the parity concept in diagram form. For the Levi Strauss & Co. treasurer to entertain investing in the German money market, he must be assured of receiving in dollar terms at least as much as he would have earned in the United States during the same period. The diagram poses the question: At what $/DM three-month forward rate would he achieve that equality? If the DM 20 million invested for three months at 4 percent per annum returned DM 20,200,000 principal and interest at maturity, and the spot equivalent of $10 million yielding 8 percent brought back $10,200,000 during the same period, the quotient of the two ($/DM) establishes the three-month forward rate. Hence,

$$\$10.2 \text{ million} \div \text{DM } 20.2 \text{ million} = \$/\text{DM } 0.5050 \quad \text{(Equation 4–4)}$$

As is the case with spatial and triangular arbitrage, any marked deviation from the $0.5050 parity rate would induce dealer buying or selling in the spot and forward markets to capitalize upon the disparity until market forces brought the rate back to its parity level.

Though an individual dealer may not himself engage in "covered interest arbitrage," as such hedged transactions are called, it is essential that the dealer be able to calculate implicit interest rates to quote correct forward rates for the currencies he or she is trading.[9] Generally, between two countries, the currency of the one with the higher interest rate of the two will be priced at a forward discount, which of course means that the currency of the lower interest rate country sells at a forward premium.

---

[8]Strictly speaking, one would sell forward the DM 20 million plus anticipated interest, as is indicated in Figure 4–5.

[9]The equation for this calculation is included in Appendix B.

Figure 4–5
Interest rate parity between German and U.S. money markets

Dec. 15: Invest DM 20 million in 90-day German Treasury bills at 4 percent per annum when comparable U.S. securities are yielding 8 percent.

Sell DM 20,200,000 three months forward at $0.5050.

Mar. 15: German Treasury bills mature, returning principal of DM 20 million plus DM 200,000 interest (DM 20 million × .04 × 3/12).

DM 20,200,000 delivered under December 15 forward sale. At $0.5050 rate Levi Strauss & Co. receives $10,201,000.

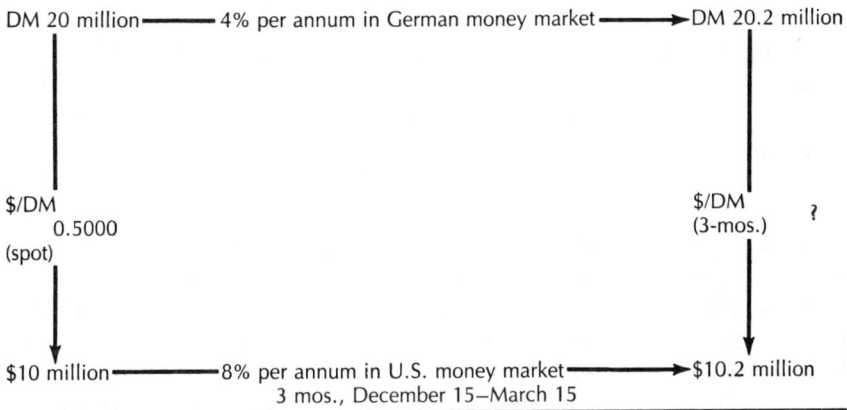

Quoting margins, not prices

When negotiating with other market-makers, bank dealers quote forward rates in terms of margins rather than as absolute prices. If, for example, the hypothetical rates listed in Table 4–4 were the current quotations, a dealer would quote three-month forward marks at 0.0050 − 0.0052 (or simply 50 − 52), indicating to the dealer's counterparties that his or her bid and offer are at those premiums over the spot rate. In most instances the spreads between bids and offers will be greater for forward rates than for spot quotations, increasing as the maturity grows longer. Not only is the effect of interest rate differentials greater on the longer maturities, but fewer dealers are inclined to quote rates that far in the future, making the market for such contracts less liquid than for the shorter maturities. An exception is when an unusual supply or demand situation affects the spot market or a near maturity, as might occur during a currency crisis or when an inordinately large purchase or sale is made. Less competitive quotes, hence wider spreads, are more often than not supplied for irregular maturity dates because banks find it difficult to cover themselves with swaps for dates that are not part of the normal maturity structure of 3, 6, 9, and 12 months.

Under the former system of fixed parities, traders' reservations concerning a particular currency usually found their expression in the forward rates because it was assumed that central banks would continue to hold the spot rate within its official intervention points. This artificial stability of the spot rate, as contrasted with greater movement in the forwards, often brought about unusually wide margins between the two, particularly during the crisis periods just mentioned. With the floating rates currently in effect, the spot rate is prone to display greater volatility as well, at least under the conditions of a relatively clean float. Under such circumstances the spot forward margins tend to remain more consistent.

To trade successfully in the forward market, a dealer must keep one eye on the interest rate differentials that affect her forward margins and the other (it would help if she had three eyes) alert to any unusual speculative or hedging activity that may touch off movement in the currencies that she customarily trades. If the forward rates are at a premium (meaning that interest rates abroad are lower than those at home) and the dealer anticipates that the spot rate will rise, she'll expect forward rates to strengthen as well if the applicable interest rate differential holds steady or shows signs of becoming narrower. If she is confronted with the reverse scenario, that is, her trading currency sells at a forward discount and her forecast is for the spot rate to weaken, steady to narrower interest differentials would indicate declining forward rates.

Conceptually, the spot rate and those for successive forward maturities each have their own supply-demand schedules, which may be viewed as five distinct albeit closely linked markets. In the absence of a currency crisis, the bulk of dealer activity takes place in the spot market and shorter forward maturities. Maturities beyond six months are more influenced by commercial hedging operations, strategic positioning of market-makers, and interest arbitrage. In this regard many traders are of the opinion that the six-month forward rate is the most accurate gauge of a currency's value because of the reason cited earlier, that most international transactions of any magnitude require at least that much time to reach completion. The six-month maturity is in most cases the applicable forward rate that determines the foreign price of goods in international trade.

Figure 4–6 illustrates the segmented market approach, with a separate supply-demand schedule and equilibrium exchange rate for each consecutive three-month maturity. Removing the supply-demand lines and linking the successive equilibrium rates, we have in Figure 4–7 the familiar term structure of foreign exchange.

In actuality, spot and forward exchange rates and interest rate differentials are established simultaneously as parts of an ongoing process that is smoothed by the several types of arbitrage activity described earlier in this chapter. Should any external event or technical market activity affect a spot rate, its influence is soon felt in the forward market, and vice versa. The action of a cracking bullwhip is an apt analogy, except that in this

Figure 4–6
Supply-and-demand schedules for spot and forward rates

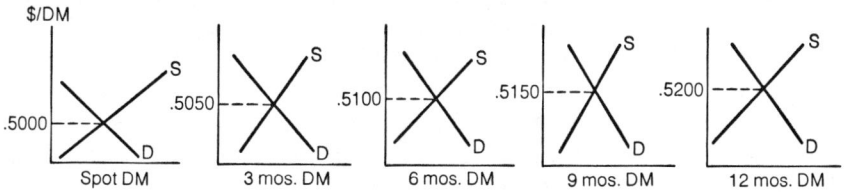

Figure 4–7
Term structure of forward exchange

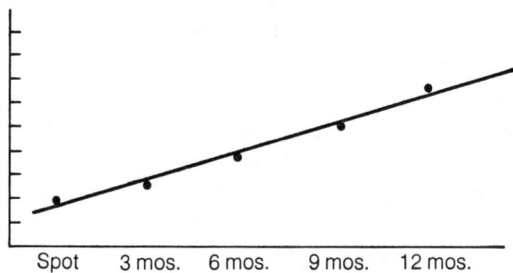

instance the moving force may originate at either end of the maturity structure and travel to the other side, causing adjustments in the successive forward maturities as it surges down the lash.

Impact of speculation

Whether they are undertaken for speculative or for hedging purposes, trading actions are influenced in large measure by expectations concerning future exchange rate movements. Though expectations are first reflected in the spot rate, they rapidly work their way through the term structure of forward rates via the interest parity link. A myriad of economic, political, social, and even psychological factors combine to shape these expectations, and there is no formula that can isolate and define the relative weight of each one.

If a speculator believes that a particular rate is likely to appreciate in the foreseeable future—$/DM 0.50 rising to 0.60, for example—he or she has an opportunity to buy that currency for future delivery. Enough of these speculative purchases will cause a forward premium to grow wider or a discount to become narrower, as the case may be. Conversely, speculators who believe that a certain rate is liable to drop will, if they follow their inclination to sell, force a discount to become wider or close a premium up.

The debate over whether foreign exchange speculation serves to moderate or exaggerate rate fluctuations is an interminable one. The best answer, though an admittedly inadequate one, is that speculation probably has both positive (stabilizing) and negative (destabilizing) effects, depending upon when and under what circumstances it is undertaken. Figure 4–8 shows how speculation can have either effect. The solid line represents the peaks and valleys of floating exchange rate fluctuations in a market environment devoid of any speculative forces, assuming that the price is set solely by the supply and demand from commercial operations. Stabilizing speculation is what purportedly occurs when selling enters the market at or near the high of the normal range and buying comes in at or near the low. The result is that rate swings are mitigated (dotted line) by this counter-cyclical buying and selling. But when buying comes into the market near the top of the cycle, on the assumption that the price rise will continue, or sellers attempt to drive the price below its customary low, rate swings become more extreme and speculation is condemned as being destabilizing. The shortcoming of such an analysis is that neither speculators nor anyone else have any way of knowing where the peak or trough of a cycle lies until it is price history. The far-from-satisfying conclusion is that individual speculators are acting along with, and contrary to, the prevailing trend at all times, so that there are always stabilizing and disruptive forces at work in the market. Which of them gains the upper hand at any given time is indeterminable, since we only know for certain the actual price, not what it might have been if circumstances were different.

Table 4–5 lists the spot and three-month dollar/DM rates at each month-end during 1979. A speculator who bought three-month forward $/DM on June 29, 1979, at .5502 would have incurred a profit of 224 points by September 28, 1979, when the spot rate was .5726. That profit represented a gain of over 4 percent over the three-month period, or about 16 percent on an annual basis, if the speculator had made a straight dollars-for-marks exchange. If, as is customary in such forward transactions, the speculator put up only a 10 percent deposit or margin, the percentage gain on his or her dollar outlay for the July 29–September 28, 1979, period would have been over 40 percent, or 160 percent annually. It should be obvious, but

Figure 4–8
Stabilizing and destabilizing speculation

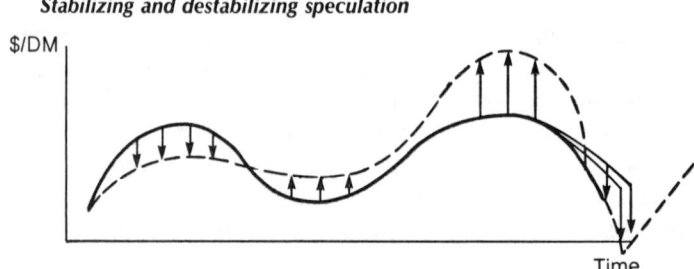

Table 4-5
Spot and three-month forward $/DM exchange rates, month-end 1979

	Spot $/DM	3-mo. $/DM	
January	.5338	.5423	
February	.5413	.5506	
March	.5357	.5432	
April	.5277	.5354	
May	.5230	.5289	
June	.5443	.5502	Bought forward 6-29-79
July	.5450	.5517	
August	.5486	.5552	
September Sold spot 9-29-79	.5726	.5802	
October	.5563	.5655	
November	.5793	.5870	
December	.5799	.5886	

Source: *The Wall Street Journal.*

nevertheless must be repeated in pointing out these handsome gains, that the indicated profit would have been a loss of the same magnitude if our trader had gone short (sold) instead of buying. The remaining entries show the profits or losses that would have been incurred on similar three-month forward transactions on each of the remaining months in 1979.

Pricing and invoicing questions

Turning from speculation to the question of pricing and invoicing for a foreign transaction, the easiest thing for a company to do is to bill in its domestic currency. But the fact remains that whatever national currency is used, one of the trading partners will have to buy or sell foreign exchange. There are in practice only three currencies used to make international commercial payments: U.S. dollar, Deutsche mark, and British pound. The Swiss franc is an important currency in terms of making purely financial transfers between countries, but for merchandise trade the other three remain the principal transaction currencies.[10]

To see how forward rates can affect pricing, consider the following situation, where the spot, three-month and six-month forward rates of dollars and marks against pounds and marks against dollars are:

---

[10]The French franc and Japanese yen are important gauges of general price levels and of specific product prices in those countries, but even in their case the majority of international transactions will be invoiced in dollars, marks, or pounds.

Table 4–6
Spot and forward rates £/$, £/DM, and $/DM

	Against pounds		Against dollars
	U.S. $	DM	DM
Spot	1.9998–2.0002	3.9925–4.0025	.4997–.5009
3–mos.	1.9668–1.9674	3.9885–3.9987	.4920–.4931
6–mos.	1.9386–1.9394	3.9832–3.9936	.4856–.4867

Given these partial term structures, a U.S. importer receiving goods from Germany and who has the choice of making payment in dollars, marks, or pounds would, if she considers the respective cross-parities, choose to pay in dollars. The merchandise she plans to import into the United States is worth $1 million, £499,950, or DM 1,996,406 at spot rates. If payment for the goods were due in six months, the present cost to her in dollars would still be $1 million, but considerably more in terms of pounds and marks. The additional cost to the importer, of being invoiced in marks, or even more so in pounds, is due to the smaller six-month forward discount in those currencies in relation to the discount on six-month forward dollars.

There may on occasion be special terms under which it would be advantageous for the importer to accept invoicing, in the above example, in marks or pounds despite the additional foreign exchange cost. One such case may be the provision of special credit facilities if the importer agrees to payment in the seller's currency. In that situation she should compare the extra cost of paying in that currency against the cost of her available sources of credit at home.

If a transaction is denominated in a foreign currency, as a matter of choice or not, it is almost always advisable to cover the exchange risk with the appropriate hedge in the forward market. A possible exception is the case of an import invoiced in a currency that is regarded as a likely candidate for devaluation. There, the importer would be better off by leaving her exposure uncovered unless the forward discount more than matched the expected size of the devaluation. If the import is denominated in a revaluation-prone currency, forward cover should be secured unless the forward premium is greater than the anticipated amount of the revaluation.

As was noted at the close of the previous chapter—and bears repeating at the end of this one—such considerations are more essential in a floating rate environment than they normally were under the fixed-parity system.

Chapter 5

The mathematics and mechanics of currency futures trading

THOUGH THE ORGANIZED FUTURES MARKET in foreign exchange is conceptually similar to the interbank forward market, the two are quite distinct in organization and operation. The forward market is an extension of the spot market described in the previous chapter, with its geographically scattered participants linked with one another by telephone and Telex. Currency futures contracts, though, are bought and sold on the same exchanges where the more traditional commodities—food, metals, and wood products—are traded.

The interbank forward market is the trading arena for the heavyweights in foreign exchange—mainly the dealer banks and their multinational corporate customers—who are accustomed to dealing in lots of $1 million (DM 2 million, £500,000, and so forth) or more. Because market-makers do not make as much profit on lesser transactions, the foreign exchange business of small and medium-sized companies has not been actively pursued by the dealer banks. The existing commodity exchanges, notably the Chicago Mercantile Exchange, saw a new business opportunity in extending to these companies the hedging and price-determining facilities they already

69

were providing to firms dealing in tangible commodities. To make the idea of introducing futures contracts on currencies even more appealing, commodity speculators would for the first time be offered a chance to try their hands at the foreign exchange trading game.

The prospects for such a supplemental hedging facility were materially enhanced by the increase in exchange rate volatility that followed the abandonment of fixed parities and intervention limits in the early 1970s. The International Monetary Market was established as an adjunct to the Chicago Mercantile Exchange on May 16, 1972, six months following the conclusion of the Smithsonian agreement. The failure of the Smithsonian reforms to revive the Bretton Woods system, and the subsequent resort to a currency float, all but assured the success of the IMM, which in turn prompted a number of other exchanges to enter the burgeoning field of financial futures.[1]

How the futures market differs

The dealers who make up the interbank spot and forward markets transact their business on a private, one-to-one basis; but members of a futures exchange operate around a common trading pit or ring, openly (and boisterously) calling out their bids and offers. Fitting the size and needs of its participants, transactions on the exchange market are less than one tenth the size of the typical contracts written in the bank market. Futures contracts also differ from bank forward contracts, in that they are all of a standard size, say DM 125,000 or £25,000, rather than being individually tailored to suit the customer's requirements. Their maturity dates are standardized as well, falling (with the exception of holidays) on the third Wednesdays of March, June, September, and December. The futures contract price, therefore, is the only variable of an otherwise fungible instrument. Maturity dates on forward contracts are, by contrast, matched to the needs of the firms that use them, and generally fall 30, 60, or 90 days or six, nine, or 12 months from the date the forward contract is written.

Bank dealers obtain their compensation for writing forward contracts from the difference between their buying and selling rates (the "spread"), whereas exchange market brokers charge their customers a set commission for each contract they buy and sell. Exchange market traders must post with their brokers a good faith deposit, known as initial margin, to guarantee their performance on each contract. Because of the limited access to the bank market and the demonstrable creditworthiness of its large-scale and well-known participants, there is no such requirement to post margin on forward

---

[1] By mid-1980, the Commodity Exchange, Inc., or Comex, had initiated trading in a variety of foreign currency and so-called interest rate futures contracts, and both the New York Stock Exchange and the American Stock Exchange had established affiliated futures exchanges to deal in similar, if not identical, contracts.

contracts.² The financial integrity of exchange traded contracts is further preserved by a clearing house system in which the exchange and its collective membership assume the opposite side to each contract and thereby share the responsibility for its fulfillment.

There is no prescribed limit to the extent a quotation may change from one day to the next in the bank dealer market. Exchange traded currency contracts, on the other hand, may not appreciate or depreciate by more than a set amount from the prior day's closing price. The interbank forward market is a true delivery market in the sense that over 90 percent of all forward contracts that are written culminate in the delivery of the actual currency specified by the contract. Exchange contracts, by contrast, are nearly always settled by a liquidating sale or purchase prior to the delivery date. The bank market is in most respects free from government regulation, whereas the IMM and other currency futures exchanges, as well as their respective members, are subject by federal law to regulation and oversight by the Commodity Futures Trading Commission.

From an investor's viewpoint

Regarding the currency futures market from the perspective of a private investor, there are a number of important differences between futures contracts and stocks and bonds. Securities are assets. They represent either a fractional ownership in a corporation, in the case of common and preferred stock, or a long-term debt owed by the issuer to the investor, in the case of bonds. Futures contracts in themselves denote neither ownership nor debt. They are binding obligations to buy or sell a particular commodity at a designated price on a specified future date. In the case of foreign currency futures, the commodity happens to be money and the contract price is the exchange rate. The eight currency contracts currently traded on the IMM, the specifications for which are summarized in Table 5–1, as well as similar contracts listed on other futures exchanges, are all quoted in U.S. dollars. Instead of being concerned with the dollar price per share of stock or per bond, therefore, currency futures traders must deal with prices expressed in hundredths (or even smaller fractions) of a cent per British pound, Dutch guilder, Mexican peso, and other units of foreign currency. The smaller that unit is in relation to the U.S. dollar—the Japanese yen, for example, at approximately 250 yen to the dollar—the more minute is the quoted unit price of the contract.

---

²There have been several notable failures of this system of mutual trust among participants that have caused severe disruptions in the interbank forward market. Among the most publicized were the default of Germany's Herstatt Bank in 1974 and the failure in the same year of the Franklin National Bank in the United States due to unauthorized and excessive foreign exchange dealings.

Table 5–1
Foreign currency contract specifications, International Monetary Market, March 1980

	British pound	Canadian dollar	Deutsche mark	Dutch guilder	French franc	Japanese yen	Mexican peso	Swiss franc
Ticker symbol	BP	CD	DM	DG	FF	JY	MP	SF
Contract size	25,000BP	100,000CD	DM125,000	125,000DG	250,000FR	12,500,000JY	1,000,000MP	125,000SF
Approx. value U.S. dollars	$55,000	$85,000	$75,000	$65,000	$62,000	$60,000	$42,000	$80,000
Minimum fluctuation	.0005 ($12.50)	.0001 ($10)	.0001 ($12.50)	.0001 ($12.50)	.00005 ($12.50)	.000001 ($12.50)	.00001 ($10)	.0001 ($12.50)
Normal daily limit change	.0500 ($1,250)	.0075 ($750)	.0060 ($750)	.0060 ($750)	.00500 ($1,250)	.0060 ($750)	.00150 ($1,500)	.0060 ($750)
Delivery months	All contracts—March, June, September, December							

Another major difference is the limited life of a futures contract. Corporate stock endures in perpetuity—or at least until the issuing company is absorbed by another firm, is dissolved, or otherwise ceases to exist. Most bonds are issued with maturities of up to 20 years. An investor is therefore able to buy and hold a stock or a bond for "the long pull" if he or she so chooses. Futures traders do not have that option. A futures contract has no value—in fact, it no longer exists—after its delivery date. Buyers and sellers have the alternatives of liquidating their contracts through offsetting sales or purchases, or of accepting or making delivery of the currency in question.[3]

Securities can be purchased outright or on margin. All futures trades are made on margin, inasmuch as neither the buyer nor the seller pays the full face value of the contract unless and until either one elects to make or accept delivery of the underlying currency—which occurs with less than 3 percent of all contracts that are originated. In futures trading, a margin deposit doesn't represent a partial payment of the purchase or selling price as it does with securities; rather, it is a good-faith or performance bond to ensure that both parties will adhere to the terms of their contract. These good-faith deposits in most instances amount to less than 10 percent of a contract's face value. Unlike the debit balance—what the investor owes the broker—in a securities margin account, futures traders are not charged interest on the remaining value of the contract. Brokerage commissions are also treated differently in a commodity account. Commissions are charged to the customer's account on the basis of a "round turn"—a purchase and a liquidating sale for a long position, or the reverse for a short position.

There are no specialists on the floor of a futures exchange who maintain a book and match buy and sell orders as there are, for instance, on the New York Stock Exchange. All floor members deal directly with one another, matching the best (highest) bids and (lowest) offers through open outcry across the trading pit or ring. Whereas an imbalance of orders—more buys than sells, or vice versa—may cause the suspension of trading in a particular stock until most of the orders can be matched at a certain price, futures exchanges deal with such a situation by imposing daily price limits above (below) which a rising (falling) contract price may not go during one trading session. A stock may be sold on another exchange than the one on which it was purchased if it happens to be listed on more than one exchange, and the sale can be handled by another brokerage firm. A futures contract must always be liquidated on the same exchange where it was initiated, and in most instances through the same broker.

Futures traders are confronted with a greater variety of market information and contract specifications than are their counterparts in the stock market. For example, they must be familiar, among other things, with the amount

---

[3]The only way in which the holder of an expiring contract is able to maintain his or her position beyond its maturity is by "rolling it over," that is, by liquidating the expiring contract and simultaneously buying or selling another contract(s) with a more distant delivery date.

of foreign exchange included in each contract, the minimum price fluctuation in points, and the dollar-and-cents value of a point in each instance. Stocks are in every case quoted in eighths of a point, which amounts to $0.1250 per share or $12.50 per round lot of 100 shares. Like stocks, foreign currency futures are quoted in fractions of a dollar per currency unit. But instead of a common denominator of 1 or 100 shares, the sizes of currency contracts vary, a frequent cause of confusion and losses to traders who fail to pay careful attention to what they're doing.

Prices and values

The purpose of having different contract sizes is to make all contracts roughly comparable in terms of their aggregate dollar value.[4] While the Deutsche mark, Dutch guilder, and Swiss franc contracts each provide for the delivery of 125,000 units of those currencies, for example, the British pound contract contains £25,000 and the Japanese yen contract contains 12.5 million yen, because the dollar values of the two latter currencies are significantly different.

Futures market rates are in most cases quoted in the same manner as are spot and forward interbank rates. The Deutsche mark contract, for example, is quoted in 100ths of a cent (four digits to the right of the decimal point), as are the British pound, Canadian dollar, Dutch guilder, and Swiss franc contracts. Because of their smaller denominations relative to the U.S. dollar, the Mexican peso and the Japanese yen contracts are carried to five and six decimal places respectively.

To illustrate the arithmetic involved, one point in the case of the Deutsche mark contract is equal to $12.50, since:

Contract size × Value of one point = Dollar equivalent

DM125,000 × $0.0001   = $12.50

To put it another way, if the dollar/mark rate ($/DM) rises from .5000 to .5100, that represents 100 points, or a $1,250 gain in the value of the DM contract. If the rate increases from .5000 to .6000, the gain on the contract is 1,000 points, or $12,500.

Figure 5–1 is a summary of the daily price activity in five IMM foreign currency contracts on November 2, 1979, as reported in *The Wall Street Journal* the following business day.[5] Following an opening trade at .5695,

---

[4] Though this was the case when the IMM contract terms were established, changes in relative currency values since the inception of trading have created a disparity in the dollar value of the eight contracts, as indicated in Table 5–1.

[5] Henceforth, for the sake of clarity and brevity, the ticker symbols *DM, BP, CD, SF,* and *JY* will be used when referring to these contracts. When alluding to the actual currencies as contrasted with the futures contracts, the words *marks, pounds, Swiss francs,* and so on, will be employed. *The Journal* did not carry comparable price information for the French franc, Dutch guilder, and Mexican peso contracts because trading activity in those currencies was relatively moderate during the period indicated.

March 1980 DM (the contract for delivery in that month) reached a high price of .5743 and a low of .5694 before closing at .5734, a gain of 39 points or $487.50 (39 × $12.50) over the previous day's closing price. During the same trading session, March 1980 CD closed at .8447. In that case, the 27-point depreciation represented a loss of $270 (27 × $10) because the size of that contract is CD 100,000, as contrasted with DM 125,000 (or DG or SF).

Figure 5–1
IMM currency futures prices, November 2, 1979, as reported by The Wall Street Journal, November 5, 1979

```
- FINANCIAL -
BRITISH POUND (IMM) - 23,000 pounds; $ per pound
Dec    2.0610 2.1020 2.0485 2.0665 -.0065 2.3145 1.9310   6,428
Mar80  2.0600 2.0730 2.0595 2.0675 -.0055 2.3050 2.0595   2,070
June   2.0650 2.0725 2.0640 2.0680 -.0050 2.2940 2.0640     584
Sept   2.0650 2.0680 2.0650 2.0670 -.0055 2.2100 2.0650     137
   Est vol 3,170; vol Thu 3,901; open int 9,219, +968.
CANADIAN DOLLAR (IMM) - 100,000 dlrs.; $ per Can$
Dec    .8430 .8437 .8422 .8426 -.0026 .8791 .8295         6,508
Mr80   .8440 .8463 .8440 .8447 -.0027 .8800 .8430         2,412
June   .8465 .8470 .8450 .8460 -.0025 .8725 .8450           619
Sept   .8495 .8495 .8495 .8495 -.0020 .8740 .8493           567
Dec                              .8523           .8750 .8500  34
   Est vol 1,395; vol Thu 661; open int 10,140, -116.
JAPANESE YEN (IMM) 12.5 million yen; cents per yen
Dec    .4300 .4319 .4295 .4304 +.0069 .6180 .4234         3,663
Mr80   .4370 .4392 .4367 .4379 +.0069 .4890 .4298           668
June   .4415 .4470 .4415 .4463 +.0073 .4750 .4368           212
   Est vol 1,325; vol Thu 743; open int 4,543, -248.
SWISS FRANC (IMM) - 125,000 francs-$ per franc
Dec    .6137 .6227 .6131 .6217 +.0072 .7610 .5977         4,617
Mr80   .6300 .6400 .6293 .6390 +.0075 .6968 .6030         3,086
June   .6425 .6535 .6420 .6513 +.0073 .7010 .6300         1,439
Sept   .6600 .6700 .6600 .6690 +.0090 .7210 .6458            55
   Est vol 3,736; vol Thu 2,506; open int 9,197, -195.
WEST GERMAN MARK - 125,000 marks; $ per mark
Dec    .5606 .5648 .5603 .5639 +.0031 .6380 .5310         4,554
Mr80   .5695 .5743 .5694 .5734 +.0039 .6037 .5360         2,633
June   .5775 .5830 .5775 .5810 +.0043 .5998 .5385           441
Sept                              .5834           .6060 .5790  24
   Est vol 3,855; vol Thu 2,667; open int 7,652, +336.
```

The profit or loss on a particular futures position is determined, therefore, by multiplying the number of contracts bought or sold by the number of points the contract price has risen or declined since the position was initiated. Assuming a long position of one March 1980 contract for each of the five currencies listed in Table 5–2, the overall gain (not considering commissions) that a trader would have accrued during the November 2 trading session is:

Table 5–2
Dollar gains and losses on five contracts, November 2, 1979

	Settlement price	Point gain (loss)	Dollar value of one point	Dollar gain (loss)
March 1980 BP	2.0675	(55)	$12.50	($137.50)
March 1980 CD	.8447	(27)	10.00	(270.00)
March 1980 JY	.4379	69	12.50	862.50
March 1980 SF	.6390	75	12.50	937.50
March 1980 DM	.5734	39	12.50	487.50

In this example the net profit on the five assumed positions after deducting the losses incurred on the BP and CD contracts would have amounted to $1,880. If, on the other hand, all five positions are assumed to have been short ones, the BP and CD contracts would have generated profits of the same dollar amount while the other positions would have registered equivalent losses.

Margin requirements

The initial margin a trader has to deposit with a broker upon initiating a long or short position is the basis on which the percentage gain or loss on a particular transaction is calculated. Assuming, for the sake of our illustration, the initial margins set by the IMM on November 2 were $2,000 per contract for each of the currencies listed in Table 5–3, the percentage gain (or loss) on each contract that day would have been:

Table 5–3
Percentage gain or loss on $2,000 initial margin

	Dollar gain	Percentage gain (loss) on $2,000 margin
March 1980 BP	($137.50)	(6.9)
March 1980 CD	(270.00)	(13.5)
March 1980 JY	862.50	43.1
March 1980 SF	937.50	46.9
March 1980 DM	487.50	24.4

The day's gains and losses expressed as a percentage of the required initial margin—the money a trader puts up to initiate a position—underscore the profit potential as well as the risk implicit in the futures market. Both are the result of the often extreme price volatility and the high leverage obtained through the low margin deposits.

As was noted previously, the purpose of requiring futures traders to deposit initial margin is to ensure that they meet the obligations set forth under the terms of the contracts they buy and sell. If the contract price moves in a trader's favor—up if he is long, down if he is short—the best guarantee that he will meet his contractual obligation is that it will profit him to do so. If the price moves the other way, however, the trader's initial margin deposit is depleted by the dollar value of the adverse movement. He must, under those circumstances, deposit additional margin. These fresh funds must be placed in the trader's account when adverse price action reduces his original deposit by a stated amount, typically 25 percent. For example, should a long position in Swiss francs decline by over 40 points (.0040), the dollar loss will exceed $500, or 25 percent of the $2,000 initial margin requirement. In that situation, the trader must deposit maintenance margin of $500, or however much is required to restore the original $2,000.

In the hypothetical futures account listed in Table 5–3, the column at the extreme right of the table indicates the paper profit or loss incurred on each position on November 2. As each of the individual contracts are liquidated—in our illustration sold, since all are assumed to be long positions—the paper gain or loss on that particular contract becomes a realized one.

The distinction between paper and realized or actual gains and losses is important in the management of a futures trading account. The initial margin originally deposited to an account represents the trader's *equity*, that is, his or her money. If subsequent price action should generate paper profits, the equity in the account is increased by the amount of that gain. Equity over and above the amount of initial margin required to carry all the contracts in the account is the account *excess*. The excess may be used to buy or sell additional contracts or may be drawn from the account. In the first instance, it remains part of the equity; in the second, it does not since the funds have been removed from the account. Should the account incur a net loss, the equity is reduced by the amount of the loss, and there is no excess since equity has fallen below the amount of required initial margin. In that case, as noted above, the trader is required to deposit additional equity to his account in the form of maintenance margin. If, however, some or all of the unprofitable contracts were liquidated—that is, paper losses are converted into realized ones—there would be no need to deposit additional margin. The account equity would be unchanged, but there would no longer be any margin required on the contracts that were liquidated.

In addition to the requirements that a futures trader deposit initial margin when initiating a position, and that he make additional cash deposits when the contract price moves against him by a stated amount, the integrity of the individual contracts and consequently of the marketplace itself is protected by an efficient clearing mechanism. Kept nominally distinct from the exchange itself for legal and financial reasons, the clearing corporation becomes the counterpart to both sides of a contract once the initial transaction between two traders is made. It is the clearing corporation to which each short contract holder looks for payment in dollars if he should elect to deliver the specified sum of foreign currency to satisfy his contractual obligation. By the same token, it is the clearing corporation that is obliged to deliver foreign currency against payment in dollars to those long contract holders who choose to settle up in that manner. Due to this system of collective settlement, futures traders are not subject to the good faith and financial capacity of the individuals with whom they trade or to that of their brokers.

In like fashion the clearing corporation daily collects from market losers and pays winners in a process known as "marking to market." By settling accounts daily, the exchange as a whole and its membership are at risk for only the dollar value of the current trading session's price variation. At yet another level of protection, the clearing corporation assesses its own membership, consisting of the largest exchange member firms, and therewith maintains a guaranty fund, which is in turn backed by the aggregate creditworthiness of the clearing members.

The delivery mechanism

Although the overwhelming majority of contracts—generally more than 95 percent—are closed out by an offsetting sale or purchase before their expiration, it is the delivery mechanism—hence the ability of futures traders to make or receive delivery of the actual currencies if they so choose—that makes the system work. Contracts change hands many times before they expire. By the time the delivery date does arrive, the original parties to a particular contract may both have long since departed from the scene. The holders of the few contracts that have not been closed out advise their brokerage firms of their intentions to make or accept delivery of the specified currencies. The brokers in turn notify the clearing corporation. By 1:00 P.M. Chicago time of the third Tuesday of the current delivery month, the long holders of contracts that expire that day deposit cashiers checks in the appropriate dollar amount with the Continental Illinois Bank in Chicago, or with other designated paying agents of the exchange in question.[6] For their part, the contract shorts arrange for the deposit of the stipulated amount of foreign currency in an approved depository bank in the country of issue.

With the dollars on deposit in Chicago (or in whichever city the futures market is located) and the foreign currency held by a bank abroad, the clearing corporation pairs the short and long delivery notices submitted to it and notifies the appropriate depository banks and customers' clearing firms of the matched commitments. The Continental Illinois Bank (or other U.S. depository) will then transfer the dollar funds from the accounts of the buyers' clearing members, who will in turn credit the accounts of their customers. The buyers' clearing members, meanwhile, dispose of the foreign currency with the overseas banks pursuant to their customers' instructions.

Nuts and bolts of trading

The accounts that futures traders maintain with their brokerage firms are similar to regular stock brokerage accounts. In fact, many of the larger

---

[6]The dollar payment is equal to the settlement price for that contract on the final day of trading times the specified contract size. If, for example, the final settlement price on a British pound contract were 2.0640, the dollar payment to the Continental Illinois Bank would amount to that price times 25,000—or $51,600.

investment firms deal in commodity futures as well as in stocks and bonds. A trader's point of contact with his brokerage firm is the registered commodity representative or account executive who is assigned to serve the trader. The representative in turn has access to her firm's research analysts and is in direct telephone or teletype contact with the IMM trading floor and other futures exchanges.[7]

Most successful traders work closely with their account representatives in reaching trading decisions and then executing them through the proper deployment of buy and sell orders. The nuts-and-bolts details of formulating and transmitting proper orders to the trading floor are as important in attaining profits as is making correct decisions about what and when to buy or sell. Giving short shrift to the mechanics of writing and sending clear and concise instructions to the brokerage firm's man on the trading floor—and, yes, a few women are beginning to appear there—can and probably will render a good trading idea useless and reduce what might have been a handsome profit to an almost certain loss.

With regard to currency futures, the basic questions of which currencies to buy or sell, why, when, and at what price will receive their due consideration in Part Two of this book. Assuming for the time being that these decisions have been made, the immediate task is to convey the proper instructions to the trading floor to make the desired trade at the best obtainable price—the lowest possible purchase price or the highest sale price. Even at that, judgment is required whether the best price is the one at which the contract is currently trading, in which case speed of execution is the prime objective, or whether a still better price may be gained by waiting. If restraint happens to be the watchword, the order must be precisely worded to reflect what it is that the customer and his account executive wish to accomplish.

The simplest and most direct order is the *market order*. It instructs the floor broker to accept the price that prevails at the moment she receives the order to buy or sell. Unlike the foreign exchange trader at a dealer bank, who is free to accept a particular quotation or not, as he sees fit, a floor broker at the IMM whose telephone clerk hands her an order to buy 1 December 1983 CD contract "at the market" when the lowest offer in the pit is .9244, has no choice but to buy at the .9244 offer price. The problem with market orders is that the .9244 price that seems attractive to the trader and his account executive sitting in, say, Baltimore could easily move to .9254 in a matter of moments, and it will be at .9254 at which the market order will be executed if that happens to be the lowest offer when the order reaches the IMM floor. That 10-points or $100 difference per contract, set against the $2,000 initial margin requirement, is a significant amount if the

---

[7]The reader is referred to Allan M. Loosigian, *Interest Rate Futures* (Princeton, N.J.: Dow Jones Books, 1980), pp. 108–42, for a more exhaustive discussion of order writing and floor trading procedures.

customer has his sights on making a quick in-and-out trade for 50 points or so.

To avoid such surprises, most commodity brokers advise their customers to use *limit orders*. In the foregoing illustration, the trader in Baltimore might have directed his account executive to wire the firm's floor broker at the IMM to:

Buy 1 Dec. 1983 CD .9245.

Such an order informs the floor broker that if she is able to buy December 1980 CD at or below the stipulated price, well and good, but she may not pay more than .9245. If the limit order were to sell 1 December 1983 CD at the same price, it would signify that the customer is willing to sell the contract at .9245 or higher, but chooses not to make the sale at all if he cannot get at least that price.

The trouble with limit orders is that they sometimes "miss the market" by a few points and leave the trader sitting empty-handed, while the price moves in the direction he anticipated. Of course, the limit price can be raised or lowered at any time, so it is not a once-and-for-all proposition. In the majority of cases, it is advisable for traders to risk losing an opportunity by using price limits and changing them, if necessary, than to surrender control through the use of market orders.

Orders are limited as to time as well as to price. Market orders must be executed immediately, so there is no question as to their duration. Unless otherwise specified, a limit order remains in force through the trading session during which it is entered. It may be valid for a shorter period, say an hour, if the trader is trying to maneuver in an exceptionally volatile market and does not care to be committed for a longer time. Limit orders may be left in force for a week, a month, or longer. On occasion the customer will instruct his broker to keep the order open, that is in effect until he asks to have it cancelled or it is executed at the designated price. Because prices and fundamental considerations change so rapidly in the futures market, open orders are not used as frequently as they are in the stock market.

The purpose of using a limit order is to secure an execution at a more favorable price than the current market price. A limit buy order will generally be entered at a price under the prevailing one; a limit sell order is usually priced above the going price. The reverse applies to *stop orders*, which are usually entered after a contract is bought or sold, to restrict the amount of loss that might be incurred on the consequent long or short position. If, to continue with the example cited above, our trader in Baltimore succeeded in buying the December 1983 CD contract at the .9245 limit price and wished to avoid losing more than 25 percent of his $2,000 margin on that position, he would instruct his broker to enter an open stop order—the one instance in which open orders are used frequently in futures trading—to sell the contract in the event the price dropped to .9195, or $500 below the purchase price.[8]

Stop orders are entered either as straight stops or as stop limits. The same problem that arises with regular market orders occurs when a straight stop order is triggered and becomes a market order to liquidate the position. The market price may be climbing or dropping too swiftly to allow the floor broker sufficient time to execute the order at or even near the designated stop price. The customer finds, therefore, that he has a realized loss far greater than the maximum loss he had in mind when he selected his stop price. The alternative is to enter a stop limit order that becomes a regular limit order when the stop price is touched. But the risk here is that if the contract price continues to rise or fall without returning to the limit, the trader is saddled with the growing loss he sought to avoid by placing the stop limit order. The problem (and loss) is compounded when the contract price moves up or down by the amount of the designated daily limit and the trader is unable to get out at any price until trading is resumed.

Phil Plunger and Dan Decimal

Having plodded our way through an unavoidably dry exposition of the ground rules—or, in this case, the floor rules—of currency futures trading, it is time to step up the tempo with an account of a true-to-life trading adventure. To disguise the dramatis personae, at least thinly, we enlist the aid of two leading players from an earlier saga: Phil Plunger, an intrepid financial futures speculator, and Dan Decimal, his keen-eyed account representative with the distinguished brokerage firm of Stable and Co.

Plunger, who has been out of the market for some time, is eager for a bit of fast-paced trading action. He has been following press reports of the decline of the U.S. dollar in the world's currency markets, and wonders whether that development might hold any profit opportunities for him, as unpatriotic as that may seem. Having just read that the Consumer Price Index rose 13.3 percent in the past year, the highest annual rate of inflation in the United States in 33 years and, even worse, several member nations of the Organization of Petroleum Exporting Countries were pressing for a further increase in the price of crude oil, he phones Dan Decimal for an expert's view of the situation.

Plunger: Listen, Dan, I've been reading about this inflation and oil price business. Why should those things affect the dollar so severely?

---

[8]If the trader had instead sold or "gone short" on 1 December 1983 CD at .9245, her risk would be that the price might subsequently rise. In that case, she would enter a stop order to *buy* the contract 50 points *above* her sale price, i.e., at .9295.

Decimal: The more dollars it takes to buy a barrel of crude oil or a gallon of gasoline at the pump, not to mention nearly every other commodity, the less each dollar is worth.

Plunger: I realize that. But why just dollars? Isn't all paper money affected the same way?

Decimal: The same way, yes. But not to the same extent. Virtually every country is dependent upon imported oil, and all are afflicted with rising prices for essential commodities. But some countries are more successful at keeping inflation in check than other countries. Therefore, their currencies have not lost as much of their former purchasing power. Add to that the fact that people in high-inflation countries want to exchange their depreciating currencies for the so-called hard currencies to preserve as much of their existing purchasing power as they can. The resulting sales of weak currencies and purchases of strong ones make their relative values, the exchange rate, diverge even further.

Plunger: Lower inflation, stronger currencies. You're talking about Germany and Switzerland, I suppose.

Decimal: Among others. The inflation rates in those countries have been appreciably lower than that of the United States, and they've nearly always managed to keep their balance of payments on the plus side, as contrasted with the deficits the United States has been running at an increasing rate over the past 15 years. As a result, the Deutsche mark and the Swiss franc have been in increasing demand while the dollar has been in excess supply, causing both the mark and the Swiss franc to appreciate against the dollar.

Plunger: What are they worth now?

Decimal: The Deutsche mark has moved between 50 cents and 60 cents during the past year, and Swiss francs have fluctuated in a somewhat higher range.

Plunger: Marks at 60 cents! The last time I was in Germany I got four to the dollar. Now you're telling me they cost more than twice as much?

Decimal: Times change. It may not be too long before the mark and dollar are equal. Then you'll be talking about the good old days when marks were worth 50 cents.

After discussing the matter further, Plunger and Decimal conclude that the purchase of one June 1981 Deutsche mark contract on the IMM would make an attractive speculation. But at what price? They consult a price chart and observe that June 1981 DM has traced a fairly consistent pattern between .5200 and .5800 during the latest six-month period. The contract is currently priced at .5340, and Plunger, true to his name is ready to push ahead and buy immediately. But Decimal notes that the price has been moving down lately, and suggests that there is more to be gained by being patient. He thinks it advisable to wait and see if they can pick a contract up 60 or so points cheaper. Plunger is willing to give it a try, and they agree to place a limit order to buy 1 June 1981 DM at .5280, good through the month.

Decimal tells Plunger that there is an $8,000 credit balance in his account with Stable and Co., so the $2,000 initial margin requirement for the June

1981 DM purchase is already on deposit. He feels comfortable about their decision, but is concerned about what might happen if the contract price should fall below what he considers a technical support level at .5200. Should that presumed support give way for any reason, Plunger could suffer a loss substantially greater than the $2,000 he committed to make the trade.[9] He therefore recommends, and Plunger agrees, placing an open stop order to sell at .5195 in the event that they succeed in buying June 1981 DM at their .5280 limit. That order, assuming it were executed at that level, would limit the potential loss on Plunger's position to approximately $1,000:

Purchase price − Sell stop price = Potential loss

Or,

.5280 − .5195 = .0085 × $12.50 = $1,062.50

Decimal adds that although there is not the same urgency about setting a profit objective as there is about limiting a prospective loss, it is good trading practice to have a target price in mind. They discuss the merit of taking their (hoped-for) profit if and when June 1981 DM reaches the vicinity of .5800, but agree to defer placing a limit sell order at that level until it becomes a more imminent possibility.

After all this talk and planning, Plunger is eager to have his order executed. Several days after the limit buy order was entered, good through the month, he calls Decimal to tell him that the morning paper carries the dollar/mark rate at .5260, and he therefore assumes that his order has been filled. Decimal, who has been monitoring the June 1981 DM price continuously, is surprised. He double-checks the futures price range for the previous day and finds that the low of .5325 came nowhere near their .5280 limit. Decimal then realizes what has happened, and tells Plunger he was looking at the spot quotation for Deutsche marks. Now it is Plunger's turn to be puzzled. He wants to know why, if they were cheaper, Decimal did not recommend that he buy spot Deutsche marks right away instead of waiting for the futures to come down in price.

Decimal explains that DM futures usually trade at a premium to the spot price, so for their purposes, spot at .5260 is no more attractive than June 1981 futures at .5340. Furthermore, he adds, trading in the spot market is unthinkable for Plunger since he would have to deal in dollar units in the magnitude of $1 million, with no provision for trading on margin.

The subject of premiums and discounts brings them to a discussion of interest rate differentials and their effect on the relationship between spot and forward exchange rates. Decimal explains that, when a currency such

---

[9]If, in the above example, June 1981 DM dropped 600 points to the .4700 area, not an unusual price movement under the floating rate system, nearly all of Plunger's $8,000 credit balance would be wiped out. If the contract price continued to fall to, say, .4300 and Plunger did not liquidate, he would have to deposit an additional $5,000 to his account, making a $13,000 loss on an original commitment of $2,000.

as the mark is priced at a forward premium in reflection of the difference between interest rates in the United States and Germany, the premium will increase as the interest difference grows wider—a development that favors the holders of long positions in DM futures.[10]

On the other hand, Decimal continues, the eventual convergence of spot and futures prices would, in the case of a premium term structure, work to the disadvantage of long contract holders. That means that there will be a structural bias against Plunger's prospective long position in June 1981 DM as the delivery date for that contract approaches. Assuming that the June 1981 DM contract is still at an 80-point premium over the spot rate if and when it reaches Plunger's prospective purchase price of .5280, both spot and futures rates would have to rise by at least 80 points by the contract delivery date for his trade to be profitable. The 80-point premium, therefore, represents a trading cost to Plunger in his role of a prospective long. If he and Decimal had, instead, decided that selling (short) DM futures was the preferred strategy, the joining of futures and spot rates—the disappearance of the premium, that is—would have worked to their advantage.[11] In that event, the 500–600 point rise they anticipate in both the spot and futures rates (*after* they manage to buy June 1981 DM, they hope) would far outweigh the cost of the vanishing 80-point premium.

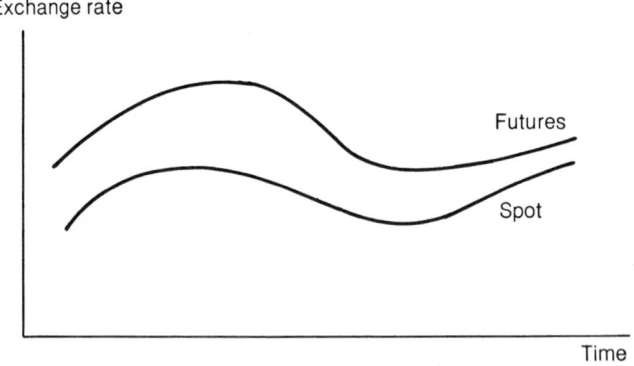

Figure 5–2
Convergence of spot and futures rates over time

Plunger's impatience starts to get the better of him. He calls Decimal a few days before the month elapses and complains:

Plunger: Where's June 1981 DM? Isn't that damned thing ever coming down to our price?

---

[10]The reader may wish, on this point, to review the example in Chapter 4, p. 63.

[11]Convergence has the opposite effect in the case of a futures discount. That is, it works to the advantage of long futures holders but to the detriment of shorts.

Decimal: It opened at .5310, the last sale was at .5305.

Plunger: That could be the low for this move. Why don't we forget about .5280 and buy it here?

Decimal: It's moving in our direction right now. We agreed that .5280 is a good price. Let's give it a few more days.

Plunger: OK, but if it turns around at .5300 and runs to .5800, you're going to have a mighty sour customer on your hands.

Decimal: It goes with the territory. I'll call you if there are any developments.

It was announced after the close of that day's trading that the U.S. balance of payments had shown marked improvement for the month just ended. Decimal calls Plunger to advise him that June 1981 DM had closed at .5290, and suggests that in view of the payments announcement they withdraw the .5280 order and try for an execution at a yet lower price the next morning. He asks Plunger for authorization to buy at the best price, up to .5280, on the opening. Plunger gives his permission, and they agree to talk again after the market opens.

Decimal calls his client the following morning with the news that he was able to execute Plunger's order at .5255—25 points below their original limit price. June 1981 DM is at that moment trading at .5260, so already they are to the good. He suggests that in light of the lower purchase price they revise their stop level downward as well. He and Plunger settle on a sell-stop price of .5170, which would maintain an 80-point, or approximately $1,000, risk level.

But now that he is finally "in the market," Plunger realizes that there is a good deal more to foreign currency futures trading than simply guessing whether a particular exchange rate is about to climb or drop. After further discussions with Dan Decimal and several members of Stable and Co.'s research staff, he is able to formulate some guidelines concerning the effect of future premiums and discounts on long and short positions:

1. When *buying* a futures contract that is quoted at a *premium* to the related spot rate, one should expect not only that the spot rate will rise but that the premium will increase through a widening of the interest rate differential between the United States and the foreign country in question.
2. When *selling* a futures contract quoted at a *premium* to spot, one should expect both the spot rate and the amount of the premium to decline. Under the best of circumstances the premium will fall to a discount to spot.
3. When *buying* a contract quoted at a *discount,* there should be the likelihood that the spot rate will appreciate, while the discount becomes narrower, and possibly climbs to a premium over spot.
4. When *selling* a contract at a discount to spot, there should be the likelihood that the spot rate will decline as the discount grows larger.

Decimal concurs with these general observations, but points out that spot rates can and do move up and down (or both) by an appreciable amount

Figure 5–3
Responding to premium-discount expectations

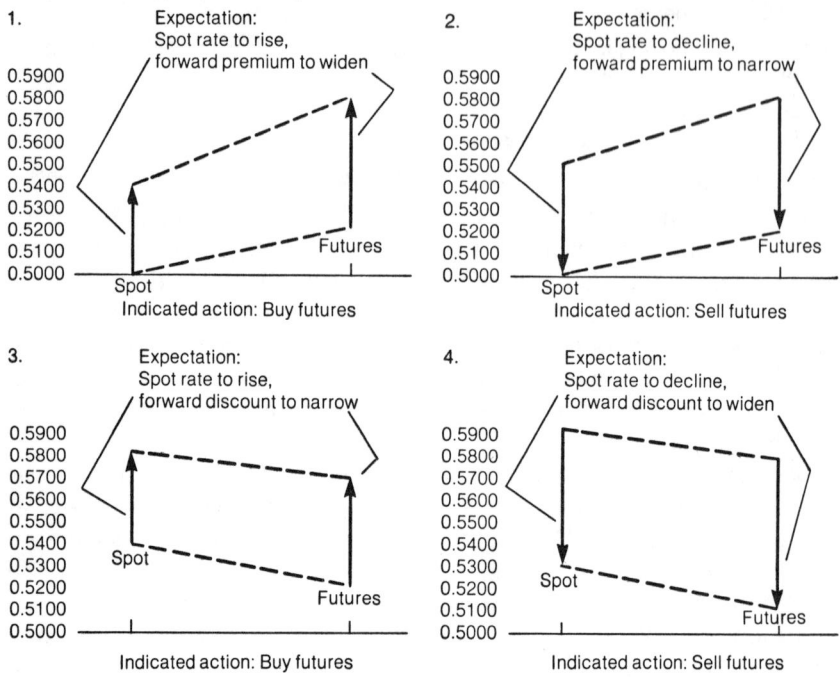

in a matter of days or weeks, while premiums and discounts change far more gradually. It usually occurs, in practice, that premiums will increase or discounts become narrower as the spot rate rises, while premiums shrink and discounts expand when the spot rate drops. The longer the maturity of the futures contract, the greater is the effect of premium or discount changes on the contract price.

Will June 1981 DM climb to the .5800 level anticipated by Decimal and Plunger? Or will their hopes be dashed when the position is stopped out at .5170? And what of the interest rate differential between the United States and Germany? Will it become wider or narrower? For the answers to these and other critical questions, read on, dear reader, read on.

PART TWO

DETERMINANTS OF FOREIGN EXCHANGE

Chapter 6

The balance of payments and how it affects currency values

THE ANALOGY WAS DRAWN in Chapter 2 between the international payments system and how money flows within a typical community. Germany might have been represented by the corner butcher, England by the owner of the hardware store on Main Street, Italy by your unemployed brother-in-law, and so on. The ordinary payments and receipts among the residents of our fictitious world would be "imports" and "exports," rainy-day savings would fill the role of monetary reserves, and trade deficits would be covered by loans granted by the kindly neighborhood banker playing the part of the International Monetary Fund.

But now it is time, for better or worse, to leave this fantasy land and come to grips with the issues affecting the real world of foreign exchange within a floating rate environment. To repeat—with good reason—the caveat stated at the beginning of this book: Exchange rate fluctuations, whether they occur in the spot or futures markets, are notoriously difficult to predict. But that is no justification for walking away from the problem. Those individuals whose businesses require them to operate in the international arena have no choice but to cope with the existing situation with the help of the best analytical tools that are at hand. Those who enter the market

89

of their own volition, for the prospect of speculative gain, do so precisely because of this uncertainty. In either case, a grasp of the theoretical concepts discussed in Part Two, and some feeling for their application, are prerequisites for survival in, let alone mastery of, the marketplace.

This chapter traces the development of the balance-of-payments theory of exchange rate movements since its origin during the bullionist controversies in 17th-century England. Against this historical backdrop we examine the effect of changes in a country's international payments position on the exchange value of its currency. Chapter 7 undertakes a review and analysis of the purchasing power parity theory—how inflation influences exchange rates—as it evolved over the same period. The two following chapters take up in turn central bank intervention, monetary policy, comparative interest rates, and market psychology, endeavoring to assess the impact of each on exchange rates. The last chapter of Part Two draws these various threads together in an attempt to establish what is admittedly an imperfect methodology for forecasting future exchange rate movements.

The balance of payments

A country's balance of international payments is the record of all economic transactions during a specified time between its own residents and those of foreign countries. (*Residents* refers to individuals, business organizations, and official government institutions or agencies.) In short, it is a statistical summary of all money payments *to* foreign entities, and of all money receipts *from* them.

"Balance of payments" is itself an imprecise description of the concept. "Statement of international transactions" or "international transactions accounts" would be a more accurate title for a tabulation of a country's economic dealings with the rest of the world. The traditional term does not make it clear that receipts are as integral a part of the statement as are payments, and the word *balance* implies an equality between the two that rarely, if ever, exists. But *balance of payments* is the term that is sanctioned by custom, and is therefore the one we are obliged to use. Whatever its label, this summary statement is indicative of the supply of (and demand for) foreign exchange that residents of various countries use to settle their respective money claims on one another. As a consequence, it has a direct and decisive effect on exchange rates.

The earliest recorded attempts to gather, document, and measure statistics pertaining to a country's economic dealings abroad arose from the controversy surrounding England's 17th-century trade rivalry with France. Businessmen and officials recognized even then that it would be purely fortuitous if the total value of the nation's purchases of goods and services from foreign countries (imports) matched precisely the total amount obtained from its sales abroad (exports).   Some means of settlement was required, therefore, to balance the difference between the sums paid and those taken.

Shipment of gold and silver was by that time established as the accepted means of settling such trade differences.   It was a cause of no little puzzlement and concern, therefore, when it was observed that bullion flowed from the country even when the balance of trade was in England's favor— that is, the money due her from total export sales exceeded the amount owed to foreigners in payment of imports.   The conclusion was soon forthcoming, that such invisible transactions—those not related to merchandise trade—because the maintenance of English troops on the Continent and the payment of shipping charges and loan interest to foreigners could and did cause specie to flow out of England in spite of her favorable trade balance. In *An Inquiry Into the Principles of Political Economy,* Sir James Steuart in 1767 made the first explicit distinction between the balance of trade and a complete account of international transactions.   In so doing, he introduced the term *balance of payments.*   Steuart's work inspired a reexamination of long-standing questions concerning the flow of goods, money, and credit between countries.

Similar questions were being raised in North America during the same period.   Following the conclusion of the War of Independence, the fledgling U.S. Department of the Treasury in 1803 was assigned the responsibility for obtaining shipping statistics and preparing statements of trade.   Ship captains were charged with reporting the amount, value, and destination of whatever goods they carried out of the country, while at the same time customs officials were given the task of compiling the identical information on merchandise that was brought into port.   The system proved inadequate because of incomplete and inaccurate reporting, problems in valuation, the lack of any customs information whatsoever on duty-free articles entering the country, and the numerous international transactions unrelated to merchandise trade.   Congress, accordingly, passed in 1820 "An Act to Provide for Obtaining Accurate Statements of Foreign Commerce of the United States."

During the greater part of the 19th century the United States was a debtor nation (it imported more than it exported) and borrowed abroad to make up the deficit.   England, the former mother country, was by contrast an international creditor; she enjoyed a steady inflow of specie in payment of interest and dividends due to her residents on their overseas investments. The United States was obliged to develop its merchandise trade to obtain the funds to service its foreign debt.   The United Kingdom was not under any such compulsion, since the income from its foreign investments was sufficient to finance its unfavorable balance of trade.

This also was the period during which national and international banking evolved, developments which hastened the replacement of specie by credit instruments for the settlement of international obligations.   The bill on

London became the predominant means of international payment during those years. Gold and, insofar as it was still used for monetary purposes, silver were relegated to use as banking reserves, rather than as the primary means of exchange that they had for so long been. Henceforth, their movement from country to country became contingent upon the requirements of the international banking system, rather than upon the flow of world trade.

World War I was a watershed in the development of international monetary relationships. The United States, in its conversion from a debtor to a creditor country, emerged on the world stage as an economic and financial power of the first rank. It was during this period that the U.S. balance-of-payments methodology and mode of presentation approached something resembling its present format. The first official U.S. balance-of-payments statement, prepared in 1923, comprised three divisions: (1) current transactions—those completed within one year and including merchandise (visible) and service and financial (invisible) items; (2) capital transactions—those expected to generate profits and/or interest payments over periods longer than one year; and (3) shipments of gold and silver. Apart from some minor rearrangements of accounts and a few additions and reclassifications, this format was used until 1946.

A bevy of balances

The problem with the present format is that there is no single figure or statement on which everyone can agree is *the* balance of payments. We have balances galore—on goods and services, on current account, on basic account, on net liquidity, and on official settlements. The purpose of this bevy of balances is to try to make the balance of payments balance. And thereby, as the dog said, wags a tale.

Those of us who struggled through a course in basic accounting were exhorted repeatedly that the opposite sides of the ledger *must* balance; that is, total receipts (credits) in the end always equalled total payments (debits). That was so, we were solemnly reminded, because it was the business of the accountant to see that they did. Now, some cynics might describe this process as one of "massaging the figures." . That attitude, combined with the fact that no country likes to admit to its own citizens—let alone the rest of the world—that it is losing money, often makes balance-of-payments analysis a very tricky business indeed.

We shall refer through the remainder of this chapter to Table 6–1, a reproduction of the 1979 U.S. balance-of-payments statement, for purposes of illustration. Readers should be cautioned, however, that the statement is simply a model, and that he or she should not become immersed at this stage in the numbers themselves, of which there will be an abundance as we move ahead. Rather, attention should be paid to the different accounts listed on each line and an effort should be made to understand the type of transaction represented by each item. Our 1979 specimen is only one of a succession of annual balances, and the United States is just one country, even though the major one, among those whose payments balances influence the behavior of leading exchange rates.

The 1979 statement lists approximately 35 accounts down the left-hand margin, and contains two columns on the right for credit and debit entries, respectively. The credit (+) column lists those amounts, expressed in dollars, which were paid or owed to American residents by non-U.S. residents, and which therefore created an actual or potential demand for dollars during the period indicated to make those payments. Entries in the debit (—) column represent the reverse flow, payments or debts owed by U.S. residents to foreign residents, thereby producing a supply of dollars to be exchanged for the currencies of those countries for which the payments were intended.

The differences between the adjacent entries in the credit and debit columns are the balances to which we have been referring. If the figure in the credit column is the greater of the two, it signifies that most revered of fiscal achievements—a surplus. If the balance falls in the debit column, it is that bane of bookkeepers and foreign exchange traders alike—a deficit. Elected government officials and their appointees don't like to reveal that their operation is running at a deficit any more than corporate officers do, and for the same reason: People tend to get the idea that they're poor managers. Most corporate shareholders supposedly "vote with their feet" when they grow disenchanted with management, meaning that they'll sell their stock, rather than become embroiled in protests, proxy fights, and the like. Foreign exchange traders behave in a similar manner. When a country posts repeated balance of payments deficits, they cast their no-confidence votes by selling its currency. That, in a nutshell, was the story of the U.S. dollar during the 1960s.

Government officials responsible for preparing the U.S. balance-of-payments statements during that decade were hard-pressed, therefore, to put the best possible face on a bad situation. The means the officials chose to achieve this cosmetic feat was to shift some of the payments accounts to different positions on the statement, and to devise the new kinds of balances mentioned earlier. Their objective was to make a convincing case that the United States was not doing so badly after all. They did, to be sure, succeed in covering the most unseemly warts and blemishes for a time. But the miracle of modern cosmetics, bookkeeping and otherwise, has not yet succeeded in transforming a crone into Miss America. To investors and foreign exchange traders, a payments deficit by any other name is still a deficit, and the prolonged weakness of the U.S. dollar during the decade indicates that they voted with their feet.

The various balances

The first balance listed in Table 6–1 is the "1. Balance on goods and services," the summary account for merchandise trade, service items (principally travel and transportation), and earnings on private and government investments abroad. It should be noted in this connection that were it not for the $37.8 billion in investment income due to U.S. residents—in the first instance to U.S.-based multinational corporations—the small 1979 surplus on goods and services would instead have been a substantial deficit. That fact refutes the often-heard charge that the primary cause of growing U.S. deficits over the past two decades was the heavy investments made abroad by American companies.

The "2. Balance on current account" is obtained by adding to the balance on goods and services the unilateral transfers accounts. These are remittances for which repayment is not expected, such as gifts and grants. In earlier years these transfers usually consisted of remittances from newly arrived emigrants to those family members who remained in their home countries. But since World War II these personal payments have been eclipsed by government-to-government grants, usually connected with reconstruction and mutual security programs that are not purely military in nature. The postwar Marshall Plan is the most widely known program of this type. The current account balance is probably the best measure of the ability of the United States to earn on a continuing basis the foreign exchange that is needed to cover its international trade and its lending and investment expenditures. It also reflects changes in the country's net international investment position, "which may well be considered more meaningful than any other measure of changes in the basic strength or weakness of our international financial position."[1]

The "3. Basic balance" adds to the current account balance those private and government transactions that fall more properly under the category of capital items than do the revenue and expense accounts cited thus far. These would include the construction of a manufacturing facility abroad (direct investment), the purchase and sale of foreign securities (indirect investment), and the issuance and repayment of long-term private and government loans. Those who favor the basic balance emphasize the importance of distinguishing between short-term, and therefore potentially volatile, financing items and those fundamental and supposedly more consistent longer-term forces that affect a country's balance-of-payments position.

All of the foregoing accounts contain "substantive" or what are referred to as "above-the-line" transactions. They consist of those items that record the day-to-day business of international trade and finance, and as such are

---

[1]U.S. Council of Economic Advisers, *Economic Report of the President* (Washington, D.C.: U.S. Government Printing Office, 1970).

Table 6–1
The U.S. balance of payments, 1979 ($ millions)

	Credits (demand for dollars)	Debits (supply of dollars)	Balance (Net supply/ demand)
Merchandise, adjusted, excluding military	$182,074	$211,524	− $29,450
Military	7,236	8,417	− 1,181
Travel	8,332	9,458	− 1,126
Passenger fares	2,156	2,969	− 813
Other transportation	9,307	10,111	− 804
Fees and royalties	6,328	667	5,661
Other private services	4,496	2,574	1,922
U.S. government miscellaneous services	520	1,713	− 1,193
Income on direct investments	37,734	6,038	31,696
Other private receipts and payments	25,859	16,346	9,513
U.S. government receipts and payments	2,269	11,164	− 8,895
1. Balance on goods and services	5,330		5,330
U.S. government grants (excluding military)		3,488	− 3,488
U.S. government pensions and other transfers		1,173	− 1,173
Private remittances and other transfers		987	− 987
2. Balance on current account		318	− 318
U.S. government loans		7,522	− 7,522
Repayments of U.S. government loans	3,713		3,713
Direct investment	7,674	24,762	− 17,088
Securities	7,599	4,967	2,632
Long-term capital	1,118	2,718	− 1,600
3. Basic balance		20,183	− 20,183
Claims and liabilities reported by U.S. banks	32,702	26,089	6,613
Allocations of special drawing rights	1,139		1,139
Statistical discrepancy	30,696		30,696
4. Net liquidity balance	18,265		18,265
Short-term, liquid capital	1,834	3,800	− 1,966
5. Official reserve transactions balance	16,299		16,299
Foreign official agencies, net		15,192	− 15,192
U.S. Reserve assets:			
Gold		65	− 65
Foreign currencies	283		283
Special drawing rights		1,136	− 1,136
IMF reserve position		189	− 189
Accounting balance			0

Source: *Survey of Current Business,* March 1980.

set apart from the so-called compensatory or "below-the-line" accounts. It is below the line, or so it is alleged, where the cosmetic balancing tricks take place, inasmuch as the accounts there are the ones designed to bring the above-the-line transactions into balance. They represent in most instances short-term capital flows, or the transfer of official reserves. A debit (deficit) above the line is usually offset by a credit below it, and vice versa. The decision to carry certain accounts above or below the line is to some extent an arbitrary one, a situation that poses the question whether a specific decision is made with the most objective of motives or as part of the attempt to achieve the desired cosmetic miracle.

The first of the below-the-line balances, and the most frequently cited measure of the U.S. international payments position, is the "4. Net liquidity balance." It is obtained by adding to, or subtracting from, the basic balance gold and foreign exchange transfers and changes in liquid (i.e., quickly realizable) claims by foreign savers and investors on U.S. residents. The latter category includes readily marketable U.S. government obligations, demand deposits, bankers acceptances, certificates of deposit owned abroad, and a catch-all errors and omissions account. Before the gold window was closed in August 1971, the net liquidity balance was regarded as the best measure of the ability of the U.S. Treasury to convert dollars into gold at the then-fixed price of $35 an ounce.

The U.S. Department of Commerce introduced in 1966 the "5. Official reserve transactions balance," which differs from the net liquidity balance in that changes in foreign claims on the United States are entered above or below the line according to the type of owner—private as opposed to official—rather than according to their maturity. This balance has acquired added significance since the adoption of floating exchange rates, because it clearly reflects any increase or decrease in claims on the United States by foreign central banks and other monetary authorities as they buy and sell dollars to maintain their own currencies at or near a desired target rate.

Table 6–2 is a summary listing of the five balances described above from 1960 to 1979. There is clearly a material difference in the official U.S. payments position during those years, depending upon the measure selected. Those public servants who were assigned the unenviable duty of defending the American payments record during the 1960s and 1970s found it less discouraging to point to the balance on goods and services and to the balance on current account than to the net liquidity balance or official reserve transactions balance. The Interagency Committee on Balance-of-Payments Statistics acknowledged the ambiguity when it recommended in 1970 that all five balances be measured and reported quarterly by the U.S. Department of Commerce.[2]

The adjustment process

Moving certain accounts from above to below the line and vice versa, and introducing new kinds of balances, cannot indefinitely gloss over a bad situation. Sooner or later some more substantive measures must be un-

---

[2]See U.S. Department of Commerce, Bureau of Economic Analysis, *Business Conditions Digest*—Monthly, $3.50 single copy, $40 per year.

Table 6–2
International balance of payments of the U.S.A. ($ millions)

Calendar year	Balance on goods and services(*)	Balance on current account	Balance on current account and long-term capital(†)	Net liquidity balance	Official reserve transactions balance
1960	$4,126	$1,834	−$1,155	−$3,655(‡)	−$3,403
1961	5,615	3,102	20	− 2,229(‡)	− 1,348
1962	5,150	2,519	− 979	− 2,845(‡)	− 2,650
1963	5,987	3,245	− 1,262	− 2,571(‡)	− 1,934
1964	8,600	5,846	28	− 2,745	− 1,534
1965	7,130	4,295	− 1,814	− 2,493	− 1,289
1966	5,300	2,410	− 1,614	− 2,148	219
1967	5,220	2,139	− 3,196	− 4,685	− 3,418
1968	2,489	− 386	− 1,349	− 1,610	1,641
1969	2,011	− 899	− 2,879	− 6,084	2,702
1970	3,592	444	− 3,038	− 3,852	− 9,821

− Net debit.
(*)Equal to net exports of goods and services in national income and product accounts of the U.S.A.
(†)Includes some short-term U.S. government assets
(‡)Coverage of liquid banking claims for 1960–63 and of liquid nonbanking claims for 1960–62 was limited to foreign currency deposits only; other liquid items were not available separately and were included with nonliquid claims.
Source: Data U.S. Department of Commerce, Office of Business Economics; table, Encyclopedia of Banking and Finance, p. 474.

dertaken to correct a fundamental imbalance. Such steps are referred to collectively as "the adjustment process," and there are a number of forms this process can take. All of them, however, work toward reducing the price of a country's goods and services in the world market. That in turn will boost its exports (which increases credits) and cut back its imports (thereby lessening debits). Should this process of adjustment continue long enough, the country's payments deficit eventually should give way to a surplus.

First, there may be a decline in the physical output of goods and services that a country in a deficit payments position produces. Such a reduction in volume will bring about a drop in aggregate income, obliging the residents to curtail their total purchases, both at home and abroad. Alternatively, the indicated adjustment may be accomplished by way of falling prices. Finally, and most germane to the subject of this book, the same end may be gained through a decline in that country's exchange rate against the currencies of its principal trading partners. In practice, payments adjustment usually occurs through a combination of all three mechanisms— changes in real income, prices and wages, and exchange rates. Theoretically, at least, these changes continue to take place until a country's economic relations with the rest of the world reach equilibrium: the point at which the credits and debits in its international payments statement can remain in an approximate balance without the benefit of a good deal of creative bookkeeping.

One consequence of abiding in an imperfect world is that balance-of-payments equilibrium is the exception rather than the rule. Above-the-line imbalances are normally corrected, at least over the short run, by additions to, or drawings on, the compensatory below-the-line accounts. During the days of fixed parities, a country had time to work toward an equilibrium position as long as it could draw down its reserves to cover its deficits on current account. The day of reckoning arrived when the reserves were exhausted but the imbalances continued.

Achieving equilibrium through an adjustment in total output, prices, wages, and exchange rates implies that a country with an above-the-line deficit loses reserves to its trading partners. Since a substantial portion of monetary reserves consists of foreign exchange, reserves flow out of a deficit country—now, as during the days of the bullionist controversy—because its private, corporate, and official residents need foreign exchange to satisfy their international obligations. The supply of the deficit country's currency in the foreign exchange market increases. Demand for the currencies of surplus countries rises as well, creating pressure on the former currency to depreciate and the latter to appreciate. Under the rules of the Bretton Woods system, reserves moved from deficit to surplus countries as a consequence of central banks' intervening in the foreign exchange markets to counteract these pressures.[3]

When, after the failure of the Smithsonian accord, exchange rates were permitted to float, and central banks were no longer committed to maintaining an official parity rate, the pressure was taken off reserves. Supply and demand were allowed—to the extent stipulated by the guidelines of a particular country's managed float—to determine the rates. In addition to this derived demand for foreign exchange, speculators who buy a particular currency for trading profits create a direct demand for it. The supply of a particular currency that is offered on the foreign exchange market is in turn a function of that country's collective taste for foreign goods, services, and investment opportunities. It is the reciprocal of its residents' aggregate demand for other currencies.

The elasticity factor

How far a given rise or depreciation of a particular currency will go toward correcting a payments imbalance depends in large measure upon its supply-demand elasticity in a floating rate environment. In other words, by how much must an exchange rate fall to reduce imports or rise to diminish exports sufficiently to achieve equilibrium? If a modest change is adequate, supply and demand are considered highly elastic. If a substantially greater change is required, they are relatively inelastic. Exchange rate elasticity is important as a practical as well as a theoretical matter. If, under floating

---

[3]The mechanics of this process are explained in some detail in Chapter 8.

rate conditions, the supply and demand elasticities of a particular currency are high, that currency probably will fluctuate within a narrower range than would be so if the elasticities were low. This is obviously a matter of prime concern for foreign exchange futures traders.

For a country's payments deficit to be erased by an adjustment in its exchange rate, its imports will have to fall by a greater amount than its exports do. In those situations where foreign demand for a country's exports is inelastic, an appreciation of its currency might, in spite of the foregoing, be more effective in achieving equilibrium since the volume of goods and services demanded would decline only moderately while money receipts rise by a more substantial amount. Exchange rates that tend to fluctuate within narrow limits because of elastic supply and demand factors are more conducive to improving a payments imbalance through this type of adjustment process than are volatile rates—implying, among other things, inelasticity—which, in more cases than not, only serve to aggravate the problem.

Taking up the German/U.S. trade model where we left it in Chapter 4, it is possible to illustrate in graphic terms how and why an increase in U.S. exports enhances the demand for dollars by, in the case of our model, private and official residents of Germany.[4] Figure 6–1A (left) shows in terms of the by-now familiar supply-demand curves what happens when there is an increase in the aggregate German demand for American goods and services from D_G to D_G^1. Assuming a constant supply schedule, Line S_{US}, an increase in German demand—represented in Figure 6–1A (left) by D_G shifting up and to the right—that signifies an increase in the dollar/mark exchange rate or, from the perspective of German buyers, higher product prices. But, as Figure 6–1B demonstrates, the demand for dollars is also influenced by the supply of U.S. exports. Here, given a constant German demand schedule for U.S. goods, the price of U.S. exports, hence $/DM, declines as S_{US} shifts down and to the right.

Similar presentations in Figures 6–2A and B illustrate the effects on U.S.[5] import prices of changes in American demand and German supply. As American residents step up their imports from Germany, more dollars are pumped into the foreign exchange market for Deutsche marks needed to pay for the imports. Figure 6–2A (left) depicts this increase as an upward shift of D_{US} to D_{US}^1. Conversely, an increase in the quantity of imports from Germany, assuming the U.S. demand curve remains fixed, would result in a decline in the import price level and, consequently, $/DM.

If there is a gap between the quantity of dollars obtained from exports and the dollar equivalent of foreign exchange paid out for exports when the

---

[4]The following analysis applies, of course, to any pair of trading nations, at least among the major OECD member countries. In fact, however, a multilateral model is a closer approximation of actual circumstances than the bilateral diagrams provided above. But for our present purpose the virtue of simplicity prevails over that of realism.

[5]Figures 6–1 A and B and 6–2 A and B are adapted from H. Robert Heller, International Monetary Economics (Englewood Cliffs, N.J.: Prentice-Hall, 1974), pp. 78–80.

Figure 6-1

A. Shift in demand for U.S. exports

B. Shift in supply of U.S. exports

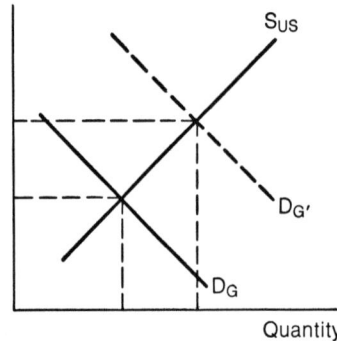
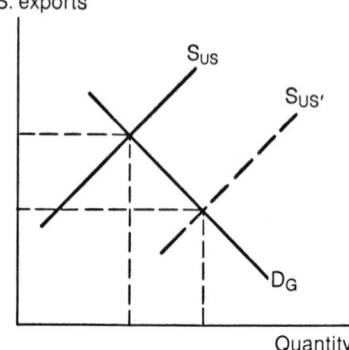

Figure 6-2

A. Shift in U.S. demand for imports from Germany

B. Shift in supply of U.S. imports from Germany

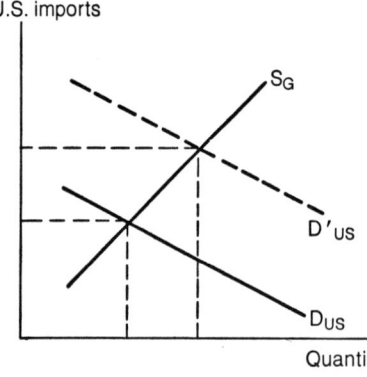
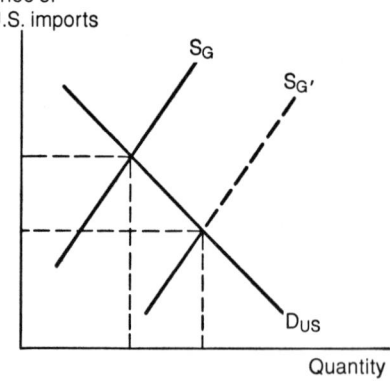

export and import supply-demand schedules are superimposed, equilibrium has not been achieved. In that case, reserves flow from the deficit to the surplus country in the manner described above until the gap on the chart is closed by a further adjustment via the total output and wage-price mechanisms.

Liquidity and forward pricing

This is where the concept of liquidity comes into play. To make an already confusing situation even more confusing, the term *liquidity* has two meanings in balance-of-payments usage. In its narrow sense, liquidity refers to the resources an individual country has at its disposal to finance its international transactions while incurring a deficit on its current account and at the same time maintaining its exchange rate at a designated level. In a broader sense it signifies the world total of monetary reserves. For our purposes, it will suffice to regard liquidity as being synonymous with reserves.

Originally intended to serve merely as a medium to finance international merchandise transactions, the short-term capital accounts from which a country draws its liquidity have, with their growth over the past two decades, assumed a life of their own. In the process, they've become commingled with—and ultimately indistinguishable from—the foreign exchange that is used by banks, corporations, and individual traders to obtain hedge protection or speculative gain. Although this latter type of trading activity is not a direct result of changes in the above-the-line accounts, therefore, its effect is reflected in the movement of the various supply-demand curves depicted in Figures 6–1 and 6–2.

Governments, during the days of the Bretton Woods system and after, have also been participants in the foreign exchange markets, either to support their exchange rates at certain levels or to promote what their official publications like to describe as "orderly market conditions." Until the mid-1950s central bank intervention was confined in most countries to the spot market. Monetary authorities avoided the forward exchange markets when they undertook official support operations because they regarded forward dealings as unduly speculative, and as an admission of economic weakness and mismanagement on their part.

This prejudicial view was to a large extent dispelled by the Bank of England's successful entry into the forward market to support the exchange value of the pound in 1957. Since then, central banks have routinely engaged in forward dealings as a regular part of their exchange management operations. They are undertaken to achieve one or several of the following:

1. Limiting fluctuations in either spot or forward rates or bringing one or both of these rates to a desired level.
2. Neutralizing what is regarded as destabilizing speculation.
3. Making adjustments in a premium or discount forward structure.
4. Carrying out stabilization operations without unduly expending official reserves.

There is a reciprocal and mutually reinforcing effect between a country's balance-of-payments position and the forward rate structure of its currency that has a direct bearing on futures market operations of any sort. The forward rates of those countries that are gaining reserves are usually quoted at premiums that grow wider as their reserves increase. Conversely, payments deficits and the loss of reserves go hand in hand with forward discounts. A substantial forward premium, as was noted in Chapter 4, is usually added to import prices quoted in that currency, a development which serves to discourage the demand for such products. A forward discount, on the other hand, is customarily deducted from the importers' posted prices, stimulating the demand for imported goods priced in the discount currency. This practice of adding forward premiums and subtracting discounts from import prices has a stabilizing effect on a country's balance of payments and, as a consequence, is an important part of the payments adjustment process.

In summary, the adjustment process operates as follows: as long as a country experiences a balance-of-payments deficit, its reserves go abroad in compensation. This outflow of liquidity pulls money out of domestic circulation, causing bank reserves to contract. The resulting decline in prices, incomes, and aggregate demand eventually lead to a reduction in imports and a rise in exports, both of which serve to reduce the deficit. When a country is in a surplus situation the reverse sequence occurs. Its volume of money in circulation and bank reserves increase as the country gains reserves. Total demand, and with it, prices, are boosted, leading to a rise in imports and a falloff in exports as foreign goods become more attractive on a price basis than competing domestic products. Either chain of events is more likely to occur in countries which, unlike the United States, maintain a major share of their official reserves in the form of foreign exchange.

It follows, therefore, that anyone who is involved, by choice or not, in the foreign exchange market and is compelled to make decisions concerning spot or forward rates should become familiar with the balance-of-payments history, current position, and outlook for those countries in whose currency that person has an interest. For good measure, he or she might become acquainted with the comparable records of their principal trading partners as well. Generally, those countries that are able to accrue payments surpluses, and therefore accumulate reserves, will enjoy the material benefits and international prestige that attach to possessing a strong currency. Countries that incur repeated deficits, and thereby lose reserves, suffer the stigma that goes with being a weak-currency country.

Four track records

The export and import performance, reserve position, and exchange rate history of four of the eight countries whose currencies are traded on the International Monetary Market, and of the United States, are charted in Figures 6–3 through 6–7. Though a country's balance of trade (exports less imports) is not, as was stated at the outset of this chapter, as comprehensive a measure as its balance of payments, its export and import figures provide a more graphic representation of its competitive position in world markets. Annual changes in a country's international reserves—com-

Figure 6–3
United Kingdom imports, exports, and reserves versus exchange rate

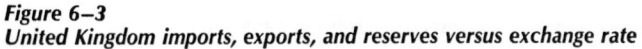

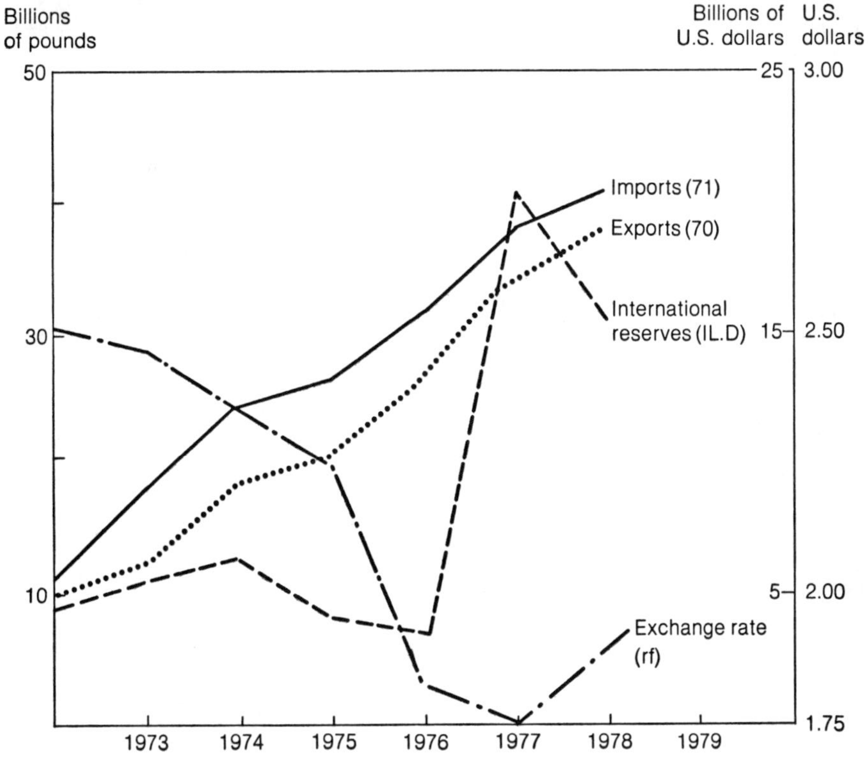

posed, in most cases, of gold, foreign exchange, and special drawing rights[6] reflect below-the-line adjustments made to compensate for the trade imbalances.

The experience of the United Kingdom since 1973 offers the clearest illustration of the concepts discussed throughout this chapter. U.K. imports exceeded exports by an increasing amount through 1975. The gap subsequently narrowed because of the receipts that were generated as the country's North Sea oil fields began producing. Great Britain's international reserves shot up nearly sixfold during this period, due primarily to offshore oil revenues. The pound, meanwhile, having declined about 30 percent, from $2.50 to around $1.75 between 1972 and 1977, scored a partial

---

[6]Special drawing rights are supplemental reserves devised by the International Monetary Fund and allocated among its member nations in proportion to their conventional gold and foreign exchange reserves. SDRs were labeled *paper gold* when they were introduced in 1971 because they are created and transferred among IMF members by bookkeeping entry. Initially valued at one U.S. dollar per unit, SDRs are now expressed in terms of a trade-weighted average of leading currencies.

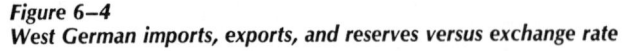

Figure 6–4
West German imports, exports, and reserves versus exchange rate

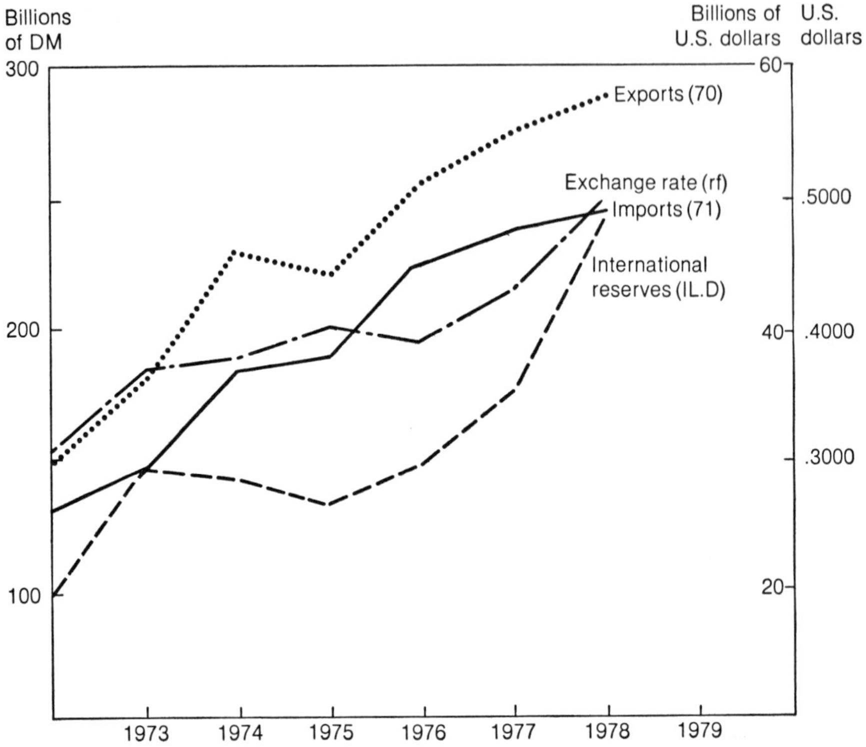

recovery back to the $2 level.[7] The appreciation of the pound after 1977 did not match the striking increase in reserves, however, because the consensus in the foreign exchange market was that the oil-induced gain was only a temporary improvement.

West Germany during the 1972–1979 period was a country with a growing trade surplus, increasing reserves, and a rising exchange rate. But the country's gain in reserves was not solely due to its favorable trade balance. Speculative capital was attracted to the country by the prospect of further appreciation of the Deutsche mark, which rose some 25 percent during 1977 and 1978 alone from an average annual rate of $0.40 to about $0.50. Switzerland was another case of "hot capital" inflows exerting a greater influence on the country's exchange rate than did its trade balance.

Of the five countries charted in Figures 6–3 to 6–7, the exports and imports of Canada were the most evenly matched. Canada's reserve position, therefore, displayed the greatest consistency. As a consequence, the Canadian dollar traced a fairly stable course between 1972 and 1976,

---

[7]Exchange rates are, in these comparisons, charted on the basis of the average rate for the years indicated. In each instance, currencies fluctuated within a range of rates around the yearly average.

Figure 6–5
Swiss imports, exports, and reserves versus exchange rate

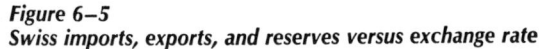

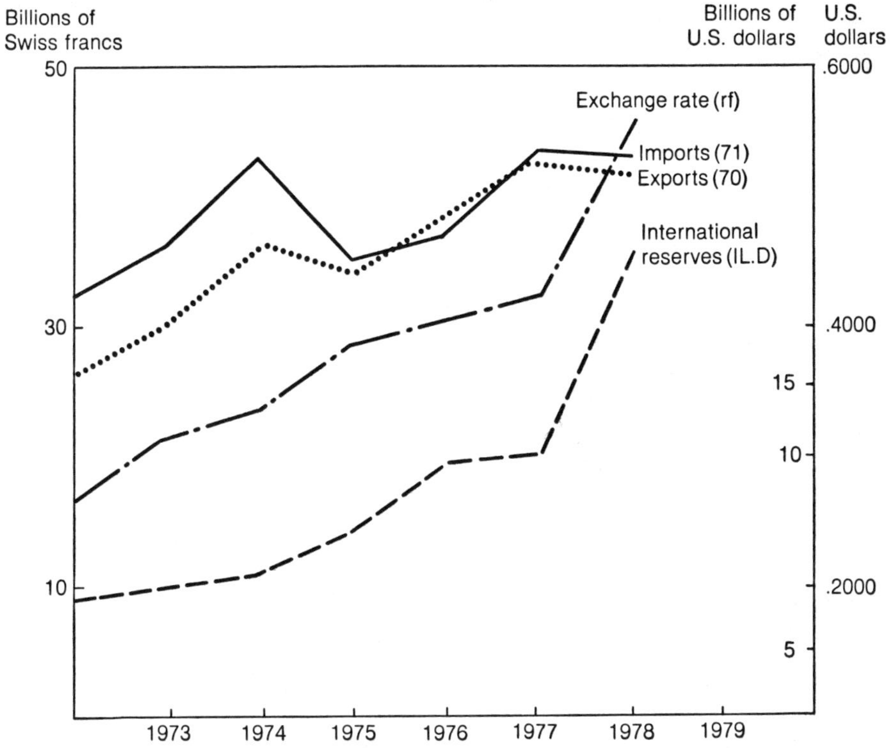

and remained close to parity with the U.S. dollar. Its appreciation relative to the U.S. dollar after 1976 was more a result of weakness in the latter currency than of any notable change in the Canadian payments position.

The exchange rates of the currencies mentioned above are expressed in terms of the U.S. dollar. Their strength or weakness, therefore, was the reciprocal of fluctuations in the dollar rate. Much of the appreciation of the Deutsche mark and Swiss franc during the latter 1970s was due as much to the problems associated with the U.S. dollar and the American international payments position as to any development peculiar to those countries.[8]

Source materials

It is helpful, indeed necessary, to study the records of trade balances, monetary reserves, and exchange rates of individual countries over past years. Historical data of this sort in itself will not suffice, however, when it comes to making trading decisions in the contemporary market envi-

---
[8]The reader may wish to refer back to Chapter 2 for an account of the difficulties which led to the breakdown of the Bretton Woods system.

Figure 6–6
Canadian imports, exports, and reserves versus exchange rate

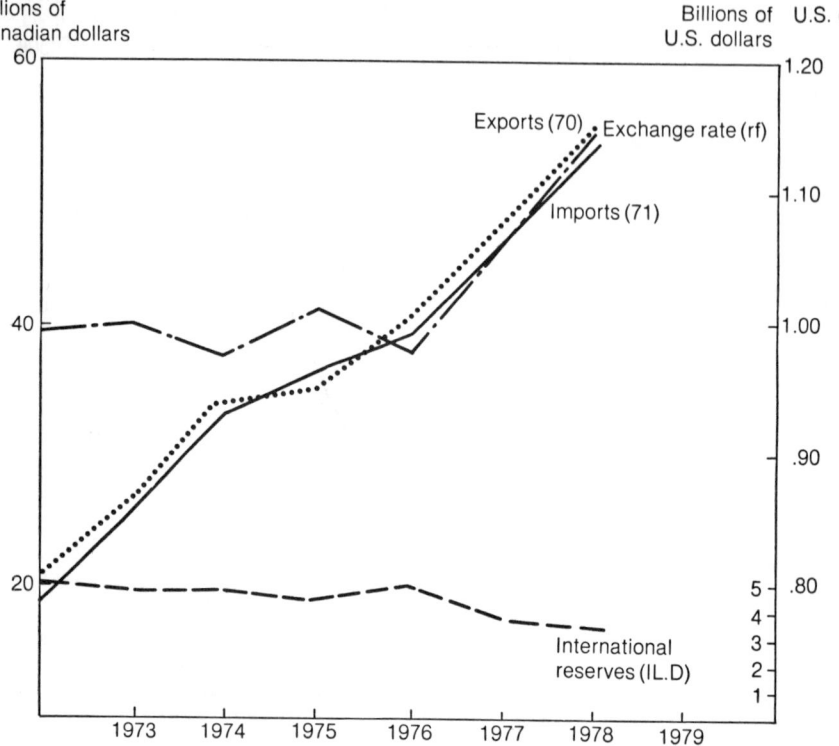

ronment. It is simply too dated as far as foreign exchange traders are concerned. Even so, it is a difficult task—for private speculators who trade for their own accounts at least—to obtain and evaluate on the spot the most recent statistics as they are released by the various countries.[9]

A valuable source that gathers recent data in a single volume is *International Financial Statistics,* published monthly at a nominal cost by the IMF.[10] Table 6–3 is a reproduction of the statistical summary for Canada from the 1981 yearbook issue of *International Financial Statistics.* For conformity and ease of comparison, the same format is used, when the relevant information is available, for each of the approximately 135 member countries of the IMF. There also is a section that lists daily spot exchange rates for the currencies of 15 countries, including, with the exceptions of the Mexican peso and Swiss franc, those for which futures contracts are

---

[9]Appendix C lists, for the guidance of traders who are determined to make an effort to track the individual reports, the sources of balance-of-payments data emanating from the various countries and an approximate timetable for the release of the most recent data.

[10]Readers who are interested in subscribing to this excellent source should write to the International Monetary Fund, Washington, D.C. 20431. The subscription price in the United States is $35 per year. Single copy price is $3.50. The publication is also available in many libraries.

Figure 6–7
U.S. imports, exports, and reserves versus exchange rate

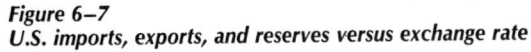

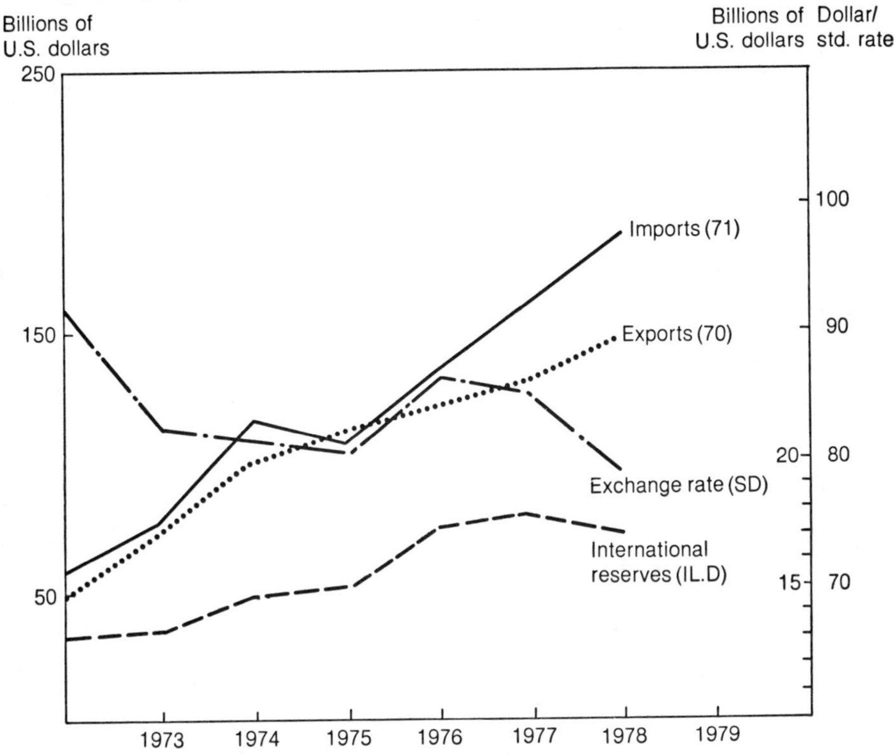

traded on the International Monetary Market. The tabulations by individual country also include such important data as international capital movements, key interest rates, and wholesale and consumer price indices.[11]

Not even this wealth of information, however, in a single source and updated monthly, is sufficiently current for daily, let alone hourly, trading. The latest issue is already old news by the time it reaches the subscriber. Consequently, a more timely source is needed. The big international banks and brokerage firms are good sources. With their far-flung branch networks, they are well situated to secure economic news soon after it is released in the originating country, accumulate it at a central point, and disseminate it with appropriate interpretation and commentary to their customers and their own trading personnel while it is still fresh. Independent economic and financial news services, such as the Dow Jones Banking Report and the Reuter International News Service, provide on a continuing basis and for a fee much the same information.

---

[11]This data also contain helpful reference material for the discussion in the succeeding chapters of the effect on exchange rates of comparative rates of inflation and interest rates in various countries.

Table 6-3
Canadian financial statistics, 1950-1979

Canada

	1974	1975	1976	1977	1978	1979	1980	1978 I	1978 II	1978 III	1978 IV	1979 I	1979 II	1979 III	1979 IV
EXCHANGE RATE: US $:NC															
RATE EXPRESSED IN SDR:NC aa	1.2136	1.1899	1.1725	1.3294	1.5451	1.5388	1.5237	1.4002	1.3939	1.5156	1.5451	1.4935	1.5077	1.5294	1.5388
													Canadian Dollars per US Dollar:		
ae	.9912	1.0164	1.0092	1.0944	1.1860	1.1681	1.1947	1.1322	1.1245	1.1831	1.1860	1.1606	1.1678	1.1606	1.1681
rf	.9780	1.0170	.9860	1.0635	1.1407	1.1714	1.1693	1.1133	1.1273	1.1438	1.1785	1.1864	1.1581	1.1663	1.1747
												Average Exchange Rate ah xn			
ah.x	104.0	100.0	103.2	95.7	89.2	86.8	87.0	91.4	90.2	88.9	86.3	85.7	87.8	87.2	86.6
am.x	104.8	100.0	106.1	98.0	87.8	84.3	84.5	91.4	89.8	86.7	83.2	83.0	85.8	84.3	84.1
									Millions of US Dollars Unless Otherwise Indicated:						
1l.d	4,885	4,426	4,964	3,672	3,560	2,864	3,093	3,019	3,788	2,681	3,560	4,425	3,179	3,495	2,864
1b.d	574	555	558	505	522	586	453	506	504	517	522	649	656	640	586
1c.d	530	648	944	852	557	391	579	824	610	603	557	530	492	467	391
1ca.d	—	—	—	44	23	—	—	45	45	41	23	22	—	—	—
1cp.d	172	289	287	206	145	24	—	202	182	173	145	124	105	70	24
1ct.d	—	—	—	—	—	10	16	—	—	—	—	—	—	—	10
1d.d	3,781	3,223	3,462	2,315	2,481	1,888	2,061	1,689	2,675	1,561	2,481	3,246	2,031	2,388	1,888
1dx.d	3,768	3,207	3,446	2,299	2,463	1,864	2,038	1,671	2,655	1,544	2,463	3,229	2,015	2,373	1,864
1a.d	21.95	21.95	21.62	22.01	22.13	22.18	20.98	22.01	22.01	22.00	22.13	22.13	22.13	22.04	22.18
1an.d	941	899	879	936	1,009	1,023	937	953	955	986	1,009	997	1,000	1,016	1,023
2f.d	1,347	1,288	1,278	1,336	1,768	1,788	2,596	1,360	1,682	1,738	1,768	1,746	1,752	1,788	1,788
7a.d	13,941	13,856	17,233	18,152	21,654	25,402	....	19,297	19,376	19,885	21,654	22,487	23,746	25,176	25,402
7b.d	13,330	14,099	16,479	18,877	24,648	32,043	....	20,511	21,569	21,354	24,648	26,107	28,588	30,041	32,043
9a.d	6,792	5,594	6,720	5,692	7,755	8,001	10,793	5,491	6,857	6,324	7,755	8,856	7,607	9,091	8,001
9b.d	3,277	3,371	3,686	4,150	7,744	8,378	9,230	4,835	5,259	5,785	7,744	8,159	7,949	8,559	8,378
									Billions of Canadian Dollars:						
11	5.77	5.41	5.90	5.04	5.42	4.54	4.81	4.50	5.33	4.34	5.42	6.29	4.88	5.24	4.54
12a	2.86	4.61	5.09	7.73	9.20	11.78	13.48	8.14	7.80	9.10	9.20	8.56	10.01	10.16	11.78
12d	.96	1.03	.86	.69	.52	.34	.17	.65	.61	.57	.52	.47	.44	.39	.34
14	9.31	10.75	11.75	13.18	14.74	16.01	17.62	12.69	13.48	13.60	14.74	14.12	14.93	15.14	16.01
14a	5.86	6.78	7.32	8.08	8.95	9.45	10.40	7.93	8.48	8.58	8.95	8.62	9.27	9.30	9.45
17r	.29	.31	.08	.29	.40	.64	.84	.60	.27	.40	.40	1.21	.41	.65	.64
									Billions of Canadian Dollars:						
20	3.44	3.95	4.41	5.07	5.76	6.54	7.20	4.74	4.97	5.00	5.76	5.47	5.63	5.82	6.54
21	13.41	13.61	16.93	19.39	25.24	29.19	41.60	21.47	21.31	23.09	25.24	25.69	27.23	28.80	29.19
22a	8.06	7.73	8.58	9.51	9.75	9.93	9.75	9.59	10.21	10.14	9.75	9.78	9.85	10.09	9.93
22b	2.45	3.04	3.05	2.64	2.64	2.73	2.88	2.61	2.52	2.52	2.64	2.65	2.53	2.81	2.73
22d	47.92	56.05	67.34	80.03	100.24	119.71	136.54	84.25	88.68	92.91	100.24	104.52	111.96	115.14	119.71
24	15.95	19.17	19.02	20.99	22.14	22.09	24.52	19.84	21.11	21.61	22.14	20.33	22.17	22.55	22.09
25	39.53	44.81	58.02	67.09	81.36	100.73	110.17	70.76	73.66	78.35	81.36	86.73	92.92	97.51	100.73
26c	11.62	12.27	14.65	18.27	26.73	34.69	48.48	21.03	21.96	22.95	26.73	28.02	30.84	32.28	34.69
26d	4.68	3.66	3.10	4.73	6.47	2.42	4.09	4.51	4.04	4.75	6.47	6.29	2.79	2.88	2.42
27r	3.49	4.47	5.51	5.57	6.93	8.17	10.69	6.53	6.92	6.00	6.93	6.75	8.48	7.45	8.17
									Billions of Canadian Dollars:						
31n	7.47	6.70	8.02	5.95	3.74	-1.19	-2.31	4.76	4.32	4.29	3.74	3.35	1.01	1.45	-1.19
32	57.55	68.77	81.79	95.84	115.85	142.05	158.67	100.71	105.75	110.15	115.85	119.58	131.98	135.68	142.05
32an	6.22	8.65	10.54	12.48	12.45	19.27	19.08	13.20	13.94	14.15	12.45	11.94	17.05	17.34	19.27
32b	2.45	3.04	3.05	2.64	2.64	2.73	2.88	2.61	2.52	2.52	2.64	2.65	2.53	2.81	2.73
32d	48.88	57.08	68.20	80.72	100.76	120.05	136.71	84.90	89.29	93.48	100.76	104.99	112.40	115.53	120.05
34	21.83	25.97	26.36	29.09	31.12	31.56	34.95	27.79	29.62	30.21	31.12	28.98	31.46	31.87	31.56
35	39.53	44.81	58.02	67.09	81.36	100.73	110.17	70.76	73.66	78.35	81.36	86.73	92.92	97.51	100.73
37r	3.67	4.70	5.40	5.62	7.10	8.56	11.23	6.92	6.80	5.87	7.10	7.25	8.60	7.77	8.56
34..b	21.32	25.34	25.67	28.33	30.30	30.73	34.42	28.80	29.30	29.68	30.30	30.03	31.09	31.34	30.73
39d	141.53	178.94	205.80	226.53	261.54	334.85	....	232.50	261.29	257.68	294.67	291.63	322.02	344.21	381.55
									Millions of Canadian Dollars:						
40	3,111	4,103	4,570	5,565	6,345	5,532	....	6,429	6,496	6,444	6,345	6,700	6,965	6,631	5,532
42b	1,266	1,271	1,265	1,368	1,376	1,313	....	1,355	1,391	1,391	1,376	1,425	1,377	1,313	1,313
42d	24,119	28,306	34,890	42,167	50,321	60,581	....	43,781	45,967	48,192	50,321	52,306	55,033	58,179	60,581
45	23,843	28,709	34,894	42,249	50,446	59,661	....	44,482	46,542	48,302	50,446	52,775	55,335	57,615	59,661
47a	3,614	4,229	4,859	5,640	6,469	6,716	....	5,896	6,158	6,395	6,469	6,485	6,695	6,784	6,716
47r	1,034	740	884	1,211	1,128	1,051	....	1,188	1,156	1,330	1,128	1,170	1,343	1,727	1,051
									Millions of Canadian Dollars:						
42d.k	1,025	1,200	1,360	1,434	1,533	1,887	1,998	1,437	1,463	1,494	1,533	1,605	1,696	1,789	1,887
46a.k	890	1,030	1,245	1,306	1,333	1,454	1,110	1,268	1,335	1,374	1,333	1,350	1,428	1,552	1,454
47a.k	106	125	162	176	248	242	751	167	178	185	248	182	329	269	242
47r.k	28	46	-48	-48	-48	191	137	2	-50	-65	-48	73	39	-32	191
									Millions of Canadian Dollars: End of Period for Annuals						
40..s	145	229	282	385	....	....	33	25	-35	68	-58	24	18	30	
42a.s	492	535	723	954	....	....	217	183	113	156	206	196	121	450	
42b.s	1,977	2,067	2,410	2,672	....	....	91	114	-19	-7	80	98	-106	23	
42d.s	15,916	17,790	19,411	21,691	....	....	357	224	511	498	737	256	593	93	
42h.s	1,186	1,273	1,396	1,465	....	....	16	16	16	49	16	26	29	44	
49z.s	1,464	2,294	2,495	....	....	....	34	-148	31	67	225	-395	74	-17	
									Per Cent or Index Numbers (1975=100):						
60	8.75	9.00	8.50	7.50	10.75	14.00	17.26	8.00	8.50	9.50	10.75	11.25	11.25	12.25	14.00
60c	7.83	7.40	8.87	7.33	8.67	11.68	12.80	7.39	8.19	8.89	10.22	10.84	10.81	11.45	13.63
61	8.90	9.04	9.18	8.70	9.30	10.26	12.49	9.13	9.20	9.15	9.73	10.01	9.72	10.17	11.14
62	105.1	100.0	101.7	92.5	101.4	146.9	200.5	89.2	95.8	108.0	112.8	126.6	139.2	155.9	165.9
63	89.9	100.0	105.1	113.4	123.9	141.8	160.8	119.0	122.4	124.9	129.1	135.3	139.5	143.5	148.7
64	90.3	100.0	107.5	116.1	126.5	138.1	152.1	122.2	125.1	128.3	130.3	133.3	136.8	139.4	142.7
65ey	86.6	100.0	113.8	126.1	135.2	147.0	161.9	131.8	133.8	135.8	138.9	142.1	145.7	148.2	151.8
66..c	106.4	100.0	105.5	107.8	112.3	117.5	115.7	109.6	111.2	112.7	115.6	116.8	116.6	118.7	118.1
67eyc	105.9	100.0	101.4	100.0	101.0	104.0	102.2	99.9	100.4	101.3	102.5	103.4	103.8	104.6	104.4

Canada 156

	1980 II	1980 III	1980 IV	1981 I	June	July	Aug	1980 Sept	Oct	Nov	Dec	Jan	1981 Feb	Mar	
End of Period															**Exchange Rates: preference indicated**
1.4907	1.5244	1.5362	1.5237	*1.4580*	1.5244	1.5240	1.5222	1.5362	1.5166	1.5187	1.5237	1.4856	1.4695	*1.4580*	Market Rate/Par or Central Rate...... **aa**
End of Period (ae) Period Average (rf)															
1.1914	1.1510	1.1705	1.1947	*1.1868*	1.1510	1.1616	1.1573	1.1705	1.1756	1.1895	1.1947	1.1940	1.2013	*1.1868*	Market Rate/Par or Central Rate...... **ae**
1.1643	1.1703	1.1586	1.1839	*1.1936*	1.1515	1.1519	1.1592	1.1646	1.1690	1.1860	1.1968	1.1907	1.1988	*1.1912*	Par Rate/Market Rate...... **rf**
1975=100															
87.4	86.9	87.8	85.9	*85.2*	88.3	88.3	87.7	87.3	87.0	85.8	85.0	85.4	84.8	*85.4*	Index of Exchange Rate ah...... **ah.x**
85.0	84.6	84.6	83.8	*84.7*	85.0	84.8	84.8	84.1	84.0	83.7	83.5	83.9	*84.8*	*85.4*	Effective Exchange Rate: MERM..... **am.x**
End of Period															**International Liquidity**
2,715	3,319	2,980	3,093	*2,816*	3,319	3,041	3,293	2,980	2,727	2,528	3,093	2,523	2,444	*2,816*	Total Reserves minus Gold...... 1l.d
745	779	745	453	*598*	779	754	747	745	726	710	453	611	595	*598*	SDRs...... 1b.d
364	385	373	*579*	*547*	385	381	374	373	367	363	*579*	565	*555*	*547*	Reserve Position in the Fund...... 1c.d
—	—	—	—	—	—	—	—	—	—	—	—	—	—	—	of which: GAB Lending...... 1cad
9	8	—	—	—	—	8	8	—	—	—	—	—	—	—	Oil Facility Lending...... 1cpd
16	17	17	16	*16*	17	17	17	17	16	16	16	16	16	*16*	SFF Lending...... 1ctd
1,607	2,155	1,862	2,061	*1,671*	2,155	1,906	2,172	1,862	1,634	1,454	2,061	1,348	1,293	*1,671*	Foreign Exchange...... 1d.d
1,589	2,135	1,840	2,038	*1,644*	2,135	1,888	2,156	1,840	1,616	1,428	2,038	1,320	1,266	*1,644*	of which: US Dollars...... 1dxd
21.78	21.31	21.11	20.98	*20.92*	21.31	21.30	21.22	21.11	21.09	21.07	20.98	20.97	20.96	*20.92*	Gold(Million Fine Troy Ounces)..... 1ad
954	988	970	937	*899*	988	978	977	970	952	941	937	913	898	*899*	Gold (National Valuation)...... 1and
															Fund Position
1,698	1,797	1,731	2,596	*2,501*	1,797	1,780	1,785	1,781	1,751	1,733	2,596	2,533	2,490	*2,501*	Quota...... 2l.d
....	....	....	....	....	....	....	....	....	....	....	....	....	....	....	Chartered Banks: Assets...... 7a.d
....	....	....	....	....	....	....	....	....	....	....	....	....	....	....	Liabilities...... 7b.d
9,198	10,070	11,029	*10,793*	....	10,070	10,198	10,145	11,029	10,809	10,717	*10,793*	*10,545*	....	....	US Liabilities to Canada...... 9a.d
8,757	8,975	9,252	*9,230*	....	8,975	8,158	8,733	9,252	8,615	*8,412*	*9,230*	*8,576*	....	....	US Claims on Canada...... 9b.d
End of Period															**Bank of Canada and Exchange Fund**
4.37	4.96	4.62	4.81	*4.41*	4.96	4.67	4.94	4.62	4.33	4.13	4.81	4.10	4.01	*4.41*	Foreign Assets...... 11
12.36	11.83	12.48	*13.48*	....	11.83	12.25	12.53	12.48	12.89	13.63	*13.48*	*13.11*	*13.13*	....	Claims on Government...... 12a
.30	.26	.22	.17	....	.26	.22	.22	.22	.17	.17	.17	.13	.13	....	Claims on Private Sector...... 12d
15.28	16.06	16.32	17.62	....	16.06	16.04	16.16	16.32	16.29	16.87	17.62	16.57	*16.38*	....	Reserve Money...... 14
9.07	9.61	9.75	10.40	....	9.61	9.72	9.91	9.75	9.92	10.03	10.40	*9.86*	....	....	of which: Currency Outside Bks... 14a
1.76	.98	.99	*.84*	....	.98	1.08	1.54	.99	1.09	1.04	*.84*	.77	*.89*	....	Other Items (Net)...... 17r
End of Period															**Chartered Banks**
6.19	6.42	6.55	7.20	....	6.42	6.30	6.22	6.55	6.34	6.82	7.20	*6.68*	....	....	Reserves...... 20
34.00	34.36	37.86	*41.60*	....	34.36	35.70	36.54	37.86	38.67	38.99	*41.60*	....	....	....	Foreign Assets...... 21
9.57	9.56	10.20	9.75	....	9.56	9.94	10.58	10.20	10.41	10.10	9.75	*10.06*	....	....	Claims on Government...... 22a
2.85	2.65	2.83	2.88	....	2.65	2.43	2.22	2.36	2.46	2.61	2.88	*3.02*	....	....	Claims on Local Government...... 22b
123.19	129.75	129.06	*136.54*	....	129.75	129.08	128.22	129.06	131.78	131.59	*136.54*	....	....	....	Claims on Private Sector...... 22d
21.51	21.57	23.23	24.52	*22.60*	21.57	22.56	22.84	23.23	24.02	24.10	24.52	*23.31*	*22.74*	*22.60*	Demand Deposits...... 24
106.09	112.26	110.94	*110.17*	....	112.26	113.78	111.68	110.94	111.90	111.69	*110.17*	....	....	....	Savings & Fgn Currency Deposits... 25
38.84	39.22	42.51	*48.48*	....	39.22	39.65	40.96	42.51	42.48	44.63	*48.48*	....	....	....	Foreign Liabilities...... 26c
2.70	1.13	1.95	4.09	....	1.13	1.45	2.28	1.95	3.36	4.46	4.09	*3.96*	....	....	Government Deposits...... 26d
6.67	8.55	7.39	*10.69*	....	8.55	6.01	6.02	7.39	7.91	5.22	*10.69*	....	....	....	Other Items (Net)...... 27r
End of Period															**Monetary Survey**
-.98	.01	-.15	*-2.31*	....	.01	.61	29	-.15	37	-1.67	*-2.31*	....	....	....	Foreign Assets (Net)...... 31n
144.59	152.91	152.36	*158.67*	....	152.91	152.46	151.32	152.36	154.31	153.61	*158.67*	....	*19.09*	....	Domestic Credit...... 32
18.25	20.25	20.72	*19.08*	....	20.25	20.73	20.66	20.72	19.90	19.24	*19.08*	*19.08*	....	....	Claims on Government (Net)...... 32an
2.85	2.65	2.36	2.88	....	2.65	2.43	2.22	2.36	2.46	2.61	2.88	*3.02*	....	....	Claims on Local Government...... 32b
123.49	130.01	129.28	*136.71*	....	130.01	129.30	128.44	129.28	131.95	131.76	*136.71*	....	....	....	Claims on Private Sector...... 32d
30.60	31.21	33.00	*34.95*	....	31.21	32.30	32.77	33.00	33.97	34.16	*34.95*	*33.20*	....	....	Money...... 34
106.09	112.26	110.94	*110.17*	....	112.26	113.78	111.68	110.94	111.90	111.69	*110.17*	....	....	....	Quasi-Money...... 35
6.94	9.44	8.25	*11.23*	....	9.44	6.97	7.17	8.25	8.81	6.07	*11.23*	....	....	....	Other Items (Net)...... 37r
31.74	30.84	32.45	*34.42*	....	30.84	31.85	32.35	32.45	33.60	33.75	*34.42*	*34.37*	....	....	Money, Seasonally Adjusted...... 34..b
398.90	445.11	437.13	....	....	438.02	449.11	405.39	456.88	511.37	*490.98*	....	....	....	....	Bank Debits (Monthly Averages).. 39d
End of Period															**Other Financial Institutions**
															Savings Institutions
6,540	7,211	*7,082*	....	....	....	....	....	....	....	....	....	....	....	....	Cash...... 40
1,388	1,531	*1,654*	....	....	....	....	....	....	....	....	....	....	....	....	Claims on Local Government...... 42b
62,217	64,284	*67,006*	....	....	....	....	....	....	....	....	....	....	....	....	Claims on Private Sector...... 42d
61,704	64,540		....	....	....	....	....	....	....	....	....	....	....	....	Time and Savings Deposits...... 45
6,762	6,670	*6,884*	....	....	....	....	....	....	....	....	....	....	....	....	Capital Accounts...... 47a
1,680	1,820	*2,343*	....	....	....	....	....	....	....	....	....	....	....	....	Other Items (Net)...... 47r
End of Period															*Federal Business Development Bank*
1,967	2,001	2,002	*1,998*	....	2,001	2,000	2,001	2,002	2,007	*1,949*	*1,998*	....	....	....	Claims on Private Sector...... 42d.k
1,606	1,737	1,205	*1,110*	....	1,737	1,753	1,231	1,205	1,152	*1,144*	*1,110*	....	....	....	Bonds...... 46a.k
200	200	690	*751*	....	200	195	698	690	693	*702*	*751*	....	....	....	Capital Accounts...... 47a.k
161	64	107	*137*	....	64	52	72	107	162	*103*	*137*	....	....	....	Other Items (Net)...... 47r..k
Millions of Canadian Dollars: Increase During Months & Quarters															*Life Insurance*
-99	14	137	*115*	....	-70	23	99	16	5	-37	*147*	....	....	....	Cash...... 40..s
280	120	22	*83*	....	31	-81	19	84	-38	74	*48*	....	....	....	Claims on Government...... 42a.s
21	9	-73	*112*	....	26	-40	-24	-9	30	29	*54*	....	....	....	Claims on Local Governments...... 42b.s
679	421	614	*516*	....	173	343	138	133	290	196	*31*	....	....	....	Claims on Private Sector...... 42d.s
47	73	40	*66*	....	19	12	11	17	21	14	*31*	....	....	....	Real Estate...... 42h.s
341	-425	189	*145*	....	-164	103	-4	-12	86	-34	*-18*	....	....	....	Incr. in Total Assets(Within Pd)... 49z.s
Period Averages															**Interest, Prices, Production**
14.79	10.67	11.02	17.26	*16.69*	10.67	10.18	10.45	11.02	11.76	13.06	17.26	17.00	*17.14*	*16.69*	Bank Rate (End of Period)...... 60
14.10	12.37	10.50	14.21	*16.71*	10.38	10.06	10.49	10.95	11.91	13.70	17.01	16.86	16.83	*16.44*	Treasury Bill Rate...... 60c
12.83	11.57	12.57	12.97	*13.27*	11.29	12.32	12.40	12.98	13.22	13.01	12.67	12.96	13.38	*13.48*	Government Bond Yield...... 61
201.4	193.3	207.7	199.6	....	200.8	211.9	205.1	206.1	197.1	207.6	194.1	197.5	*193.0*	....	Industrial Share Prices...... 62
156.0	157.7	162.1	*167.2*	....	158.6	160.2	162.2	*164.0*	*166.4*	*167.5*	167.7	169.9	....	....	Prices: Industry Selling...... 63
145.8	149.9	154.2	158.5	....	151.6	152.7	154.2	155.5	156.9	158.8	159.8	161.8	*163.5*	....	Consumer Prices...... 64
156.1	159.3	163.0	*168.6*	....	160.5	161.5	162.1	165.8	*168.0*	*168.6*	*169.0*	*171.1*	....	....	Wages: Hourly Earnings (Mfg)...... 65ey
117.3	114.4	114.1	*116.9*	....	*113.4*	*112.8*	113.8	*115.7*	*116.4*	*117.0*	*117.2*	*116.2*	....	....	Industrial Production, Seas. Adj.... 66..c
103.7	101.9	101.0	102.1	....	101.6	100.9	100.6	101.5	101.7	101.7	102.9	....	....	....	Mfg. Employment, Seas. Adj....... 67eyc

Table 6-3 (continued)

Canada

		1974	1975	1976	1977	1978	1979	1980	1978 I	1978 II	1978 III	1978 IV	1979 I	1979 II	1979 III	1979 IV
CONSUMER PRICES INDUSTRIAL COUNTRIES◼ WORLD◼																Millions of Canadian Dollars
	70	33.740	34.661	40.015	46.337	55.311	68.134	78.970	12,213	14,605	13,129	15,365	15,702	16,767	16,925	18,740
	70aa	3,420	3,052	2,287	1,751	1,578	2,418	2,902	432	355	364	414	520	599	606	692
	70b	494	1,092	1,617	2,028	2,191	2,897	3,983	603	569	480	539	683	650	647	918
	70d	2,123	2,128	1,862	2,001	2,065	2,318	3,906	320	518	655	571	356	467	683	812
	70rl	1,970	1,513	2,344	3,337	4,500	5,482	5,135	952	1,206	1,160	1,182	1,239	1,396	1,486	1,361
	70sl	1,889	1,834	2,186	2,158	2,181	3,085	3,867	487	551	544	599	751	737	759	838
	70ul	1,726	1,746	2,003	2,382	2,886	3,222	3,677	651	781	728	727	739	785	811	886
	71	33,654	36,834	39,778	44,943	53,155	66,544	73,179	11,379	14,452	12,392	14,932	15,762	16,735	16,290	17,756
	71aa	2,646	3,302	3,269	3,254	3,434	4,450	6,868	876	809	864	885	978	876	1,279	1,317
	71.v	32,674	35,761	38,619	43,634	51,607	64,606	71,048	11,048	14,031	12,031	14,497	15,303	16,248	15,816	17,239
																1975=100
	72	107.8	100.0	111.9	122.0	134.1	136.4	134.2	122.4	145.0	125.7	142.9	136.0	138.0	131.1	140.4
	72d	95	100	99	139	134	112	152	86	141	172	137	80	101	131	134
TREASURY BILL RATE	72rl	127	100	146	189	204	203		182	230	210	195	190	212		195
GOVERNMENT BOND YIELD	72sl	132	100	123	122	133	142	145	122	142	136	132	149	141	138	142
	72ul	124	100	110	114	124	123	118	118	135	122	117	118	123		126
	72kr	102.7	100.0	102.2	104.8	104.9	96.5	94.2	98.5	103.3	98.8	102.8	95.8	94.3	99.1	107.1
	73	105.8	100.0	107.9	108.4	112.0	124.1	117.1	99.9	125.3	103.2	119.0	123.1	130.9	118.5	123.9
	74	90.3	100.0	102.4	109.0	118.6	143.3	167.6	115.0	115.9	120.2	123.6	132.5	139.3	148.1	153.3
	74d	107	100	88	69	73	103	123	68	70	72	81	88	90	101	122
	74sl	77	100	96	98	88	118	145	87	82	85	98	109	113	120	128
	74ul	80	100	104	119	133	151	179	126	132	137	143	143	147		161
	75	86.3	100.0	100.1	112.4	127.5	145.4	169.1	122.4	124.0	129.1	134.8	138.9	138.8	149.1	155.6
																Millions of US Dollars
	77aa.d	34,335	33,910	39,844	42,962	47,625	57,278	66,932	10,957	12,448	11,289	12,931	13,019	14,249	14,095	15,916
	77ab.d	-32,396	-34,288	-38,130	-40,049	-44,064	-53,467	-59,576	-9,886	-11,910	-10,294	-11,976	-12,475	-13,752	-12,797	-14,443
	77ac.d	5,545	5,841	6,428	6,415	7,336	8,161	9,676	1,337	1,932	2,330	1,679	1,499	2,075	2,734	1,853
	77ad.d	-9,541	-10,531	-12,556	-13,787	-15,336	-16,876	-19,406	-3,525	-3,736	-3,749	-4,327	-3,919	-4,163	-4,179	-4,615
RESERVE MONEY	77ae.d	429	373	430	326	234	372	680	44	61	94	35	32	73	150	117
INDUSTRIAL COUNTRIES◼	77ag.d	141	-1	106	58	-203	193	379	-264	26	-29	64	37	79	26	51
WORLD◼	77ba.d	34	-185	-1,070	-580	-1,382	-366	-2,200	-29	-597	58	-814	173	-624	-173	258
	77bd.d	1,806	4,394	8,770	5,039	4,383	3,091	4,579	879	2,547	242	715	1,178	632	1,192	89
	77be.d	-784	-349	166	-796	-1,916	-947	-1,569	-18	-1,470	149	-576	-659	142	-189	-241
	77cc.d	1,337	1,610	240	756	696	3,579	1,081	-380	1,157	-1,213	1,132	1,824	-171	-117	2,043
	77d.d	-881	-1,174	-3,673	-1,693	-2,476	-3,311	-2,146	-548	-1,396	-1,197	665	-1,380	215	-478	-1,669
	78c.d	—	—	—	—	—	—	—	—	—	—	—	—	—	—	—
	78b.d	—	—	—	—	—	182	186	—	—	—	—	182	—	—	—
	78d.d	18	-59	-30	72	72	22	-42	22	-5	43	13	2	-1	23	-2
	78ta.d	—	—	—	—	1,995	603	—	—	1,264	—	731	603	—	—	—
	78fb.d	—	—	—	—	188	749	—	—	188	—	—	749	—	—	—
	78tc.d	—	—	—	—	2,728	—	913	758	261	1,108	601	—	—	—	—
	79x.d	—	—	—	—	—	—	—	—	—	—	—	—	—	—	—
	79k.d	-43	459	-525	1,277	120	737	513	653	-770	1,109	-873	-865	1,246	-287	643
MONEY INDUSTRIAL COUNTRIES◼ WORLD◼																Billions of Canadian Dollars
	80	-1.63	-6.28	-4.95	-9.08	-10.47	-10.40	....	-3.27	-3.29	-2.86	-2.13	-2.18	-4.11	-1.91	-2.01
	81	33.40	36.12	39.99	40.52	43.55	49.31	....	10.88	9.51	10.53	11.09	12.42	9.95	11.87	12.85
	82	31.46	37.47	41.34	46.70	51.05	56.38	....	13.92	11.90	12.34	12.68	14.13	12.93	12.82	14.26
	83	3.57	4.93	3.60	2.90	2.97	3.33	....	.23	.90	1.05	.54	.47	1.13	.96	.70
	84	4.11	5.46	5.52	10.02	12.41	7.72	....	3.04	2.85	3.90	3.52	2.14	.57	1.98	1.67
	87	-2.48	.82	-.56	-.92	-1.94	2.69	....	.23	.45	-1.04	-1.40	.05	3.54	-.06	.44
																Millions of Canadian Dollars
	88	33,267	37,179	41,300	49,108	63,121	69,693	81,685	50,976	54,488	57,475	63,121	66,156	64,908	66,982	69,693
	88aa	7,039	7,880	8,452	10,305	12,046	13,754	16,093	10,923	10,417	11,946	12,046	12,790	12,194	13,192	13,754
	88ab	8,122	7,771	8,643	9,537	11,481	10,418	10,668	10,433	11,377	11,473	11,481	11,133	10,511	10,776	10,418
	88ac	1,998	1,605	2,069	2,724	3,966	5,270	....	2,929	3,752	3,635	3,966	4,221	5,078	4,871	5,270
	88ae	15,372	18,949	20,383	24,270	29,218	33,359	....	24,526	24,988	25,253	29,218	29,793	30,144	30,908	33,359
	88c	737	974	1,753	2,272	6,410	6,892	....	2,165	3,954	5,168	6,410	8,219	6,981	7,235	6,892
	88s	680	741	852	1,064	1,189	907	974	1,128	1,145	1,321	1,189	1,131	1,101	1,052	907
EXPORTS (IN $) INDUSTRIAL COUNTRIES◼ WORLD																Billions of Canadian Dollars
	90c	37.61	38.78	44.00	50.85	60.51	74.38	86.61	54.87	59.41	60.99	66.78	69.45	70.14	76.83	81.10
	91f	27.82	33.38	38.32	43.40	47.49	51.21	57.39	45.87	46.97	47.88	49.25	49.78	50.48	52.00	52.61
	93e	34.26	40.04	44.89	48.19	52.21	59.73	67.55	49.69	51.92	52.80	54.45	55.90	57.78	61.99	63.25
	93i	3.45	-.24	1.56	.36	.22	4.44	-.97	-.42	-.56	1.23	.63	3.62	3.05	3.14	4.96
	96f	83.39	96.99	110.89	122.47	135.36	150.49	167.31	130.22	133.66	137.25	140.30	145.09	148.00	153.06	155.81
	98c	-37.27	-4.25	-45.03	-51.01	-59.92	-72.74	-81.09	-53.24	-59.49	-60.98	-65.96	-69.18	-74.87	-77.24	
	99b	149.88	168.01	194.37	213.36	235.38	267.70	296.45	226.09	231.56	238.47	245.42	254.22	263.53	272.32	280.73
	98e	-2.35	-2.67	-3.34	-4.55	-5.68	-7.39	-8.31	-5.04	-4.98	-5.27	-7.45	-6.72	-7.27	-7.60	-7.98
	99a	147.53	165.34	191.03	208.81	229.70	260.30	288.14	221.05	226.57	233.20	237.97	247.50	256.26	264.71	272.76
	99e	148.18	147.07	170.29	185.75	204.63	232.25	257.33	196.52	202.07	207.79	212.12	220.98	228.64	236.45	243.37
	99a.r	120.09	165.34	174.40	178.17	184.27	189.30		181.79	183.28	185.63	186.38	188.33	187.95	190.04	190.90
							Millions; Mid-Year Estimates									
	99z	22.40	22.73	23.02	23.28	23.48	23.69	....	....	....	....	Population				99z

IMPORTS, CIF (IN $) INDUSTRIAL COUNTRIES◼ WORLD

Standard Sources:
B: Bank of Canada, *Review*
S: Statistics Canada, *Canadian Statistical Review*.
Exchange Rates: Exchange rates provide conversion factors. Depending on the purpose, preference might be for market rates, if available, or for par rates, or par or central rates, if effective. See Introduction.
Market Rate (End of Period and Period Average): midpoint rate for noon transactions between banks from 1948.
Par or Central Rate: Par value for 1948 and 1949 and from May 1962 through April 1970.

International Liquidity: Line 1a.d, Gold (National Valuation), is the U.S. dollar value of official holdings of gold as reported in the country's standard sources.
Lines 7a.d and 7b.d comprise Canadian dollar and foreign currency accounts of nonresidents booked in Canada, beginning June 1973. Data for earlier dates agree with lines 21 and 26c and comprise only the foreign currency accounts of nonresidents. Hence, lines 21 and 26c, converted into U.S. dollars, are smaller than lines 7a.d and 7b.d, respectively, from June 1973 onwards.
Bank of Canada and Exchange Fund: Exchange Fund foreign assets and Treasury IMF accounts and coin issues are consolidated with Bank of Canada accounts. The counterentry is included in line 12a.

SEMI-LOG SCALE. ALL SERIES DRAWN WITH DECEMBER OR QIV 1978=100
1977 1978 1979 1980 1981
◼See Introduction and World Tables

1980 I	1980 II	1980 III	1980 IV	1981 I	1980 June	1980 July	1980 Aug	1980 Sept	1980 Oct	1980 Nov	1980 Dec	1981 Jan	1981 Feb	1981 Mar	Canada 156
Millions of Canadian Dollars															**International Transactions**
19,408	19,735	18,513	21,314	....	6,852	6,275	5,755	6,482	7,517	7,117	6,680	6,980	6,526	....	Exports ... 70
866	759	642	635	....	251	219	209	215	224	199	213	253	....	....	Crude Petroleum ... 70aa
1,151	1,009	807	1,017	....	315	275	268	264	269	332	416	452	....	....	Natural Gas ... 70b
552	1,022	1,286	1,046	....	563	398	457	311	474	276	....	....	....	....	Wheat ... 70d
1,378	1,216	1,315	1,226	....	....	....	....	....	....	....	....	....	....	....	Wood ... 70rl
915	1,016	993	943	....	364	311	331	350	331	298	314	348	....	....	Wood Pulp ... 70sl
916	963	837	961	....	328	264	299	274	314	325	322	336	....	....	Newsprint ... 70ul
18,089	19,023	16,573	19,496	....	6,101	5,850	5,079	5,643	7,157	6,305	6,034	6,302	6,243	....	Imports, cif ... 71
1,841	1,616	1,747	1,664	....	386	576	443	728	678	475	520	745	520	....	Crude Petroleum ... 71aa
17,562	18,469	16,090	18,928	....	5,923	5,680	4,931	5,479	6,949	6,121	5,858	6.118	6,061	....	Imports, fob ... 71.v
1975=100															
133.9	137.0	125.5	143.6	....	142.4	127.8	115.4	133.3	154.3	144.3	132.2	....	....	....	Volume of Exports ... 72
89	169	205	146	....	....	....	....	....	....	....	....	....	....	....	Wheat ... 72d
193	188	....	....	....	231	....	....	....	....	....	....	....	....	....	Wood ... 72rl
148	152	145	136	....	160	137	145	153	144	129	136	149	....	....	Wood Pulp ... 72sl
128	128	106	108	....	129	103	120	95	109	107	108	111	....	....	Newsprint ... 72ul
91.9	97.1	96.6	94.0	....	95.4	100.1	84.3	96.8	96.1	94.9	91.0	76.3	....	....	Volume of Gold Produced ... 72kr
118.8	123.4	104.6	121.4	....	120.7	112.2	96.8	104.8	134.6	120.3	109.3	....	....	....	Volume of Imports ... 73
166.1	164.9	168.7	169.9	....	165.6	168.6	171.1	166.6	167.3	169.1	173.3	....	....	....	Unit Value of Exports ... 74
121	114	120	136	....	113	112	122	124	133	138	139	140	....	....	Wheat ... 74d
135	146	149	150	....	149	149	150	150	148	151	152	153	....	....	Wood Pulp ... 74sl
164	173	181	203	....	175	176	172	199	197	208	204	209	....	....	Newsprint ... 74ul
164.2	166.3	171.5	174.5	....	163.7	169.1	170.3	175.2	173.1	170.5	179.8	....	....	....	Unit Value of Imports ... 75
Minus Sign Indicates Debit															Balance of Payments
16,355	16,452	15,893	18,232	....	....	....	....	....	....	....	....	....	....	....	Merchandise: Exports fob ... 77aad
-14,787	-15,569	-13,663	-15,557	....	....	....	....	....	....	....	....	....	....	....	Merchandise: Imports fob ... 77abd
1,726	2,544	3,207	2,199	....	....	....	....	....	....	....	....	....	....	....	Other Goods,Serv.&Income:Cred 77acd
-4,734	-4,853	-4,710	-5,109	....	....	....	....	....	....	....	....	....	....	....	Other Goods,Serv.&Income:Deb. 77add
83	180	248	168	....	....	....	....	....	....	....	....	....	....	....	Private Unrequited Transfers ... 77aed
129	121	-7	136	....	....	....	....	....	....	....	....	....	....	....	Official Unrequited Trans.nie ... 77agd
-478	-3	-632	-1,087	....	....	....	....	....	....	....	....	....	....	....	Direct Investment ... 77bad
1,262	1,609	1,060	649	....	....	....	....	....	....	....	....	....	....	....	Portfolio Investment, nie ... 77bdd
-248	-259	-528	-534	....	....	....	....	....	....	....	....	....	....	....	Other Long-Term Capital, nie ... 77bed
-25	-32	59	1,079	....	....	....	....	....	....	....	....	....	....	....	Other Short-Term Capital, nie ... 77ccd
161	93	-1,385	-1,016	....	....	....	....	....	....	....	....	....	....	....	Net Errors and Omissions ... 77d.d
—	—	—	—	....	....	....	....	....	....	....	....	....	....	....	C'part to Mon./Demon. of Gold ... 78c.d
186	—	—	—	175	—	—	—	—	—	—	—	175	—	—	Counterpart to SDR Allocation ... 78b.d
-50	63	-12	-43	....	....	....	....	....	....	....	....	....	....	....	Counterpart to Valuation Change 78d.d
—	—	—	—	....	....	....	....	....	....	....	....	....	....	....	Security Issues by Govt. ... 78fad
—	—	—	—	....	....	....	....	....	....	....	....	....	....	....	Deutsche Mark Loan ... 78fbd
3	—	—	911	....	....	....	....	....	....	....	....	....	....	....	Revolving Credits ... 78fcd
—	—	—	—	....	....	....	....	....	....	....	....	....	....	....	Liab.Const.Fgn Author. Reserves 79x.d
417	-346	470	-28	....	....	....	....	....	....	....	....	....	....	....	Total Change in Reserves ... 79k.d
Year Beginning April 1															**Government Finance**
-2.26	-3.80	-3.24	-1.62	....	-1.52	-.86	-1.06	-1.30	-.37	-.84	-.42	-.76	-1.47	....	Deficit (-) or Surplus ... 80
14.64	12.93	13.75	15.85	....	4.91	4.85	4.38	4.52	5.44	5.06	5.35	5.15	4.27	....	Revenue ... 81
16.36	15.67	16.21	17.03	....	5.92	5.50	5.29	5.41	5.78	5.69	5.56	6.25	5.66	....	Expenditure ... 82
.54	1.06	.78	.44	....	.51	.21	.15	.41	.03	.21	.21	-.34	.08	....	Lending Minus Repayments ... 83
															Financing
3.49	1.27	4.06	3.73	....	.67	1.17	1.99	.90	1.72	1.90	.11	.72	1.47	....	Net Borrowing ... 84
-1.23	2.53	-.83	-2.11	....	.85	-.30	-.93	.40	-1.36	-1.06	.31	.04	.01	....	Use of Cash Balances ... 87
Year Ending December 31															
71,686	73,834	76,580	81,685	....	73,834	74,733	76,157	76,580	77,771	79,547	81,685	80,654	81,195	....	Total Debt ... 88
14,581	14,408	15,216	16,093	....	14,408	15,060	15,569	15,216	15,042	15,119	16,093	15,147	15,043	....	Held By: Bank of Canada ... 88aa
10,080	9,686	10,333	10,668	....	9,686	10,071	10,547	10,333	10,581	10,275	10,668	10,249	....	....	Chartered Banks ... 88ab
6,405	7,102	7,426	7,436	....	....	....	....	....	....	....	....	....	....	....	Other Finan. Inst. ... 88ac
33,487	35,013	35,391	....	....	....	....	....	....	....	....	....	....	....	....	Other Domestic Investo 88ae
7,133	7,625	8,214	....	....	....	....	....	....	....	....	....	....	....	....	Foreigners ... 88c
1,035	876	916	974	....	876	890	946	916	941	938	974	983	1,019	....	Intragovernmental Debt ... 88s
Quarterly Data Seasonally Adjusted at Annual Rates															**National Accounts**
84.94	82.22	85.89	93.40	....	....	....	....	....	....	....	....	....	....	....	Exports ... 90c
54.23	56.52	58.50	60.30	....	....	....	....	....	....	....	....	....	....	....	Government Consumption ... 91f
66.02	65.32	67.70	71.17	....	....	....	....	....	....	....	....	....	....	....	Gross Fixed Capital Formation ... 93e
3.26	3.91	-4.87	-6.16	....	....	....	....	....	....	....	....	....	....	....	Increase in Stocks ... 93i
159.44	162.83	170.16	176.80	....	....	....	....	....	....	....	....	....	....	....	Private Consumption ... 96f
-80.46	-79.59	-79.46	-84.84	....	....	....	....	....	....	....	....	....	....	....	Less: Imports ... 98c
287.64	291.32	297.07	309.76	....	....	....	....	....	....	....	....	....	....	....	Gross Domestic Product ... 99b
-8.94	-8.31	-8.07	-7.93	....	....	....	....	....	....	....	....	....	....	....	Less: Net Factor Pmts Abroad ... 98e
278.70	283.01	289.00	301.83	....	....	....	....	....	....	....	....	....	....	....	Gross Nat'l Expenditure = GNP ... 99a
249.12	252.60	257.77	269.84	....	....	....	....	....	....	....	....	....	....	....	Nat'l Income, Market Prices ... 99e
189.81	187.72	188.49	....	....	....	....	....	....	....	....	....	....	....	....	Gross Nat'l Prod. 1975 Prices ... 99a.r

Chartered Banks: Beginning 1967, data for *lines 24* and *25* refer to averages of Wednesdays since an adequate classification at month-ends is not available.

Other Financial Institutions: Savings Institutions cover Local Credit Unions and Caisses Populaires, Quebec Savings Banks, Mortgage Loan Companies, and Trust Companies. The Federal Business Development Bank commenced operations on October 2, 1975. Prior to that date, data refer to the Industrial Development Bank.

Life Insurance: Annual data relate to end of year assets of all companies. Quarterly and monthly data are for 16 representative companies doing about 75 per cent of total business.

Interest, Prices, Production:

Bank Rate (End of Period): Source B data. It is the rate at which the Bank of Canada is prepared to respond to requests of chartered banks for temporary advances and enter into purchase and resale agreements with money market dealers. Beginning March 13, 1980, the rate is set at one-fourth of one per cent above the latest average rate on three-month Treasury bills established at the preceding weekly tender. *Treasury Bill Rate:* Source B data. Monthly data relate to the tender rates of the last Thursday of the month. Quarterly and annual data are averages of the monthly data. *Government Bond Yield:* Source B data on average yield to maturity of issues ten years and over.

Industrial Share Prices: Source B data on closing quotations at the end of the month on the Montreal Stock Exchange for 65 industrial shares, base 1956. *Prices: Industry Selling:* Source B data on aggregate industry selling prices (gross weighted), base 1971. *Consumer Prices:* Source B data for all cities with a population of over 30,000, with weights corresponding to family expenditure patterns of 1967, base 1971. *Wages: Hourly Earnings:* Source S data in dollars per hour, covering manufacturing firms employing 20 or more persons. Data refer to the last pay period of the month including overtime, vacation pay, cost of living, allowances, etc.

Those futures traders who are attuned to longer-range trends, as contrasted with attempting to anticipate or react to transitory news reports—but both are valid strategies if they are executed properly—can usually get the same information that is carried by the wire services the following morning in the leading financial newspapers. *The Wall Street Journal, New York Times, Financial Times* of London, *Frankfurter Allegemeine,* and so on, routinely report the newswire releases in their next issue. Whether that delay of 12 hours or so imposes an unacceptable handicap on an individual trader is a matter that one should evaluate within the context of his or her particular trading plan.

Plunger's yen for profit

The Phil Plunger saga draws on. Since his initial forays into the foreign exchange futures market, Plunger has pursued his study of its inner workings and of the big-picture forces that affect it. He often feels as if the deeper he becomes immersed in his subject, the more confused he gets. There is, he soon discovers, no well-ordered grand design, but rather a series of cross-currents that make the alleged currency float a very choppy passage in fact.

Plunger also realizes a mutual economic dependency exists among trading nations, so that an analysis of one country's currency is not complete without giving due regard to conditions throughout the rest of the world. The bigger part a country's export-oriented industries and products play in its overall economy, the greater the influence circumstances abroad have. It is, Plunger thinks, as if his own customers were experiencing hard times. Sooner or later, their troubles would become his troubles. For the rest of the world, the concept was summed up by the expression, "If the United States catches cold, everyone else comes down with pneumonia."

Plunger's problem is to determine how this interdependence affects currency values, if in fact it does. As before, he turns to Dan Decimal as an interlocutor:

Plunger: How would a recession, here in the United States, say, affect the economies of other countries?

Decimal: That's something you'd have to look at on a country-by-country basis. In general terms, the more dependent any country is on exporting to the United States the more adversely it would be affected by a slowdown here.

Plunger: What are the most dependent countries?

Decimal: For many years West Germany and Japan were prime examples of the cold–pneumonia syndrome. Exports comprised a high proportion of total GNP in both countries, and the United States was in each case the single largest export market. Both have since enjoyed an expansion of their domestic sectors, however, and therefore are no longer as susceptible to economic sneezes from the United States as they once were.

Plunger: Are there any countries that are still heavily dependent on U.S. trade, then?

Decimal: Canada has long been, and remains, the largest trading partner of the United States. Since easily a quarter of its GNP and 70 percent of its merchandise exports go to the United States, Canada would feel the effect of a recession here almost immediately. Hong Kong, Taiwan, and South Korea are other examples of export-led economies that are vulnerable to slumps in other countries, particularly in the United States.

Decimal and Plunger discuss the matter further. They concur that any development, such as a recession in a major customer country, that leads to a curtailment of foreign demand for a country's goods and services will result in a dropoff in demand for its currency as well. A pickup in foreign demand, however, would enhance the demand for the currency. Any indication that a country's trade balance is improving—that is, a growing surplus or a narrowing deficit—would therefore be bullish news as far as its exchange rate is concerned. Signs of a country's trade position deteriorating would by the same token be a bearish factor, an intimation that futures prices for that currency are falling, or are about to fall.

Decimal points out that, because foreign currency futures are quoted in U.S. dollars, the foregoing precepts are turned around when it comes to evaluating the trade and payments position of the United States. Any bullish development pertaining to the U.S. balance of payments is bearish news for Swiss franc or Japanese yen contracts, say, while reports indicating dollar weakness are positive items as far as the latter and other dollar-priced currency contracts are concerned.

Plunger, ready to put his knowledge to a practical test, reads in *The Wall Street Journal* that Japan's trade surplus was sharply lower for the first 20 days of the month than during the comparable year-earlier period. Exports fell 17.6 percent while imports were down only 7.1 percent. A surplus on the order of $765 million had shrunk, therefore, to about $140 million. Plunger regards this as a bearish development for the yen. He asks Decimal about the feasibility of selling one or more yen contracts short on the basis of the trade balance news. Decimal is somewhat hesitant. He points out to Plunger that yen futures dropped some 90 points the day of the announcement, and suspects that it might be too late to sell futures on the basis of that particular news item. He suggests to Plunger that, instead of going short immediately, they await a possible rally in the contract price back to the .5400 level and seek to establish a short position there. Plunger agrees, and Decimal enters an order good through the remainder of the month to sell 1 December JY at .5410. There is equity of $11,500 in Plunger's trading account, so the $2,000 initial margin required to sell one contract is amply covered. They select .5560 as an appropriate level at which to enter a protective buy stop order in the event they execute their sell order at .5410.

A week later Decimal phones Plunger to tell him that the order has been executed at .5410, and not at all too soon. Shortly after he received confirmation of the sale from the IMM trading floor, Decimal says, an announcement came over the newswire that the United States had posted a narrower-than-expected trade deficit for the previous month, and that the dollar rallied strongly on the news. Instead of the whopping deficit most traders had been predicting, the figure came in at $1.9 billion, a slight improvement, but an improvement nevertheless, from the earlier $2.1 billion deficit. To spark the dollar rally further, and thereby depress December JY even more to Plunger's great delight, the U.S. secretary of commerce announced that the nation's trade outlook was improving, with continued gains expected through the remainder of the year.

As December JY drops to .5250, Plunger grouses to Decimal that they should have sold more than one contract. The broker cautions his client in less-than-gentle terms that greed has been the undoing of too many futures traders. Instead of lamenting the fact that his profit is not even greater, Decimal warns Plunger, he should act to protect the tidy one he already has by lowering his buy stop limit order. Plunger, a bit abashed, concedes the propriety of this advice and agrees to let the stop be moved down to .5350. The earlier strength of the yen continued to have a dampening effect on Japan's foreign trade position. Tokyo announced that exports to the United States fell 9.4 percent during the same period that Japanese imports from the United States jumped 18 percent. December JY plummeted another 120 points on the news. Plunger was beside himself with joy. Decimal, also pleased but having learned to restrain his exuberance, counseled locking in the additional paper profit by lowering the stop once again.

During the two months following, the dollar continued to rise against the yen and other currencies. A number of Japanese analysts predicted the dollar's strength would be a short-lived trend because Japanese exports, now that the yen was dropping, would be enhanced just as imports would be curtailed. There was, though, increasing concern among foreign exchange traders that a cutback in oil shipments to Japan from the Middle East would severely hamper Japanese economic growth. What, Plunger asked, was Decimal's opinion? The account executive granted that Japan's total dependence on imported oil was indeed a critical factor, but felt that this vulnerability was already amply reflected in the futures price. Moreover, Decimal believed, the oil dependency issue might already have depressed the yen below the level that the actual circumstances warranted. He suggested that Plunger consider taking his profit on any further decline in the JY contract. Plunger was amenable to the recommendation and authorized Decimal to enter a good-through-week limit order to buy (back) 1 December JY at .4760.

The .4760 limit buy order was executed three days later, as the yen dropped further on news of an oil well fire off Saudi Arabia. Even though the fire was not expected to affect oil shipments to Japan, nervous traders regarded the news as an excuse to reduce their long yen positions. Contemplating his realized profit of $8,125, Plunger wondered aloud whether they might not have covered the short position prematurely. Once again, Decimal reminded his client of the pitfalls of greed, and pointedly suggested that, instead of wondering why a big profit was not bigger, Plunger might better direct his attention to planning their next move.

Chapter 7

Inflation and purchasing power parity

IT IS HARDLY NECESSARY in this day and age to define the term *inflation*. Everyone who has not inhabited the densest jungle for the past quarter-century knows perfectly well what it is. But for the benefit of readers who do not believe that a book on finance can be "serious" unless it's chock-full of statistics, we have inserted the following table:

Table 7-1
Price increases on consumer products in the United States, 1960-1980

	Price 1960	Price 1980	Percent increase
Gallon of gasoline at pump	.27	1.25	363
McDonald's hamburger	.20	.50	150
Buick Skylark	3,100.00	4,400.00	42
Hershey bar	.10	.25	150
Cup of coffee	.15	.50	233
Pack of Marlboro	.35	.85	143
New York City subway fare	.15	.60	300
First-run movie	2.00	4.50	125

117

Speaking of movies, there was one released in 1974 entitled, *That's Entertainment!* It featured old clips of Judy Garland, Gene Kelly, Ginger Rogers, and other musical stars singing and dancing across the silver screen. Well, ladies and gentlemen, that's not entertainment, that's inflation!

Prices and exchange rates

Inflation, therefore, is a process of continually rising prices. One old saw invariably quoted by writers on the subject—and we would not dare be the first to ignore the convention—says that it is a case of "too much money chasing too few goods." That's a shorthand way of describing the tendency of consumers and businesses to use their available purchasing power to bid up the prices on a limited supply of raw materials, labor, and finished products.

The proposition that there is a causative relationship between a country's overall price level and the exchange rate of its currency was first advanced around the start of the 19th century, when the expression "par of produce" was introduced by the English economist John Wheatley to describe the differences in general price levels among a group of countries. Wheatley stated that "if the currency of one country increased above the required quantity, commodity prices would increase, and the same quantity of money would no longer be the measure of equivalency between two countries for the same quantity of produce." This was the first formal expression of the purchasing power parity theory.

The theory was developed and given official sanction in the 1810 report of The Bullion Committee:

> In the event of prices of commodities being raised in one country by an augmentation of its circulating medium [an increase in the note issue] while no similar augmentation in the circulating medium of a neighboring country has led to a similar rise in prices, the currencies of those two countries will no longer continue to bear the same relative value to each other as before . . . the exchange will be computed between those two countries to the disadvantage of the former.

In other (and fewer) words, the exchange rate will move against the country with the bigger money supply and higher inflation rate.

These and subsequent formulations of the purchasing power parity theory left several important questions unanswered. First, was the causation unilateral from product prices to exchange rates, or was the process reciprocal in nature? Second, if it was in fact a one-way street, did prices have a direct influence on exchange rates or did they work through the balance-of-payments adjustment process discussed in the preceding chapter? Third, what prices should determine purchasing power parity, a general index, or only prices of goods traded between the two countries in question? Finally, could the purchasing power parity theory explain short-term exchange rate fluctuations as well as long-range trends?

The nature of inflation

Putting aside, however reluctantly, the frivolous tone with which we opened this chapter—if comic relief was good enough for Shakespeare, why not for writers of finance, which is sufficiently tragic?—it is necessary to take a closer look at the phenomenon of inflation before addressing such complex questions.

It is easy to understand why inflation occurs during wartime. A fully employed work force is earning high wages to produce guns, tanks, aircraft, and other war matériel. But, at the same time, workers are frustrated by their inability to enjoy fully the fruits of their new prosperity because industry has converted from turning out consumer goods to producing weaponry. Resorting to the hoary analogy—this chapter is reserved for the "oldies, but goodies"—the more guns the economy produces the fewer resources there are available to make butter, or automobiles or TV sets for that matter. It truly is a case of too much money chasing too few goods, since the bulk of industrial production is either being blown up at or over battlefields or is being used to feed, clothe, and equip the forces doing the blowing up. After peace (of sorts) is declared and most of industry goes back to producing for a consumer economy, the deprived citizenry embarks on a buying binge with the earnings they were unable to spend during the war. Production cannot be geared up fast enough to meet the demand, and so prices continue to be bid up during the immediate postwar period.

Such was the U.S. experience during and after World War II: Consumer prices increased by about 20 percent throughout the war itself, and continued to rise another 35 percent during the years immediately following. Unlike previous wars, however, prices just kept on climbing after the war-induced demand was for the most part satisfied. There was a good deal of talk during 1946 and 1947 about the "inevitable" recession, but those years were only the start of the greatest and longest consumer boom in the country's history.

Several new elements set apart the years following World War II from earlier postwar periods. The upward attraction that intense and persistent consumer buying exerted on prices—demand-pull inflation, in economists' jargon—was joined for the first time by the so-called cost-push factor, in particular labor unions' newly achieved power to demand, and obtain, wage increases designed to keep pace with rising prices. The ability of big business and big labor to move consumer and wholesale prices ever upward in tandem—the infamous wage-price inflationary spiral—was tolerated, indeed encouraged, by government policy. The Full Employment Act of 1946, which was intended, incidentally, to cushion the effect of the inevitable postwar recession that never occurred, committed the federal government to following expansive monetary and fiscal policies. These policies kept prices inflated during the years when they might otherwise have fallen back to lower levels. Once an inflationary spiral is launched, it is difficult and not particularly useful to apportion the blame among demand-pull, cost-push, or government-induced forces. Beyond a certain point, the three tend to reinforce one another and eventually they become indistinguishable.

There is, to be sure, a linkage between the volume of money in circulation and the rate at which prices increase. A government's control over the country's money supply gives it, therefore, an effective tool with which to influence, if not actually determine, the nation's inflation rate.[1] The catchphrase about too much money chasing too few goods is simply a shorthand way of saying that the money supply is too great and the level of production is too low. The implication, therefore, is that policies which succeed in curtailing the growth of the money supply or increasing productivity, or both, will go a long way toward reducing the rate of inflation.

Economic growth versus inflation control

Academic economists and government policymakers have long debated how those two goals may best be achieved with the available tools of monetary and fiscal policy. They are constrained in their decision making by the fact that a certain amount of money expansion is necessary to achieve the desired rate of economic growth, and to maintain overall employment at the high level stipulated by the Full Employment Act. Ultimately, there is a trade-off between a country's inflation rate and its level of economic activity. If economic growth, and with it a high level of employment and wages, is the desired goal, some inflation is, according to the trade-off theory, part of the price that must be paid for it. But if reducing the rate of inflation is the top-priority policy objective, politicians who must answer to the electorate run the risk, if they are to succeed, of precipitating a recession, thereby incurring the wrath of millions of unemployed workers, and after the next election, joining them.

A. W. Phillips, the British economist, is credited with measuring the statistical relationship between inflation and unemployment. Claiming that wage rates and the general price level are closely linked, Phillips held that his measurements of the rate of change in wages against the percentage of the labor force unemployed in the United Kingdom between 1861 and 1913 established a negative relationship between unemployment and the rate of

---

[1]See Allan M. Loosigian, *Interest Rate Futures* (Princeton, N.J.: Dow Jones Books, 1980), pp. 228–44, for a discussion of money creation and measurement of monetary aggregates.

inflation. Economists and officials have since pointed to the Phillips curve—the scatter diagram which embodies his statistical results—as proof positive that price stability and a high level of employment are essentially incompatible. Inasmuch as the Phillips curve has been found to apply to other developed countries than the U.K. as well, government officials have, until recent years, been resigned to what in their view was the lesser of the two evils. Accordingly, they have administered policies to boost employment, with the hope that the inflationary consequences would be moderate at the very worst. Lately, they've been sadly disillusioned.

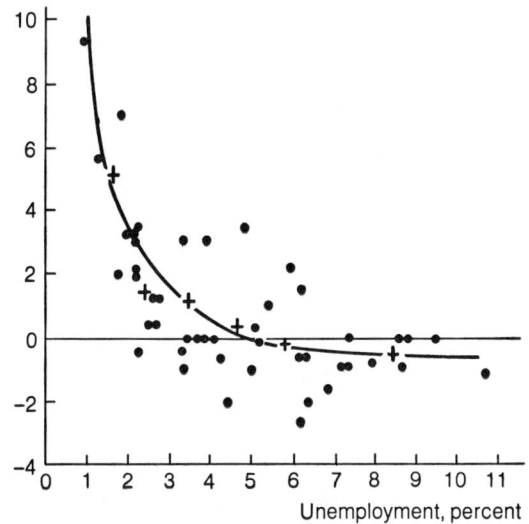

Figure 7-1
The Phillips curve—annual percentage change in money wage rates versus percentage change in unemployment

Source: Geoffrey Maynard and W. Van Ryckeghem, *A World of Inflation* (New York: Barnes & Noble, 1975).

Most economists agree that the only lasting solution to the Phillips curve dilemma is to keep increasing productivity. But agreement is a far cry from accomplishment. If manufacturing and service workers, executives, and every other category in the labor force can all increase their output—however each may be measured—no one would deny them their fair share of a growing gross national product. It is difficult, however, to persuade any work group, let alone its collective bargaining agents, that it is not entitled to wage increases in excess of productivity gains, particularly when prices seem to be rising everywhere whether productivity increases or not.

Like many other contemporary economic and public policy issues, analyses of inflation and recommendations for curing it divide along monetarist and Keynesian lines. The former approach, not surprisingly, emphasizes the money supply and the effect that its change has on available spendable income. Analysts who build econometric models along monetarist lines believe there is a link between a country's money supply and its balance of payments. They then proceed to the conclusion that prices of similar goods in different countries tend to move to equality. This convergence of real prices creates a transmission effect that carries inflation from one country to others with which it maintains trade relations.

The Keynesian analysis builds on the Phillips curve thesis. In so doing, it emphasizes the connection between changes in the general wage level and the unemployment rate. Economists who subscribe to this brand of analysis refer to a foreign trade multiplier to explain why different inflation rates in different countries tend to converge toward an approximate average world rate.[2] A corollary of the Keynesian-Phillips view of inflation is that real output and unemployment rates in different countries will adjust in accordance with this convergence of inflation rates.

The monetarists base their case on the fact that any sustained rise in the general price level of most developed countries has always been accompanied by a rise in their money supply. Their conclusion, as was noted earlier, is that the monetary authorities have it within their power to control inflation through their ability to restrict the money supply. If, however, the Keynesian assumption that forces other than the money supply contribute to rising prices is valid, closer attention must be given to the trade-off between economic growth (including employment) and price stability.

The Keynesian approach, with its emphasis on output and employment, was the doctrine subscribed to by most governments during the 1950s and 1960s. Inflation, which during those decades averaged slightly higher than an annual 3 percent rate, was not considered a serious cause for concern. Of greater importance to policymakers was stimulating demand—that is, boosting economic growth, not restraining it. The sharp acceleration of inflation during the 1970s, coupled with more rather than less unemployment, raised doubts concerning the continued validity of the Keynesian-Phillips curve analysis, and prompted a reconsideration of the monetarist approach. But unlike earlier analyses, attention this time was focused not on the domestic money supply of any particular country but on the international money supply. This shift in emphasis to the world level underscored the fact that inflation had by then become a shared problem of increasingly serious proportions.

---

[2]The foreign trade multiplier is an algebraic expression of the concept that fluctuations in a country's imports or exports or both, may cause significant variations in its national income. Interested readers may refer to H. Robert Heller, *International Monetary Economics* (Englewood Cliffs, N.J.: Prentice-Hall, 1974), pp. 125–35, for a detailed analysis of the multiplier effect.

Table 7-2
OECD annual inflation rate (GDP deflator)

	54	55	56	57	58	59	60	61	62	63	64	65	66	67	68
Belgium	0.9	0.4	3.5	3.5	1.5	0.6	0.7	1.2	1.7	2.9	4.8	5.1	4.5	3.0	2.7
Canada	2.5	−0.5	4.3	2.9	1.8	2.8	1.3	0.6	1.3	2.0	2.5	2.9	4.5	3.8	3.6
Denmark	2.4	3.7	4.8	0.9	1.8	3.9	1.6	4.7	6.8	5.7	4.7	7.3	7.3	6.0	5.7
France	1.0	2.3	4.9	6.1	11.8	6.4	3.0	3.3	7.7	6.6	4.7	3.8	3.0	2.7	4.8
Germany	0.1	2.0	2.9	2.9	3.6	1.3	2.6	4.3	4.4	2.9	2.7	3.6	3.8	0.6	1.7
Italy	1.5	4.4	3.9	1.8	2.6	0.0	2.5	2.7	5.8	8.6	6.3	3.9	2.1	2.8	1.5
Ireland	−0.9	2.7	2.8	3.2	6.3	2.1	0.7	2.6	4.6	2.7	9.5	4.4	3.8	3.1	4.0
Japan	0.0	5.5	3.1	4.5	−1.1	2.3	3.8	6.8	4.2	4.4	4.1	5.5	4.5	4.2	3.8
Netherlands	4.0	5.2	4.0	5.4	2.0	2.0	2.7	2.5	3.2	5.2	7.9	5.8	6.0	3.8	3.7
Norway	3.5	4.9	6.3	−0.8	1.7	2.6	2.7	2.4	3.0	2.5	5.4	4.8	4.3	4.4	2.5
Sweden	0.0	4.3	1.3	4.3	7.1	0.4	4.7	3.0	4.6	3.5	3.4	5.7	5.5	4.9	2.6
U.K.	3.8	1.9	6.4	3.8	3.8	1.3	1.1	2.9	4.0	1.6	2.9	4.8	4.1	2.7	3.2
U.S.	1.9	1.3	3.3	3.9	2.2	1.9	1.7	1.2	1.0	1.4	1.8	1.8	2.3	2.9	4.1
Average	1.6	3.0	4.3	3.8	2.4	2.1	2.4	3.1	4.0	3.8	4.6	4.7	4.2	3.4	3.1

Note: 1954–68 GDP at factor cost; 1969–1972 GDP at market prices.
Source: Yearbook of National Account Statistics.

Table 7-2 (continued)

	69	70	71	72	73	74	75	76	77	78	79	Annual Average 1954-1968	Annual Average 1969-1979
Belgium	4.3	4.7	5.7	5.9	7.0	12.6	12.7	9.2	7.1	4.5	4.4	2.5	7.1
Canada	4.5	3.7	3.3	4.4	7.5	10.9	10.8	7.5	7.9	8.9	9.2	2.4	7.1
Denmark	5.1	8.1	6.0	8.8	9.3	15.2	9.6	8.9	11.1	10.1	9.6	4.5	9.2
France	6.6	5.5	5.2	5.7	7.3	13.9	11.7	9.2	9.5	9.1	10.7	4.8	8.6
Germany	3.5	7.1	7.7	6.1	6.9	6.9	5.9	4.5	3.9	2.7	4.0	2.6	5.4
Italy	4.3	7.4	7.6	5.7	10.8	19.1	18.5	16.7	17.0	12.1	14.7	3.3	12.1
Ireland	8.1	9.6	10.3	14.3	11.3	16.9	20.8	17.9	13.6	9.6	13.2	3.4	13.2
Japan	4.2	6.7	4.4	4.9	11.8	24.2	11.8	9.2	8.0	3.8	3.6	3.7	8.4
Netherlands	6.2	5.4	8.1	9.3	8.0	9.6	10.1	8.7	6.6	4.1	4.2	4.2	7.7
Norway	3.0	—	6.0	4.3	7.4	9.3	11.6	9.1	9.0	8.1	4.8	3.3	7.3
Sweden	3.4	7.1	7.3	6.2	6.7	9.8	9.8	10.3	11.4	9.9	7.3	3.7	8.1
U.K.	5.6	7.3	8.8	7.8	9.1	16.0	24.2	16.5	15.8	8.3	13.4	3.2	12.1
U.S.	4.7	4.7	4.7	3.3	6.2	11.0	9.1	5.7	6.4	7.5	11.3	2.1	6.8
Average	4.7	6.4	6.4	6.5	8.4	13.4	12.6	10.2	9.1	7.4	8.5	3.4	8.5

Note: 1954-68 GDP at factor cost; 1969-1972 GDP at market prices.
Source: Yearbook of National Account Statistics.

Effects on exchange rates

Before looking at the problem of worldwide inflation and assessing its impact on exchange rates, it would be well to review the effect of inflation in one country on its exchange rates with its principal trading partners. The primary linkages in this regard are:

1. Immediate and delayed changes in import prices.
2. Changes in domestic prices caused by altered demand.
3. Changes in the composition of financial portfolios.
4. The effect of the factors noted above on wages.

When the currency of country X depreciates vis-à-vis other currencies, foreign production costs measured in terms of X's currency rise. Foreign producers have the option, therefore, of absorbing some of the higher costs and thereby giving up some of their profits, or of raising their prices in X. They normally would favor the latter course, and in so doing subject the residents of X to higher import prices. The latter group has in turn the option of rejecting what have become higher-priced foreign goods in favor of more attractively priced domestic products. That is in fact the basis for the argument that floating exchange rates provide the most effective adjustment mechanism for what the textbooks refer to as international payments disequilibria. If, in our example, foreign producers are of the opinion that the decline in country X's exchange rate is merely a temporary phenomenon, they may well decide to adhere to their existing price schedules and tolerate a period of reduced profitability rather than risk losing their market share in X.

In the event that import prices are raised, whether or not the amount of the increase fully reflects the amount of currency devaluation, many consumers in X are likely to turn to a domestic product if it is in fact less expensive in terms of their home currency. Their decision to switch will lift X's general price level by raising aggregate demand in its domestic sector. In accordance with conventional balance-of-payments theory, moreover, country X's exports should increase as a consequence of its currency's depreciating, though this increase may not occur for some time inasmuch as consumers do not generally alter their buying habits immediately in response to price changes. In any event, the extent to which domestic prices rise as a consequence of increased demand depends upon the ease and speed with which producers are able to expand their output. In those industries where output can be increased without high incremental costs and effort, any ensuing price increases may be insignificant. In such sectors as agriculture, where output, at least over the short term, cannot easily be stepped up to any appreciable extent, the impact of increased demand on domestic prices is likely to be considerable.

If we take country X to be the United States, we have a situation in which the currency in question, the dollar, also happens to be an international transactions and reserve currency. Any change in the dollar's value, therefore, will affect the value of dollar-denominated investments throughout the world. The propensity to avoid or to switch out of a financial asset which is suspect is greatly facilitated and therefore magnified by the ease with which investors are able to move out of a currency they believe to be depreciation-prone. If all currencies are suspect, investors are motivated to convert their money holdings into physical commodities, precious metals in particular. If the prices of such commodities are established in worldwide competitive markets the resulting price increases will be reflected in the inflation rates of all countries.[3] In the case of the dollar, the amount of dollar-denominated assets held by private and official entities throughout the world is so vast that even the slightest suspicion of its weakness can spur a sharp rise in the dollar prices of most world-traded commodities, especially raw materials.

Finally, the depreciation of a country's exchange rate has an inflationary impact through its effect on the general level of wages. Workers strive to sustain their purchasing power, (i.e., their real wages) in the face of inflation by demanding higher nominal wages. Such demands are now almost routinely incorporated into collective bargaining contracts in the form of cost-of-living escalator provisions or "reopener" clauses. In the latter case, there normally will be a time lag until an existing contract expires and is renegotiated to reflect the higher price level. These contractual wage increases, when they do go into effect, work their way through the wholesale and consumer price structure and, in so doing, perpetuate the wage-price spiral.

To answer the first of the questions posed earlier in this chapter, then, the interaction between price levels and relative currency values is not one-directional. The purchasing power parity theory, as it was originally formulated, recognized that inflation—anticipated as well as actual—serves to depress a country's exchange rate. There are, therefore, reciprocal or mutually reinforcing elements at work. With the causality running both ways, it is difficult to measure precisely the impact that a certain acceleration or slowdown in inflation has on a country's exchange rate, particularly when the expectation of a further advance or decline also may have a determining effect. It is equally difficult to predict with statistical accuracy the extent to which a given rise or fall in the exchange rate will affect inflationary expectations, and thereby speed or slow the shift from money to tangible commodities or the reverse.

---

[3]Precious metals are but a few of the commodities individuals and business entities regard as a hedge against depreciating currency values, in themselves a consequence of inflation. The process becomes, in essence, a self-fulfilling prophecy.

A recent study estimated that the 12 percent depreciation of the U.S. dollar during 1977 and 1978, as measured against the weighted average of 10 other major currencies, caused an increase of about 9.5 percent in U.S. import prices, and ultimately an increase in the overall consumer price level of about 2.4 percent.[4]   Figure 7–2 plots the trade-weighted value of the dollar against the U.S. consumer price index from 1975 through 1979. There clearly is a negative relationship wherein periods of rising inflation coincided with periods of dollar weakness.

Figure 7–2
Value of the dollar versus United States inflation, 1975–1979

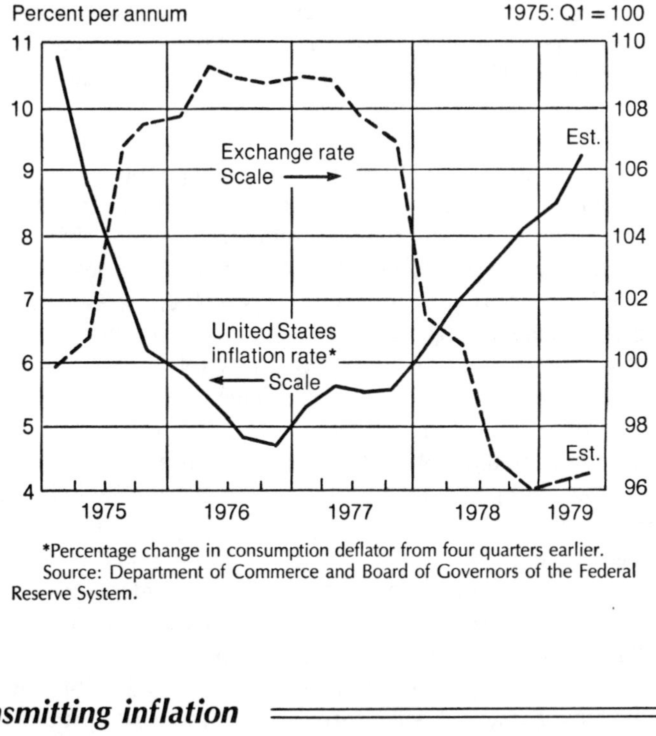

*Percentage change in consumption deflator from four quarters earlier.
Source: Department of Commerce and Board of Governors of the Federal Reserve System.

Transmitting inflation

The fact that inflation in the major industrial countries demonstrated similar rates of change during the post-World War II period suggests the existence of some common forces and linkages between the various countries.   Evidence pointing to such a community of experience became more marked during the 1970s, when inflation in nearly all of the countries in the OECD area increased more than twofold, and each country underwent its sharpest price gains at virtually the same time.

---

[4]Joel L. Prakken, "Exchange Rates, Import Prices and Domestic Inflation," Research Paper no. 7817, Federal Reserve Bank of New York, October 1978.

That export prices in most major trading nations exhibit a higher degree of uniformity than do overall price levels seems to confirm the logical assumption that inflation is transmitted from one country to another via the foreign trade sector. This is reasonable enough—one country's exports are another's imports. Countries that are enjoying boom times are most likely also experiencing demand-pull, or buyer's, inflation. During such periods, residents are inclined to import more, acting to satisfy some of the excess demand pressures with foreign supply. Escalating demand thereby moves from country to country like some invisible hot potato, boosting prices in each country where it lands.

Fixed parities were the medium through which this inflation transmission process worked during the Bretton Woods era. Higher prices on goods exported from one country became, by definition, higher import prices in the countries to which they were shipped, hiking up their general price levels. If the importing countries were themselves experiencing significant rates of inflation, the effect of rising import prices was all the greater.

Conversely, increased worldwide demand for a country's principal export products—food, for example—may boost the domestic prices of such goods if they are consumed as extensively at home as they are abroad. If such is the case, the general price level of the exporting countries will be subject to additional inflationary pressures which, as with the foregoing, will eventually filter through to wages and other types of income. The greater a country's foreign trade sector is relative to its total GNP, the greater the consequences this imported inflation will have on its economy.

Under the present system of floating rates, according to current theory at least, inflation should not be transmitted from a country to its trading partners. Now, the principal adjustment is made through changes in exchange rates, rather than via a country's reserves and money supply. Although a country experiencing an economic boom would most likely have higher inflation than would have been the case under the former parity system, it would by and large be confined to that one country.

Since the adoption of a floating rate system, countries with economies that are heavily export-oriented usually try to prevent or limit the appreciation of their exchange rates for fear that key industries would lose their competitive edge in world markets. Also situations may arise where the monetary authorities accept the need to allow their home currency to appreciate against that of a second country, but not against third-country currencies. That was the major problem confronting the countries that established the joint European float in the early 1970s. All of the members wanted to float their currencies jointly against the U.S. dollar; that was indeed their purpose in forming the snake. But those countries that felt they were being asked to assume more than their fair share of U.S. deficits and inflation—Germany was the outstanding example—believed there should be a more equitable division of responsibility in keeping the joint float intact.

Though floating exchange rates are thought to eliminate the transmission of inflation—or deflation for that matter—it does not necessarily follow that the level of inflation throughout the world will be reduced thereby. The exchange rates of countries with relatively high inflation rates will decline as a consequence of the diminished purchasing power of their currencies at home. The prices of imports quoted in the currencies of high-inflation countries will rise and the cost of their exports expressed in the currencies of nations with lower inflation rates will drop. Both forces contribute to the balance-of-payments adjustment process. Theoretically, at least, countries that suffer from the opposite difficulty—a deficiency in domestic demand—will find that their deflationary problems are aggravated by floating rates. Declining domestic prices will cause the exchange rates of these countries to float upward, which in turn discourages exports and boosts imports which are priced more attractively as a result of the rate appreciation. The fact that exporters come under pressure to reduce their costs and prices to remain competitive will reinforce the deflationary pressures.[5]

But to confound all of these elaborately reasoned theories, the 1970s experience of a sharp, concurrent rise in inflation in virtually all nations, developed and less-developed alike, suggests that there is an international transmission mechanism at work within the floating rate environment as well. Though the Keynesians and monetarists each have developed their interpretations of why this is so, the most reasonable explanation seems to be that the old linkages are still at least partially intact because the major nations do not allow perfectly free, or "clean," floating. Under the conditions of a managed float, central banks continue to intervene in the exchange markets to uphold what is to them a desirable rate, even though they may choose to describe their actions as quelling disorderly market conditions. Moreover, all of the nations during this period were faced with a common set of inflationary circumstances, most notably sharply higher energy costs owing to the rise in the cartelized price of imported oil, and attempted to resolve the situation with the same kit of monetary and fiscal policies. It is not surprising, therefore, that they all achieved similar degrees of success—or failure, depending on one's inclination to be critical—in their handling of the problem.

Focus on OECD nations

Inflation accelerated to unprecedented levels in every industrialized country during the late 1970s and early 1980s. Between 1969 and 1972, the average annual rate of price increases among the member countries of the Organization for Economic Cooperation and Development was over 6

---

[5]Inasmuch as deflation has not been a severe problem in the post-1945 world, one must go back to the Great Depression of the 1930s to identify actual examples of this scenario.

percent, double the average annual rate over the preceding 15 years. By the end of 1979 the figure had reached 8.5 percent for the OECD area as a whole.

Table 7–3 presents the most frequently cited measures of inflation during three succeeding periods: 1954–68, 1969–73, and 1974–79. The indicators listed are indexes of consumer prices, money wages, productivity, export prices, import prices, and money supplies in the 24 OECD countries. Foreign trade prices, for both exports and imports, show the most striking comparisons over the three time frames. Having remained relatively stable during the 1954–68 period, import and export prices in most OECD countries began to rise markedly after 1968. Confirming our earlier analysis, they climbed farthest and most rapidly in the United States and England, the two countries whose currencies substantially depreciated immediately prior to, or during, the time that foreign trade prices rose. Those countries whose currencies appreciated, with the exception of Japan, enjoyed relatively stable export and import prices. In Japan, prices declined for the most part during the 1950s and 1960s, owing to a stringent monetary policy, but then rose quite rapidly after 1968.

Other statistics in Table 7–3 indicate that, although the rate of increase in money wages (unadjusted for inflation) was not excessive in relation to productivity growth in the more advanced economic sectors of the various OECD countries, it was excessive as far as many of the lagging or obsolete industry sectors were concerned. That was due, in large part, to the aforementioned determination of collective bargaining agents to secure for their constituents wage gains equaling those obtained by groups that may have been more deserving of them in terms of increased productivity. Some econometric studies suggest that part, though by no means all, of the disparity in national inflation rates can be attributed to different rates of productivity growth among the member OECD countries.

Since a substantial portion of the foreign trade within the OECD area is conducted among the various member countries themselves, export and import prices within the area as a whole are essentially identical. It will not suffice, therefore, simply to blame the post-1968 acceleration of worldwide inflation on a rise in import prices, since they were to a great extent the mirror image of export prices of other OECD member countries.

This general aggravation of the inflationary condition throughout the industrial world coincided with major changes in long-standing currency relationships among the major trading nations. The question raised, therefore, was which was the cause and which the effect. In November 1967 the British pound was devalued 14 percent ($2.80 to $2.40) against the U.S. dollar and other currencies. The French franc was devalued by about 11 percent ($0.20 to $0.18) in August 1969, a drop soon followed by an upward float and formal 10 percent revaluation ($.0.25 to $0.273) of the Deutsche mark. The Canadian dollar was floated in mid-1970, to be joined again by the Deutsche mark and Dutch guilder in that lighter-than-air state in May

Table 7-3
Indicators of inflation 1954–1968 and 1969–1973 (percentage increase per annum)

	Inflation rate (GDP deflator)		Money wages (hourly earnings)		Productivity (manufacturing)		Export prices (national currency)		Import prices (national currency)		Money supply	
	1954–68	1969–72	1954–68	1969–73	1954–68	1969–73	1954–68	1969–73	1954–68	1969–73	1954–68	1969–73
Belgium	2.5	5.1	6.4	12.4	4.7	3.2	−0.1	2.0	−0.1	1.5	5.3	8.3
Canada	2.4	4.1	4.4	8.3	3.8	3.9	1.4	4.5	1.5	3.8	7.5	12.0
Denmark	4.5	4.7	8.3	12.2	3.0	5.6	0.6	5.7	0.5	4.3	9.5	12.0
France	4.8	5.7	8.2	11.5	6.1	7.6	2.3	6.8	2.1	5.6	10.5	7.7
Germany	2.6	5.8	7.4	10.5	4.5	4.5	0.3	1.6	−0.8	0.5	9.0	9.6
Ireland	3.4	10.7	6.3	14.7	3.4	4.6	1.3	8.6	1.3	7.5	6.4	7.5
Italy	3.4	5.8	5.5	10.8	7.3	2.6	−0.9	5.8	−0.4	7.0	12.5	17.6
Japan	3.7	5.2	7.7	15.8	9.7	9.7	−0.7	3.3	−0.7	2.1	15.5	18.9
Netherlands	4.1	7.2	8.1	11.7	5.3	7.5	0.1	3.0	−0.1	4.2	6.2	12.4
Norway	3.5	4.4	6.5	10.7	4.1	?	0.4	4.0	0.2	4.2	5.7	12.8
Sweden	3.7	6.0	7.0	9.8	5.1	4.4	0.8	5.2	0.7	5.2	4.4	6.3
U.K.	3.2	7.3	4.5	11.5	3.0	4.0	2.0	7.5	1.1	7.9	3.4	9.6
U.S.	2.2	4.6	3.7	6.1	3.4	3.2	1.2	6.2	0.1	8.2	3.1	6.1
Average	3.3	5.9	6.7	11.2	4.9	5.1	0.7	4.9	0.4	4.8	7.6	10.8

Source: Maynard and Van Ryckeghem, *A World of Inflation*.

1971. There ensued the distress selling of the U.S. dollar, which culminated in the cessation of its gold convertibility in August 1971, and the consequent chaos in the foreign exchange markets.

A formal devaluation of the U.S. dollar of 11 percent and a further revaluation of the Deutsche mark and Japanese yen were the cornerstones of the short-lived Smithsonian agreement of December 1971. Once again, uncooperative market forces quickly rendered these revised relationships obsolete. The British pound was floated in June 1972, and the dollar was devalued again the following February. The yen, mark, and guilder were driven to still higher levels.[6]

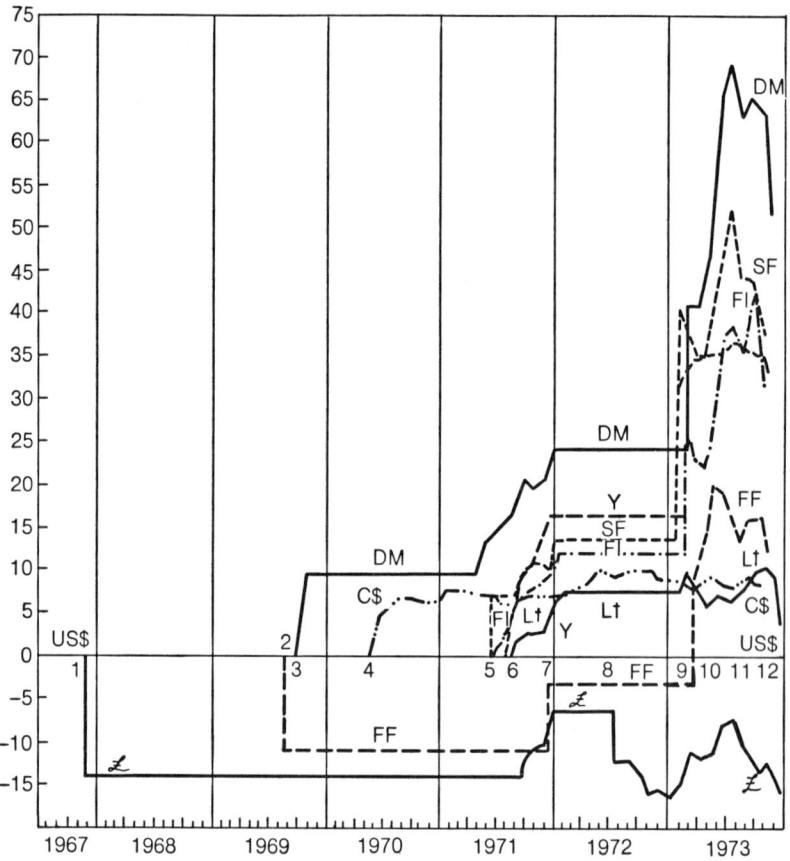

Figure 7–3
Foreign exchange rates of major currencies (percentage deviation with respect to dollar parities of October 1967)

Source: Maynard and Van Ryckeghem, *A World of Inflation*.

---

[6]Readers may wish to review the account of these events in Chapter 3.

By the close of 1973, the cumulative appreciation of the Deutsche mark since 1967 had amounted to over 50 percent ($0.2500 to $0.3846), that of the Swiss franc ($0.2286 to $0.3340) by nearly as much, and of the Dutch guilder ($0.2760 to $0.3700), and Japanese yen ($0.00277 to $0.00367) to more than 30 percent. The pound, on the other hand, had depreciated by 18 percent ($2.80 to $2.30), compared with its dollar parity in 1967. It is, as was noted, impossible to isolate and to measure the exact effect of exchange rate levels on price levels and vice versa. It is clear, however, that such drastic revisions in long-established rates, unprecedented in the post World War II period, were bound to have a decisive effect on foreign trade prices in the OECD community and, via the transmission process, on the domestic price levels of the member countries as well.

We have explained why a substantial depreciation in the exchange rate of a country's currency against the currencies of its principal trading partners will stimulate an increase in the prices of internationally traded goods within that country. It stands to reason, therefore, that there will be a price decline of similar proportion in countries whose currencies have appreciated. But because of the so-called ratchet effect—greater rigidity of wages and prices on the down side than on the up side—the 1967–73 period produced disproportionately greater price increases in the depreciating countries cited above (the U.S. and U.K.) than any insignificant price declines that may have occurred in the appreciating countries (Japan, Switzerland, Germany, and the Netherlands). On balance, therefore, the general level of world prices rose markedly during the period.

Inasmuch as the output of the United States comprised nearly one third of total OECD production during the 1967–73 period, the argument that the United States "exported" its inflation to the rest of the world carries some weight. However, it should also be noted that the general world price level expressed in dollar terms had until 1968 lagged considerably behind U.S. export prices. A decade later, no country was in a position to point an accusatory finger at any other for not guarding its state of economic health more assiduously. As the 1980s began, it was no longer a question of which countries had the inflationary disease, but rather of how badly each was stricken.

There are formidable technical problems involved in creating a single worldwide inflation index. While it is possible in theory to create a weighted average of the consumer price index in each major country, such an average would be less than ideal because, from country to country, the CPI has a somewhat different composition and meaning. Even with this qualification, however, the CPI remains the best available means of comparison.

Briefly reviewing the record in several selected countries, high demand was the cause for accelerating inflation in the United States during the peak years (until then) of 1956–57 and 1966–69. In both periods, the inflation rate rose after the nation's gains in gross national product slowed. Government expenditures to fund the Vietnam War, which was financed for the most part by budget deficits, were blamed for the latter experience. The early 1970s witnessed a different mix of inflationary forces. There were, to be sure, continuing demand pressures which, when taken in conjunction with the two devaluations of the dollar in 1971 and 1973, pushed up the prices of export and import products alike. But a new factor was the inflationary effect on finished goods of higher prices for crude oil, food, and other internationally traded raw commodities. There was also, for the first time, an overt attempt by certain occupational, social, and ethnic groups to wrest income shares from other groups. By 1975, it was clear to most thoughtful observers that inflation no longer was—if it had ever been—a purely economic phenomenon. Analysts were referring more frequently to the effect that various national and international institutions, public attitudes and traditions, and social and political pressures were having on the inflationary process.

The United States saw the decade of the 1980s open with an inflation rate approaching double-double digits, which is 20 percent. The administration's principal response to what was belatedly perceived as a crisis was to attempt to balance the federal budget for only the third time in 22 years. Should that remedy fail to retard inflation, the alternate hope was that an economic slowdown would provide some relief. Asked by a reporter whether the government's policy might not hasten recession and higher unemployment, the chairman of the Federal Reserve Board replied, "Yes, and the sooner the better!"[7]

Casting about for a bright spot in an exceedingly grim picture, economists pointed to an ample supply of gasoline and other petroleum products, and indications that interest rates had reached their cyclical peak as possible precursors of lower consumer prices. But further wage increases, reflecting through escalator clauses the existing inflation, threatened to limit any such slackening to one of modest proportions. Any prospective gains in productivity were also held to be minimal. A continued expansion of the nation's money supply at a 10 percent annual rate, as well as the likelihood of increased military expenditures, combined to make, skeptics maintained, the outlook for any substantial decline in the U.S. inflation rate highly uncertain.

West Germany succeeded in keeping its inflation rate under far tighter control during the 1960s and 1970s. The memory of the post-World War I hyperinflation that lingered with the older generation, an influx of refugees from East Germany and "guest workers" from other countries, an accommodating attitude on the part of the labor unions, and the government's conservative fiscal policy—all combined to hold consumer price increases to less than 4 percent during most of those years. Even at that, most of West Germany's inflation was imported—in the sense that it was fueled by

---

[7]*The Wall Street Journal*, April 9, 1980, p. 18.

an expansion of the country's domestic money supply, which in turn swelled with the inflow of foreign capital attracted by the amount and quality of its exports, relatively low inflation rate, and the consequent strength of its currency.

Every German boom period since 1958 was export-led in the sense that rising foreign demand for its products created trade surpluses at the same time that the central bank pursued a tight monetary policy to check the expansionary effect of incoming capital. The purported advantage of floating rates was that the monetary authorities could achieve the same end by allowing the mark to appreciate.

But in fact inflation increased in Germany as the mark floated higher. The heightened wage militancy of German labor unions and the new willingness of the government to resort to deficit spending to maintain employment at high levels served to bring the country's inflation rate closer to that of other countries. While still a rate to be envied by most other countries, the 5.6 percent figure reported for the first quarter of 1980 suggested a trend which was becoming increasingly discomforting for most Germans. Critics of the government's policies complained of conflicting signals, in that the central bank was boosting interest rates to curtail economic activity at the same time that the economics ministry was embarking on an expansive spending program as the contribution it had agreed to make toward continued worldwide growth. For the first time in a number of years, the Deutsche mark declined against the U.S. dollar by an appreciable amount. As a consequence, international capital flowed out of the country to take advantage of higher interest rates in the United States and elsewhere. Compelled for the first time in recent history to create money to finance a deficit on current account, Germany's monetary authorities discovered that the policies they had relied upon in the past to contain inflation no longer seemed to work.

The inflation record of Japan has differed from that of most other countries, in the sense that while its wholesale prices have increased during boom periods the country's excess industrial capacity prompted price softening during business downturns. The government relied on monetary policy as its principal economic tool during the 1960s and 1970s. From 1960 to 1968 the Japanese central bank pursued a policy of declining interest rates and an expanding money supply to stimulate business investment in plant and equipment. As occurred in Germany and other countries, Japan became subject from 1969 on to imported inflation when sharply rising prices elsewhere pushed her own export and import prices higher, and also sparked a domestic inflation rate unprecedented in the country's post-World War II experience. The escalating cost of imported raw materials is estimated to have caused between one third and one half of the total increase in wholesale prices adjusted for the higher value of the yen.

Still sensitive to the after-effects of the 1974–75 worldwide recession, nearly all major OECD nations remained preoccupied with stimulating economic growth through the remainder of the 1970s. Their hope was that the inflation problem could be reduced to manageable proportions by rising productivity. The two countries having then what were considered the most robust economies, Germany and Japan, were imported by the other nations into taking the lead in applying stimulative policies which would sustain economic growth throughout the OECD area. This undertaking, combined with a commitment by the United States to trim its trade deficit and inflation rate, were the best available means, it was thought, to continue raising the total of world trade and at the same time to foster exchange rate stability. Unfortunately, given the conditions prevailing during 1978–79, this game plan resulted in overstimulation and accelerating inflation. European central banks absorbed more than $30 billion during the course of their exchange market intervention in support of the U.S. dollar, an operation which in each case prompted an excessive expansion of their own money supplies. By early 1980, OECD-area statesmen and their economic advisors were forced, in the face of what was clearly an inflationary crisis of runaway proportions, to alter their priorities and deal with this problem even at the risk of throttling economic growth and courting another worldwide recession on the order of the 1974–75 experience.

Plunger is pound-ed

Still basking in the glow of his successful Japanese yen trade, Phil Plunger has been seeking new worlds, or rather currencies, to conquer. Lately, he has concentrated his studies on the effect of a country's inflation rate on its currency. He ponders a statement by the U.S. Treasury secretary: "The dollar's value can't be protected at home if it is weak abroad, and we can't maintain its integrity abroad if it is shrinking at home." Plunger endeavors to fit together the links between monetary policy, money supply, the inflation rate and, finally, the domestic and international value of a country's currency. Becoming hopelessly lost amidst the jargon-ridden debates between academics of Keynesian and monetarist persuasions, he turns to Dan Decimal for a translation.

Plunger: What in blue blazes do those professors mean by "national income adjustment costs to external disequilibria caused by disturbances originating in the country's foreign sector are equal to the inverse of the marginal propensity to import times the disturbance"?

Decimal: I don't really know, and can't say that it would do either of us much good if I did. The crux of the Monetarist-Keynesian debate is, in practical terms, to which policy should the government give priority—creating and spending more money than it takes in through taxes to spur economic growth and sustain a high level of employment, or maintaining a balanced budget and keeping a tight lid on the money supply to contain inflation? The two policies are in the final analysis contradictory, and the one which the government tilts toward is, for our purposes, the decisive factor.

Plunger: You mean, the bottom line is—inflation up, sell the currency, inflation down, buy it?

Decimal: You have a gift for oversimplification, my friend. That's the other extreme from your "external disequilibria disturbances . . ." business. Yes, that's a pretty good rule of thumb, but don't forget that inflation is just one of the factors that affect exchange rates.

But Plunger is only half listening. He is eager to repeat his Japanese yen triumph, and thinks he's found a way of doing it. He scours the financial press for news pertaining to inflation and soon seizes upon what he believes is the right opportunity. Britain's National Institute of Economic and Social Research has announced, he reads, that the prospects for inflation in the United Kingdom have worsened appreciably, a rise in consumer prices of about 16 percent being forecast for the current quarter while economic growth during the same period is projected at less than a 2 percent annual rate.

Plunger asks Decimal for a current quotation on British pound futures. Decimal tells him that March BP is trading at 2.0160. Flushed with his earlier success, Plunger decides to increase the ante and tells Decimal to sell 2 March BP contracts at 2.0150 or better. Decimal is wary. He notes that the contract rose 135 points the day the National Institute made its announcement—what Plunger took to be bad news—and feels that a 16 percent inflation rate is not sufficiently above earlier forecasts to warrant a short position on the basis of that estimate alone. But Plunger has made up his mind, and Decimal enters the order as directed. He insists, however, that a buy stop order be entered above the sale price to prevent a ruinous loss. Plunger agrees to that, and an order is so placed at 2.0460. With the profit on the earlier yen trade added to Plunger's previous equity, there are more than ample funds in the account to cover the $3,000 initial margin requirement for the sale of two contracts.

A week after the short position in March BP is taken, the finance ministers of Western Europe announce at the conclusion of a mini-summit conference that they agreed to make the inflation battle their highest policy priority, and to put less emphasis on economic growth in their respective countries, even at the risk of rising unemployment. The pound, in the company of other European currencies, rallied on the news. Decimal calls Plunger to advise him that March BP is 2.0300. What should they do, Plunger asks. "Nothing," is the reply. "The buy stop is still in force at 2.0460. Let's just hope it isn't hit."

But it was. Two weeks later, the British prime minister emphasized in a speech before the House of Commons his determination to resist labor union demands for what he considered unjustified wage increases. The pound climbed as high as 2.10, triggering Plunger's stop on the way up.

His loss on the two March contracts essentially consumed the profit on his earlier yen trade. What did he do wrong, Plunger laments. "Nothing," is Decimal's laconic reply, except for "upping the ante" to two contracts on the strength of one profit. Even so, consoles Decimal, they had done the right thing in using a protective stop order to limit the loss and keep enough equity intact to fight again another day. A chastened Plunger resolves not to overreach himself the next time.

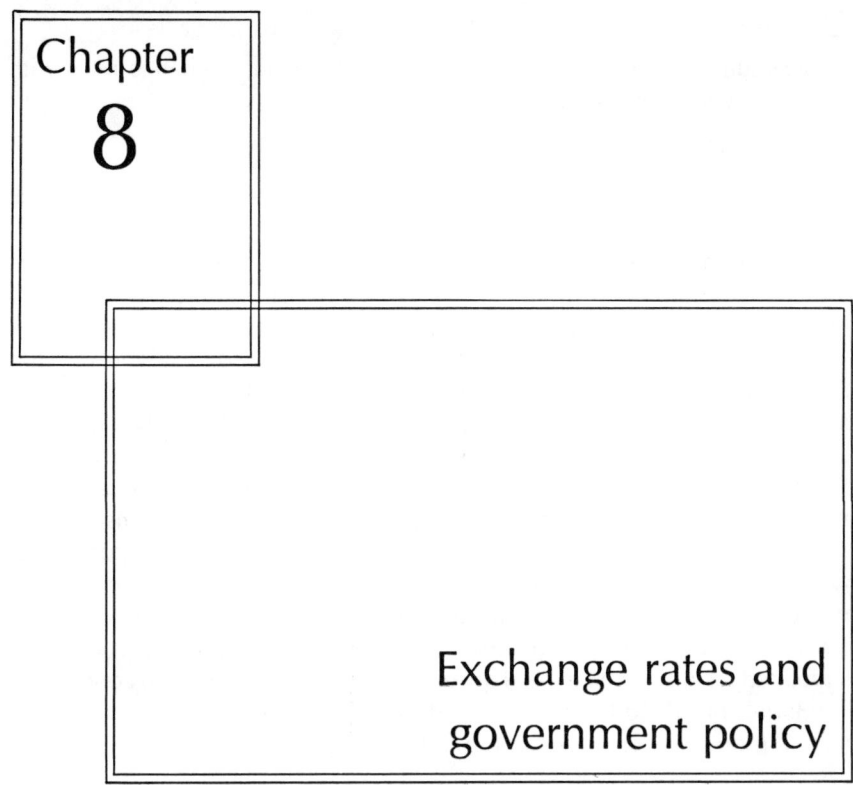

Chapter 8

Exchange rates and government policy

THE SUPPLY-DEMAND CHARTS that economics writers use to illustrate their points—and I am no exception, as the foregoing chapters repeatedly reveal—are possibly misleading in that they impart a sense of precision that is seldom the case. With regard to foreign exchange, they also suggest that exchange rates are set by the unbridled interplay of supply and demand. That was certainly not so during the fixed-parity years, nor is it completely true nowadays with floating rates. Governments continue to believe that the exchange value of their respective currencies is too much a matter of national interest to leave solely to market forces. They persist, therefore, in employing a variety of techniques to modify, and in some instances to contravene, the rates the market would establish if left to its own devices.

Government authorities seek to influence exchange rates indirectly through their exercise of monetary policy, with predictable effects on interest rates and the money supply, and directly through buying or selling large quantities of foreign exchange. Private traders, whether they are active in the spot or in the futures exchange markets, therefore must understand the implications of government policy and attempt to anticipate the likely effects of any number of official measures on the particular exchange rates with which they are concerned.

Econometric modeling

The purchasing power parity theory, which argues that currency values are chiefly determined by relative rates of inflation in different countries, holds reasonably true over the long run. But it is not of much use to traders whose time horizon extends to tomorrow, or perhaps to next week. That applies as well to the topics to be discussed in this chapter. But once again, it is a good idea to paint the backdrop with a broad brush before examining the fine points. To obtain this overview of the monetary factors that determine exchange rates, we turn to econometric modeling, a subject not as forbidding as that term might suggest. A model in this sense is a set of mathematical equations that represent an economist's best guesses of what actually happens in the real worlds of production, trade, and investment. A computer is generally used to incorporate the large volume of relevant data and to perform the many calculations required to produce simulated results of what would occur under a variety of assumed conditions.

Models of this sort vary in their degree of complexity. For example, a simple model might consist of the following equation:

$$\$/DM = A + B(BTUS) + C(BTGER) \qquad (8-1)$$

According to this expression, the dollar/Deutsche mark exchange rate is determined primarily by the trade balances of the United States and Germany respectively, with A; B, and C representing arithmetic constants derived from past data. When estimates of the two variables BTUS and BTGER are entered into the equation, the model projects a $/DM rate on the basis of those estimates. By entering additional variables and such nuances as adjustment time lags and multiple equations, models can be made to incorporate greater types and amounts of data, and thereby deal with broader assumptions. To include a purchasing power parity calculation in our basic $/DM model, therefore, we add the expression:

$$D - E(CPIUS) - F(CPIGER) \qquad (8-2)$$

containing the U.S. and German consumer price indexes.

Moving the modeling concept beyond the most basic of formulations, the economics faculty at the University of Chicago linked the purchasing power parity theory with an analysis of money supply trends to advance the so-called monetary approach. Their primary thesis is that the exchange rate between two currencies is determined on the whole by the relative money supplies, money velocities—the frequency with which a dollar, mark, pound, and the like, changes hands over a certain period—and levels of real income in the countries involved, with the expectation that the exchange rate will move against that country with the higher rate of money supply expansion. Contrary to the generally held theory that a country's interest rate and exchange rate levels rise and fall together, the monetary approach holds that an increase in a country's interest rate level will cause its currency to depreciate.

The monetarists have developed their own model, which holds that:

$$P = V\frac{M}{Y} \qquad (8-3)$$

Where

M = money supply
P = overall price level
V = velocity of money
Y = real income

Translated into ordinary English, this equation says that when the velocity of money remains constant, an increase in a country's money supply will lead to a proportionate rise in its price level.[1] If the rate of turnover increases while the supply is unchanged, that, too, will cause a rise in the price level.

The monetary approach to exchange rate determination also incorporates into its model the expression,

$$P = P^*E \qquad (8-4)$$

It states the purchasing power parity hypothesis that a country's domestic price level, P, is equal to the price level(s) abroad, P*, translated into the domestic currency at the exchange rate, E. Combining Equations 8–3 and 8–4 we have:

$$E = \left(\frac{1}{P^*}\right)V\frac{M}{Y} \qquad (8-5)$$

This awesome cluster of algebraic symbols says that an increase in a country's money supply or in its velocity of circulation will lead to a depreciation in the exchange value of its currency, whereas an increase in production will bring about its appreciation.

The builders of the monetary model are among the first to point out its limitations. If, as we noted at the beginning of this chapter, the purchasing power parity theory is itself too indefinite to be of much analytical value over the short term, simply incorporating the theory into a broader model does not make it any the more precise. Moreover, as described above, the model makes no provision for the effect on present and future exchange rates of investor and trader expectations. Finally, the monetary model does

---

[1]See Allan M. Loosigian, *Interest Rate Futures* (Princeton, N.J.: Dow Jones Books, 1980), pp. 228–36, for a description of the manner in which the Federal Reserve System initiates changes in the U.S. money supply through open market operations and other policy tools. The central banks of other countries employ similar techniques to the same end.

not allow for the effects that exchange rate changes have on the domestic price level.

Another approach, which endeavors to place greater weight on expectations, is the portfolio balance model. Unlike most other models, which assume that domestic and foreign investments are perfect substitutes for each other, and that capital is totally free to move from one country to another in response to interest rate differentials, the portfolio balance model strives to identify the variations in the supply and demand for interest-bearing securities denominated in different currencies.

The following chapter treats the subject of trader psychology and expectations at some length. It is sufficient to remark at this point that the role of expectations is central to any theory of exchange rate behavior inasmuch as the spot rate is indicative of the course market participants expect it to take over the near and intermediate-term future.

If, according to the portfolio-balance model, interest rates rise in the domestic money market of country X, domestic demand for X's money market instruments—government bills and notes, certificates of deposit, bankers acceptances, and the like—should increase in proportion. A rise in interest rates in money markets abroad, though, is likely to divert demand away from country X's investments, thus contributing to an excess supply of money and securities there. Country X's exchange rate, as well as that of other countries, is determined, therefore, by the relative supplies of, and demand for, financial assets in the major domestic money centers. An increase in the ratio of the money supply in country X to the supply of domestic investments there will lead to a depreciation in X's exchange rate. An increase in the ratio of domestic securities available in X to foreign securities will have essentially the same result.

Some general observations

The foregoing descriptions of monetary and portfolio balance models are fleeting by design because, expressed in precise mathematical terms as they invariably are, they and other such models seem to bear little relation to the highly subjective, frequently emotional markets with which exchange market participants are familiar. Some general observations drawn from these exercises in logic do have practical value, however, in preparing would-be traders for the real test—anticipating exchange rate movements or, failing that difficult task, recognizing them in their early stages.[2]

---

[2]For a fuller discussion of these points as well as a more detailed description of the monetary and portfolio-balance models, see Rudiger Dornbusch, "Monetary Policy Under Exchange-Rate Flexibility," in *Managed Exchange Rate Flexibility: The Recent Experience* (Boston: Federal Reserve Bank of Boston, 1978), pp. 90–126.

1. In the present environment of flexible exchange rates and high capital mobility, monetary policy in country X affects the exchange rate not only through its influence over interest rates but also via its impact on the merchandise account. The latter effect is so because any policy-induced changes in the overall price level will serve to enhance or impede X's international competitiveness, thereby boosting or retarding its net exports.
2. Although an expansionary monetary policy will temporarily improve country X's trade posture by raising exports, there eventually may be an offsetting negative development as lower interest rates spur domestic spending for consumption and business investment, which in turn would lead to a higher level of imports.
3. The effect that country X's monetary policy has on its interest rates will also have an immediate effect on the exchange rate because of the resulting change in the interest rate differential. If, as is likely, the monetary tightening or relaxation produces a change in expectations as well, its effect on exchange rates will be all the more pronounced.
4. A primary cause of exchange rate volatility is the low interest rate elasticity of money demand. That means that fluctuations in the demand for, or supply of, money produce disproportionately greater fluctuations in interest rates, which then call for larger exchange rate movements to maintain international interest rate parity.
5. Depending upon the magnitude of country X's imports, the effect which exchange rate changes have on import prices will in turn affect domestic producer and consumer prices as well. The greater the overall effect of exchange rate changes on X's domestic price level, the more inflationary any monetary expansion will be.
6. The impact of exchange rate changes, if any, on X's trade flows and direct investment abroad will occur after a considerable time lag. The net export effect will therefore not be one of the immediate consequences of monetary policy.

Effect of money-supply growth

The rates of money supply growth and the (presumably) resulting changes in dollar exchange rates for the United States, United Kingdom, Germany, Switzerland, and Japan are listed in Table 8–1 on an annual basis for 1976–77 and quarterly for 1978–79. It is noteworthy, since it casts some doubt on the monetarist theory, that during those periods when the dollar was experiencing its most severe weakness in foreign exchange markets, the growth in the U.S. money supply was among the lowest of the five countries listed. At the same time, German monetary growth was among the highest, but that did not hinder the appreciation of the mark to any noticeable degree.

To the contrary, it was largely the conversion of dollars into Deutsche marks during the years covered in the table that was a primary cause of the German monetary expansion.

Table 8-1
Monetary growth and exchange rate fluctuation

	Monetary growth					Effective $ rate versus S.D.R.
	U.S.	U.K.	Ger.	Switz.	Jap.	
1976	5.1	11.4	10.3	7.7	14.2	-5.0
1977	7.1	21.5	8.3	.5	7.0	1.1
1978						
I	-6.2	2.5	-1.0	7.6	-3.2	1.8
II	5.5	2.0	5.5	2.2	4.5	.2
III	-.3	5.2	1.3	-1.6	-1.1	3.3
IV	8.7	5.7	8.3	10.6	13.5	1.7
1979						
I	-7.6	-.1	-4.1	1.7	-3.3	-1.2
II	4.7	1.4	3.2	-3.4	1.6	.4
III	.3	3.2	-1.3	-2.7	-.5	2.1
IV	8.0	3.8	6.1	2.5	5.6	Unch.

Bearing out the contention of the portfolio-balance model proponents—even though their own approach by no means provides all the answers—one must go beyond comparing the bare money-supply figures for a complete explanation of how and why exchange rates behave as they do. Perhaps, as American car buyers were for many years led to believe, success comes to those who buy bigger and better models. On the other hand, that may not be the answer at all.

The multicountry model

Obviously, modeling is in this context no mere child's play. Staff members of the U.S. Federal Reserve System have themselves assembled a number of econometric models to project and evaluate the probable effects of monetary policy actions under a variety of assumed conditions. A leading example is their multicountry model (MCM), which is in essence a collection of individual country models grouped around one of the U.S. economy at the center. The other nations included are the U.K., Canada, Germany, and Japan, with a residual model representing the rest of the world.

Simulations are conducted to project the likely effect of a particular policy action on exchange rates under the assumptions programmed into the model. One such simulation might be to measure the probable effects of a monetary contraction in the United States isolated from the rest of the world. A follow-up program might then be to link the United States with the other country models to estimate the effects of restrictive monetary policies in other countries, such as, say, an increase in the Bank of Japan's discount rate or the imposition of higher reserve requirements on commercial banks in Germany.

In carrying out such simulations, a number of variables are entered into each component of the multicountry model: real and nominal GNP divided into their constituent parts, consumption, investment, exports and imports, price deflators for the foregoing items, as well as for wage rates, percentage of productive capacity currently being utilized, and the unemployment rate. Variables in the monetary sector would include short- and long-term interest rates, the aggregates M_1 and M_2, and the primary vehicles of monetary and fiscal policy—the discount rate, reserve requirements, reserve holdings of domestic and foreign financial assets, and government expenditures. Trade and capital flows between countries and interest rate parities are then used to link together the monetary sectors of each country represented in the model so that the effects of changes in one on all others can be projected and evaluated.

The key variable in such a program during the Bretton Woods years would have been changes in the level of each country's international reserves. Under the present flexible rate system, the central variable, and for our purposes the object of the entire exercise, is the projected change in each country's exchange rate.

The four panels of Figure 8–1 trace, according to the multicountry model, the projected results of a restrictive monetary policy in the United States on (A) real GNP, (B) overall price level, (C) trade balance, and (D) interest rates. The solid lines represent the projected changes taking the U.S. model alone, while the adjacent dotted lines link the U.S. model with the other five country models. The charts display a significant difference in the two projections in each instance. In the case of GNP (panel A) the depressing effect of a tight monetary policy is much greater with all the countries included than with the U.S. model by itself. Seven calendar quarters after the assumed tightening was initiated, the U.S. GNP would have fallen by an additional .2 percent when the international repercussions of this tightening reverberated back to the United States.

The most marked difference occurred in the case of the price level (panel B) where the divergence between the projected result for the United States alone and for the entire multicountry model was about .3 percent at the end of eight quarters. The impact on the trade balance (panel C) is also greater when the feedback into the United States is taken into account.

Taken together, Figure 8–1's four panels suggest that the effect of monetary policy changes on important U.S. variables is greater when the international consequences of the assumed policy actions are considered. According to the multicountry model, an appreciation of nearly 3 percent in the dollar exchange rate caused by monetary contraction produces a 1½ percent decline in the average price of U.S. imports, which in turn works

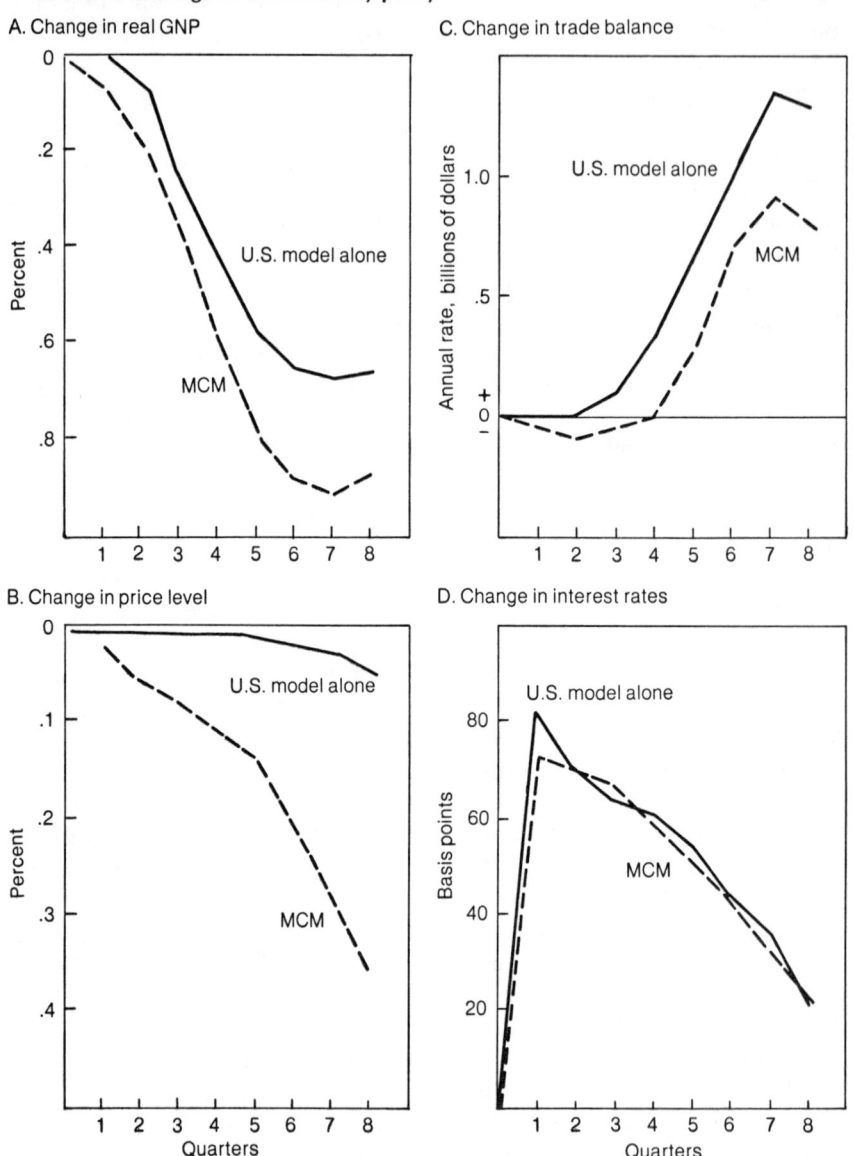

Figure 8–1
Effects of a change in U.S. monetary policy*

*All changes are measured relative to conditions that would prevail in the absence of policy action.
Source: Ernesto Hernándes-Catá et al., "Monetary Policy under Alternative Exchange Rate Regimes: Simulations with a Multi-Country Model," in *Managed Exchange Rate Flexibility: The Recent Experience* (Boston: Federal Reserve Bank of Boston, 1978), p. 129.

its way through and depresses the aggregate price level. The dollar appreciation simultaneously reduces the volume of U.S. exports and stimulates a boost in the volume of imports. The consequent net deterioration in the

U.S. trade balance depresses GNP below the level to which the initial monetary contraction pushed it, while the feedback effect from abroad diminishes foreign demand for U.S. exports even more.

Figure 8–2 traces the multicountry model's projected effects of a 1-percentage-point increase in the Bank of Japan's discount rate. As is indicated

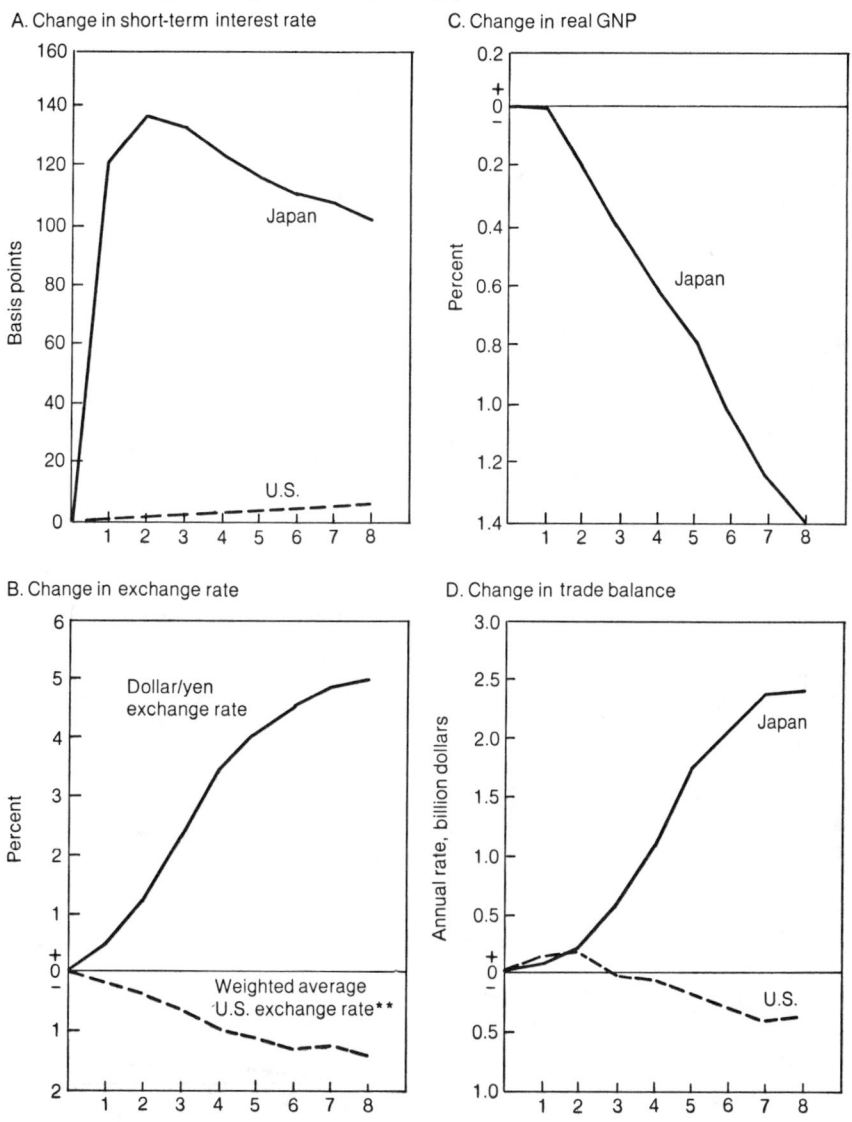

Figure 8–2
Effects of a 1 percentage-point increase in Japan's discount rate*

*All changes are measured relative to conditions that would prevail in the absence of policy actions.
**Units of foreign currency per dollar.
Source: Ernesto Hernández-Catá et al., in Managed Exchange Rate Flexibility: the Recent Experience (Boston: Federal Reserve Bank of Boston, 1978), p. 133.

in panel A, short-term interest rates in Japan would have risen sharply for the two quarters following the discount rate increase, and would then have fallen off gradually. Though short-term interest rates in the United States also rise moderately, the interest rate differential between the two countries initially moves in favor of Japan, thereby reducing the relative attraction of

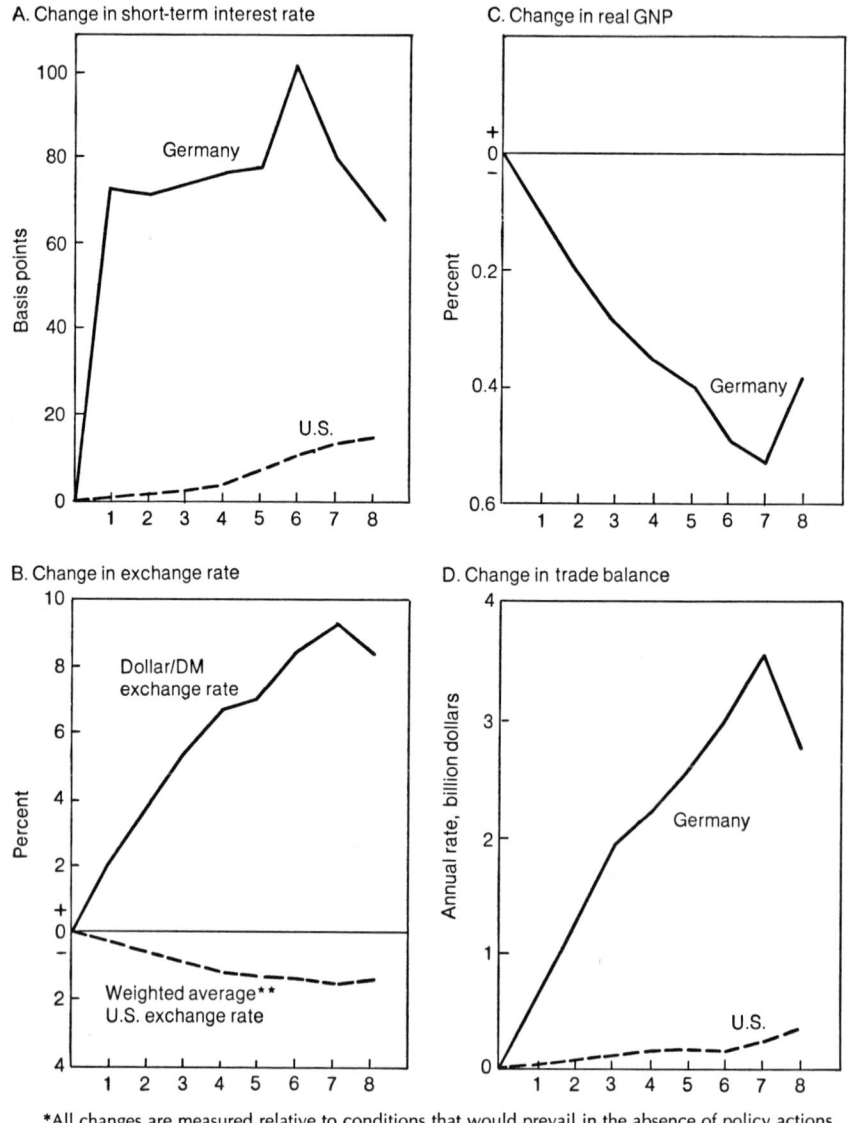

Figure 8–3
Effects of a 1 percentage-point increase in German reserve requirements*

*All changes are measured relative to conditions that would prevail in the absence of policy actions.
**Units of foreign currency per dollar.
Source: Ernesto Hernández-Catá et al., in *Managed Exchange Rate Flexibility: The Recent Experience* (Boston: Federal Reserve Bank of Boston, 1978), p. 135.

investing in the United States and in the Eurodollar markets, and causing the yen to appreciate versus the dollar.

A similar result follows a 1 percentage-point increase in the German central bank's reserve requirements for commercial bank deposits in that country.   In the multicountry model simulation, however, the U.S. trade balance improves as a result of the monetary contraction in Germany because U.S. exports will eventually rise in response to the sharp depreciation of the dollar.   In the prior case of a projected increase in the Japanese discount rate, the ensuing dollar depreciation is more than offset by the depressing effect on U.S. exports of a large reduction in Japanese GNP.

Effect of interest rates

Notwithstanding the limitations of the multicountry model and others like it, especially about measuring investor expectations of future rate movements, such models are useful in highlighting certain relevant linkages. The most important relationship for our purposes is that exchange rates tend to move *over the long run* by some multiple of the change in a country's interest rates, but that there is a marked lag in the completion of this process. Recent studies suggest that a determining factor in the relationship is whether the interest rate change is caused by a permanent or merely a temporary change in the size of a country's money supply or is due to a variation in its growth rate.   The multicountry-model simulations indicate that a temporary change in the money supply brings about only a temporary change in interest rates, and that the extent and ultimate effect of these changes on the exchange rate depends upon their duration.[3]

Once again the difficulty remains that, important though such observations might be in terms of theoretical research and long-range policy planning, they are not of much immediate value to the trader who must cope with the daily vicissitudes of the market place.   The problem of sharp "overshoots" or overreactions by market participants to specific news items continues to bedevil traders who act on the basis of what they believe, and, in the long run, turn out to be perfectly correct analyses of interest rate patterns and other fundamental factors.   But, as Keynes observed, we are all dead over the long run, and in the meantime traders are subjected to repeated figurative deaths as they are whipsawed by the market's jittery responses to what often prove to be fleeting and in retrospect inconsequential events.

There is also the academic problem of determining what formula most accurately represents the linkage between exchange rates and the various money supply and interest rate variables.   Two workable approaches are either to extrapolate expected future exchange rates as a function of past

---

[3]Charles Freedman, "Discussion of Hernández-Catá Paper," in *Managed Exchange Rate Flexibility*, pp. 143–47.

rates or to divide the domestic country's export price level by an average export price level of other countries.

The conventional wisdom that an increase in a country's interest rate level would, by attracting investment funds from abroad, induce a proportionate increase in its exchange rate was a valid analysis in the days when interest arbitrageurs could rely on reasonable exchange rate stability. At that time, there was minimal risk of a substantial rate change between the times they converted their funds into another currency for the sake of a higher interest return, and when the investment matured and the funds, plus interest, were to be reconverted into the original currency.

Five case examples

Flexible exchange rates are, as they say in less somber circles, a different ballgame altogether. Now, the exchange rate risk usually overshadows the interest advantage to be gained by switching from one currency to another. To make the picture even more obscure, relative interest rates are but one of several factors that affect exchange rates at any given time. A certain rate may respond to a balance of payments statement one day, a price index figure the next, and only on the third day get around to reflecting relative interest rates, and for only a few hours at that. The five charts in Figure 8–4 fail to reveal any sustained positive relationship between interest rates and exchange rates during the 36 months between mid-1977 and mid-1980. The dollar rates of the Deutsche mark, British pound, Swiss franc, and Japanese yen, as well as the average trade-weighted rate of the U.S. dollar,[4] displayed as much a tendency to decline during periods of rising interest rates in those countries as they did to appreciate. Moreover, the recent record refutes conventional interest rate parity theory inasmuch as exchange rates during the months indicated were as likely to move against countries with an interest rate advantage as they were to move in their favor.

In the case of Germany (panel A), the $/DM rate rose on balance during the 17 months from September 1977 to February 1979, while the interbank loan rate in that country remained close to the 4 percent level. After short-term interest rates in Germany did start to rise in March 1979, the mark leveled off, having risen from around 42 U.S. cents during the preceding months while interest rates remained stable. For the remainder of the period, spot marks traded in a lateral range between 52 and 55 U.S. cents each. The Swiss interest rate/exchange rate comparison is similar, yet more pronounced. Here, the $/SF rate appreciated by over 60 percent from about

---

[4]The trade-weighted dollar is a cumulative index which reflects the U.S. dollar's value in terms of 15 other currencies with each component weighted for the level of U.S. trade with that country. By means of such a weighing of trade components, the dollar's decline against some currencies is partially offset by gains against others.

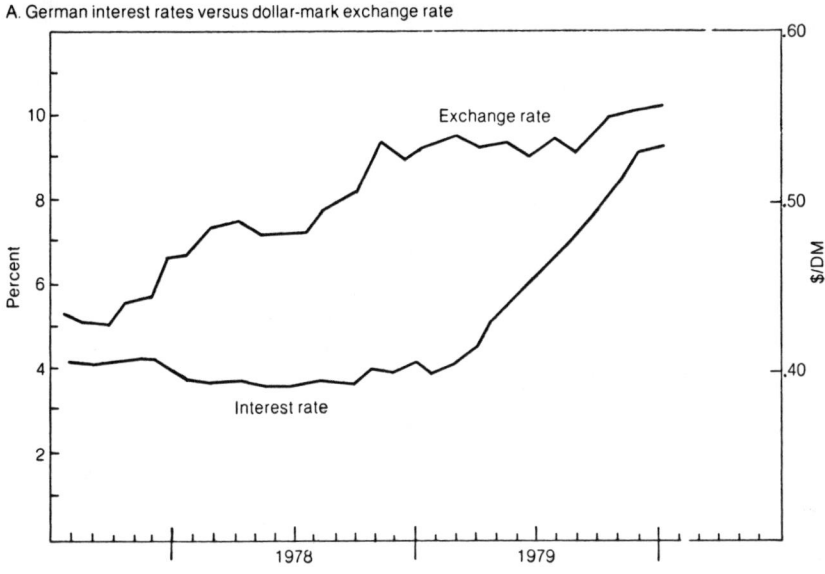

Figure 8–4
Exchange rates versus interest rates—five cases 1977–1980

A. German interest rates versus dollar-mark exchange rate

B. Swiss interest rates versus dollar-Swiss franc exchange rate

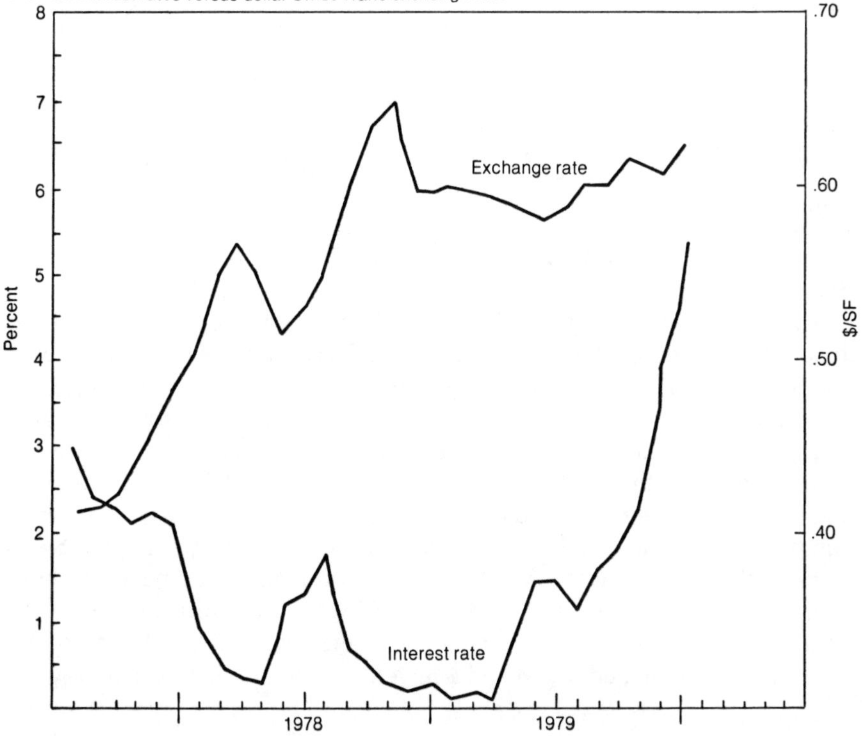

Figure 8–4 (continued)

C. Japanese interest rates versus dollar-yen exchange rate

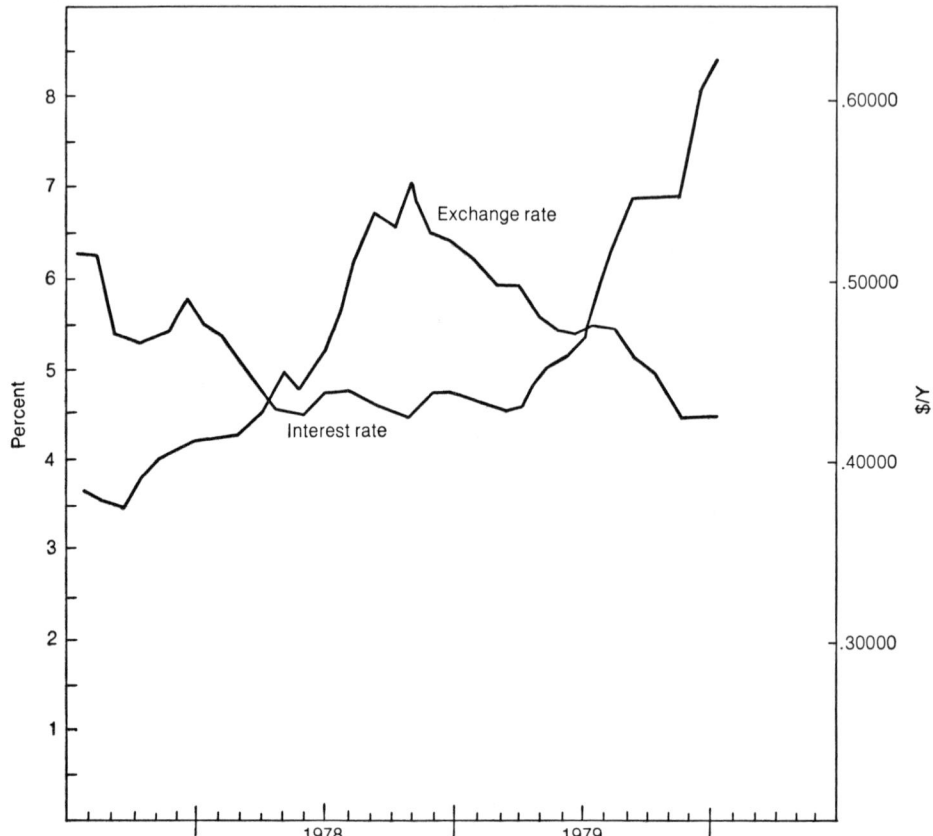

40 to 65 cents during the 20 months from July 1977 to March 1979 as the Swiss interbank loan rate was declining from an already low 3 percent to what was in effect a negative interest rate of 0.25 percent. Then, as the loan rate climbed back to 5½ percent, the Swiss franc leveled off at about the 60 cent area. In both the Swiss and German cases, then, interest rates were by no means the principal determinants which drew foreign capital into those currencies and boosted their exchange rates to record high levels. To the contrary, the central banks of both countries deliberately reduced interest rates in their efforts to discourage the swelling inflow of investment funds. Their efforts were to no avail because the soaring mark and Swiss franc exchange rates were the consequence of unabated demand for those currencies. Rather, rising $/DM and $/SF were the mirror images of the sharp dollar decline between early 1977 and late 1978. As the dollar subsequently stabilized $/DM and $/SF reflected this by leveling off as well.

Figure 8–4 (continued)

D. United Kingdom interest rates versus dollar-pound exchange rate

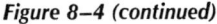

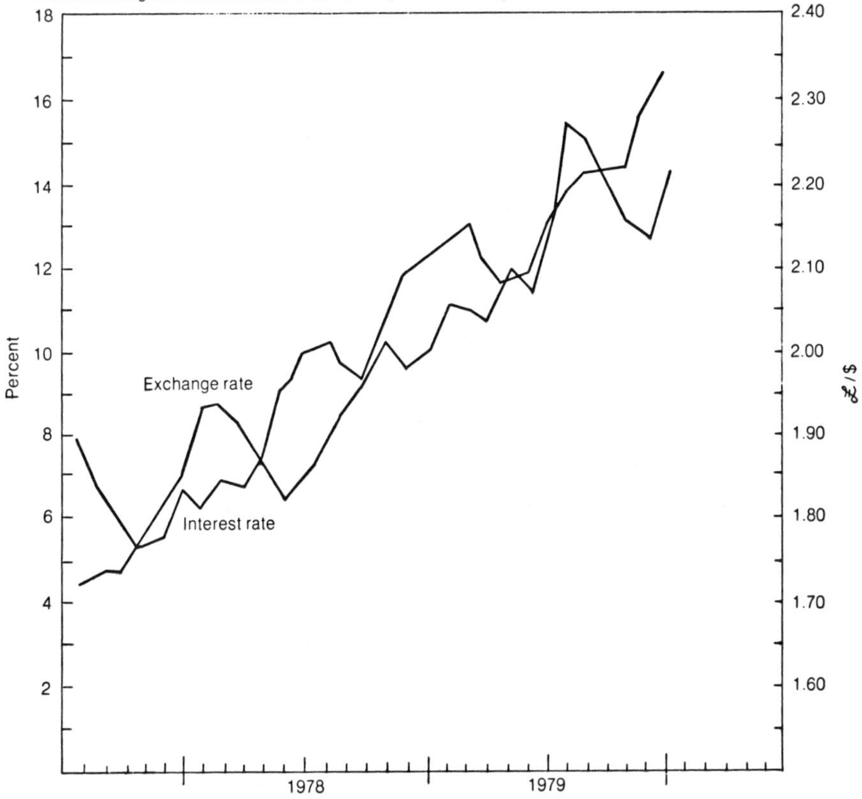

The Japanese yen traced a similar pattern, appreciating from September 1977 to October 1978 as interest rates in Japan dropped from about 6.25 percent to 4.25 percent. Again, as interest rates turned up on their way to 8½ percent by the end of 1979, the $/JY rate moved in the opposite direction, falling back to the .00400 level, where it stood at the onset of 1978.

The British pound provided the only instance among the five of a rough correlation between interest rate and exchange rate trends. During the 26 months that the U.K. interest rate rose from 4½ percent to 16½ percent, the pound followed suit in climbing from $1.75 to around $2.25. There were, however, intermittent periods of three to six months when interest rates were rising and the pound was falling, or vice versa, confirming our contention that interest rate trends taken by themselves are an incomplete and often a misleading indicator of future exchange rate behavior.

Figure 8–4 (concluded)

E. U.S. interest rates versus trade-weighted dollar

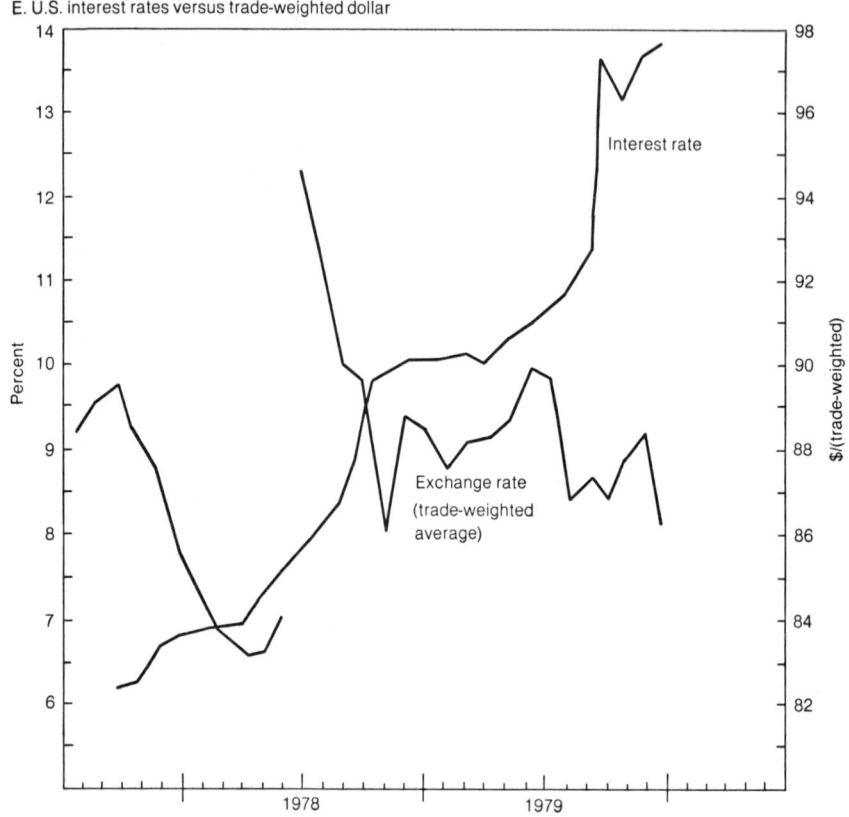

Source: International Financial Statistics.

Interest rate parities

An analysis of interest rate parities between several countries provides a more promising avenue of study, but the data are still inconclusive. Table 8–2 lists short-term interest rates for the United States, United Kingdom, and Germany at each month-end in 1979 as well as the effective interest rates between three-month forward dollars and forward pounds and Deutsche marks, respectively.

To reiterate the concept of covered interest arbitrage, the effective interest rate on an investment denominated in a foreign currency is the nominal (reported) rate of interest plus the premium, or minus the discount, on the forward contract used to hedge the exchange rate risk during the term of the deposit.[5] This relationship prevails because of the supply-and-demand

---

[5] Readers may refer back to Chapter 4, p. 63.

pressures created by the conversion of a substantial volume of funds from one currency into another. Such pressures are in turn produced by arbitrageurs covering their exposed foreign exchange positions in the forward market. They bring the interest rate differential between the two countries involved and the premium or discount on their forward exchange rate to parity, where it is no longer advantageous to exchange currencies for a yield advantage and cover the risk in the forward market. Even this covered interest rate parity theory is to some extent dated. With the substantial increase in exchange rate volatility in recent years, funds are likely to be switched from one currency to another for other reasons than to obtain a higher yield.

Table 8–2 bears this out. Of the 12 month-end intervals listed, interest parity prevailed within 0.5 percent between the dollar and the pound on only four of the dates indicated (January, April, July, and November). In the case of the dollar/mark relationship, the forward premium on the mark represents a forward dollar discount, hence a cost in exchanging marks for dollars to invest in U.S. interest-bearing instruments.[6] During 1979, according to the table, an approximate $/DM parity occurred in 5 months of the 12 (January, March, June, July, and August). During those months that there was a significant advantage after computing the costs of forward covering in converting dollars into pounds for the sake of a higher yield, spot and forward pounds appreciated the following month about half the time and declined the other half. Nominal U.S. interest rates ranged three to six percentage points above the comparable German rate throughout 1979. This premium on the 90-day forward Deutsche mark (again, a cost as far as switching marks into dollars is concerned) was sufficiently high, due to the expectation of continued mark appreciation, that there was no month in which it would have been profitable to convert marks to dollars for the sake of the higher nominal yield after taking the cost of covering into account. For example, in July three-month rates in the United States stood at 11.29 percent versus 6.77 percent in Germany, but subtracting the 4.70 percent annualized cost of cover from the nominal U.S. rate brought the effective rate down to 6.59 percent, slightly less than the German rate. Mark holders were actually better off investing at home, therefore, unless they accepted the risk of holding an uncovered dollar position for three months.

---

[6]The formula for computing the effective or implied interest rate obtainable by covered interest arbitrage is:

$$\frac{\text{Future rate} - \text{Spot rate}}{\text{Spot rate}} \times \frac{360}{T} \times 100 = \text{Percent per annum}$$

where T is the number of days remaining to maturity of the forward exchange contract equal in duration to the interest-bearing instrument under consideration. If the foreign currency involved is priced at a forward discount, the resulting figure is negative and must be subtracted from the interest yield of the instrument. If the currency is selling at a premium, the calculation is positive and should be added to the rate of interest.

Table 8-2
Comparative interest rates and forward cover parity—United States, United Kingdom, and Germany, 1979

1979 month-end	U.S. 3-mo. nominal interest rate	U.K. 3-mo. nominal interest rate	3-mo. forward pound discount	U.K. 3-mo. effective interest rate	Ger. 3-mo. nominal interest rate	3-mo. forward D-mark premium	Ger. 3-mo. effective interest rate
January	10.06%	12.61%	.0124	10.13%	3.85%	.0091	10.63%
February	10.09	13.28	.0096	11.39	4.13	.0093	11.00
March	10.01	11.98	.0064	10.74	4.42	.0075	10.02
April	10.24	11.64	.0062	10.45	5.50	.0077	11.33
May	10.35	11.76	.0063	10.55	5.89	.0059	10.40
June	10.47	13.02	.0180	9.72	6.40	.0059	10.73
July	10.94	13.87	.0183	10.62	6.77	.0067	11.68
August	11.43	14.06	.0105	12.21	7.04	.0066	11.85
September	13.77	14.11	.0067	12.90	7.82	.0076	13.12
October	13.18	14.12	(.0017)	14.44	8.84	.0092	15.45
November	13.78	16.09	.0118	13.95	9.57	.0077	14.88
December	13.82	16.71	.0120	14.55	9.54	.0087	15.54

Source: *Federal Reserve Bulletin*, and *The Wall Street Journal*, various issues.

Three exchange rates

There are at any given time three relevant exchange rates for any pair of currencies. There are, of course, the rates printed in the newspapers, the quotations at which currencies are bought and sold in the interbank market and futures contracts change hands on the organized exchanges. Then there are the theoretical rates at the intersecting points on the line charts where supply and demand for a particular currency are believed to be in equilibrium. Finally, there are the rates at which the monetary authorities of each country believe their currency should be valued. Under Bretton Woods and the fixed-rate systems of earlier eras, the latter would have been the official parity rates maintained through a variety of active and passive government measures.

Under the present flexible-rate system, these separate views of the same exchange rate rarely coincide. When they do, it is usually fortuitous. The primary justification for allowing currencies to float—apart from the very compelling reason that it no longer was possible to sustain the Bretton Woods parities or their Smithsonian replacements—was that the actual market rate and the theoretical equilibrium rate would coincide if only governments did not interfere by attempting to impose their notions of what the proper rate should be. A practical benefit was that countries would cease to lose reserves in endeavoring to enforce a rate at variance with the other viewpoints. But, despite these arguments in favor of flexible exchange rates, the very term *managed floating* reveals the inability of governments to keep out of the marketplace. If any group of private traders attempted to do what governments—or, more precisely, central banks—do to influence exchange rates, they would be indicted and probably convicted of conspiracy to manipulate the market. Since this official manipulation or rigging is purportedly in the national interest, it is not described in such pejorative terms, but rather as foreign exchange market intervention, an expression doubtlessly selected for its connotation of authority and legitimacy.

Central bank intervention

Until the final abandonment of fixed parities in 1973, central bank intervention was intended to accomplish two ends that were not always compatible. The monetary authorities assumed in the first instance an obligation to maintain stable and orderly market conditions. Second, they undertook to hold the exchange rate within its official IMF band with the least loss of reserves. Even after the abolition of parity rates per se, the preservation of orderly market conditions and the encouragement of a desirable exchange rate remain the dual purposes of central bank intervention.

Central banks, depending upon the situation and their objectives, may either buy their own currency with foreign exchange to raise the exchange rate, or at least to prevent it from falling further, or, conversely, sell their domestic currency to hold the rate down. Their three major considerations are: the appropriate time and exchange rate at which to intervene, and the amount of foreign exchange reserves they're prepared to commit to a particular support (buying) operation. If the authorities are striving to sustain a particular rate, the condition of the market will determine how much buying or selling is necessary, and for how long. If the amount of foreign exchange held in reserve is limited, they will not have the wherewithal to intervene for very long. For that reason, the central bank's intervening agency sometimes attempts to mask its activity to give dealers and traders the impression that supposedly natural forces are actually behind the particular buying or selling pressure it is attempting to exert. If, on the other hand, it suits their purpose to do so, the authorities may publicly announce the amount of funds at their disposal in the hope that market participants will be impressed by their seriousness of purpose and by the resources at their command.

Once the target exchange rate and the amount of funds earmarked for the intervention have been established, the authorities must decide in which market, spot or forward, they will act, the direction and speed of the rate change they are striving either to achieve or to prevent, and the effect of their actions on the spot-forward rate structure. The latter hinges directly, as we have recently seen, upon relative interest rates, and thus upon the respective monetary policies of the governments involved. Beyond the decisions concerning spot versus forward markets and open versus covert action is the question whether to intervene in that country's foreign exchange market, in markets abroad, or in more than one market.

Central banks' use of modern communications technology to intervene outside their domestic exchange markets has at the same time made their task more complex. Just as their scope of operations has expanded, so, too, has that of the market's other participants. Both the large international banks and their multinational corporate customers have increased their deposits in foreign financial centers. The corporations, having become accustomed to keeping deposits and credit lines with a number of different banks, also have grown more adept at managing their cash balances, transferring them from one national money market to another (thereby engaging in currency conversion) whenever they spy an opportunity to increase their investment income without unduly increasing their risk exposure. The volume and frequency of these transfers, changes in the centers where corporations keep their funds on deposit and where they borrow, changes in the timing of foreign payments and in the repatriation of foreign receipts all affect, and are in turn affected by, exchange rate movements. Thus, they also affect the selection and execution of intervention strategies central banks employ to influence such movements.

Four intervention strategies

There are four basic intervention strategies which may be implemented individually, or in combination. The objective of the first is to hold the spot rate at or near a specific level, and by so doing to impress other market participants that there is little likelihood of their profiting from abrupt changes in spot or forward rates. This strategy places the highest priority on orderly markets. Its principal cost is the drain of foreign exchange reserves that results from holding the rate stable in the face of large-scale currency conversions for the purpose of covered interest arbitrage or exchange rate speculation. This strategy was well-suited to the conditions that prevailed during the Bretton Woods years, but it has become increasingly difficult to execute successfully in the much more volatile climate inherent in a floating rate system, whether it is a managed or a clean float.

The second strategy is one of "leaning against the wind" to retard, if not entirely prevent, sweeping changes in the exchange rate. This strategy stipulates that the central bank will buy its domestic currency when the exchange rate is falling, and sell it when the majority of the other market participants is buying. This strategy is less rigid than the first because there is no effort to hold the exchange rate at or near any particular level. Because of that, it is less costly in terms of lost reserves.

The third strategy seeks to keep the exchange rate within a definite target range not unlike the intervention bands of the Bretton Woods system. The important difference, however, is that the upper and lower limits of the band are not in this case fixed, nor are they usually a matter of public knowledge.

This approach offers the benefit of conserving reserves. On the other hand, the central bank's tolerance of rate movements within the target range often gives rise to the appearance, if not the fact, of disorderly market conditions as the rate swings from the upper to the lower limit.

The fourth strategy is the seldom-used one of provoking uncertainty about the central bank's intentions, in the hopes that their inability to frame firm expectations will dissuade speculators and arbitrageurs from shifting funds from one center to another.

How strategies are picked

Just as private market participants must incorporate into their own particular trading strategies their impressions of what the central bank(s) concerned are doing or may do in the way of exchange market intervention, the central banks must take into account the likely behavior of the private participants in selecting and, after the fact, evaluating policy measures. An unexpected reaction by the dealer community may prompt officials to modify their intervention strategy. Possible tactics and techniques therefore affect, and are in turn affected by, the anticipated reactions of the various types of market participants, requiring their reliance on market "feel," or intuition if you will, as much as on objective calculation.

As was noted above, the monetary authorities may elect to implement a particular strategy by dealing in the spot market, in the forward market at one or more maturities, or in both spot and forward markets simultaneously. Should officials at the Bank of Japan, say, wish to discourage an appreciation of the yen above .005050, they might sell spot yen at that rate. They may decide, however, that their purpose would be better served by acting to hold the rate on three-month forward yen at whatever level would induce the flow of interest arbitrage funds in the volume necessary to hold spot yen at .005050. Intervention in the forward market has the advantage in the eyes of the authorities of allowing them to operate in greater secrecy than is generally the case in the spot market, where they may be required to report publicly any changes in reserves that occur as a result of their activity.

Much depends, as the portfolio-balance model discussed earlier suggests, on the actual availability of arbitrage funds and the facility with which they move from center to center. If the supply of such funds is not unlimited, the forward rate will very likely deviate from its interest parity if intervention is confined to the spot market. If the currency involved should be subject to heavy selling, actual forward rates are almost certain, as our foregoing review of the 1979 experience (Table 8–2) bears out, to drop below the effective interest parity rates. Should the central bank choose to intervene in the forward market, its buying there could force the forward rate to a premium above interest parity. The premium would in turn disappear as private arbitrageurs bid up the spot rate to take advantage of the incremental return.

U.S. monetary authorities did not intervene actively in the foreign exchange market during the Bretton Woods years until 1961. They met their IMF obligations as they perceived them by buying gold from and selling it to foreign central banks at $35 an ounce. The burden thereby was put on the latter institutions to intervene to hold their own currencies at their assigned dollar parities. With the onset of steadily increasing balance-of-payments deficits and the consequent loss of monetary gold reserves, U.S. Treasury officials felt compelled by March 1961 to shift their passive policy to one of active intervention. They were joined in their dollar-support operations by the Federal Reserve a year later.

Intervention techniques

Over the past two decades, the U.S. Treasury and the Federal Reserve have resorted to a variety of intervention techniques: purchases and sales in both spot and forward markets; transactions in the New York foreign exchange market and, through foreign central banks, markets in other centers; currency-swap arrangements with foreign central banks, and the issue of foreign currency-denominated securities to absorb excess dollars held abroad. As was noted earlier, the Federal Reserve Bank of New York serves as the agent of the entire Federal Reserve System and of the Treasury department in carrying out these transactions. The New York Fed's exchange market posture varies from aggressively bidding for, or offering foreign exchange to, most of the major dealer banks in the New York market to one of simply responding to the bids and offers of other participants. The New York Fed also acts as agent for foreign central banks, carrying out their instructions in its home market just as it in turn uses them to execute orders in its behalf in their own domestic exchange markets.

Other central banks apply similar techniques in managing their own currencies, though the operational details may vary from country to country. The Bank of Canada, for example, serves as that country's official intervention agency on behalf of the Finance Minister's Exchange Fund Account. It may also act in the Canadian exchange market for its own account or for those of other central banks and government authorities. The bank, like most central banks, does not as a rule make it a matter of public knowledge at what rate or up to what volume of funds it is intervening or would intervene in the market. Most of the transactions are in the spot market using the U.S. dollar, as do most other major central banks, as an intervention currency with which to buy Canadian dollars in a support operation, and for which to sell them when the bank is attempting to dampen the appreciation of its domestic currency.

German Bundesbank (federal bank) officials meet with representatives of that country's leading commercial banks at the Frankfurt Bourse (stock exchange) twice daily to set official buying and selling rates for the Deutsche mark, although dealings among the German banks continues throughout the trading day via telephone and Telex as it does in other exchange markets. The tradition of setting prices on the bourse floor—though not entirely unlike a modern futures exchange—is something of an anachronism in that the preponderance of foreign exchange trading is conducted off the exchange floor. Except under what it describes as "special circumstances," the Bundesbank does not carry out intervention operations in the forward market.

The Bank of England works through the U.K.'s Exchange Equalization Account for the purposes of "checking . . . undue fluctuations in the exchange value of sterling" and for ". . . the conservation or disposition in the national interest of the means of making payments abroad," which means the U.K.'s international reserves. The bank has the authority to operate freely in both spot and forward markets, but usually restricts its activities to the London exchange markets. The Swiss National Bank was not empowered to engage in forward exchange dealings until 1969, when special legislation was passed specifically authorizing the bank to make such transactions. Until that date it was able to circumvent the restriction by instructing the Federal Reserve Bank of New York to buy or sell for its account forward Swiss francs in that market.

What makes them so smart?

As was noted earlier, the justification for the monetary authorities' interference in the foreign exchange market is that, if it is left unregulated, private trading tends to get out of hand, and potentially contrary to the national interest. Hence, private manipulation is considered to be evil, but official manipulation is good, and therefore deserving of the more responsible term "intervention" in the sense that an adult intervenes to prevent a misbehaving child from injuring itself. Yet the question remains: Who intervenes with the interveners? What gives government officials a clearer insight to what the "correct" exchange rate should be than, say, bank dealers or their corporate customers? Or what is to prevent them from deliberately depressing the rate through intervention to gain an unfair competitive advantage in that country's trade with other countries?

The situation was more clear-cut during the Bretton Woods years. It then was the obligation of the monetary authority to maintain an orderly exchange market and to hold the exchange rate within the relatively tight limits of the designated IMF band. When that was no longer possible without extreme efforts and the prohibitive drainage of reserves, those officials who had the responsibility would eventually bow to the inevitable and declare a devaluation, or a revaluation in those rare instances when a currency was unacceptably strong.   But with flexible exchange rates, central bank intervention is a more arbitrary and undefined matter. Someone, it is argued, should be delegated the responsibility and authority to monitor the intervention policies of central banks and then intervene in some fashion when a particular policy is deemed to be improper.   Since it has been largely at a loss for meaningful work since the abolition of official parities, the IMF has frequently been advanced as a candidate for the job.

Several methods have been proposed as means by which the IMF or some other international agency might undertake the surveillance of central bank intervention policies.   Among the various approaches that have been suggested are: overseeing changes in the level of a country's international reserves, establishing target zones much like the former IMF parity bands, requiring central banks to lean against the wind to mitigate extreme and volatile rate movements, and evaluating each intervention policy and its results on a case-by-case basis.   Some free-market zealots have gone so far as to propose that central bank intervention be eliminated entirely, and that the same ends be achieved through official borrowing from private markets, monetary policy, capital controls, and other quantitative limits on reserve changes.

As jealous of their sovereign powers as independent nations are, the question remains open whether IMF member states would tolerate such supranational surveillance of their intervention activities.   The IMF has attempted to assert itself in this area by issuing a statement pertaining to surveillance, which holds among other things that a country should avoid manipulating its exchange rate to gain an unfair competitive trade advantage over other fund members.   But as of mid-1980 the members had not accorded the IMF any explicit authority to enforce that statement of principle.

Chapter 9

Expectations, news, and rumors: The effects of market psychology

WE CONCLUDED IN THE LAST CHAPTER that a major shortcoming of econometric modeling stems from the difficulty of reducing trader expectations to a mathematical formula. How does one express in numerical terms an opinion about the future, let alone a variety of opinions? The subject is even more prone to conjecture than it is to objective measurement, because every participant in the market knows that it is not the individual opinion that moves prices but the opinion of the majority of his or her fellows.[1]

Short of attempting to probe traders' psyches, we can defend the proposition that the dual motives underlying financial operations of various sorts are the hope for profit and the fear of loss. Whether the market participants are dealing in foreign exchange, managing an exposed or hedged foreign exchange position, or are otherwise engaged in arbitrage or speculation, the

---

[1] John Maynard Keynes, who was himself a highly successful securities and futures trader as well as an eminent economist and writer, likened the situation to a newspaper's pick-the-picture-of-the-prettiest-girl contest, where the prizes are given not to the readers who correctly guess the beauty queen but to those who correctly guess the girl who receives the most votes.

relative importance they attach to the profit and safety motives color their perceptions and determine the manner in which they decide to translate their expectations into market action. To the extent that such an appraisal is possible, it is worthwhile knowing how these attitudes affect specific exchange rates.

The Eurocurrency market

Before venturing into such murky waters it is necessary to introduce a new element into our analysis. Second only to the advent of floating rates themselves, the ease, speed, and frequency with which financial officers of multinational corporations transfer bank balances from one national money market to another has been the consequential development of the past decade in the foreign exchange market. The transition from fixed to floating exchange rates was accompanied by the rapid growth of the Eurodollar market—an interbank market for dollar balances held in banks situated outside the United States. Although the Eurodollar market remains the most important of such offshore credit markets in terms of volume, similar markets for loans and deposits denominated in other currencies have emerged alongside, but distinct from, their respective domestic money markets. Taken together, they comprise the Eurocurrency markets, a term that is misleading in that it implies that the market is in Europe or that it deals primarily in European currencies. Neither of these assumptions is correct.

The Eurocurrency market is not a regional component of the foreign exchange market, but one in which investing and borrowing is conducted in other currencies than those of the countries in which the transactions are made. There are, to be sure, close ties between each of the market's subsidiary parts—Eurodollars, Euromarks, Euroyen, and the like—and both its related domestic credit market and the foreign exchange market. In fact, dealers in those banks active in these markets often work side by side because of this close connection. There need not be a foreign exchange transaction involved in a Euroloan or deposit per se, however.

A Eurodollar deposit, for example, is a dollar-denominated balance held by a bank located outside the United States, while a Eurodollar loan is likewise made by a bank situated abroad. Apart from their geographic place of origin, there is no difference between such transactions and comparable ones made within the United States. The same applies to credit transactions denominated in other Eurocurrencies. Eurocurrency loans and deposits differ from their domestic counterparts in that the interest rates for the former are more attractive to both borrowers and depositors, and they are not subject to many of the restrictions and regulations governing domestic banking transactions. It is, in fact, the relative freedom from regulation which in large part accounts for the more competitive Eurocurrency rates.

The more attractive rates available in the Eurocurrency market on the borrowing and lending sides have lured a considerable number of bank asset managers and corporate treasurers from their domestic money markets. It is the need to convert currencies before transferring them from one market to another which binds the foreign exchange and Eurocurrency markets closely together. An even greater volume of funds would flow from a domestic to Eurocurrency market were it not for the fact that the latter is predominantly a wholesale market dealing in equivalent amounts of $1 million or more, and reserved for the largest and most credit-worthy corporate and government borrowers.

By way of illustration, let us reassemble our earlier cast of characters from Levi Strauss & Co. in San Francisco, Citibank in New York, and Commerzbank in Frankfurt. Holding $10 million on deposit with Citibank, the ever-vigilant treasurer at L.S. & Co. sees that he can earn an additional 2 percent annually by transferring the funds from a regular dollar account in New York to a Eurodollar deposit in Frankfurt (or, for that matter, some other non-U.S. money center). If the treasurer should decide to make the transfer—remember, there is as yet no foreign exchange transaction—Citibank would lose a $10 million deposit, of which Commerzbank would become the recipient. Total U.S. domestic deposits as a result would fall and the overall size of the Eurodollar market would increase by $10 million.

Having gained a $10 million deposit upon which it has committed to pay a specific interest rate, Commerzbank naturally enough wishes to earn something for itself on the funds. It therefore arranges to "place" them in the interbank Eurodollar market at a slightly higher rate, an increase on the order of 1/8 percent. The sequence continues, with L.S. & Co.'s original $10 million deposit being loaned from bank to bank, each time for an additional 1/8 percent until one of the banks in the chain has a call from a corporate customer for a loan of that amount. Maturities on Eurocurrency loans run from three months at the short end of the range to as long as 10 years. When a loan carries a maturity longer than six months, the interest rate is usually set on a rollover basis, being thereafter redetermined at the start of each new six-month period at the then-current rate.

Significance of Eurocurrency

The significance of Eurocurrency loans and deposits for the foreign exchange market is that they comprise an alternate interest rate structure which has an important bearing on the interest parity relationships discussed in Chapter 8. We stated there that the premium or discount on a particular forward rate tends to remain close to the interest rate differential between two domestic money markets. We can now extend that proposition to include the comparative interest rates prevailing in separate components of the Eurocurrency market, say between Eurodollars and Euromarks. With this qualification, we are able to propose a means by which the trader expectations described at the beginning of the chapter can be incorporated into a general theory of exchange rate determination.

As the release of new information on trade balances, inflation rates, and so on, alters foreign exchange traders' expectations regarding projected spot rates, the premium or discount on the pertinent forward rate will also change in reflection of the fresh data. The problem, as mentioned earlier, is one of first expressing and then measuring these subjective changes in numerical terms to incorporate them into the information that more easily lends itself to statistical analysis.

One proposed resolution of the measurement problem proceeds on the convenient assumption that the forward rate is itself a statistically unbiased gauge of the generally expected future spot rate. That is not to say, of course, that the prevailing view regarding a particular rate, six months hence, say, will turn out to be anywhere near the mark when that projected date is reached. That presupposes an ability to forecast exchange rate movements which very few, if any, traders possess. Rather, it is meant to convey the idea that the forward rate is at any given time an accurate measure of the consensus expectation. If that should be the case, all is solved. Analysts would then simply need to crank the existing premium or discount into their models and they're set to roll.

But, as is usual in this life, the situation is not quite so simple. The statistical nitpickers maintain that allowance should be made for transaction costs in such an arrangement. They contend that currency traders will not act unless the profit they perceive to be attainable exceeds what they must pay to make the transaction. If that is so, a statistical bias creeps into the calculation, in that the forward rate will under- or overestimate the actual expected future spot rate by the amount of the projected transaction cost. Other nitpickers add that there must also be included a determination of risk, which may deter traders from taking action. According to these qualifications, then, the forward exchange rate is an accurate representation of the real expected future spot rate only after transactions costs and the appropriate risk premium is taken into account.

Statisticians—nitpickers, after all, is an unduly harsh description of what is usually an honorable profession—debate these fine points within a framework of what are to nonmathematicians a mindboggling array of formulas. Since the contending parties themselves concede a lack of conclusive evidence to prove or disprove any of the theories they put forth, we don't feel remiss in sparing readers (on compassionate grounds) an equation-by-equation account of their contest.[2] It is in any event easier to grasp the important relationships if they are presented graphically. Figure 9–1 indicates that when the expected future spot rate (solid line) of the Deutsche mark is rising, the forward rate (dotted line) underestimates it by a constant factor of K, which represents the combined transactions cost and risk premium. This relationship holds because when currency traders expect the spot rate to

---

[2]Those readers who are of a statistical turn of mind may refer to Gunter Dufey and Ian H. Giddy, *The International Money Market* (Englewood Cliffs, N.J.: Prentice-Hall, 1978), specifically chap. 11, pp. 48–106. The author acknowledges this material as the principal source for the following analysis.

rise within a specific time period to an extent greater than that projected by the current spot rate, they will bid the latter rate up until it differs from the former by an amount equal to the transaction risk premium, K. When, on the other hand, the future spot rate is expected to fall, the forward rate overestimates it by K.

The assumption that K in Figure 9–1, the transaction cost and risk premium, is a constant need not always apply. It may in fact widen or narrow over time, but in today's highly competitive foreign exchange markets, transactions costs are likely to be small, and the variation of the risk premium from a positive to a negative value would tend to hold the mean figure close to zero.

An important formula

The conclusion to be drawn from the countless formulas that we've omitted for humanitarian reasons, and from the visual representation in Figure 9–1, is that the premium (discount) of a given forward exchange rate above (below) its related spot rate is equal to the expected annual rate of change in the spot rate. If, for example,

$$\$/DM_{Spot} = \$0.5000$$

and

$$\$/DM_{3\text{-mos.}} = \$0.5050$$

Figure 9–1
Relation over time between forward rate and expected future spot rate with transactions premium of k

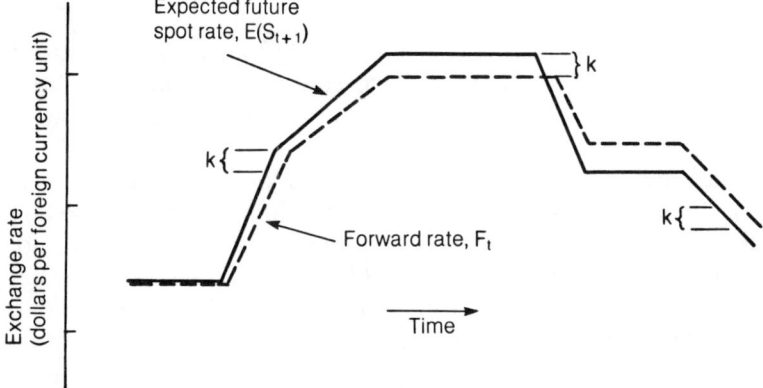

Source: Adapted from Richard M. Levich, "Tests of Foreign Exchange Forecasting Models and Market Efficiency," *New York University Business School Working Paper, no. 75–88*, November 1975.

The 1 percent three-month forward premium multiplied by four is the annual rate at which "the market" then expects $/DM$_{Spot}$ to appreciate. So states the "unbiased forward rate theorem."

"But wait just one nitpicking minute!" some of our more retentive readers might be heard to exclaim—or is it cotton-picking?—"Isn't that essentially the formula for interest rate parity you fed to us in the last chapter? And if it is, what kind of hocus-pocus are you trying to put over on us?" Well, it is not *essentially* the formula for interest rate parity. It *is* the formula. Here is the magic trick which fits everything neatly into place:

The differential between interest rates on different denominations of Eurocurrency deposits and/or in different domestic money markets and the expected annual rate of change in the spot exchange rate are one and the same.

"Well," you might say, "that is indeed a pretty neat stunt if you can manage to pull it off. Just how do you propose to prove that statement?"

To do so, let's go back to our friend, the sharp-eyed corporate treasurer at Levi Strauss & Co., as he ponders the interest yields available in the various markets, Eurocurrency and domestic, in which he has the option of depositing his company's $10 million. Since he intends to leave the $10 million on deposit for only 90 days he does not feel himself obliged to obtain forward cover for his funds, should he choose to place them in an account denominated in a currency other than dollars. If he elects not to hedge a foreign currency denominated deposit, therefore, our treasurer's practical method of comparing the effective yields on alternate investment opportunities is to respond to his gut feel concerning the future prospects for the one or more currencies he may have under consideration. Gut feel is not a particularly elegant expression. "Risk premium" and "expected rate of exchange rate change" sound far more professional and precise. Or, heaven help us, there is also

$$\$1(1 + I_n, E\$)^n = (\$1/s_t)(1 + I_n EDM)^n E(S_t + n)$$

which we could not resist tossing in for effect after all, and is, we're assured, the value at $t + n$ of $1 converted into Euro-Deutsche marks (EDM) and earning interest rate I_n, EDM until $t + n$, when it is converted back into dollars at the expected future spot rate, $E(S_{t+n})$.[3]

It is doubtful whether Levi Strauss & Co.'s treasurer would attempt to make such an agonizing calculation, either in his head or with the help of a pocket calculator—lest readers get the idea, however, that we're not *au courant* with the latest fads, we shall get to desk-top computers a bit farther along in our narrative—nor would most other corporate financial officers or foreign exchange traders do so. Rather, he compares, say, three-month Eurodollar interest rates at 8 percent per annum with three-month Euromark

---

[3] Dufey and Giddy, *The International Money Market*, p. 102.

rates at 4 percent.[4]   It is in fact his gut feel, or subjective opinion if you will, that in large part conditions his decision as to where he is able to receive the best overall return on his company's funds.   He reckons that he would be better off keeping the money in Eurodollars unless and until the lower yield available on Euromark deposits is offset by an appreciation in $/DM at a rate equal to ¼ (for the 90 days out of the 360-term of the deposit) the 4 percent differential between the two yields.   It would strike prospective borrowers, on the other hand, as less costly to take marks rather than dollars unless and until they believed they'd have to repay the loan in marks which had appreciated by more than a 4 percent annual rate.

If our treasurer, or any other prospective investor, arrives at the guesstimate that $/DM will appreciate at an annual rate of 2 percent over the 90-day term of his contemplated deposit, his inclination would be to keep his available funds in Eurodollars rather than shifting them into Euromarks. That would be the rational decision of everyone who subscribed to that forecast for $/DM.   The preference for, and resulting transfer of funds into, Eurodollar deposits would normally cause interest rates on such deposits to decline, while prospective depositors' avoiding Euromarks would force interest rates in that market to move higher.   The resulting sale of marks for dollars will therefore depress $/DM until interest rate parity between Eurocurrency interest rates and forward exchange rates is achieved.   Or, in terms of our example:

Annualized rate of forward premium—

$$\frac{\$0.5050 - 0.5000}{\$0.5000} \times \frac{360}{90} \times 100 = 4 \text{ percent}$$

Eurodollar/Euromark interest rate differential: 8% − 4% = 4%

Thus, the expected annual rate of exchange as indicated by the forward premium (or discount) and the interest rate differential between Eurodollar and Euromark deposits both equal 4 percent, and are therefore equal to each other.

A simulation

That is the theory, whether it strikes you as convincing or not.   But, first and foremost, we are traders, and our primary interest in such concepts remains whether an understanding of them will enable us to trade more successfully.   If forward premiums and discounts do in fact fully reflect trader expectations viscerally if not statistically, it is possible then to return to our model kit and create a pair of simulations to assist us in following the

---

[4]It is convenient to continue with the dollar/mark example for consistency and, therefore, greater ease of comprehension.   There is nothing to say, however, that some other Eurocurrency may not offer the best return under the circumstances we are here describing.

sequence of developments in the credit and foreign exchange markets arising from changes in: (1) domestic credit conditions, and (2) exchange rate expectations. To begin, assume the following structure of interest and exchange rates:

U.S. domestic 90-day interest rate	= 7.5%
Eurodollar rate	= 8.0%
German domestic 90-day interest rate	= 3.5%
Euromark rate	= 4.0%
Spot $/DM rate	= $0.5000
90-day forward $/DM rate	= $0.5050

Anticipating these figures, we established on the previous page the equality of the (annualized) forward $/DM premium and the Eurodollar/Euromark interest differential at 4 percent. Proceeding from this scenario, assume further that the Federal Reserve adjusts monetary policy to boost U.S. domestic short-term interest rates to 10 percent.[5] This 2½ percentage-point increase pushes the U.S. domestic interest rate out of line—or into disequilibrium if you want to get fancy about it—prompting the transfer of funds along the lines of the Levi Strauss & Co. example cited earlier. The resulting adaptation of the remaining variables acts to restore equilibrium at a different interest and exchange rate level roughly as follows.

Because the U.S. domestic money markets for the moment yield more than the Eurodollar rate (10 percent versus 8 percent) depositors gravitate to the former and would-be borrowers to the latter. The supply of Eurodollar deposits falls off at the same time that the demand for loans in that market is increasing, forcing an increase in the Eurodollar interest rate to, say, 11 percent or higher, depending upon the volume of funds that are shifted from one market to the other. Next, and in a similar manner, Euromark interest rates are likely to rise as arbitrage and speculative funds move out of Euromarks to pick up the more attractive Eurodollar yield. The same movement will drive the spot $/DM rate down as marks are sold for dollars to effect the transfer of deposits. Finally, forward $/DM will be bid up as hedgers buy forward marks (the equivalent of selling dollars forward) to hedge their dollar investments. According to the unbiased forward rate theorem, forward $/DM is for all practical purposes equal to the expected future value of spot $/DM, so that if the original U.S. domestic interest rate change does not alter exchange rate expectations, the forward premium will adjust through a change in the spot rate rather than through the forward rate. Summarizing the process, a change in credit conditions within a particular market produces a change in interest differentials between it and

---

[5]There are at any given time somewhat divergent interest rates on different types of money market instruments and short-term deposits. The two bellwether rates most applicable to the ensuing discussion are the discount yield on 90-day U.S. Treasury bills and the 90-day Eurodollar certificate of deposit rate.

other markets. The resulting arbitrage and speculative money flows, in bringing interest differentials back into equilibrium, will at the same time cause adjustments in differentials between spot and forward rates to restore interest rate and expectations parity. Hence, in our first simulation, the rise in U.S. domestic short-term interest rates may have brought about the following changes in the related variables:

U.S. domestic 90-day interest rate	from 7.5%	to 10%
Eurodollar rate	from 8	to 11
German domestic 90-day interest rate	from 3.5	to 4
Euromark rate	from 4	to 5
Spot $/DM rate	from $0.5000	to $0.4990
90-day forward $/DM rate	from $0.5050	to $0.5065

$$\text{Adjusted forward premium} = \frac{0.5065 - 0.4990}{0.4990} \times \frac{360}{90} \times 100$$

$$= 6\% \text{ per annum}$$

$$= \text{Eurocurrency interest rate differential}$$

A second simulation

We now come to the heart of the matter with a second simulation, this time incorporating a change in exchange rate expectations. We carry on with the structure of exchange and interest rates that resulted from the first simulation. The specific event that precipitates the change in expectations is for the moment immaterial. It may be an unexpected jump in the German inflation rate or an equally unexpected improvement in the U.S. trade balance.

In this case a change in expectations will induce a change in forward $/DM. The exchange rate change will in turn bring about a widening or narrowing of the forward premium or discount. We calculated in the first simulation that the 6 percent Eurodollar/Euromark interest rate differential equaled the .0075 90-day forward $/DM premium ($0.5065 forward minus $0.4990 spot). To adjust to whatever situation prompted the change in expectations, 90-day forward $/DM will drop from $0.5065 to $0.5045 as a result of sales by speculators who hope to cover at the lower rate what they are currently able to sell forward for the 90-day period at a rate 20 points higher. At the same time, corporate treasurers become uncomfortable with their uncovered Euromark deposits and undertake to hedge such positions by selling marks forward until the 90-day $/DM rate drops to or near the revised expectations of $0.5045, where they feel there is little to be gained by engaging in further hedge sales.

With a declining forward mark compressing the forward premium, the Euromark interest rate will tend to rise, possibly pulling the domestic German interest rate up along with it, as arbitrageurs shift their funds from Euromarks to Eurodollars. Conversely, Eurodollar rates will drop. Interest arbitrageurs earn a higher return than the 5 percent offered on Euromark deposits by buying spot dollars at $/DM 0.4990, selling them forward at 0.5065, and thereby substantially enhancing their interest return by depositing the covered funds at, say, 11 percent. As arbitrageurs and other depositors switch their deposits into Eurodollars, their spot sales of marks for dollars will tend to depress spot $/DM. In this instance, it is the spot rate that bears the brunt of the adjustment even though the change in expectations initially affected the forward rate. The manner of monetary policy and central bank intervention have a marked effect on the precise type and degree of exchange rate changes that occur within the overall adjustment process. If, in the foregoing simulation, the monetary authorities hold interest rates fairly well in check, the entire structure may change along the following lines:

90-day forward $/DM rate	from $0.5065	to $0.5045
Euromark rate	from 5%	to 5.75%
German domestic 90-day interest rate	from 4	to 4.75
Eurodollar rate	unchanged	at 11
U.S. domestic 90-day interest rate	unchanged	at 10
Spot $/DM rate	from $0.4990	to $0.4980

$$\text{New forward premium} = \frac{0.5045 - 0.4980}{0.4980} \times \frac{360}{90} \times 100$$

$$= 5.25\% \text{ per annum}$$
$$= \text{Eurocurrency interest rate differential}$$

Real world is different

To reiterate, we are in the first instance concerned with the day-to-day trading ramifications, if any, of the foregoing associations. A likely reaction of an experienced currency trader would be something on the order of: "Terrific! If it's only a matter of plugging in the right numbers, why isn't this guy making money in the market with his bright ideas instead of writing about it?" And he would be perfectly justified in making that dig. Simulations such as the two we've just taken the trouble to describe in some detail are theoretical laboratories in which analysts may piece together and then observe the interaction of the elements that determine broad exchange rate movements. That certainly does have value in its own right, but seasoned traders know—and neophytes soon learn—that such broad-based data is of marginal value to them on the trading floor.

The real foreign exchange world is very different. It is an extremely nervous and capricious organism, and those participants who hope to survive and prosper there must learn to adapt to its whims. The intervention strategy of leaning against the wind sometimes pursued by central banks would be a sure-fire formula for disaster for private traders who attempted it. With the frequent price reversals brought about by the endless stream of new information and rumors of same that flow through the market daily, if not hourly, it is agility as much as analytical skill that is required of a successful trader. That is the requisite quality which cannot be stated algebraically nor be fitted into a mathematical model.

The following headlines from several foreign exchange market reports in *The Wall Street Journal* offer a more immediate, and a more realistic, sense of the game we're describing than do our earlier theoretical simulations.

Dollar sinks on fear of an oil price rise, U.S. Treasury denies seeking IMF aid [October 31, 1978]

Dealers attributed weakness in Canadian dollar to anticipation Canada's foreign exchange reserves for December will be sharply lower reflecting intervention by central bank [January 3, 1979]

but then,

Canadian dollar gained in moderate Toronto trading. Dealers attributed the rise to better-than-expected Canadian monetary reserves for December [January 5, 1979]

[U.S.] dollar surged against other currencies, apparently fueled by reports, later denied by the White House, that President Carter would hold a news conference later this week after his return from Guadeloupe [January 10, 1979]

and the following day,

Dollar gives ground after White House denies rumor of Carter news conference. Tuesday's rumors had spurred speculation U.S. might be planning further steps to defend the dollar [January 11, 1979]

Dollar pummeled as Japan central bank backs yen and rumors fly about mark [August 31, 1979]

Dollar mostly declines in nervous market buffeted by rumors of Iran [hostage situation], Yugoslavia [President Tito's failing condition] [January 24, 1980]

Why, one wonders, would any rational person want to be in this business? One good reason is that it's exciting as hell! But no one other than Evel Knievel and some lesser-known movie stunt men have managed to make a living out of excitement per se. And the world hasn't heard much from Evel of late. Somehow, we must make an effort to impose a rational sense on what all too often appears to be a totally irrational situation. Put another way, how does the treasurer of Levi Strauss & Co. and his counterparts at other corporations reconcile the logic of the unbiased forward rate theorem with tumultuous and fickle markets buffeted every which way by incessant rumors, only the most prominent of which are reported in the newspapers? The flip answer is that they are paid very handsomely to cope with such dilemmas. We shall make a more serious attempt to answer that question in Part Three of this book.

Like waiting that extra split second for your intended receiver to get into position before letting fly with the football while half a ton of the Green Bay Packer line is bearing down on you, or sensing the correct moment to close on the sale of a multimillion-dollar corporate jet, what amounts to the instinct to trade successfully cannot be gleaned from a book. One trader who possesses the gift put it perhaps too bluntly: "Why bother to write a book? They either have the touch or they dont." There is admittedly much to be said for having the touch, but those of us who are not so fortunate must make do with the most effective analytical tools and trading principles that are at hand. One way to give a newcomer to foreign exchange trading a hint of what lies before him or her is to put the abstract models to one side for the time being and to undertake a blow-by-blow account of how exchange rates, and in this case futures contract prices, respond to the day-to-day influx of fact and rumor. The two series of circumstances we've chosen to recount are those affecting the British pound between June and October 1979, and the Deutsche mark during August and September of the same year.

Up and down with the pound

By mid-June 1979 the British pound had risen to its highest level in over three years. Spot $/£ stood at the $2.10 level, up from about $2 at the beginning of that year and more than a 25 percent appreciation from its September 1976 low of about $1.65. The March 1980 British pound contract was at that point priced at about $2.0800, or approximately at a 200-point discount under spot. The 2½ percentage-point differential between domestic short-term interest rates in the U.K. (13 percent) and in the U.S. (10½ percent) was roughly twice that of the 200-point spot $/£–March 1980 BP discount. The pound's strength that week, spurred by an increase in the Bank of England's discount rate from 12 percent to 14 percent, carried the spot rate to $2.1130 and March 1980 BP to $2.1300 before purported profit taking and official intervention to check the strength brought spot $/£ back to the $2.1000 level. The euphoria started to subside the following day, according to London dealers, because traders were reassessing the government's proposed budget. Spot sterling remained more or less stable, but March 1980 BP fell to $2.1055, off 245 points from the prior day's high.

The first week of July saw the pound propelled to further highs by the rumored discovery of another major oil deposit in Britain's sector of the North Sea. Spot pounds by then had risen to $2.2360, and March 1980 BP to $2.2020, thereby opening the spot futures discount to 340 points. U.K. interest rates (14 percent) rose 1 percentage point while U.S. rates (11%) gained ½ percentage point, opening the interest differential between the two money markets as well. It was alleged the Bank of England was intervening modestly to slow the rise "for purposes of stability" rather than to establish a specific spot or forward $/£ rate.

By the last week of July, spot pounds in the London market hit their peak of $2.3250, with the March 1980 BP contract following suit to $2.2975. British exporters complained that this surge was too much of a good thing, adversely affecting the competitive standing of their products in the international market. The chairman of Courtlandts, the country's largest textile firm, said that the pound was at that point overvalued by about 25 percent, and that its current strength was having an adverse effect on his company's earnings. The Bank of England, declaring that it was sympathetic but that it had no intention of intervening to halt the pound's advance, suggested that, rather than complaining about a healthy currency, British industry direct its efforts to making its products more competitive on the basis of design, quality, prompt delivery, and service.

By the beginning of August, the pound passed from its smooth upward course into choppy waters as both spot and futures rates fluctuated erratically in response to a spate of contradictory rumors concerning the condition of the economy, policies of the Conservative government, rising interest rates, and North Sea oil. During two successive trading sessions, July 30 and 31, spot pounds fell 725 points from $2.3190 to $2.2465 as traders seemed to realize overnight that the recent rise had been overdone. On August 1, buying poured into the market at $2.2400 on the assumption that the sell-off had in turn been too extreme. As these gyrations were taking place, the forward discount opened from 310 to 415 points, then narrowed back to 345 points. The recovery continued, carrying spot $/£ back up to $2.2755 the following day on the news of a sharp rise in foreign exchange reserves. The Bank of England finally felt compelled by the end of July to intervene in the market as a seller to dampen the sometimes frenzied speculative buying of sterling. Between July 20 and August 2, March 1980 pound futures rose 445, plummeted 830, and rallied 365 points. Traders who ventured to establish a long or short position were whipsawed as the market almost immediately reversed itself each time and raced headlong in the opposite direction.

By August 7, spot sterling had dropped back to $2.2440, chiefly on the news that the U.K. wholesale price index for the month of July had soared to a 28 percent annual rate of increase. The July euphoria concerning the pound continued to dissolve amid increasing pessimism over the outlook for the economy as a whole. Spot $/£ dropped to $2.21 before recovering

Figure 9–2
March 1980 British pound versus spot pound rate, June–December 1979

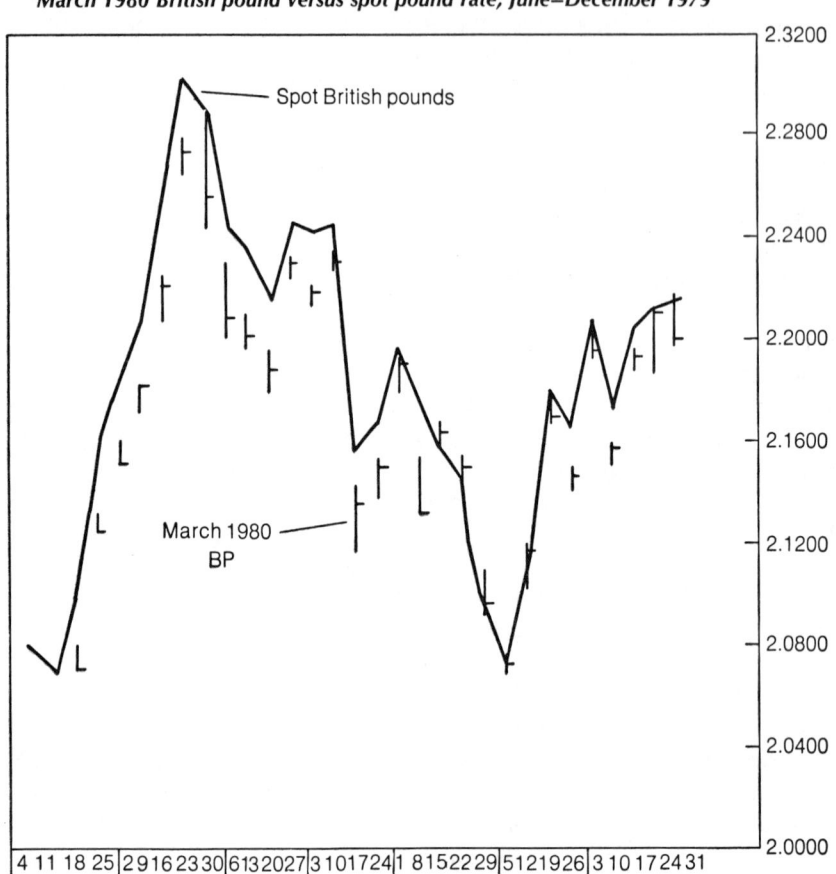

somewhat on a report that the sale of North Sea oil would contribute twice as much to Britain's balance of payments in 1979 as it had in the previous year. Despite this injection of good news, traders continued to vote with their feet by selling pounds because they apparently concurred with the country's industrial leaders that good news for the pound was, as it rose above a certain level, bad news for British exports.

The pound continued to sink during the late summer and fall, reaching, with intermittent flurries of strength, $2.10. The announcement at the end of October that exchange controls which had been in effect for 40 years and during that time had sharply limited overseas spending by British residents would be lifted, pushed the spot rate down to $2.06. Restrained by limits on daily futures price changes, March 1980 BP fell a total of 450 points on October 29 and 30 to $2.0695, thereby moving for a brief period to a small premium over spot.

Virtually all of the factors discussed thus far in Part Two—balance of payments, inflation, the effect of exchange rate changes on export prices, interest rate differentials, monetary policy, and central bank intervention—were operative during the five-month period just described in pushing the dollar price of the British pound from approximately $2.10 to as high as $2.32, and then driving it right back down again. The important point to note is that while there occurred no fundamental changes in the underlying condition of the British economy during that brief time, "the market" seemed to react to each news item or rumor as if that particular bit of information was heralding such a change. In the final analysis, there were no one or two specific reasons for this roller coaster activity in the pound between June and October save the fact that traders realized around the first of August that they had become carried away by their own enthusiasm and had consequently stuck their necks out too far.

Buy on the rumor, etc.

Turning to the circumstances surrounding the Deutsche mark during a part of the same period, the first six months of 1979 had seen the faltering start-up of the European Monetary System (EMS)—a modified version of the joint currency float—after a succession of delays and squabbles among the participating countries about the terms and conditions of membership. The most picaresque if not profound dispute was the two-week pork war in which French hog raisers destroyed pork products imported from West Germany, Belgium, and the Netherlands to protest what were in their view inequitable Common Market subsidies that enabled growers in the latter countries to post lower prices.

As in earlier attempts to harmonize national monetary policies and thereby to promote greater exchange rate stability among the member countries of the Common Market, France, whose sentiments were this time shared by Italy, the U.K., and Ireland, complained that under the proposed terms of this supersnake she would be compelled to pursue deflationary policies, which would in turn lead to greater unemployment. The Germans for their part worried that the EMS administration would adopt the Deutsche mark in lieu of the U.S. dollar as its primary intervention currency, a move which would exacerbate inflation in their country by requiring the monetary authorities to create more marks. Should the mark become a full-fledged reserve currency in the proposed EMS currency grid, they feared it would fall prey to many of the problems that had beset the dollar over the past two decades.

By the end of August, spot marks stood at .5486 and the IMM March 1980 DM contract was at .5620, a forward premium of 134 points or 4.2 percent annualized at a time when the dollar/mark interest differential was about 4½ percent higher (11.4 percent to 7 percent). Rumors were rife that the mark would be adjusted—what, in the fixed-rate days, would have been called a revaluation—due to the pressures imposed on it within the EMS grid. During the first three weeks of September spot $/DM climbed about 200 points to .5680, and March 1980 DM followed suit to .5811, keeping the forward premium nearly unchanged. This time the rumors proved to be well founded. Throughout the month EMS officials repeatedly denied that a mark adjustment was in the wind (they always do under such circumstances) but as speculation to the contrary continued unabated, the finance ministers of the member countries met in an extraordinary session on September 23 and formally raised the value of the mark 2 percent against the other six EMS currencies. On the heels of the announcement, spot and futures $/DM did—nothing. The official EMS action was regarded as a mere ratification of the fait accompli brought about by market speculators. In fact, any Johnny-come-latelys who went long either spot or forward marks at the time of the announcement would in all likelihood have incurred a loss when, a month later at the end of October, spot was at .5535 and March 1980 futures at .5650.

Attitudes and conventions

Both the British pound and Deutsche mark developments during the summer and fall of 1979 bear out our contention that fast footwork has as much if not more to do with trading successfully in the foreign exchange market than does assiduous study and sound reasoning. That is not good news for those who are of a scholarly bent, but such is the way of the real world, the one in which profits and losses are tallied at the end of each day.

There are also certain attitudes and conventions pertaining to the operational side of foreign exchange trading which play an important role in determining the psychological set of the market. Dealer banks that regard themselves as market leaders endeavor to be among the first to respond to a new development, while others prefer to wait for the trendsetters to point the way. Small institutions with limited access to foreign money centers are at a disadvantage when it comes to obtaining timely information. The better-informed dealers are often in and out of a situation before many of the laggards are even aware that anything of consequence has taken place.

As was noted in Chapter 4, the length of time that a dealer bank's management authorizes its foreign exchange traders to carry open positions—overnight, over a weekend, or, rarely, for longer periods—as well as the manner in which the traders balance their books have a bearing on the ways in which they respond to breaking news. Traders may balance their spot and forward transactions separately, or one against the other with large open spot positions offset overnight by equivalent forward positions. Such practices have a cumulative and considerable effect on daily trading patterns as dealers square their books at the end of each day.

The conventions governing the initiation and response to inquiries between dealers for rate quotations are also significant. Dealers consider the amounts which their counterparts are willing to buy and sell (they must be prepared to deal from either side of the market) and the size of the spreads between their bids and offers important attributes of their reputation and market standing. The dealer who calls and asks for a quotation normally expects the contacted party to respond with a firm bid and offer at which he is ready to deal. This custom works to the advantage of the calling dealer because the burden is on the contacted dealer to reveal his buying and selling rates before knowing which side of the market he'll be asked to take. To maintain his reputation in the dealer community, therefore, the trader who is contacted must quote binding rates for at least a minimum amount, and then transact that minimum amount if so requested, even if he is obliged to buy a currency he would as soon sell.

There are, as was indicated in Chapter 4, no hard and fast rules regarding spreads. A spread between a bid and offered rate which might be considered excessive under normal market conditions would be looked upon as acceptable when the market is unduly erratic. If a dealer persists in quoting spreads that are wider than others are quoting under the same market conditions, she will be passed by in favor of the more competitive marketmakers. The readiness with which an interbank market dealer quotes competitive buying and selling rates and the minimum size of the transactions she normally makes is indicative of her institution's standing in the dealer community, and determines the frequency with which she is contacted by other trading departments. These factors in turn condition her probable reaction to specific market developments of the sort related in our British pound and Deutsche mark episodes. These are elements which are all but impossible to incorporate into a pre-programmed model or trading strategy; they fall under the heading of market feel and tone, a proper appreciation of which, like so much else in the foreign exchange market, can only be gained through time, observation, and experience.

Chapter 10

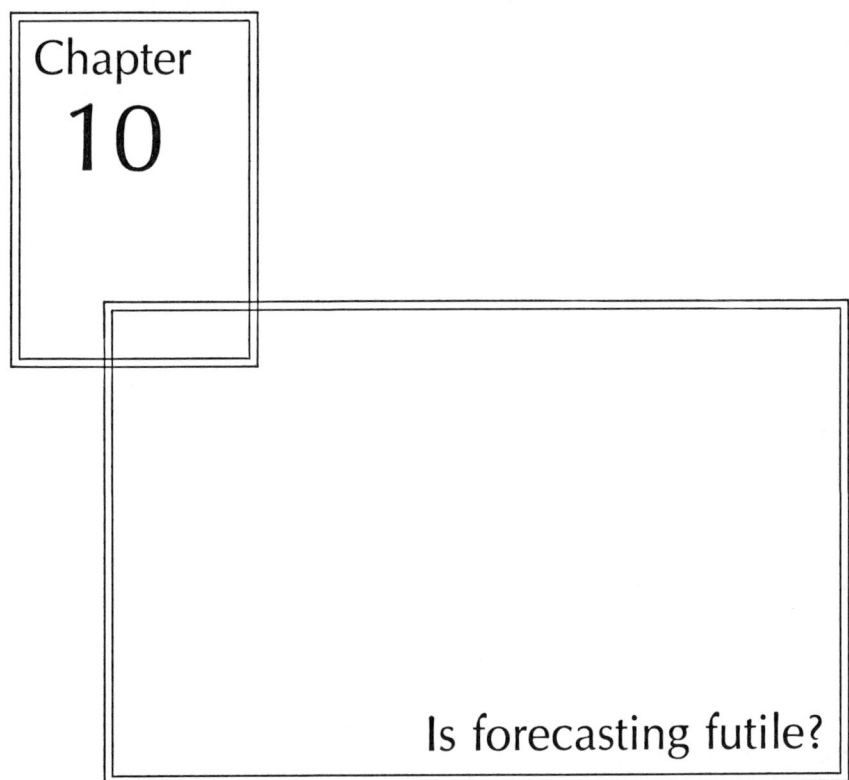

Is forecasting futile?

OUR DISCUSSION about purchasing power parity, risk premiums, "leaning against the wind," and so on is to the point, and will doubtlessly stand readers in good stead. But, as we noted in the last chapter, this information is not in itself sufficient to enable would-be traders to make money in the currency futures market. The passport to fame and fortune—preferably the latter—is to have a pretty good idea of the direction prices are heading tomorrow and thereafter. Our ticket to success, therefore, is a good exchange rate forecast.

The question which has bedeviled foreign exchange analysts for some time is whether it is possible to predict future exchange movements, and if it is, what is the best way of going about it? Or are those skeptics who call themselves "random walkers" correct in their contention that tossing darts at newspaper quotations is as good a method as any?

Forecasting exchange rates during the years that the Bretton Woods system was still intact was an easier task than it is today for the simple reason that the rates did not move about as much then. The surprising thing is that more speculators did not realize what a low-risk game foreign exchange trading was when central banks were committed to maintaining fixed parities in relation to the dollar. Under those conditions forecasting consisted chiefly of studying a country's balance-of-payments position and its inflationary trends, and determining from that data the direction from which speculative pressure on a currency would come and how intense that pressure was likely to be. That, coupled with an estimate on the basis of known reserves of the central bank's ability to resist such pressure through exchange market intervention gave traders ample forewarning that a change in parity was possible, or perhaps imminent.

Should they conclude that a devaluation was indeed in the offing, their selling that currency short was essentially a one-way bet inasmuch as the worst that could happen was that the exchange rate would rise to the upper limit of the parity band, where the central bank could be counted upon to intervene and thereby check any further appreciation. When enough speculators became aware of that simple fact, their widespread expectation of a devaluation became in many such instances a self-fulfilling prophecy as their cumulative sales forced the besieged central bank to do just what the speculators predicted it would do.

Forecasting today's flexible exchange rates is a far riskier proposition. By definition, they are more volatile and the actions of the monetary authorities are more difficult to anticipate. Because the central banks' role under these circumstances has become more limited and less visible, the dominant influence over exchange rates is now what is exerted by the private participants in the market. The aim of foreign exchange forecasting has changed as a consequence from one of predicting how a handful of central banks might react to speculative attacks on their currencies—with a modest penalty if one guessed incorrectly—to that of assembling and evaluating an outpouring of economic data of the sort described in the foregoing chapters. Beyond that, it is necessary to formulate an opinion about how hundreds of corporations, banks, and other commercial entities are themselves likely to interpret and respond to that data.

Tough predictions

Forecasting price changes is a formidable task in any market. But in foreign exchange, the factors that shape supply and demand are less precise and therefore less understood by the very participants whose market activity determines spot and forward rates. Predicting the future level and direction of exchange rates under such nebulous circumstances is bound to be a highly uncertain undertaking. More than one player has walked away from the game a loser, muttering that it's no better than betting on a horse race. While conceding that there is more than a slight amount of chance involved, and that it is easily as much an art as a science, we nevertheless take a more constructive view of the prospects.

It is a difficult task even for those firms which make up the small forecasting industry that has developed since the onset of floating currencies to gather and evaluate the mass of pertinent data that is scattered, imprecise, and becomes available in such an unpredictable fashion. The fact that the prime corporate prospects for such services are themselves influential in determining the supply-demand balance for a particular currency makes the job of a forecaster-for-hire all the more difficult.

The availability of information and the speed with which market participants act upon it, and thereby affect prices, determine what economists like to call "the efficiency of a market." When all of the information that can be known concerning a particular security, commodity, or, in this case, currency is reflected in the current price, the market for that item is held to be efficient and defies prediction. Each subsequent price change is determined by random events—hence the name *random walk theory*—and we come back to throwing darts against the wall. All attempts to forecast random events are doomed to failure. Only when a market is not fully efficient, so the theory goes, is it possible to get ahead of the crowd by acting on information which is not generally known.

In academe and business, as in the world of high fashion, certain styles are in vogue for a time and are then displaced by the next hot idea. The theory of efficient markets is still respected, but it's been modified of late to be less despairing of price forecasting. The theory, as amended, recognizes different gradations of market efficiency—strong, semistrong, and weak—and admits to occasions when the best forecasters may get a jump on the crowd by digging out previously undisseminated if not unknown information, and are therefore entitled to their fancy fees. The $600 billion question, not to mention pounds, marks, francs, et al., then, is: Who are these people and how do they work?

Three approaches

Foreign exchange forecasters-for-hire tend to favor one of three general approaches: econometric, judgmental, or technical. Some attempt to combine two or all of these methods in arriving at their forecasts. The econometric approach is further broken down among the variables that individual forecasters consider the most consequential in determining exchange rates. Traditionally, the emphasis usually has been on some type of balance-of-payments analysis. By projecting past and present international payments trends, an effort is made to estimate future developments and thereby anticipate likely changes in the supply and demand for a particular currency over a one-to-five-year period. Broader models incorporate additional variables, such as rates of inflation, but they generally operate in much the same fashion. These models all have the common shortcoming that, while they can and do extrapolate what should theoretically happen to a given exchange rate as a consequence of projected changes in the supply and demand for the currency in question, they cannot project the responses of market participants to unforeseeable economic and political events.

Forecasters who are of the monetarist persuasion regard foreign exchange as the domestic money of foreign nationals, a reasonable view since that is precisely what it happens to be. Their models are constructed according to the concept of purchasing power parity, and therefore concentrate on changes in price levels, money stocks, and monetary reserves, as well as monitor various monetary policies as they are implemented by central banks to bring about the desired changes in those variables.

Forecasters who adhere to the judgmental approach also study the various factors mentioned above, but they interpret the data in the light of their own attitudes and experience, rather than simply inserting it into one or more equations and automatically accepting the solutions that are generated. Some judgmental forecasters subscribe to the fully efficient market theory, that all of the relevant information concerning a currency is at any point already reflected in the prevailing spot rate. They become in effect pollsters who arrive at their forecasts by sampling the opinions of prominent traders, bankers, and corporate financial officers, noting the reasons for those opinions and attempting to meld them into what they hope represents a widely held consensus. An obvious problem with this polling method is that if the individuals included in the sample really believed the opinions they express, presumably they've already taken the appropriate market action. That in turn casts considerable doubt on the validity of using such opinions as a basis for predicting future exchange rates.

Then there are the chartists, or, as they prefer to be called, "technicians." They're generally analysts with stock or commodity market backgrounds who believe that charts of exchange rate movements tend to form repetitive patterns, and therefore comprise the best available forecasting tools. The particular trends, cycles, momentum measurements, or time-series models that each of them favors are all expressions in one way or another of the so-called K percent rules, which are based upon what the statisticians, our nitpicking friends from Chapter 9, call "the theory of speculative runs." This theory holds that a price which has risen or fallen by a predetermined percentage—the analyst provides his or her own estimate of K to fit the circumstances—will in all likelihood continue to move in the same direction. In the present context, the appropriate action then would be to go long a currency as soon as it's risen by whatever percentage is selected for K, or to sell it short after the exchange rate has fallen by the specified amount.

Whichever factor a forecaster believes is the principal determinant of exchange rate behavior, it must be established that there is a consistent time lag between it and a consequent rate change to confirm that there is a cause-and-effect relationship at work. To take but two possible examples, if it should be observed that there is an improvement in the U.S. trade balance, or a rise in the U.K. inflation rate, there should be a fairly constant interval between when these events occur and the resulting strength in the dollar or weakness in the pound, as the case may be. If no reliable time lag can be demonstrated, it remains uncertain which of the two events is the cause and which is the result.

Interpretations of forecasting

The efficient market theory holds that a successful forecasting model cannot be kept secret for very long. Given the closely knit and highly competitive nature of the foreign exchange market, the word is bound to leak out and spawn imitators, depriving the original of its competitive edge. A number of analysts have tried to reconcile the apparent contradiction of attempting to forecast prices in an efficient market by regarding trading profits as compensation for the cost of digging up and acting on new information before it becomes common knowledge. One hypothesis is that, given the cost in both time and money of securing generally unknown information, and the reluctance or inability of some traders to pay this cost, the market will not be strongly efficient because not all of the participants will be equally informed.[1]

Another interpretation assumes that all traders have access to sufficient information but that differences in their ability to evaluate it correctly, and the degree of risk aversion each has, the trading skills and available capital make it inevitable that traders will have varying degrees of success—and that, as a consequence, expert advice is worth paying for.[2] That, of course, is the viewpoint that the forecasters-for-hire are most eager to have accepted.

As was discussed at some length in Chapter 9, the forward rate is itself indicative of prevailing expectations about the future spot rate. That is a forecast which may be had for the price of a newspaper. The burden is therefore on the advisory services that charge their clients considerably more to demonstrate that their forecasts come closer to the mark, yen, lira, or what-you-will than does the applicable forward rate.

Interest rate differentials between domestic and Eurocurrency markets also provide ballpark forecasts of the possible trend of a particular exchange rate. The general rule of thumb is: The higher a country's interest rate, the weaker its future spot rate is expected to be. Conversely, the lower the interest rate level, the higher the forward premium will be, and along with it the expected appreciation of a future spot rate. The do-it-yourself fore-

---

[1]Sanford J. Grossman and Joseph E. Stiglitz, "Information and Competitive Price Systems," *American Economic Review* 66, no. 2 (May 1976): pp. 246–53, cited in Richard M. Levich, *A Progress Report on Research into the Accuracy of Foreign Exchange Advisory Service Forecasts,* New York University and National Bureau of Economic Research, Inc., 1979.

[2]Stephen Figlewski, "Market Efficiency" in a Market with Heterogeneous Information," *Journal of Political Economy* 86, no. 4 (August 1978): pp. 581–97.

caster—as well as the for-hire professional—therefore may use the applicable interest differential as a test of his own forecast, satisfying himself that there is a valid reason for any disparity that there may be between them.

The currency futures trader encounters the further complication of having to reconcile the trader's own forecast with the price that prevails in the market. If this forecast on or about June 15, say, is that Swiss francs should appreciate from their current spot rate of 0.6100 by about 100 points a month, there is no immediate profit opportunity apparent to the trader if September SF is at 0.6400, since the futures price already is projecting a rise of the same magnitude. It is only when a marked disparity exists between the futures price and the trader's own forecast that he or she sees a possible profit to be gained by going long or short that particular contract.

There is also the broader problem of reconciling the long-range factors that lend themselves to statistical comparison, such as trade and capital flows and changes in interest rates and price levels, with unquantifiable psychological elements that serve to exaggerate exchange rate movements over the short to intermediate term. It becomes increasingly apparent, in light of the numerous long-range factors that must be considered, that no single forecasting approach by itself can do justice to them all. A more effective attitude would appear to be regarding the foreign exchange market as a segmented rather than cohesive entity and, accordingly, employing the forecasting technique best suited to each particular aspect of the market.

Who the forecasters are

Having made that profound observation, it is time to identify the practitioners who are in the foreign exchange forecasting business and to take a closer look at how they operate. Given the extreme volatility of exchange rates and the consequently high level of foreign exchange risk to which multinational corporations have been exposed in recent years, many of these corporations place a high value on a service that is able to provide them with accurate forecasts and, beyond, to incorporate such forecasts into a plan for effectively reducing their foreign exchange exposure. Even so, an equal number of prospective users are asking themselves what such services are worth, in general terms and, specifically, whether they justify the handsome fees they're asked to pay.

The nature, quality, and cost of the forecasting services that are on the market are as varied as the firms which offer them. In terms of their approach to forecasting, the majority of firms fall into one of the three categories described before: judgmental, econometric, technical (charting), or some combination thereof. The most readily recognizable names in the business are those of a dozen or so of the major international banks, most of whom seem to favor the judgmental approach. The handful of securities or commodities—oriented firms, which include foreign exchange forecasting in a broad line of brokerage and investment banking services to corporations, have adapted many of the charting techniques that traditionally have been employed in those other markets. The equally few independent consulting firms, which have been established expressly to develop and market currency forecasts, tend to lean toward the mathematical approach and associated econometric modeling. The format that any of these several types of firms use in forming their forecasts may be a specific estimated spot rate for a particular time horizon, a quarterly average over, perhaps a one- to three-year period, or simply an indication of the probable future trend of a currency.

Table 10–1 lists the principal firms that offered foreign exchange forecasting services in 1979, as well as their annual fee schedules, methods of analysis and length of forecast, number of currencies covered, and the number of clients each of them claimed at that time.[3] The "kitchen sink" approach embraces, as the name implies, a host of economic, political, and psychological factors. It is basically judgmental in nature, but some econometric techniques may on occasion be applied to supplement the qualitative evaluations. Of the 20 or so firms listed, 9 are U.S.-based commercial banks, although one, the European-American Bank, is capable of calling on the resources of its 6 parent banks situated throughout Europe. Advisory fees range between $5,000 and $40,000 annually, on the whole, though the figures listed are not strictly comparable in that a particular fee may include special consulting work in solving clients' foreign exchange-related problems.

The big banks are especially sensitive to, and vigorously deny, the charge (usually leveled by their competitors) that they encourage their forecasting units to promote the banks' other services, their foreign exchange trading departments in particular, and that their advice is on this account biased toward excessive turnover. There is also the suspicion that the forecasting units may pass along to other departments inside the bank, trust management or commercial lending, for example, confidential information concerning a client's financial position and future plans to which they must of necessity be privy. To forestall such serious, and potentially damaging, criticism, the banks point to the "Chinese walls"—i.e., administrative safeguards— they've instituted to cordon off their consulting and loan sections from other areas that could conceivably benefit from the confidences those functions entail.

Each of the bank forecasting services strives to maintain its own style and structure. Citibank's 80-member organization is dispersed throughout five U.S. cities in addition to the bank's New York headquarters and is divided into three operating sections: International Financial Advisory (the traditional corporate counseling service), the Market Analysis Unit (money market eval-

---

[3]"Is This How Corporate Treasurers View Their Foreign Exchange Advisors?" *Euromoney*, August 1978, pp. 12–41. Adapted with permission.

Table 10–1
Who the forecasters are, and what they offer

Service	Fees - Annual	Fees - Other	Method and length of forecast	Number of currencies	Number of customers
Amex Bank Limited	Negotiated individually		Kitchen sink* Time period according to client requirements	All major currencies	n.a.
Brown Brothers Harriman	$18,000 to $45,000		Kitchen sink Up to 12 months	50, half in limited scope	55
Chase Econometrics	$10,000	$12,500 including time-share access to models	Econometric Up to eight quarters; monthly model out to five years.	11 monthly, additional 2 quarterly, others on request	n.a.
Chase Manhattan Bank	No fee for forecasts produced internally and available on request to bank's clients. Foreign exchange management is separate service		Kitchen sink Up to 18 months, or two to seven years, for general planning	12, others occasionally	Any bank clients, on request, and staff
Chemical Bank	$10,000 to $50,000		Momentum model, one week to one month, three months to 12 months, Five years	26	200
Citibank	$30,000	Negotiated according to intensity of service	Kitchen sink and momentum model Up to 12 months	All of interest to clients	90
ContiCurrency	$25,000	$10,000 to $40,000 for special projects or fewer demands	Kitchen sink 12 months and up to five years for budget and planning rates	33, others on request	52

Eurofinance	FF 1600 for 11 currencies, one year FF 5500 for six currencies, five years FF 50,000 for full corporate finance service	Econometric One year and five years	11	100, all services
European American Bank	$10,000 basic $18,000 maximum Projects at $550 a day	Momentum for short term, kitchen sink for up to five years	All, emphasis on Europe	80
Harris Bank	No fee for forecasts produced internally and available upon request to bank's foreign exchange customers.	Kitchen sink Up to 12 months	All major currencies	All bank clients on request
IFC	$8000 for 10 currencies against the dollar. $15,000, for above, plus eight currencies against Can$ and DM	Momentum	10 against $; eight against Can$ and DM; Yen against Swfr, £; £ against Skr	20+

Table 10–1
Who the forecasters are and what they offer what they offer (continued)

Service	Fees		Method and length of forecast	Number of currencies	Number of customers
	Annual	Other			
Marine Midland Bank: International Treasury Treasury Management	$25,000	Price unbundling for special softwear and information products. Major projects $50,000 to $500,000	Judgmental One, three, six and 15 months	22, also special studies for other	70
Morgan Guaranty: Foreign Exchange Services Group	No fee to bank's corporate clients		Kitchen sink	All leading currencies	Any of bank's corporate clients
Patterson, Little & Desmartin	$1500 (one currency) $1100 (2nd to 4th currency) $7500 (all currencies)		Econometric One, two, three and six months	16	32

Predex	$12,000 (planning service) $11,000 (trading service) $19,000 (planning plus trading service) $25,000 (planning and trading plus on line services)	Econometric	Predex, forecast, 20, up to 22 months. Predex trading service 10, up to 3 months	60+
N M Rothschild & Sons Limited	$75,000 minimum	Judgmental	Up to five years	55	22, plus "undisclosed number of Central Banks."
Waldner & Co.	$15,000 minimum plus $2,500 for every additional currency	Momentum	8	n.a.

n.a.: Not available.
*Kitchen sink may include the use of econometric models, but is mainly judgemental, taking economic, political, and psychological factors into account.
Adapted from *Euromoney*, August 1978, p. 28, with permission.

uation and forecasting) and the Financial Transaction Unit (specialized research and analysis). The Citibank service has approximately 90 corporate clients and mounts an on-going marketing effort to add more multinationals to its customer roster. As a principal selling point, it stresses the many local treasury operations throughout the Citibank worldwide network of offices which, according to the bank, affords its forecasting service a broader and more intensive coverage of foreign exchange markets and regulations than its competitors are capable of maintaining.

Brown Brothers Harriman, an old-line private banking house, one of the few such institutions surviving in the United States, first offered a currency forecasting service to its clients during the 1967 sterling crisis and subsequent devaluation of the British pound. Unlike the self-contained Citibank unit, Brown Brothers draws on a number of departments for the information and advice that the bank provides to its clients. The basic service consists of written monthly forecasts of exchange rate, interest rate, and balance-of-payments changes in the 50 or so countries the bank monitors, with an accompanying commentary on relevant international economic and political events. Brown Brothers currently does not seek to increase its client list of 55 large multinational corporations. Says a bank spokesman: "We are happy with 10 percent of the *Fortune* 500."[4]

Morgan Guaranty Trust Co. also draws on various departments throughout the bank to provide what it terms "foreign exchange market-related assistance to multinationals." The International Money Management (IMM)[5] group performs an initial analysis of a new corporate client's overall financial posture, including its foreign exchange exposure, and then advises the client of the options that are available in managing that exposure. The International Financial Management (IFM) group then comes aboard to advise on such matters as financing possibilities and related foreign exchange regulations imposed by the particular countries involved. A third group, Foreign Exchange Services (FXS), is comprised of 23 of the bank's personnel in 10 locations around the world. It produces the bank's daily rate cable, listing all of the leading exchange rates and summarizing that day's international financial news. The FXS group also conducts research on specific strategy and exposure management issues, either in response to a client's inquiry or on its own initiative.

Morgan Guaranty asserts that it doesn't make specific exchange rate forecasts—an interesting position for a firm listed as being among those that are in the forecasting business. The bank regards its proper role rather as one of providing service than advice. In fact, most of the banks that have established foreign exchange consulting services maintain that they should be judged on the basis of the complete package of services they provide

---

[4]*Euromoney*, ibid, p. 27.

[5]Not to be confused with the International Monetary Market division of the Chicago Mercantile Exchange, where futures contracts on eight currencies are traded.

their clients, rather than solely on their ability to predict exchange rates.[6] They perceive their function as being one of helping companies to assess their foreign exchange exposure, determine the best means by which to manage that exposure and, finally, deal with such foreign exchange regulations of various countries as may impede such steps. These are, not coincidentally, the topics that will be treated at some length in Part Three of this book.

The nonbank forecasters more frequently restrict their activities to predicting exchange rate trends and future rates. They have tended to be more mathematically oriented than the banks, a condition that the latter group has been endeavoring to redress of late. Predex Corporation and Eurofinance are two such independent services. Predex offers several combinations of corporate planning and trading advisory services and maintained, at last count, a customer list of about 60 corporate clients.

The forecasts made by Paris-based Eurofinance in a like manner are based on traditional analysis that stresses economic growth, balance of payments, relative rates of inflation, export prices, and other important exchange rate determinants. The service issues one-year and five-year forecasts that are updated every six months. The principal criticism made of the independent services as a group is that they rely too heavily on the econometric models, and are not sufficiently in touch with day-to-day market conditions. Another of their alleged shortcomings is that their standard reports are framed in such general terms as to be of little help in resolving a client company's particular exposure problems.

Though still in a minority, the reputation of technical and momentum analysis forecasters has been on the rise of late. Chicago-based Waldner & Company tested its technical model for five years in-house before offering it to clients. Waldner's principal innovation is the Dyna line, or what the firm calls the "progressive dynamics" of a currency. The Dyna line is plotted on a price chart in relation to a base line, signaling a change in trend when the two cross. The sale of a currency is indicated when the Dyna line drops beneath the base line. The Dyna line moving up through the base line constitutes a buy signal. This technique is said to have been reasonably successful in identifying major turning points, in currency movements, but there is some concern that it, like many such systems, lends itself to overtrading.

New York-based Eurocurrency Management Corporation, or EMCOR, relies primarily on the technical-momentum analysis approach to forecasting but, like other services, blends with it fundamental and geopolitical analysis. The company provides its multinational corporate clients with several levels of service, including total management of a corporation's exposure, specific exposure management, and general advice on currency and interest rate

---

[6]Perhaps that, better than anything else, answers the question posed by the title of this chapter.

trends. In addition to its forecasting and exposure management functions, EMCOR supplies international investment banking services that encompass the Eurocurrency, foreign exchange, and financial futures markets.

Forecasters' track records

Such splendid-sounding techniques as Dyna lines, momentum studies, FXS services, and all the rest are most impressive, to be sure—but what the prospective users really want to know is how well have these firms performed. What are their track records? Not surprisingly, the replies of those who have bought and used such services are colored by their experiences with them. The opinions range from disdainful to favorable, with several gradations of approval in between. There is, of course, the inevitable wisecrack that if forecasters were so smart, why aren't they rich? Or, with the panache that foreign exchange market denizens like to affect, "They [the forecasters] wouldn't be on the train commuting to the City [of London], they'd be in the south of France." Then there's the misery-likes-company, or scapegoat, argument: "When the flak hits the fan, it should be someone else's flak." Some users take the hopeful view that, "If we have to make point forecasts, the [forecasters] should do it for us. They're the pros." Others are more definite in their praise: "There have been a number of transactions we have gone ahead with on the bank's advice, which have in turn made measurable differences in the amount of savings and profits."[7]

Some company treasurers question the need to pay a bank, or anyone else for that matter, for their forecasts when they're able to call up the trading departments of the major dealer banks and get these opinions without charge. Others take the attitude that the fee is a minor consideration. With so much money at stake in just one sizable transaction, good advice, they say, is well worth the relatively modest amount they're charged. Some clients have expressed the view that the banks have been remiss in ignoring technical-momentum studies, since such methods are believed to have produced more consistently accurate forecasts than either the judgmental or the econometric approaches during the recent past.

The acid test, of course, is not criticism or testimonials, but the forecaster's unvarnished track record. The services themselves, as noted, would like their clients, actual and prospective, to think otherwise, maintaining that simply comparing the actual spot rate on a certain date with a past forecast takes their work out of the context of the specific financing problem for which the forecast was intended. Well they might protest. Doing what the forecasters say one should not—namely, matching the spot rates for the Canadian dollar, British pound, and Deutsche mark, as of July 1, 1979, against the predictions they made a year earlier—produces results that can be described only as abysmal.

---

[7]*Euromoney*, ibid., p. 34.

The three panels of Figure 10–1 tell the sorry story. In the case of the Canadian dollar (left), of the dozen services, whose one-year forecasts could be obtained, only one, Amex Bank, came anywhere near the July 1, 1979, spot rate of .8560. And even that was barely achieved by projecting a possible range of .8500 to .9000. The point forecasts made by the other services were all much too high. Their record with the British pound was even worse. Of the 13 point forecasts made public for the same period, not one came within 400 points of the 2.1870 spot rate on July 1, 1979. The remaining forecasts were miles away, bunched between 1.65 and 1.85. The outcome of the Deutsche mark forecasts (right) was equally disheartening. Predex, the firm that came within shouting distance of the actual pound rate was approximately 300 points above the July 1, 1979, dollar mark rate of .5425, while Bi/Metrics, Citibank, and European-American Bank were about the same number of points under the mark, so to speak.[8]

The services just cited would no doubt protest, with some justification to be sure, that such a spotty check—not even a poor pun can make those records look good by comparison—does them an injustice. A fairer test, they would maintain, would be to take a broad statistical sampling of their forecasts over an extended period and see how they turned out.

There have been at least two such studies conducted in the past several years, one from an academic and the other from a corporate perspective.[9] Comparing an extended history of published forecasts and their results, both studies set out to determine whether:

1. Forecasts that were made by the advisory services were more accurate than those indicated by the applicable forward rate.
2. The accuracy of those forecasts varied according to their analytical method and time horizon.
3. Substantial speculative profits could have been derived by following the recommendations of any advisory services.

The two surveys, like the forecasters themselves, varied somewhat in their conclusions. The findings of the academic study were moderately positive. Those of the corporate survey were predominantly negative. The former found that:

1. Over short-time horizons, the judgmental forecasters performed better than those who are econometrics-oriented. For periods of one year or longer, the relationship was reversed, with the econometrics approach faring better than the judgmental.

---

[8]Source of forecasts, *Euromoney*, ibid., pp. 19–22.
[9]Stephen H. Goodman, "Foreign Exchange Rate Forecasting Techniques: Implications for Business and Policy," *The Journal of Finance*, 34, no. 2 (May 1979): 415–27, and Richard M. Levich, "A Progress Report on Research into the Accuracy of Foreign Exchange Advisory Service Forecasts," New York University and the National Bureau of Economic Research, Inc., 1980.

Figure 10-1
Faulty forecasts, predicted versus actual exchange rates, July 1, 1979

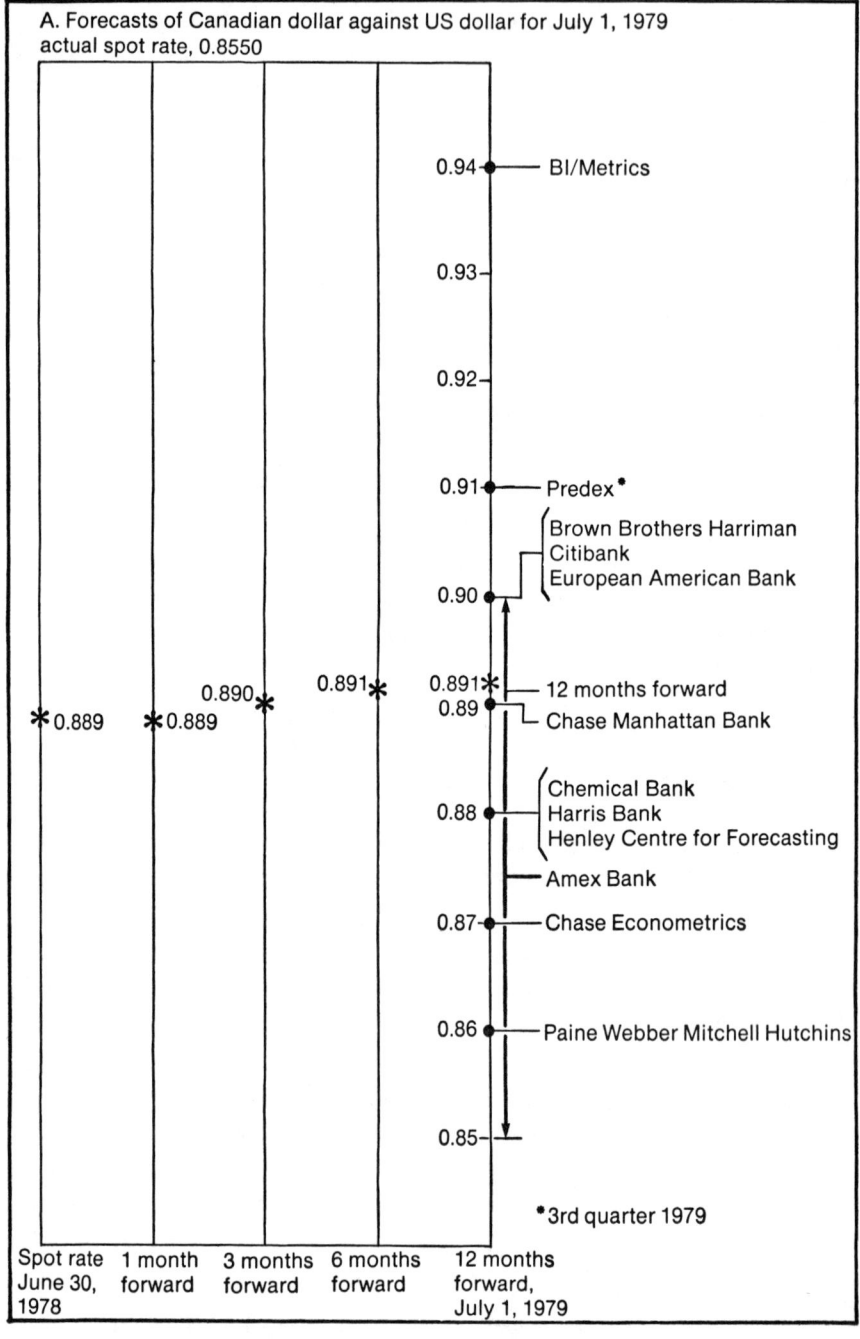

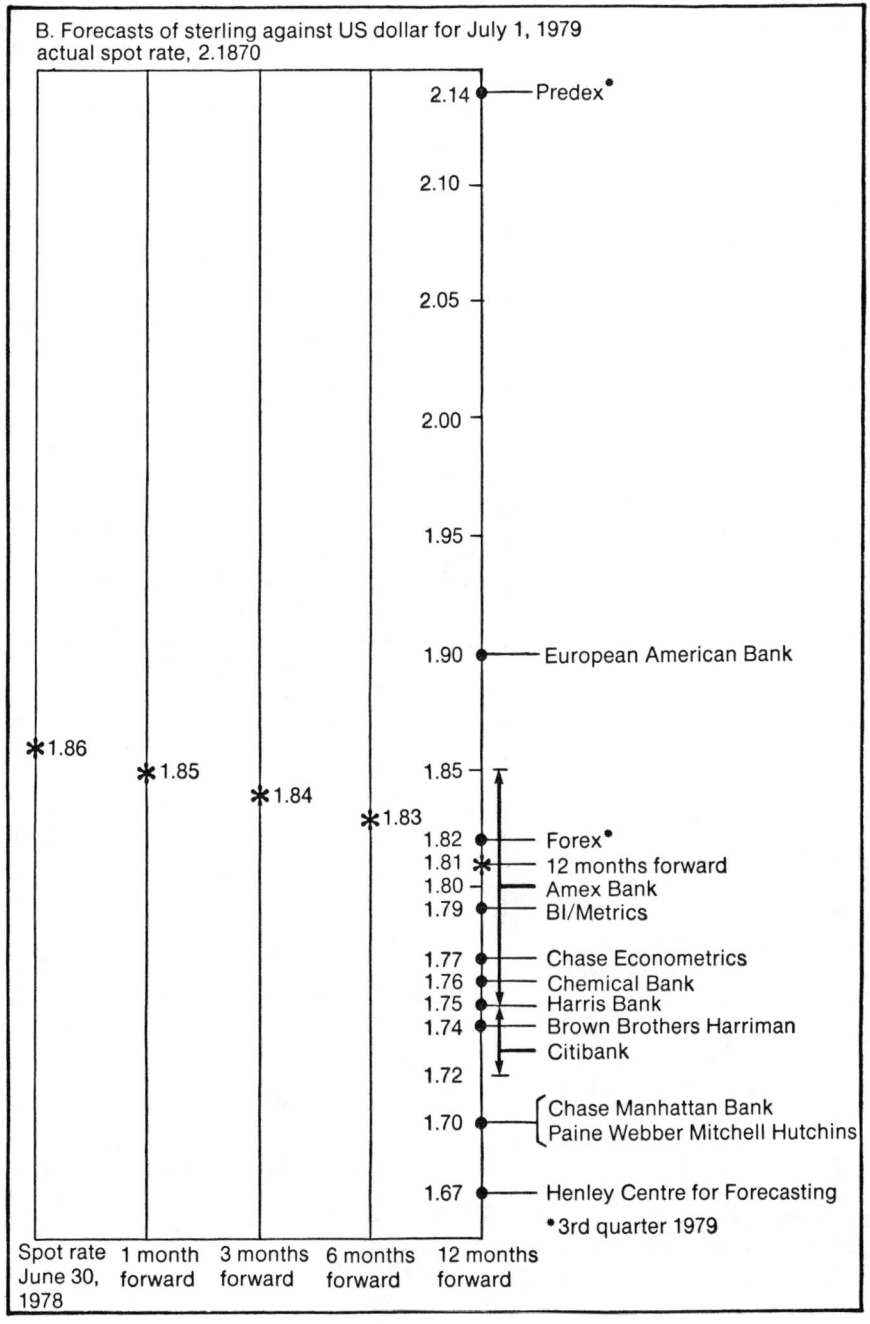

Figure 10–1 (continued)

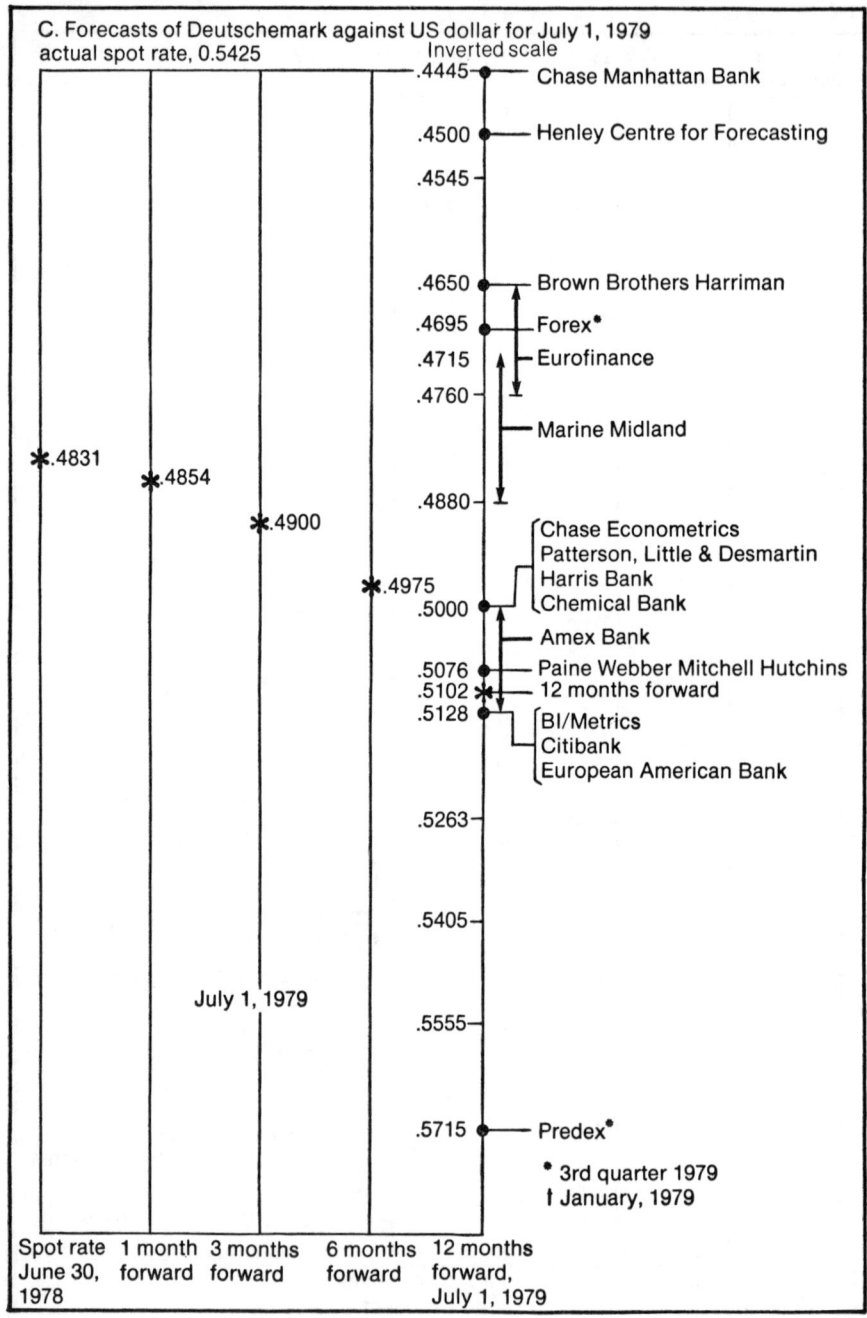

Adapted from *Euromoney*, August 1978, pp. 19–21.

2. Most advisory firms failed to outperform the present forward rate as predictors of the future spot rate.
3. The proportion of accurate forecasts were generally higher for shorter-time horizons, although some services did perform better over a longer horizon.
4. Following some advisory recommendations was profitable over the short run. Results fell off markedly beyond a 12-month horizon, especially the predictions of the judgmental forecasters.

To make substantial speculative profits from trading foreign exchange, according to the above conclusions, it would have been necessary to have had access to information and analytical skills that were not available to all market participants. That conclusion merely confirms the Figlewski model, and is hardly a conceptual breakthrough. Though such prior access to information is always theoretically possible, it is not so easily attained in the close-knit and highly competitive foreign exchange market. Yet the survey just cited concluded that the track records of some forecasting services, and the profits that could have been made by following their advice, were too consistent to have occurred by chance, and that it was therefore possible on occasion to beat the forward rate as a forecast.[10]

The second study did not hold out much hope that such superior performance was attainable over an extended period. Its survey of six econometric and four judgmental-technical services reached the same conclusion that the econometric services fared poorly over a short (three-to six-month) time horizon. They were found to have predicted the direction of trend for spot rates accurately 50 percent of the time over a three-month forecast horizon, and 61 percent of the time over a six-month horizon. In both cases the study found that the applicable forward rate provided a somewhat better, though still not very reliable, indication of the direction of trend.

The corporate study also determined that the track records of the services surveyed, both on an absolute basis and relative to the forward rate, improved as the forecast horizon was stretched from three to six months. It held that the performance of the econometric services supported the contention that the foreign exchange market is strongly efficient, and that such services were of little value in helping a multinational corporation to manage its foreign exchange exposure. The ultimate condemnation was that, "blindly following any of the econometric services would have led to intermittent periods with considerable losses for most currencies, periods that would dishearten, if not bankrupt, most individual speculators."[11] Of course, the corporate clients were not exactly thrilled either.

The study was more favorably disposed toward the technical momentum forecasters, asserting that their record upholds the view that stock market

---
[10]Levich, *A Progress Report*, p. 24.
[11]Goodman, "Foreign Exchange Rate Forecasting," p. 422.

type charting can be applied profitably to the analysis of exchange rate movements, and that multinational corporations were well advised to subscribe to one or more of the services that favor such an approach.

Value of charting

It is clear, finally, that we are not the only ones who are vexed by the difficulty of reconciling the emotional, and essentially unpredictable, near-term gyrations of exchange rates with the long-range forces that analysts, with good reason or not, feel more comfortable about measuring with their econometric models. Corporate treasurers, professors of international finance, and the full-time forecasters-for-hire all apparently have the same problem. It would appear reasonable, then, for private traders to follow the lead of those who should know and utilize the types of analysis that the statistical studies suggest are best suited to the circumstances at hand.

The indications are that charting and other types of technical and momentum analysis are the best available means of dealing with irregular, short-term exchange rate fluctuations—because they're geared not so much to predicting future swings as they are to helping the trader identify and move with the current trend. There is an extensive literature devoted to describing and interpreting the patterns that have been observed to recur with some regularity in stock and commodity futures price histories.[12] The evidence indicates that many of the same techniques apply to spot and forward exchange rates as well.

With the minimum outlay required to commence charting—consisting of paper, pencils, an eraser (no one is perfect) and a straight edge—there is much to be said for a speculator developing his or her own technical skills and depositing the $5,000 to $20,000 annual advisory fee one might otherwise pay to a forecaster-for-hire in the trading account. Even a corporate hedger who would be disposed toward engaging a professional forecaster in any case would find a grasp of fundamental charting principles of value in fully utilizing a service that employs such methods.

Table 10–2 is a summary trend analysis of the price movement of the IMM September 1980 Deutsche mark chart during the first half of 1980. It is another application of the K percent rule described earlier in the chapter where it is assumed that a price advance or decline of a predetermined degree is likely to continue for a longer duration. If a chart-watching trader goes long as soon as the contract price rises K percent, or however many points that represents, or goes short after a price drop of the same magnitude,

---

[12]One of the most comprehensive books on the subject is R. D. Edwards and John Magee, Jr., *Technical Analysis of Stock Trends*, 5th ed. (Springfield, Mass.: Stock Trend Service, 1973).

Also, the discussion of chart analysis of futures price trends in Allan M. Loosigian, *Interest Rate Futures* (Princeton, N.J.: Dow Jones Books, 1980), pp. 284–314, is applicable to foreign currency futures price analysis as well as to that of government and corporate debt obligations.

Table 10–2
Trend analysis—March 1981 Deutsche mark contract (IMM), September 2–December 29, 1980

Date	Settlement price	Minor trend	Major trend	Minor support	Major support	Minor resistance	Major resistance	Minor objective	Major objective	Comment—recommendation
September 2	.5734	Up	Down	.5720	.5550	.5750	.5760	.5750	.5550	Enter limit order to sell at .5750 for 200-point decline to major objective at .5550.
8	.5730	Up	Down	.5700	.5550	.5740	.5750	.5750	.5550	Minor objective not yet reached. Leave limit sell order in force at .5750.
15	.5718	Down	Down	.5700	.5530	.5740	.5740	.5740	.5550	Contract trading in 40-point, 5700-5740 range. Reduce sell limit order to .5740
22	.5635	Down	Down	.5600	.5510	.5700	.5730	.5650	.5550	Minor support is violated. Major downtrend continues. Reduce limit sell order to .5650
29	.5633	Down	Down	.5600	.5500	.5650	.5700	.5600	.5500	Sell order executed at .5650. Enter open buy stop order at .5720.
October 6	.5658	Up	Down	.5600	.5475	.5670	.5700	.5600	.5500	Contract trading laterally around .5650 sell point. Maintain short position.
13	.5608	Down	Down	.5600	.5450	.5650	.5700	.5600	.5500	Contract testing minor support at .5600. Maintain short position.
20	.5485	Down	Down	.5450	.5450	.5550	.5600	.5450	.5450	Downtrend accelerating. Lower buy stop order to .5550. Enter limit buy order at .5450.
27	.5423	Down	Down	.5350	dk*	.5450	.5580	.5350	.5200	Limit buy order executed at .5450 for 200-point realized gain. Cancel buy stop order at .5550.

Table 10–2 (continued)

Date	Settlement price	Minor trend	Major trend	Minor support	Major support	Minor resistance	Major resistance	Minor objective	Major objective	Comment—recommendation
November 3	.5348	Down	Down	.5250	dk	.5375	.5550	.5250	.5200	Minor trend reversal. Enter open sell order at .5500.
10	.5371	Up	Down	.5250	dk	dk	.5520	.5500	.5200	Rally subsiding. Leave sell order in force at .5500.
17	.5300	Down	Down	.5250	dk	.5400	.5500	.5500	.5200	Contract trading laterally in 5400–5450 range. Leave sell order in force. Await developments.
24	.5344	Up	Down	.5250	.5100	.5400	.5450	.5400	.5200	
December 1	.5268	Down	Down	.5250	.5100	.5300	.5425	.5250	.5200	Missed sale on rally. Cancel sell order, too far from market.
8	.5221	Down	Down	.5200	.5100	.5270	.5400	.5200	.5200	Minor support violated. Contract approaching major objective. Make another attempt to sell on rally.
15	.5142	Up	Down	.5100	.5100	.5200	.5350	.5200	dk	Contract rallied from .5100. Try to reinstate short position around .5300.
22	.5210	Up	Down	.5170	.5100	.5270	.5340	.5300	dk	Enter open limit sell order at .5290. Leave open sell order in force at .5290.
29	.5216	Down	Down	.5150	.5100	.5250	.5300	.5300	.5100	

*Don't know.

he or she stands a good chance, so the theory says, of making money. On the corporate side, the same rules would give a signal to cover the company's long or short exposure, as the case may be, in a particular currency.

Basic econometric modeling

If a layperson is capable of becoming a chartist, there is no reason why she shouldn't try her hand at basic econometric modeling and exchange rate forecasting as well. But here, the necessary tools are more elaborate than a pencil and straight edge and, of course, much more expensive. As one might guess, a computer and a specialized program to feed into it are required. The current boom in small, self-contained computers designed for use in homes and offices makes this not such a far-fetched idea. Some computer enthusiasts go so far as to claim that within several years nearly every "serious" investor of substantial means—ostensibly in contrast with frivolous ones of negligible means—will have such a unit at one's disposal. The computer stores that seem to have opened on practically every street would appear to bear out this glowing forecast.

The basic components of a so-called personal computer cost between $1,000 and $2,500, with some of the more advanced and versatile systems running as high as $10,000 or more. The hardware for such systems is produced and marketed by a number of equipment manufacturers, including Apple Computer, Inc., Tandy Corporation, Atari, Digital Equipment Corporation, and Hewlett-Packard.

A beginning user will need, as a minimum, a central processor (the computing unit itself), a typewriter keyboard for communicating with the computer, and a video display screen that allows the computer to communicate with the user. Beyond these basic components, an advanced minicomputer user may wish to add such accessories as a hard-copy printer to record the information that appears on the screen and at least one of an assortment of devices that stores information in a computer's memory. The softwear, or the programs themselves, is contained in audio tape cassettes, plug-in cartridges, or plastic discs called "floppies."

Among the hardware manufacturers, Apple Computer has been the most resourceful in developing and marketing prefabricated programs to assist individuals in analyzing and managing their investment portfolios. Relatively little has been done along these lines in the area of foreign exchange trading, however, and the trader who cares to use this modern technology has until recently been left largely to his or her own devices in designing a personal program.

The initial problem is one of reducing the abundant data pertaining to exchange rates to those critical elements the trader believes are most consequential in determining future spot rates. Then follows the task of expressing and linking these elements in terms of a mathematical formula—

what we have earlier referred to as an econometric model—which will, after digesting the variables that are fed into it, produce an exchange rate forecast.

The principal variables are, of course, those which we identified in Part Two as the primary determinants of rates of exchange—balance of payments trends, particularly trade and capital movements, productivity, changes in national income and money supply levels, relative rates of interest and inflation, central bank intervention policies, and so forth. To be sure, there is no single, everlastingly correct formula for assessing this mass of information. But even if such models fall short of pinpointing future rates, there are ways of arranging the essential data to identify currency trends early on and, possibly, signal likely changes in exchange rate patterns.

One simple example of a forecasting model follows the monetary approach to exchange rate analysis. The model is formulated on the premise that an equilibrium condition exists when the nominal supply of money is equal to the nominal demand for money—nominal demand being defined as the product of a country's domestic price level times the real demand for money. This premise is expressed by the formula:

$$M^s = e\, p\, l(y, i)$$

where M^s represents the nominal supply of money; $e\, p$ that country's exchange rate times the world price level, which is in turn equal to the domestic price level of the country, and $l(y,i)$ the real demand for money, a function of the level of real income y and the prevailing interest rate i.

Developing these concepts, the monetarist model is further refined to the proposition that the percentage change in an exchange rate will be equal to the percentage change in the nominal money supply minus the percentage change in the real demand for money minus the percentage change in the world price level, a concept which can be expressed algebraically and programmed into a minicomputer as:

$$g_e = g_m s - (n_y g_y + n_i g_i) - g_p$$

A major uncertainty in this instance, as with most formulas of this type, concerns the accuracy of the data to be entered into the formula. In the case of the monetary model outlined above, it is problematical whether the projected rate of money supply growth that is central to the equation can be forecast with any greater degree of accuracy than the exchange rate itself, which the formula is intended to predict. As a model grows in complexity and encompasses a greater number of variables, the less is the likelihood that all or even most of the incorporated variables contain reliable data.

Even accepting these shortcomings, a do-it-yourself econometrician can switch on the personal computer, enter one or more combinations of assumed variables, and then sit back and let the computer tell how future rates are likely to react in the event that the data materialize as it's assumed that they will.

Currency futures traders who have access to a computer terminal but who lack the inclination or mathematical background to construct their own models may, for a fee, plug into one prepared by a professional forecasting firm. Predex Corporation, one of the companies cited earlier in this chapter, offers its own model and proprietary forecasts to subscribers through the Control Data Corporation's Cybernet time-sharing system. The system's users may accept the forecasts generated by the Predex model or enter their own assumptions regarding balance of payments, industrial production, changes in money supply, and other determining factors to develop forecasts of what future exchange rates might be under the conditions they foresee.

Successful futures trading must be closely attuned to the daily—and in some instances, hourly—exchange rate fluctuations that the broad econometric projections do not take into account, a condition which prompts traders to rely heavily on charting and technical analysis. Even here, a personal computer can be of assistance. There are time-sharing programs available that allow the user to retrieve frequently updated charts on one's display screen, sparing the chore of keeping such charts manually. Interactive Data Corporation, and Stock Market Softwear, two Massachusetts-based companies, and Commodity Systems, Inc., of Boca Raton, Florida, offer technically oriented computer programs from which the subscriber can derive trading ideas. For a fee, the Personal Computer Commodity Analysis Group provides its members with a five-disc package, which enables them to do their charting electronically. This program is compatible with the Apple II system, as is the Dow Jones News Service, which provides news stories and other market information via a telephone link.

CMT Tradecenter Corporation of Moonachie, New Jersey, offers institutional and corporate traders a highly sophisticated visual display system that incorporates price data seconds after it originates on the exchange floor. The Tradecenter service, for which CMT supplies the programs and Hewlett-Packard the hardware, generates on an ongoing basis a broad array of charts and graphs to assist its subscribers in identifying trend lines, price support and resistance levels, and (hopefully) enable them to spot contract price reversals in the incipient stages. At a monthly charge beginning at $2,000, the Tradecenter system is priced beyond the means of most private traders. For a somewhat lower monthly rate, Stamford, Connecticut-based Comtrend offers traders a somewhat less-sophisticated system.

Like manual tools, such advanced equipment and softwear are only as good as the use to which they are put. Computer enthusiasts maintain, however, that they have more time to devote to profitable analysis and predict that before too many years have passed, a personal computer will be a "must" for all traders and investors who are determined to make money.

PART THREE

THE FUTURES MARKET FOR FOREIGN EXCHANGE

Chapter 11

Futures trading versus the interbank forward market

PART ONE OF THIS BOOK traced the historical evolution of the foreign exchange market. Part Two examined the principal determinants of exchange rate movements. This third and final part turns to the primary users of these markets: the arbitrageurs who seek to capitalize upon the small price disparities that arise between what are essentially the same forward contracts traded in different markets; the multinational corporate treasurers, who engage in forward pricing to reduce their companies' foreign exchange risk; and, in the concluding chapter, the private speculators who court that very risk by trying to guess which way exchange rates will move next.

This chapter describes the relationship, which appears to be at the same time competitive and complimentary, between the currency futures exchanges and the interbank forward market. Chapter 12 takes up the subject of foreign exchange exposure, what it is, and the methods by which companies identify and measure it. Chapters 13 and 14 arrive at the heart of the matter, as far as this book is concerned, namely the use of forward pricing, among other techniques, to hedge that type of risk and the accepted means of dealing with the accounting, tax, and related problems associated with hedging. Finally, for the benefit of those would-be traders who do not believe that currency speculation is tantamount to gambling—or perhaps are attracted to it because they do—we conclude with a chapter of what we hope are helpful hints on how to emerge from this wild and woolly game with one's ego and bank account (not necessarily in that order) intact.

The differences

Although the organized financial futures exchanges and the interbank market in forward exchange—the nomenclature gets a bit confusing here—both deal in contracts for the future delivery of foreign currency, the two markets are structured and operate differently.[1] The interbank market is an informal network of foreign exchange traders in banks throughout the world who do business with one another over the telephone and via Telex, in what stock and bond investors would properly think of as an international over-the-counter market. The futures market, on the other hand, is similar to a stock exchange; in one instance, a currency futures market is affiliated with a stock exchange. Wherever in the world orders to buy or sell futures contracts may originate, they are executed on the exchange floor by member brokers.

Though most of the forward contracts negotiated in the interbank market happen to be in amounts of $1 million or its equivalent in another currency, there is no fixed contract size. Exchange traded futures contracts are both smaller and of a standard size, falling in the $100,000 to $150,000 range depending on the dollar value of the underlying currency. Interbank forward contracts don't carry uniform delivery dates. They simply mature 3, 6, or 12 months from the day they're made. Futures contracts do expire on fixed dates, and so do not have a standard longevity of, say, six months when they're first undertaken.

Interbank market quotations are expressed as bids and offers. Orders are executed "flat"—that is, without a commission added to purchase orders at the offer and deducted from sells at the bid. There also are bids and offers made between brokers in exchange trading; but orders are executed at the best prices obtainable in this competitive two-way auction, with a commission added to the total purchase price or subtracted from the amount of the sale.

Interbank contracts are relatively informal, though scrupulously observed, deals struck over the telephone or Telex, and confirmed by the crossing of simple notification receipts. The contracts are settled in full at their maturity, with no initial or intermediate payments required of either the buyer or seller. Exchange market trading, by contrast, entails the payment by both parties to a transaction of initial and variation (maintenance) margin

---

[1]See Chapter 5.

deposits. The exchange's "mark to the market" accounting procedure requires of market losers that they pay off to the benefit of winners via the clearing corporation on a daily basis.

The two markets also differ with respect to their daily price fluctuations and contract delivery procedures. The exchanges set limits on the extent to which their contracts may advance or decline in price during the course of a single trading session. There are no such daily fluctuation limits in the interbank market. Whereas approximately 95 percent of the forward contracts negotiated in the interbank market are settled by delivery of the underlying currencies, the reverse ratio is the norm in the futures market, where deliveries are made on less than 5 percent of the open interest, or total contracts in force.

How the futures market evolved

In spite of these operational differences, both markets were designed in principle to accomplish the same purpose, to provide a mechanism by which an advance rate may be set on a contemplated foreign exchange transaction. But, one might ask, what is the point of having two markets when one would serve just as well, other than to provide employment for more people? Is this duplication of effort really necessary? The answer to these questions harkens back to our discussion in Chapter 10 about exchange rate forecasting, and specifically about the one-way bets that arose when central banks were committed to maintaining fixed parities in the face of speculative attacks. Under those relatively straightforward circumstances, it was obvious on which side of the market the principal risk lay. The great majority of bank dealers were, as a consequence, prevailed on by their corporate hedge customers to assume the same short position in the currency under attack, leaving the intervening central bank in not-so-splendid isolation on the other side. The situation resembled that of the audience pushing toward the solitary exit in a crowded theater after someone has shouted *"FIRE!"* Only in this case, the stampede was all the more frantic because there almost always really was a fire.

It was recognized in the wake of these chaotic conditions that the much-maligned speculator plays a useful, indeed an indispensable, role in a situation where "the trade" all want to stand on the same side of the market. The idea was floated—no doubt by the speculators themselves—that there were speculators a plenty in the traditional futures markets, which had served for over a century to hedge price fluctuations in agricultural and other physical commodities. Why couldn't these same speculators act as the risk offset for hedgers in currencies as well? Those who believed they could, proposed to establish an alternate market where forward cover could be more easily obtained in the event of a currency crisis within the existing futures market, thereby having immediate use of exchange facilities and trading expertise that were already in place. The major drawback to the plan was that such crises occurred relatively infrequently, even during the latter years of the Bretton Woods era, and a market such as the one proposed would have difficulty sustaining itself during the intervening periods of relative tranquility.

The situation changed with the conclusion of the Smithsonian agreement in December 1971. With the expansion of the parity limits between which exchange rates were allowed to fluctuate from 2 percent to 4½ percent, currency risk even under noncrisis conditions became substantial enough to make the notion of an alternate hedging facility more compelling. That was especially so for those companies whose foreign exchange dealings were not large enough to afford them ready access to the interbank market. Earlier plans were revived, and achieved fruition when the International Monetary Market affiliate of the Chicago Mercantile Exchange commenced trading in contracts for six major currencies in May 1972. It is an ill wind that blows no good. The subsequent failure of the Smithsonian agreement to keep the fixed-parity system intact, and the largely involuntary drift by most countries to flexible exchange rates was due to, and in turn aggravated by, the turmoil in the foreign exchange markets during the early and mid-1970s. The timing for the establishment of a currency futures market became propitious.

Efficiency and lags

If a prospective hedger has his choice of two essentially equivalent markets, which then should he use? Is there a possibility of his securing a better rate in one market as opposed to the other, or are they so closely meshed as to make any disparities between them negligible? These questions hinge on what are known in economic jargon as price correlation and relative liquidity. The answers revolve in turn around the efficiency of each market. We defined market efficiency in Chapter 10 as the extent to which current market prices, in this case forward exchange rates, reflect all of the known information which can affect those prices. Since the interbank and exchange markets both price the same "commodities"—that is, currencies—any price change in one should be matched by an identical change in the other if the two markets are equally efficient. In other words, they should be mirror images of one another.

To determine whether and to what degree that mirror image condition exists, it is necessary to resort to some rather rarefied statistical analysis. As if the subject were not already prone to too much mumbo jumbo, and difficult enough to understand in English, our friends the nitpickers from Chapter 9 force us to start conversing in Greek. To obtain a precise measurement of the degree to which comparable contracts in the two markets vary in price over an extended period, we need to introduce the concepts of alpha (α) and beta (β).

Alpha and beta are the products of attempts to measure and express statistically price volatility and the resulting risk implicit in a particular security or commodity. The two concepts have become integral parts of modern portfolio management theory.

Beta is a measure of the volatility of a specific security, commodity, or currency in relation to the aggregate market in which that asset is traded. If, for example, Canadian dollars exhibit half the volatility of all IMM-traded currencies, they would be assigned a beta of 0.5. Or, to take another hypothetical case, if Swiss francs are twice as volatile as the overall currency futures market, their beta would be 2.0.

As with most such attempts to attach precise values to market behavior, actual performance does not always match that which the beta says it should be. Price changes at variance with beta are therefore in turn expressed in terms of alpha—the difference between actual price performance and what the beta indicated it would have been. A popular admonition among portfolio managers who subscribe to these concepts is to "keep your alpha high and your beta low."

Figure 11-1 is the graphic representation of such an analysis.[2] A statistical comparison was made of nine sets of price data for various IMM and interbank British pound contracts between May 1972 and June 1973, the first year of currency futures trading. An alpha on the IMM-interbank regression series equal to zero and a beta of one would have indicated an absolute identity of contract prices in the two markets. If that had been the case, both the solid and diagonal lines in Figure 11-1 would have passed through the origin of the vertical (IMM rates) and horizontal (interbank rates) axes and their plots would have coincided. The fact that they did not signified that there was a statistical variance between the two price series. The analysis of 1972-73 prices did in fact confirm a high degree of correlation between IMM and interbank rates during that period, but also revealed significant variations between prices in the two markets in the range represented by the shaded areas on the chart.

As we've had to do with previous statistical measurements of this sort, it is necessary to translate the alphas and betas into a language which can be meaningful to a currency trader. To claim perfect identity of the two markets, it must be demonstrated that the closest match-ups were between contracts of the same maturity, such as, for example, 90 days to the delivery date on an IMM futures contract versus a comparable interbank forward contract. Actually, the survey of 1972-73 British pound forward prices

[2]The above analysis and supporting chart in Figure 11-1 are drawn from Jack Denis, Jr., "How Well Does the International Monetary Market Track the Interbank Forward Market?" *Financial Analysts Journal*, January/February 1976, pp. 2-7. Permission granted to reproduce Figure 11-1.

Figure 11-1
Statistical comparison between IMM and interbank rates

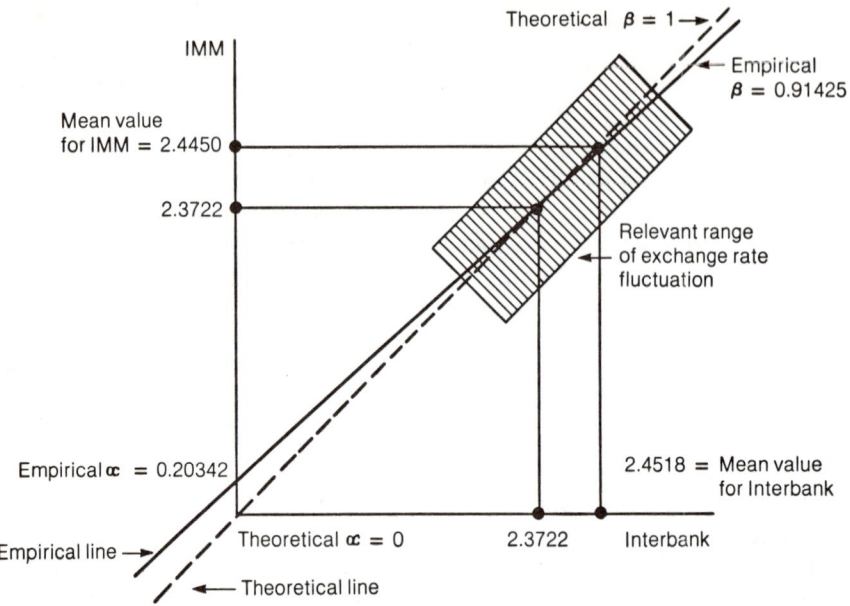

revealed a closer match between each day's interbank quotation and the parallel IMM price for the day following. These results were taken to comprise strong evidence of a consistent lead-lag relationship between the two markets. Although the variations recorded were minimal, they were statistically conclusive. All of our feeble jokes about nitpicking aside, in the 13-month period surveyed, at least, IMM prices followed the lead of the interbank market by one day.

One would think that a full day's lag between the interbank market and the IMM would offer savvy traders—and even some who were not so savvy—a sure-fire way of making money. Simply do in the futures market what would have scored a profit in the interbank market the day before, right? Wrong. Those readers who are thinking that there must be a hitch are quite correct. Unfortunately, there always is a hitch. In the first place, the interbank market hugely overshadowed the IMM in size when the pound contract comparisons were made. That, as well as the novelty of commodity futures contracts on currencies at the time, and the consequent inexperience of exchange members in trading them, made it reasonable to expect that the larger and senior of the two markets would lead the fledgling market by at least a day.

Second, any apparent profit opportunities in playing the one-day lag dwindle when transaction costs are taken into account. As was noted earlier, the interbank market operates on a spread between the bid and asked quotations, as contrasted with the commission charged on the purchase and sale of futures contracts on the exchange. If, for example, an interbank foreign exchange trader were bidding 2.0452 to buy three-month forward pounds and offering to sell them at 2.0456, he or she could in principle earn four points per round turn all day, every day, by buying pounds at the lower of the two rates and selling them at the higher. Expressed in percentage terms, that comes to a spread of 0.10 percent to 0.15 percent, depending upon the value in U.S. dollars of the particular currency being quoted. In practice, it does not work out so neatly.

With quotations being adjusted up or down by the minute in volatile markets, there is scarcely enough time for an interbank trader to complete a round-turn transaction at his original bid and offer. If the quote is raised, the trader's profit increases if the position is a long one and diminishes if it is a short. The reverse applies if the quote is lowered. Market exposure and therefore risk have entered the picture, making the transaction cost greater—or less—than the amount obtained by simply subtracting the bid price from the offer.

The only way, under these volatile circumstances, in which an interbank trader may assure herself of capturing her entire spread is by simultaneously pairing off a buy and sell order of the same size and for the same maturity date. Since that rarely occurs in the real trading world, the dealer will find herself taking on an exposed position, either to accommodate a customer or to protect a position in another currency. The futures broker charges a commission on each contract that he buys or sells for a customer's account. But if he is a so-called local, trading for his own account, he, too, will almost certainly incur a profit or loss on each transaction that will affect the price comparison between the two markets we're discussing.

The profiles of its participants also affect the composition and character of a market. The smaller standard sizes and uniform maturities of futures contracts lend themselves—were in fact expressly designed for—trading by individual speculators and smaller companies with foreign exchange exposure. The interbank market, on the other hand, is geared to large multinational corporations of the *Fortune*-500 stripe. Given this difference in the size of the players and of their market impact, it is not surprising that interbank rates would lead those on the exchanges. Trading in the interbank forward market also has a substantial and immediate impact on the spot foreign exchange market, inasmuch as the two are actually branches of the same market, while a currency futures exchange is an entity apart.

Table 11–1 shows the rapid growth in currency futures trading from the early years of the IMM to the recent past. As it and other futures markets for foreign exchange continue to develop, they should outgrow their junior status and operate more on a par with the interbank market. At that point, the lead-lag relationship between the two markets will diminish and very likely all but disappear.

Table 11–1
IMM currency futures contracts traded first five months of each year

1974	96,007
1975	91,689
1976	71,838
1977	175,643
1978	498,816
1979	675,205
1980	1,662,054

Types of arbitrage

Even though no automatic windfalls are to be reaped from the existing lead-lag, there are still profit opportunities open to those traders who are sharp-eyed and (literally) fleet-footed enough to seize them. This type of intermarket trading is labeled *Class B arbitrage*, so named for the membership category futures exchanges put firms that engage in it.

We described early in this book the several kinds of arbitrage that at various times in the past have been conducted in the foreign exchange market. *Spatial arbitrage* seeks to exploit exchange rate discrepancies between geographic centers, simultaneously buying, for example, the same currency in London, say, and selling it in Tokyo. *Trilateral arbitrage* is similar in technique, but concentrates on temporary aberrations in cross rates between three or more currencies. *Interest rate arbitrage* is the movement of funds from one domestic or Eurocurrency market to another in response to yield differentials. It was described in Chapter 8 how these differentials affect and in turn are affected by the premiums and discounts on forward exchange quotations.

The establishment of an organized futures market in foreign exchange has created yet another type of arbitrage, this one between the futures and interbank markets. The technique and objective remain the same, namely the simultaneous (or nearly so) purchase and sale of the same forward contract in the two markets to capture any rate difference that may arise between them. If, for example, on December 15 an arbitrageur is able to buy for three-months forward delivery in the interbank market DM 1.25 million at 0.5436, while at the same moment selling 10 IMM March DM contracts (for the equivalent number of marks) at 0.5440, he or she clears before commission charges a profit of four points per contract, or a total of $500.[3] Although in most cases the arbitrage operation is completed by separately "unwinding" both sides of the transaction well before the maturity date of the contracts, the procedure works in practice because in theory the

---

[3] Readers may wish to refer back to Chapter 5, for an explanation of how contract points are translated into dollar gains or losses.

1.25 million forward marks purchased in the interbank market could be used to meet the trader's commitment to deliver the same number of marks in satisfaction of his 10 short March DM contracts.

What a trader needs to excel at this sort of arbitrage are a quick numerical sense to spot the discrepancies between the markets before anyone else, and a strong set of legs to race from the pit where the futures contracts are traded to the telephone stations at the edge of the floor to execute the other "leg" immediately over a direct line to a bank's foreign exchange desk. If he doesn't move fast enough, he runs the risk of having the blip disappear before he's able to execute both sides of the transaction. He's then left with an unintended and undesired open short or long position. As a practical matter, and because exchanges do not permit the use of roller skates on the floor, an arbitrageur usually works with a partner who makes the necessary transactions in the pit while he himself mans the direct line to the bank.

The key to successful arbitrage trading of this sort is a constant turnover of trades. The narrower the spread between the two markets becomes, the greater the number and frequency of contracts traded must be to maintain the same level of profits. As in any such operation, the more players who are competing for a dwindling number of profit opportunities, the more difficult the game becomes—a sort of Darwinism in the pits. That is precisely what has happened in Class B arbitrage. As the number of players has swelled, the game has become a great deal more competitive and the average profit has shrunk from $50 a trade to about $30. In the words of one survivor, "It's just about over for the inefficient guys."[4]

Banks' role

Even so, a growing number of dealer banks apparently have decided that if anyone is going to make money at the currency arbitrage game, it may as well be they. Rather than fight the rival market, they've decided to join it. Many have gone so far as to buy exchange memberships and put their own people on the floor to operate the direct lines to their trading rooms.

Banks also become involved in Class B arbitrage in their capacity as lenders to the extent they finance a fair percentage of the positions carried by brokerage firms and individual exchange members. In so doing, they are exposed to five types of potential risk:

1. *Delivery risk* is incurred when on contract settlement date the opposite party to the original transaction does not honor his commitment to deliver the designated currency even though the bank has met its obligation. The exchanges' clearing and delivery procedures were designed to elim-

---

[4]Laurie Cohen, "Arbitrage: Pennywise, Pound Rich," *Chicago Tribune,* June 11, 1980.

inate this type of risk and thereby to protect banks and other market participants from losses on that account.
2. When a bank advances to its customer the dollars with which to pay for and receive delivery of foreign exchange at the expiration of a futures contract, it is subject to *delivery financing risk* until the foreign exchange is converted back into dollars.
3. *Position risk* is the possibility that a foreign exchange position financed by the bank will depreciate during the time its customer is long the currency, or appreciate while it is short. As was noted earlier, the exchanges enforce a daily computation of contract values and require the deposit of additional margin when it is necessary.
4. *Margin variation loan risk* stems from position risk. When the bank extends credit to its customer to meet these margin calls, repayment of the loan, apart from the borrowing firm's creditworthiness, depends upon the market turning back in the customer's favor.
5. Banks issue letters of credit on behalf of their customers to the exchange to be drawn on in the event the customer defaults or otherwise fails to meet its variation margin requirements. If default occurs, the lending bank is subject to *letter-of-credit risk*.

To reduce these risks and thereby encourage more banks to engage in currency arbitrage financing, futures exchanges have established the special Class B clearing memberships mentioned above. They were so designated to set them apart from the exchange's regular Class A clearing members. The Class B category was designed to apply to partnerships and corporations that are formed solely for the purpose of conducting currency arbitrage between the exchanges and the interbank forward market. Class A firms that choose to engage in this type of business also are required to establish separate "B" entities strictly for that purpose to segregate their two types of trading.

Exchange approval, contingent upon its satisfaction of certain legal and financial requirements, is required before a member firm may commence operations as a Class B arbitrageur. To provide further assurance to potential bank lenders, Class B firms are required to operate under a closely monitored system of guarantees and controls. In the first instance, each position assumed by a Class B firm must have the full guarantee of a regular Class A clearing member firm. Second, the Class B firm is limited to arbitrage only, and may trade with only one sponsoring bank that is registered as such with the exchange. The purpose of this limitation is to ensure that each one of a firm's positions on the exchange will be offset by an equivalent and opposite position with the sponsor bank. As a further control, the designated bank receives directly from the exchange a daily position report listing the member firm's foreign currency futures positions with the exchange. The bank's insistence that every position on the daily listing corresponds with a matching position carried by the bank effectively limits the bank's single greatest risk: that its customers will overstep the restrictions and speculate in the market by assuming uncovered positions. Finally, collections and disbursements of margin funds and other money move directly between the exchange and the bank, removing such funds from the immediate control of the Class B firm.

These comprehensive controls make it difficult, if not impossible, for the arbitrage firm to assume uncovered positions in the futures market even if it wished to do so. Banks feel more comfortable about extending credit for this type of limited-risk trading, allowing the market to achieve higher levels of volume and liquidity and providing smaller-scale hedgers with a viable alternative to the interbank forward market. The only positions which the exchange and sponsor bank cannot fully monitor and control are those which the arbitrageur assumes during the course of the current trading session. There, the burden is on him to ensure that he can offset his intended exchange position by a matching opposite position with the bank. Should the desired price spread disappear while he's in the process of taking both positions, the arbitrageur should back away and decline to do either side until the profit opportunity reasserts itself. He is sometimes simply unable to act fast enough to execute both sides before the spread evaporates. If he is left standing on one leg, the arbitrageur's best move is to close out the side that he did execute, at a loss if need be. Even under those circumstances it is unusual for the loss to exceed $1,000 unless the position was exceptionally large, roughly 50 contracts or more. Then, the arbitrageur should have made it his business to ensure that the two transactions were capable of being executed simultaneously. Another potential cause for loss is the "outtrade," when during the course of active trading two floor brokers misunderstand each other. Losses arising out of such error trades are customarily divided between the two brokers involved, and generally amount to several hundred or occasionally several thousand dollars.

Arbitrageurs in most cases restrict their trading activity to the nearby delivery month, since that is where the most worthwhile profit opportunities for them occur. Bank financing is also something of a problem here, in that while a bank may extend total credit to a Class B firm amounting to, say, $20 million, it will in most instances limit the portion of that total credit line the borrowing firm may use for trading in any single delivery month. These so-called settlement limits have been the greatest constraint on banks' financing of Class B arbitrage.

Champagne or beer profits?

To get a flavor of what this is like, put yourself in an arbitrageur's shoes for the first two weeks of January 1980. You're on the direct line to the bank, while your partner is standing 100 feet away in the pit, waiting for your signal to complete the trade the two of you have rehearsed. What

Table 11-2
IMM currency futures—New York interbank forward market arbitrage, January 1980

Date January	90-day British pound	March 80 BP	Range	90-day Canadian dollar	March 80 CD	Range	90-day Japanese yen
2	2.2325	2.2380 2.2140	$137.50 -$462.50	.8583	.8604 .8577	$210.00 -$ 60.00	.4269
3	2.2238	2.2385 2.2215	$362.50 -$ 62.50	.8567	.8573 .8540	$ 60.00 -$270.00	.4258
4	2.2288	2.2330 2.2250	$100.00 -$100.00	.8581	.8585 .8562	$ 40.00 -$190.00	.4342
7	2.2540	2.2590 2.2395	$125.00 -$362.50	.8561	.8580 .8547	$190.00 -$140.00	.4397
8	2.2462	2.2565 2.2445	$250.00 -$ 50.00	.8553	.8570 .8555	$170.00 +$ 20.00	.4322
9	2.2543	2.2630 2.2510	$225.00 -$ 75.00	.8569	.8577 .8561	$ 80.00 -$ 80.00	.4313
10	2.2415	2.2545 2.2440	$325.00 $ 62.50	.8593	.8603 .8586	$100.00 -$ 70.00	.4304
11	2.2525	2.2570 2.2445	$112.50 -$200.00	.8600	.8606 .8580	$ 60.00 -$200.00	.4306
14	2.2730	2.2775 2.2560	$112.50 $425.00	.8589	.8594 .8575	$ 50.00 -$140.00	.4294
15	2.2720	2.2860 2.2640	$350.00 -$200.00	.8588	.8599 .8572	$110.00 -$160.00	.4231

March 80 JY	Range	90-day Swiss Franc	March 80 SF	Range	90-day Deutsche mark	March 80 DM	Range
.4260	$112.50	.6517	.6485	$400.00	.5944	.5934	$125.00
.4240	$362.50		.6438	$987.50		.5894	$625.00
.4278	−$250.00	.6506	.6516	−$125.00	.5943	.5956	−$162.50
.4239	$237.50		.6457	$612.50		.5906	$462.50
.4336	$ 75.00	.6501	.6475	$325.00	.5940	.5925	$187.50
.4279	$787.50		.6420	$1,012.50		.5892	$600.00
.4395	$ 25.00	.6525	.6504	$262.50	.5951	.5935	$200.00
.4336	$762.50		.6449	$950.00		.5912	$487.50
.4329	−$ 87.50	.6481	.6463	$225.00	.5921	.5909	$150.00
.4297	$312.50		.6425	$700.00		.5877	$550.00
.4318	−$ 62.50	.6498	.6474	$300.00	.5928	.5911	$212.50
.4291	$275.00		.6451	$587.50		.5897	$387.50
.4296	$100.00	.6469	.6454	$187.50	.5899	.5895	$ 50.00
.4284	$250.00		.6410	$737.50		.5863	$450.00
.4292	$175.00	.6479	.6450	$362.50	.5907	.5885	$275.00
.4282	$300.00		.6422	$712.50		.5865	$525.00
.4290	$ 50.00	.6474	.6436	$475.00	.5909	.5886	$287.50
.4272	$275.00		.6414	$750.00		.5873	$450.00
.4261	−$375.00	.6420	.6422	−$ 25.00	.5878	.5881	−$ 37.50
.4201	$375.00		.6356	$800.00		.5836	$525.00

would you have done? That's not really a fair question for anyone who wasn't on the exchange floor and familiar with the futures and interbank rates at the time. To give you more than a sporting chance, then, we've provided a sort of crib sheet in Table 11–2, which lists the closing interbank three-month forward rate on five currencies between January 2 and 15, along with the daily range of the nearby IMM futures contracts, in this case for March 1980 delivery of those currencies. We've also computed the profits or losses that would have been incurred on one contract if the interbank rate had been paired against both the daily high and low prices for each trading session on the comparable IMM contracts.[5]

On January 2, and for most of the subsequent trading sessions listed, three-month forward Swiss francs would have provided you, the arbitrageur, with the greatest profit opportunities. You might, had you been able to capture the low price of the day, have bought March 1980 SF at 0.6438 while at the same time selling three-months forward via your sponsor bank at 0.6517 for a 79-point spread, or a profit per contract of $987.50.

$$0.6517 - 0.6438 = 79 \text{ points} \times \$12.50 = \$987.50$$

If you had executed the interbank side of the arbitrage at the same rate, but managed to buy the futures contract at its daily high of 0.6485, your profit per contract before brokerage commissions—which, as an exchange member, you pay to yourself—would have amounted to $400.

$$0.6517 - 0.6485 = 32 \text{ points} \times \$12.50 = \$400$$

In either case, the interbank $/SF_{3\text{-mo.}}$ rate was above the March 1980 SF daily price range, assuring you of a profit on the transaction at whatever rate you managed to get.

It's a pretty easy game, buying low and selling high at the same instant, right? Everyone should get into the currency arbitrage business. Certainly for the two-week period under review, it was smooth sailing for the Swiss franc arbitrage. On most days you'd have made between $300 and $700 a contract, sometimes a bit less but occasionally a good deal more. On only two days, January 3 and 15, would you have lost $125 and $25 per contract, respectively, if you'd been unlucky enough to catch the high futures price of the day. Should you have elected to play with the "heavy hitters" and traded 10 or more contracts at a clip, there'd have been profits galore to pay for plenty of filet mignon and Chateau Rothschild to restore your depleted energy and powers of concentration between trading sessions.

The same would have held true, albeit to a lesser extent, of the arbitrage in three-month forward Deutsche marks. You'd have earned upwards of $600 a contract on days when you caught the best quotation, and perhaps $100 or $200 on those days when you weren't so fortunate. Like the Swiss

---

[5]The price comparisons included in Table 11–2 are not strictly accurate in the sense that they do not take into account intraday fluctuations in the interbank three-month rate for each currency listed. But for the purposes of our training exercise, they will suffice.

franc arbitrage, there were two days out of the 10 in which you might have lost money, a maximum of $162.50 on January 3 and $37.50 on the 15th. Who needs to work for a living with odds like that? Off-track betting doesn't pay off nearly as well.

There must be a fly in the ointment, you say? Well, there is, so don't rush off to put a second mortgage on your home to buy an exchange seat just yet. Remember, those contracts you've been racing from post to pillar, or phone to pit, to buy and sell simultaneously—or, to spare wear and tear on your heart and legs, have your henchman standing at one of those locations to do half of the job—must either be carried to their maturity, involving charges on the financing discussed above, or else unwound at an opportune time. Either way, the filet mignon profits start, if you will excuse the expression, to get eaten away. Your friendly banker, however much she may like you and remember your children's birthdays, did not persuade her top management to get into Class B arbitrage financing for the fun of it. And the higher interest rates are, the greater the cost of carrying contracts to maturity becomes and the smaller the profits on the arbitrage become.

Should you have elected to unwind both positions before the delivery date, you'd immediately realize that the relationship which worked to your advantage going in, selling at the higher price and buying at the lower, is now reversed. Thus, after placing the Swiss franc arbitrage on January 4, your arbitrage trading account with the bank reflects a breathtaking profit of $1,012.50 per contract. But when you unwind at the appropriate rates on January 7, $950 of that goes right back into the market, leaving you with a less-than-princely gain on the deal of $62.50.

$$0.6449 - 0.6525 = -76 \times \$12.50 = -\$950$$

It's a profit, to be sure, but one that is more befitting a Burger King and a Miller Lite than the aforementioned menu.

All of which puts us back to the old and rather tiresome Horatio Alger moral that there ain't no easy way to make a buck—mark, pound, yen, or what you will. Watching the numbers and beating the crowd to the phone is still the only way to make a living as an arbitrageur.

Chapter 12

Foreign exchange exposure— what it is and how it's measured

THERE WOULD BE NO FORWARD MARKET in foreign exchange, either between banks or on futures exchanges, were it not for the need of companies to cover the risk of financial losses that arises from their transacting business in currencies other than their own. Foreign exchange exposure can lead to profits as well as to losses. But no one looks a gift horse in the mouth. It's the pig in the poke that they're worried about.

Foreign exchange risk is, so long as we're in the mood to coin fresh phrases, a twin-edged sword. There is the risk of being long—owning or contracting to receive—a currency that is liable to depreciate in relation to one's own. The reverse risk is that of being short, which is owing or otherwise having a liability in an appreciating currency. Forward covering is a standard technique to hedge such risks, either by selling for future delivery a depreciation-prone currency or buying a rising one. To explain such maneuvers, most textbooks that deal with international trade and finance include one or more examples of an exporter, say, selling forward X amount of currency Y for delivery in Z months' time to offset the risk of receiving payment in a depreciated currency. Unfortunately, most of these examples are vastly oversimplified, merely providing the barest bones of a

225

hedging situation. We shall, to be sure, concoct a few examples of our own, but only as models with which to treat some of the complex problems that arise when the various currencies that pass through an international company's trade and financial accounts change in their relative values.

Given the size, scope, and variety of the business of today's giant multinational corporations, it is a task of some magnitude simply to determine how, where, and to what extent throughout the world these companies are exposed to exchange rate risk. That is the subject of this chapter. The one following takes up the ensuing problem of how this exposure may best be reduced, or else managed in such a way that is profitable to the company.

Figure 12–1
IBM's worldwide operations

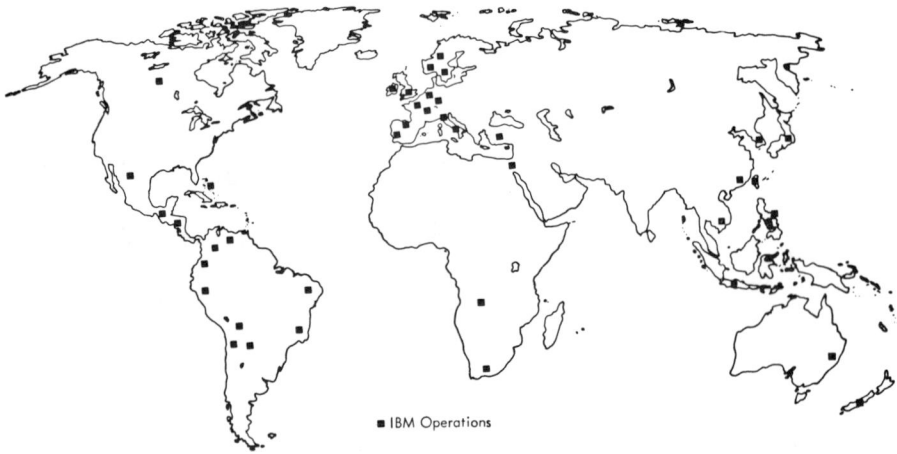

■ IBM Operations

Three classifications

Accepting the fact that a currency can depreciate or appreciate (and with flexible exchange rates it may do both within a relatively brief period) there are three general classifications of exchange rate risk: accounting risk, economic risk, and (stock) market risk. *Accounting risk* is, logically enough, the effect which exchange fluctuations may have on a company's financial statements. It is in turn further divided into *translation risk* and *transaction risk*. The former is the possibility that currency fluctuations may cause changes in the valuation of various items in a company's balance sheet—cash, accounts receivable, short and long-term debt, and so on—from one accounting period to the next. Transaction risk occurs when the parent company or any of its subsidiaries or affiliates abroad contracts to make or receive payment in a currency other than its own. One of those corporate entities, and possibly the entire group when their respective statements are consolidated, is subject to financial loss (or gain) if the applicable exchange rate changes before the contracted payment is made.

Economic risk is a broader concept than accounting risk, in the sense that it includes many operating and financial consequences of exchange rate fluctuations that will not appear, initially at least, on a company's balance sheet or income statement. A growing number of corporate treasurers have come to the conclusion that economic risk is for them the most important type of exchange rate risk because it is the most far reaching. The third sort of exchange risk, *market risk,* is the possibility that a company's stockholders and the investment community at large may react unfavorably (and perhaps sell their stock) if reported earnings decline as a result of untoward exchange rate movements. Some investors may become disenchanted by currency-induced changes in earnings per share, where others may simply shrug them off as an unavoidable cost of doing business abroad.

These several types of exchange risk are not necessarily compatible, in the sense that the appropriate action to reduce one will always have a limiting effect on the others. It may in fact serve to increase them. For example, a company may succeed through its use of forward cover and other techniques in maintaining a rising trend of earnings, to the satisfaction of its stockholders and of security analysts; but as a consequence, may incur negative economic effects that could prove to be more harmful over the long run than a less impressive near-term earnings record. The firm's first task, then, is to ascertain which of the exchange risks cited above is potentially the most damaging in its case, and only then to shape a protective strategy on the basis of that determination. Far from being confined to the specific area of foreign exchange, such a determination will of necessity affect other spheres of corporate activity, including cash management, short-term borrowing, financial reporting, declaration or repatriation of subsidiary dividends, and direct long-term investments.

Translation and transaction risk

Examining each of these concepts in greater detail, transaction risk is perhaps easier to understand than translation risk because it is the more visible of the two. It arises whenever the parent company or any of its subsidiaries undertakes a commitment to pay or to receive at a future date funds that will be denominated in a currency other than the one in which the parent customarily transacts its business. Since it is the intention of the corporate entity concerned to exchange its domestic currency for the foreign currency of payment when that payment is due, or else upon its receipt to convert the foreign currency into its own, it will not know the rate of exchange until the actual conversion of funds is made. Just suppose, for the sake of our first action-packed example, that IBM's German subsidiary booked an account receivable of £500,000 on June 15 when the spot £/DM rate was 4.0. The receivable initially would have been entered at DM 2 million, but by September 15 the pound had suffered a 10 percent depreciation against the Deutsche mark, making the receivable worth in that latter currency only DM 1.8 million. The transaction loss to the German subsidiary would have been accounted for as follows:

          June 15 £/DM = 4.00   £500,000 = DM 2,000,000
          September 15 £/DM = 3.60   £500,000 = DM 1,800,000
                                         Transaction loss = (DM 200,000)

The £500,000 exposure therefore led to a transaction loss to the German subsidiary of DM 200,000. The same type of exposure also occurs at the level of the parent company. In either instance, the liquidity of the corporate entity to which the receivable is due will be directly affected because ultimately it may get more or less in its own currency than was indicated by the spot exchange rate when the receivable was initially booked.

Translation exposure affects only the parent company. It arises when the financial statements of the entire group are consolidated and the results are expressed in the domestic currency of the parent. Proceeding with the above example, from the viewpoint of IBM, the receivable carried on its German subsidiary's books on June 15 at DM 2 million was worth in dollars on that date $1,200,000. But by September 15 spot $/DM had declined to 0.5600, reducing the value of the receivable in dollars to $1,008,000. The accounting result was a translation loss of $192,000 reported as:

          June 15 $/DM = 0.6000   DM 2 million   = $1,200,000
          September 15 $/DM = 0.5600   DM 1.8 million = $1,008,000
                                         Translation loss = ($ 192,000)

Translation exposure doesn't arise in the case of intercompany accounts that exist within the multinational group, such as an account payable owed by the parent to one of its subsidiaries. Since upon consolidation the parent is at the same time long and short in the same currency, by the same amount and for the same maturity, the two equal and contrasting exposures are balanced and are therefore neutralized.

Bookkeeping treatments

The bookkeeping treatment of transaction and translation exposure varies from country to country, and even between firms in the same country, depending upon the accounting convention observed by the parent company. The three methods most commonly employed in the United States and in Western Europe in the past have been (1) the closing rate method, (2) the working capital method, and (3) the historic rate method.

Its choice of accounting method will, like the firm's definition of exchange risk, determine in large measure how that risk is to be managed. The closing rate method translates all of the parent's and subsidiaries' foreign currency items at the spot rates prevailing as of the closing date of the group's consolidated balance sheet. The rationale underlying this method is that it is most equitable to treat all items alike, including liquid assets, long-term debt, and fixed plant. The closing rate method is the easiest of the three to understand and apply. The result of including all of the group's assets and liabilities at their closing rates is that only the net equity of each subsidiary and the foreign currency positions of the parent firm are exposed, inasmuch as all of the other items are balanced out. The practice of carrying the group's fixed assets at the current spot rate, rather than at their historic cost, is held to provide a more realistic appraisal of the current earning power of those assets.

Yet, even though the closing rate method is the one most commonly used in the United Kingdom, and is widely followed on the Continent as well, a growing number of corporate treasurers in those areas have begun to question the validity of its assumptions. Their primary objection is that cash or short-term investments carried in a foreign currency do not logically entail the same degree of risk as do fixed assets denominated in the same currency. By the same token, so the argument runs, a subsidiary company's short-term debt should not be viewed in the same light as should its long-term debt or bonds issued in that currency. Moreover, translating all types of assets and liabilities at the same exchange rate doesn't conform with accounting practices that do not pertain to foreign exchange.

Table 12–1
German subsidiary balance sheet—closing rate method

	DM (000)
Cash and accounts receivable	1,200
Inventory	1,350
Fixed assets	1,050
Total assets	3,600
Current liabilities	1,350
Long-term debt	750
Net worth	1,500
	3,600

Table 12–1 depicts the closing rate method as it is applied to a German subsidiary balance sheet where the items were booked at $/DM 0.6000. If $/DM had declined to 0.5600 by the statement's closing date, total assets, liabilities, and net worth would be restated to reflect the change.

The working capital method, also known as the current/noncurrent method, has been the foreign exchange accounting convention most frequently followed in the United States, though less so abroad. This method segregates for the purpose of translation consolidated balance sheet items on the basis of their maturity, with one year the customary dividing line. Assets and liabilities slated to be received or paid out within the current year are treated according to the closing rate method. Fixed assets, depreciation, long-term debt, and other items of longer than one year's maturity are translated at the exchange rates in effect when they were booked originally.

The use of two different rates introduces an element of discretion into the computation of exchange exposure. The purpose of doing so is to distinguish between those short-term balance sheet items whose actual value does in fact vary with exchange rates, and items such as fixed plant and long-term debt, which do not. Their separation does not imply that the short-term items are any more or less subject to exchange risk than are the long-term ones, but it does acknowledge in an accounting sense that different maturities should as a practical matter be dealt with differently.[1] The working capital method is intended to provide financial officers with a more realistic framework within which to make their foreign exchange hedging decisions. It was the method endorsed by the American Institute of Certified Public Accountants Committee on Accounting Procedure, until new guidelines were introduced in 1975. The German subsidiary's balance sheet is restated in Table 12–2 to reflect the working capital method.

Table 12–2
German subsidiary balance sheet—working capital method

	DM (000s)	Items translated at closing rate (000s)
Cash and accounts receivable	1,200	1,200
Inventory	1,350	1,350
Fixed assets	1,050	
Total assets	3,600	2,550
Current liabilities	1,350	1,350
Long-term debt	750	
Net worth	1,500	
	3,600	1,350

Translation loss on DM assets of 2550 × 0.5600: $1428
Translation gain on DM liabilities of 1350 × 0.5600: $756

The net translation loss that would be reported by the parent corporation under the working capital method would be the difference between the loss on assets and the gain on liabilities or $672,000.

The historic rate, or monetary/nonmonetary accounting method, is another hybrid approach. The physical assets of the parent company and its subsidiaries are translated at their historic rates, while the financial items in the consolidated statement are translated at the closing spot rate. The justification for this approach is that the exchange rate, or the currency for that matter, in which a subsidiary's plant and equipment were purchased

---

[1] That treatment also applies to the portion of long-term debt due to mature within one year, and is included for the purposes of exposure management in the working capital segment of the balance sheet.

years earlier has little or no bearing on the group's current financial condition. Long-term debt, on the other hand, is booked as a financial item at the closing rate. The latter is a critical item that can represent the group's largest single element of foreign exchange exposure. Including such debt in the consolidated balance sheet at the closing rate can result in extremely large translation losses, whether it is carried by the parent company or by one of its subsidiaries. A problem created by the widespread use of this method is that it increases substantially the accounting exposure of firms which have a high proportion of foreign currency-denominated debt in relation to companies which do not. That exposure can in turn have highly adverse effects on the current earnings of the former group, as a number of U.S.-based multinationals that undertook heavy Swiss franc and Deutsche mark borrowings during the early 1970s discovered to the dismay of management and investors alike.[2]

Another difficulty with this method arises from the fact that some items are not strictly monetary or nonmonetary in nature, but overlap the two categories. Inventory is a leading example. Some firms take the position that, as a replenishable commodity, inventory is as exposed to exchange rate risk as is any purely financial item, and should be so treated. Other firms, pointing to the physical nature of inventory, disagree. A similar disagreement arises over the appropriate accounting treatment of foreign currency-denominated stock and bonds. Investments in such long-term marketable securities may with justification be translated at either the appropriate historic or closing rate.

Table 12–3
German subsidiary balance sheet—monetary/nonmonetary method

	DM (000s)	Items translated at closing rate (000 s)
Cash and accounts receivable	1,200	1,200
Inventory	1,350	
Fixed assets	1,050	
Total assets	3,600	1,200
Current liabilities	1,350	1,350
Long-term debt	750	750
Net worth	1,500	
	3,600	2,100

---

[2]Among the companies whose current earnings were adversely affected by foreign currency borrowings made a decade or more earlier were Firestone Tire & Rubber Company, R. J. Reynolds Industries, Inc., and Burlington Industries, Inc. All were faced with repaying Swiss franc or Deutsche mark loans at exchange rates substantially different than those in effect when the loans were incurred. See "Dollar's Decline Spurs Many Firms to Avoid Deals in Foreign Funds," *The Wall Street Journal*, December 1, 1977, p. 1.

Translation loss on subsidiary's

DM cash and accounts receivable of 1,200 × 0.5600: $672

Translation gain on current and

Long-term liabilities of (1,350 + 750) × 0.5600: $1,176

Under the monetary/nonmonetary method there is a net gain on translation of $1,176,000 minus $672,000, or $504,000.

Translating income

The translation of income is a more straightforward matter, subject as it is to more universally accepted accounting principles. The controlling factor here is the extent to which a subsidiary's income is consolidated with that of the entire group. If the parent company directly owns over 50 percent of a foreign subsidiary or affiliate, that entity's entire income, along with all of its balance sheet items that are not of an intercompany nature, are according to U.S. practice brought into the consolidated statement of the group. If the foreign entity is 20 percent to 50 percent owned, a proportionate share of its income for the accounting period is consolidated. An ownership interest of less than 20 percent may be carried on the parent's books as an investment, in which case its share of the subsidiary's income is remitted to it in the form of dividends. In the event of full or partial consolidation, a foreign subsidiary's income is accrued over the course of a year and translated at the average of spot rates at each month-end, a simple method of hedging month-by-month exchange rate fluctuations in and of itself.

A number of multinational corporations have in the past established special accounting reserves as a method of handling foreign exchange gains and losses. One argument in favor of such reserves is that they provide a means by which firms with different amounts of foreign currency-denominated debt may be regarded on a comparable basis. The use by U.S.-based corporations of special foreign exchange reserves was disallowed in 1975, however, by the Financial Accounting Standards Board's *Statement No. 8*, "Accounting for the Translation of Foreign Currency Transactions and Foreign Currency Statements." The document, which together with its interpretations became known throughout the world simply as *FASB 8*, includes the following provisions:

1. All U.S. nonfinancial companies must adhere to uniform accounting methods in booking their foreign exchange-related transactions and in consolidating subsidiary statements.
2. Special reserves created for the purpose of transferring the income effects of exchange gains and losses into another accounting period are disallowed.

3 Companies must value all forward and futures contracts assumed to hedge foreign exchange exposure as of the statement's closing date. Moreover, any profits or losses incurred on such contracts must be included as income for the accounting period in which they occurred. The only exceptions permitted are those contracts which exactly match in amount and maturity the foreign exchange exposure they are intended to cover.

The Accounting Board therefore required that any gains or losses on outstanding futures or forward contracts, other than those that perfectly offset an existing or pending foreign exchange position, must be included in the determination of current income. The practical effect of this ruling is that contracts which are bought or sold as hedges are to be accounted for as transactions apart from the exposed currency positions they were meant to offset.

FASB 8 imposed upon U.S.-based multinational corporations a new accounting convention—the temporal method—which differs somewhat from the monetary/nonmonetary or historic method. This method of foreign exchange accounting provides that those items carried in financial statements at past prices be translated at historic exchange rates, while those that are carried at current or future prices—forward contracts are an example of the latter—be converted at closing spot rates.

More troublesome has been the provision that companies show all foreign exchange gains or losses, whether they are realized by the close of the accounting period or not, in their current income statements. Widespread dissatisfaction with this rule arose almost immediately among corporate financial officers as foreign exchange fluctuations prompted unanticipated and sometimes inordinate changes in their companies' operating earnings. In the case of International Telephone & Telegraph Corporation, for example, strength in the U.S. dollar during the first quarter of 1980 was in large part responsible for the 64 percent increase in ITT's earnings per share for that period, as compared with the comparable earnings figure for the first quarter of 1979. ITT estimated that without the accounting treatment stipulated by *FASB 8,* its operating earnings per share would only have risen about 4 percent. Because of such extreme earnings distortions, the corporation's executive vice president and comptroller criticized the rule as being "so bad they couldn't have made it much worse."[3]

Similar criticism expressed by many corporate financial officers as well as by a number of accountants themselves prompted the Financial Accounting Standards Board in 1980 to reconsider *FASB 8* and to propose certain revisions which would mitigate its alleged inequities.

The Accounting Standards Steering Committee of the U.K.'s Institute of Chartered Accountants issues from time to time statements of recommended

---

[3]Tom Herman, "Accounting Body Seeks to Change Currencies Rule," *The Wall Street Journal,* April 11, 1980, p. 12.

accounting practice. The committee has not released to date a circular comparable to *FASB 8*. It did however, prepare in 1975 a study paper entitled "Extraordinary Items and Prior Year Adjustments," in which it proposed that translation gains and losses be carried directly into the profit and loss accounts, rather than being treated as extraordinary items.

The conventions described above are variously observed by European-based multinationals as well. Companies in a number of European countries are not required by statute or decree to consolidate subsidiary statements or to issue public reports to the extent that their U.S. and U.K. counterparts are. Balance sheets and income statements are consolidated for internal use, however, and the closing rate is the method most commonly used in these private reports.

Economic risk

The economic exposure to which a company with multicurrency dealings is subject is a good deal broader and more difficult to define in quantitative terms than are the transaction and translation risks we've discussed thus far. At issue here are the effects which immediate and prospective exchange rate movements may have on a company's future business, taken over both the short and long range. These effects are first reflected in a firm's current liquidity and operations, and ultimately on its financial structure and profit margins. All of them fall under the heading of economic exposure.

An example of economic exposure is a transaction or translation loss which impairs a company's liquidity, and which in turn affects its operations and profitability. Others would be situations in which an appreciating currency hampers a company's export sales, or the reverse, depreciation, jeopardizes its profits. A multinational company may have decided to establish a subsidiary in a particular country to take advantage of such favorable economic conditions as a positive trade balance, a low inflation rate, an ample labor supply at low and stable wage levels, and a moderate corporate tax rate. The positive features that first attracted the corporation to that country may slide with the passage of time into negative circumstances. The balance of payments could go into a deficit, in which case the rate of inflation would most likely rise, carrying wages and taxes up with it. As a consequence of this economic deterioration the domestic currency in all likelihood would depreciate against those of healthier countries. The subsidiary may be forced to raise the prices of its finished products, particularly if they contain a large proportion of imported raw materials. Credit conditions in the local money market and banking system would become tighter under such conditions, with interest rates climbing on whatever funds that were available for lending. It is conceivable that price controls would be imposed, making it impossible for the subsidiary to recoup its rising costs through price increases, at the same time that the labor pool is drying up and the wage level is rising.

These changes do not immediately appear to be directly associated with exchange rate movement, and are not reported in the firm's financial statements as such. Moreover, as was observed in an earlier chapter, it usually is impossible to ascertain which of these events are the causes and which are the effects.[4] Even so, there can be no question but that such developments are critical to the well being, if not the very existence, of the subsidiary, and are therefore of vital importance to the parent corporation itself. Clearly, this type of exposure goes beyond the current balance sheet and income statement, and may not even be directly linked to a particular foreign exchange gain or loss.

One of the areas that is the most susceptible to economic exposure are the intercompany accounts within a multinational group. Yet, that is the segment most often ignored in exposure management because of the prevailing belief that transactions between a corporate parent and its subsidiaries, or among the subsidiaries themselves, cancel each other out in consolidation. But even though no net exposure is thought to exist, such transactions can be of major consequence to the subsidiaries that are directly affected. To make the matter even more perplexing, the most effective strategy to counteract a particular economic exposure, once it has been identified as such, may not be the action that is called for under any of the three accounting methods described earlier. The monetary/nonmonetary method might, for example, indicate an extensive and costly hedging program to neutralize an anticipated depreciation, while the economic view of exposure would encourage increased investment in the country affected to capitalize on the additional export opportunities such a devaluation would logically create. It may, under certain conditions, be possible to fashion a strategy which takes both kinds of exposure into account, using the temporal accounting method to pinpoint the shorter-term transaction and translation risks, and the economic view to focus on longer-range issues along the lines of those mentioned above.

A good many corporate treasurers agree to the need to take the latter, longer view in evaluating the probable effect of future exchange rate movements on their companies' operations and financial condition. But most of them admit that as a practical matter they have more than they can comfortably handle to stay abreast of developments within the customary three- to six-month time frame. They may speculate on the one-year outlook when there is a major financing or direct investment that would entail substantial exposure. For most of them, going beyond one year is just so much blue-skying.

---

[4]Readers may refer to the earlier discussion of international transmission of inflation in Chapter 7, pp. 127–129.

The reporting system

Whether a firm chooses to plan on the basis of its accounting exposure, its perceived economic exposure, or both, the first step in identifying that exposure is to devise a reporting system to collect and monitor the relevant data, and to fit it within the company's existing system of financial planning. In view of the magnitude of the exposure risk that is all too often involved, a surprising number of multinational corporations have not yet developed an organized approach to identifying and evaluating this risk on a systematic basis.   Most of the required information is usually already at hand within the group's existing reporting and accounting structure; it is largely a matter of locating and bringing it to bear on the exposure issue.   Conventional corporate accounting systems, however, are usually static, historical, and oriented to assets, liabilities, and income.   As such, they lack the timeliness, detail, and anticipatory quality needed to manage exchange exposure effectively in the face of today's rate volatility.   The systems that are in place for reporting from the subsidiaries to the accounting and treasury departments of the parent company as a matter of course may omit much of the intercompany information that is necessary in assessing the group's overall economic exposure.

The information required for an export/import firm differs from that which is needed for a manufacturing/service corporation.   The former type of business is primarily concerned with the effects of exchange rate changes on its liquidity, accounts receivables, import payables, and possibly certain foreign currency-denominated borrowings, as well as on its income statements.   The emphasis is on exposure from import and export orders booked and grouped according to currency, amount, and maturity.   In the case of a large, decentralized trading firm organized by products or divisions, the hazard exists that the firm's net exposure in each currency is not identified, and that the appropriate covering action would not be taken in time to avoid substantial losses.

The reporting problem is greater and more complex when it comes to multinational operating companies.   Corporations need in such cases to identify as closely as possible the position of each subsidiary, and consequently that of the entire group with respect to each currency in which they deal.   Balance sheets as well as reports and forecasts by each subsidiary should identify those items that are denominated in that subsidiary's domestic currency, and those that are for its foreign currencies.   That distinction is often overlooked in the process of consolidation.

Companies may elect to list their exposed positions by country or by currency.   Though the end results of the two methods of computation are, or should be, the same, they have different organizational implications. The country-by-country approach is the outgrowth of a decentralized management structure, which gives subsidiary managers wide latitude in dealing with their local exposure problems.   The currency breakdown implies a centralized structure, where the control resides and the major decisions are taken at the treasury level of the parent.

The matter of timing also entails some choices. Quarterly consolidation of subsidiary statements is still practiced by some companies, but monthly reporting has become the norm, and is in fact the minimum needed for satisfactory exposure control. Even when monthly statements are prepared at the subsidiary level, ordinary delays in forwarding them to the parent make them immediately dated for the purpose of controlling exposure risk. To keep corporate headquarters as current as possible, "flash" summaries of exposed items and other pertinent data are wired from the subsidiaries as frequently as may be required.

The critical subject of exchange rate forecasting was discussed at considerable length in Chapter 10, where we reached the conclusion that, under the turbulent conditions that have prevailed over the past decade, such forecasting yields highly problematical results at best. Even so, to define a hedging strategy on the basis of present exchange rates, let alone past ones, seriously will hamper the effectiveness of the strategy at the outset. It is important to have some projected rates in mind, even if they are admittedly little more than educated guesses.

Monitoring economic risk

In the area of economic exposure, a number of variables should be subjected to continuous review, including most of the exchange rate determinants discussed in Part Two of this book. To reiterate an earlier point, it is as important to consider factors which do not appear in the consolidated statements as it is those which do. The more far-reaching and complex a company's international business becomes, the more difficult it gets to estimate its future exposure, either by country or by currency. But when their limitations are understood, a series of forecasts can aid the corporate treasury section in estimating the magnitude and likely direction of change in the company's exposure by currency. From the monthly reports that are normally submitted to corporate headquarters, the treasury section should be able to project:

1. The present balance sheet position of the group, both by subsidiary and by currency.
2. The balance sheet position in the next accounting period, again by subsidiary and by currency.
3. The expected income and dividend stream of the group by the same breakdowns as above.
4. The estimated economic exposure of the group.

Table 12–4 is a summary of such a group forecast performed by currency for two upcoming closing dates, as compared with the most recent actual result. The indicated forecasts, expressed in dollars as the home currency of the U.S. parent, represent the net long position in each currency of exposed assets over exposed liabilities or, in parentheses, the net short positions of liabilities over assets if such happens to be the case. A similar format may be used in forecasting income flows.

Table 12–4
Group exposure report by currency exposed assets over (under) exposed liabilities ($ million equivalent)

	Actual 12/31/79	Estimated 6/30/80	Estimated 12/31/80
Deutsche mark	$ 6.9	$ 5.7	$ 3.9
Dutch guilder	(4.9)	(4.9)	1.5
British pound	(7.4)	(3.4)	(5.2)
French franc	2.7	1.5	3.6

A supporting calculation is a ratio analysis by currency of each item in the group balance sheet. This classification is performed for each subsidiary company in the group in conjunction with the net exposure computation summarized in Table 12–4, and should bring into closer focus the currency risks incurred by the subsidiary and for the entire group on a consolidated basis:

Table 12–5
Working capital breakdown by currency German subsidiary

Percentage	Deutsche mark	Dollar	Pound	Dutch guilder	French franc
Cash	90	5	0	5	0
Short-term investment	100	0	0	0	0
Accounts receivable	75	10	5	5	5
Accounts payable	50	20	10	10	10

Combining the working capital percentage breakdown summarized in Table 12–5 with projected changes in the group's liquidity and that of each subsidiary will bring a clearer overview of currency risks foreseeable over the coming accounting period.

A multinational corporation that has exchange exposure in a variety of countries and currencies should prepare up to seven reports in maintaining an effective information collection and evaluation system. Not all companies will adopt the format and sequence suggested below, but some combination of the following reports is a precondition for identifying and controlling the accounting and economic risks described in this chapter.

1. Detailed balance sheets should be obtained from each of the group's subsidiary companies on a monthly basis, including all intercompany positions and a breakdown by currency as was illustrated in Table 12–4.
2. Balance sheet forecasts projecting the latest reported figures for each subsidiary, again on a currency-by-currency basis.
3. Separate exchange exposure reports may be prepared either as substitutes for or as supplements to the monthly balance sheets. Outstanding futures or forward contracts are also entered on the exposure reports to identify those exposed positions which are fully or partially hedged.
4. Reports prepared on a cash-flow basis are another alternative to the subsidiary balance sheets. The cash flow reports identify the specific sources of the subsidiaries' accounting risks, and provide a framework for measuring that exposure.
5. Hedging reports are required, whether or not monthly balance sheets are prepared. These reports list each hedged position by currency, amount, maturity, and, of course, rate. They may be included in the balance sheet report or prepared as a separate form. As was noted earlier in this chapter, such a breakdown by contract was required under *FASB 8*, and the gains or losses thus reported had to be included in the consolidated profit and loss statement unless the outstanding contracts matched exactly the exposed positions they were intended to cover.
6. Cash forecasts are needed to identify the liquidity positions of the subsidiaries, and thereby to provide further insight into the economic exposure of each subsidiary.
7. Inventory evaluations are undertaken as an additional check on economic exposure. The customary practice is for a subsidiary to divide its inventory positions between those that involve foreign exchange exposure and those that do not.

An operating multinational corporation has more flexibility in managing its exchange exposure through adjustments in the currency, timing, and to some extent the price of transactions within the group than most export/import firms do. As viewed from the perspective of each subsidiary, any intercompany adjustments of this sort would conceivably work to the detriment of one and possibly both of the individual entities that are directly affected. There are, however, regulatory and accounting constraints on such adjustments which make them a controversial aspect of exposure management.

Time frames and predictions

The object of these admittedly involved reporting and measuring procedures is to give the multinational corporate treasurer and his staff the information they require to assess the likely impact of potential exchange rate changes on the group's finances and, ultimately, on its operations and earnings. In addition to their in-house economics research departments, the large companies may draw on the foreign exchange trading departments of the major dealer banks and, for a fee, the specialized forecasting services that were described in Chapter 10. As was noted there, the three primary analytical approaches these forecasting firms take—judgmental, econometric, and technical—have produced varying degrees of success, and have each shown themselves to be best suited to predicting exchange rate movements within a particular time frame. The approach that proves to be most useful to a corporation, and which will in turn likely determine the type of forecasting service it retains, if any, depends mainly upon the time period with which the firm is most concerned.

The time horizon that is of greatest concern to most corporate treasurers is the one extending three to six months from the present. That period happens to coincide with the one within which most export/import transactions are conducted, and the term for which trade credit is usually made available. The extended horizon, up to one year ahead, anticipates exchange rate movements which will be reflected in the next balance sheet closing. Relatively few corporate financial decisions with foreign exchange implications—they usually involve direct investment in plant and equipment in a foreign country or the sale of foreign currency-denominated bonds—go beyond the three-to-six-month and one-year horizons. It is debatable in any event whether exchange rate considerations per se are accorded very much weight in arriving at truly long-range foreign investment decisions. In such a case the underlying economic and political conditions in the proposed country of investment should be the dominant considerations, although the currency of that country will of course reflect such factors. Under the monetary/nonmonetary accounting convention, long-term debt denominated in a foreign currency is a significant exposure item in that such debt is booked at the closing rate for each accounting period.

The fact that exchange rate movements up to a three-month time horizon, and even beyond, are notoriously difficult if not impossible to predict points up the need for a corporation to apply effective exposure management procedures. Given the alternatives within the uncertain exchange rate environment of the past decade—and very likely that of the coming one as well—of covering exposed positions or of leaving them uncovered, there is in fact no realistic choice but to cover them by one or more of the means to be discussed in the following chapter. Despite the difficulties involved, and the high incidence of error of most short-term forecasts, there is a great deal at stake. The task, even more so than during the relatively placid Bretton Woods days, remains one of estimating the most probable direction and magnitude of future exchange rate movements, and of preparing a strategy to neutralize the adverse consequences, both accounting and economic, of such movements.

Given the demonstrated fallibility of point forecasts of exchange rates over both the near and long-term, firms are disposed toward tailoring their exposure strategies and projections to target ranges of future spot rates, and then making a further determination of the relative likelihood of the specific rates that fall within the estimated range matching the actual spot rate at the stipulated time horizon. The histogram in Figure 12–2 illustrates such an evaluation of projected $/DM spot rates three months from the date of the forecast. Within a range between 0.5200 and 0.6000, the forecast assesses a 30 percent likelihood that spot $/DM will fall between 0.5400 and 0.5600 after three months, 25 percent that it will be between 0.5600 and 0.5800, and so on. That is about as guarded a projection as it's possible to make, but it does provide the corporation's exposure management group with a quantitative framework for estimating the magnitude of exchange rate risk with which it is, according to its best estimate, likely to be confronted.

Figure 12–2
Histogram of projected $/DM spot rates within three months of forecast

Table 12–6
Effects on present exposure of projected exchange rate changes

Currency	Projected range	Percent expected maximum gain	Maximum gain (loss) ($000)
British pound	2.24–2.26	1– (2)	150
Canadian dollar	.8450–.8550	0– (1)	(55)
Deutsche mark	.5450–.5600	2–+3	120
French franc	.2000–.2050	1– (3)	(6)
Italian lira	.0950–.1050	0– (10)	(65)
Japanese yen	.4900–.4950	0– (50)	90

Within such a framework of estimated exposure, Table 12–6 shows the translation of special currency forecasts, whether they are of the pinpoint or target range variety, into the estimated gains or losses that would accrue in the company's various net exposed positions, should the projected exchange rates come to pass. The table summarizes the translation effects on the group's consolidated statements at what are from its point of view the best and worst of the projected rates for each currency in which it has exposure. The supposition is that in each case the actual result will fall somewhere between those extremes. The specific hedging program which the company may choose to initiate in response to these possibilities—and they are at this point no more than that—will in turn be determined by a number of factors. Among them are the cost of forward cover, top management's attitude toward such covering—namely does the act of hedging or the exposure itself comprise what it considers the greater risk—and the possible effects of intercompany adjustments within the group.

Chapter

13

Hedging foreign exchange exposure: Options, strategies, and tactics

THE CHAPTER JUST ENDED told more about foreign exchange exposure than most readers probably ever cared to know. Admittedly, it hardly makes for exhilarating reading. Not even a Harold Robbins could make a discussion of accounting methods seem exciting, sexy—we at least managed to get the word in—and all the other things that readers usually enjoy. That is, no doubt, why Robbins chooses to write about something else. But our bed is made—of thorns, though, it sometimes seems—and lie in it we must. Covering foreign exchange exposure through the purchase or sale of forward and futures contracts and other techniques is not much more titillating, but we can at least try in this chapter to do the topic justice in a less irksome fashion.

To begin, the expressions *covering* and *hedging* require some clarification. The broader term, *hedging,* usually refers in the context of foreign exchange to any one of a number of methods by which companies may reduce or eliminate exposed positions in one or more foreign currencies. *Covering,* in its strictest sense, applies specifically to the use of futures or forward contracts to accomplish that end. Aspiring to a relaxed, or what has become known as a "laid back" attitude—though that is probably not the best posture to assume on a bed of thorns—we shall here employ the two terms interchangeably. No nitpickers, we!

Fluctuation insurance

A company's purpose in initiating a hedging—or a covering—strategy is to reduce the variations in its earnings and financial condition that can arise from dealing in currencies other than its home-grown variety. If a U.S. aircraft manufacturer, for example, books an order to sell a widebodied jet to Air France for the French franc equivalent of $10 million, it wants to be assured of receiving $10 million upon delivery of the plane, whatever may happen to the $/FF rate by the payment date. Expanding the example beyond a single transaction, if worldwide sales for the aircraft company amount to $1 billion in a given year denominated in a variety of currencies, the company wants to count on actually receiving $1 billion after all of the foreign currency payments are made and converted into dollars.

It is often held that hedging foreign exchange exposure amounts to taking out an insurance policy against losses arising from exchange rate changes. But apart from referring to insurance in a very general sense as a protective measure, the use of a futures contract or any other covering device does not constitute insurance in the most commonly understood meaning of the word. Whereas an insurance policy represents a small ownership share in a pool organized by persons and companies that are subject to a common risk for the benefit of those among them who actually fall prey to that risk, there is no pooling of funds or sharing of risk in the case of hedging foreign exchange exposure. In the latter situation, everyone involved looks out for himself as best he can. To be sure, the premium (or discount) on a futures contract represents, according to some interpretations, the cost of hedging an exposed foreign exchange position, but here again any similarity between that and an insurance premium lies mainly in the choice of terminology.

A company's selection of a hedging strategy and of the particular technique with which it seeks to implement that strategy depends in the first instance upon the type of business in which the firm is engaged, and in the second on the corporate objectives of its senior management. The primary objective of most companies in the latter regard is the stabilization and maximization of cash flow. Ancillary goals may include the preservation of the translation value of the firm's foreign-held assets and maintenance of its sales or market share. Management that seeks to avoid all risks unconnected with its conventional production and sales functions would be prone to cover its transaction and translation risks completely and at all times.   Other companies may adopt a more aggressive, semispeculative attitude that prompts them to regard exchange rate changes as profit opportunities as well as risks.   They would tend toward a more selective hedging strategy in seeking to capitalize on these perceived opportunities. In other words, they are of a mind to become foreign exchange traders of a special sort when they think that the time is opportune.

Risks and strategies

Export/import firms, inasmuch as they don't usually maintain fixed plant and other facilities or investments abroad, are almost exclusively concerned with transaction risk and typically seek to hedge all of their exposure of that type.   Exporters and importers are both upon occasion compelled, for marketing as well as other reasons, to invoice or to accept billing in currencies other than their own.   In either case, the firm is exposed to exchange rate changes between the time the orders are booked and their scheduled payment dates.   An exporter, say a French firm selling ball bearings to Fiat in Italy, for which it has agreed to be paid in lira, has the alternatives of selling the contracted amount of lira forward, or else engaging in some other type of hedging operation to avoid a loss (or the greater part thereof) should the lira depreciate relative to the French franc before the date Fiat contracted to pay the exporter for the ball bearings.   An importer may find himself in the opposite situation, namely that of having to pay a higher price for merchandise because the currency of payment appreciated prior to the settlement date.   Take the case of a U.S. importer of pork products from Germany (remember the pork war of 1979?),[1] who commits to pay in Deutsche marks.   He would be perfectly content to have the Deutsche mark decline versus the U.S. dollar before the payment date insofar as he'd profit from such a decline.   But the importer in the United States realizes that the mark could appreciate just as easily.   If that happened, the German pork price would rise in terms of dollars, making it advisable for him to buy marks forward to offset the deleterious effect such a rate appreciation would have on the projected profit on the transaction.

The latter consideration, the projected profit margin, is critical in determining whether a particular transaction should be hedged.   If the anticipated profit does not exceed the estimated hedging cost, chances are that the firm will elect to remain unhedged.

The typical exposure of a multinational group consisting of a parent company and a number of subsidiaries scattered throughout the world is more complex than that which is normally encountered by most export/import firms.   Instead of dealing with a series of one-shot transactions, the

---

[1]Chapter Nine, p. 177.

multinational operating firm must juggle a number of balls, so to speak, including various currencies, countries, transactions, and balance sheet exposures that are all up in the air at the same time. Under such circumstances, a multinational firm may discover that the cost of hedging all of the exchange risk, to which it is always subject, is prohibitive. In some instances, cover may not be obtainable at any price. A number of countries, many of those in South America, for example, do not have forward markets in foreign exchange, and such alternate hedging methods as are available may again be considered too costly in relation to the perceived risk. Given these conditions, a multinational company may not have any other choice but to adopt a strategy of selective hedging, or else resort to unconventional methods to obtain the desired protection.

In the face of such constraints, companies are likely to assess their exchange exposure on a currency-by-currency basis, weighing the estimated risks in terms of their domestic currencies against the costs of covering those risks if the facilities to do so are in fact available. Some firms may conclude that all exchange risks are worth covering insofar as possible, whatever the cost. Others may determine that, in view of the projected expense and management effort which a fully hedged policy would entail, they are better off only covering their transaction exposure. In the latter instance, management may elect to cover the company's estimated future cash flows as well, believing that approach is more economical than hedging potential translation gains or losses.

Hedging with futures

The primary thrust of this chapter, indeed of the entire book, is of course the hedging of exchange exposure through the purchase or sale of futures contracts for the same currency, in the same amount and of the same maturity as the position those contracts are intended to offset. The controlling words here are *same* and *offset*. In this respect the two standard definitions of a futures contract hedge, whatever the underlying commodity happens to be, are:

1. A futures contract position *equal* and *opposite* to an existing or pending position in the actual commodity.
2. The purchase or sale of futures contracts as *temporary substitutes* for contemplated cash (spot) positions.

Both definitions apply in hedging exchange exposure. Take the earlier example of the U.S. importer of German sausage, and assume that his commitment was to pay in Deutsche marks three months from the time he placed his order. The importer isn't obligated to convert dollars into marks until then, but he is open to the risk of the latter currency's appreciating if he does nothing in the meantime. Should that possibility occur, the longer he waits to cover and the higher the mark climbs versus the dollar, the more the bratwurst shipment will cost him in dollars when the date of reckoning arrives.   As in our prior examples concerning American aircraft and French ball bearings, the more the applicable exchange rate, in this case $/DM, moves against him, the smaller the importer's realized profit will be.

But, by buying three-month forward marks at the same time that he closes the bratwurst deal, the importer can fix the $/DM rate at which he'll convert dollars into marks at or about the date he is obligated to pay for the wurst. Relating this to our previous definitions, he is using the DM futures contracts as temporary substitutes for the actual marks with which he'll make payment in three months.   By buying DM contracts instead of waiting until the last moment to convert his dollars, he has determined in advance what his rate of conversion—the exchange rate—will be.   Regarding the equal and opposite definition, by purchasing the DM contracts the U.S. importer assumes a long futures position to offset the short spot mark position implicit in his commitment to pay his German sausage supplier.

The equal part of the definition is not as easy to satisfy as the opposite part.   One can be either short or long.   The only other possibility is to be short and long at the same time, which very simply is what this discussion is all about.   Whichever way the market moves, one side is making money and the other side is losing, so the net effect is a standoff.   But to achieve a total standoff, the two sides must be evenly matched.   Exchange traded futures contracts specify a standard currency amount.   Although interbank forward contracts are not of uniform size, they too tend to be made in round amounts.   Perfect matches are usually a matter of coincidence, therefore, but the relatively small futures contract size—such as DM 125,000 in the case of Deutsche marks—allows a reasonably close fit.

The bratwurst hedge

Let's say that the sausage contract called for the payment of DM 1 million. That's an awful lot of bratwurst, but imagine for the fun of it that Oktoberfest is just around the corner.   People eat (and drink) a lot then.   If that were the case, our hedge would work out very nicely because eight DM contracts would cover the million-mark commitment exactly.   But, if the bratwurst invoice came to DM 900,000, eight contracts would be too many; and they would be too few to cover a DM 1,100,000 commitment entirely.   Since a futures contract cannot be divided, the customary practice is to select the number of contracts that most nearly matches the actual commitment, and therefore to be somewhat underhedged or overhedged.   Let's keep our lives as simple as possible for now and stay with DM 1 million worth of premium bratwurst, granting us in our illustration, at least, the happy condition of being perfectly hedged.   There is an obligation to pay the sausage maker DM 1 million in three months, offset by eight long DM futures contracts calling for the delivery at that specified future date an equivalent number of Deutsche marks.

Now, all we have to worry about is the rate of exchange, our old friend $/DM, which is what the entire fuss is about to begin with. At what is then the $/DM spot rate of 0.6250, the importer calculates that at the converted dollar price of $625,000 (DM 1 million × 0.6250) he will be able to turn a tidy profit by feeding all of those hungry Oktoberfest celebrants in the United States. But he knows that he is limited for competitive reasons to a profit of 8 percent or $50,000. The best price he can expect to receive for all that sausage stateside is $675,000. The retail bratwurst peddlers won't pay any more, and the German supplier certainly won't accept less than his contracted DM 1 million if $/DM should rise in the meantime to, say, 0.6500. If that happens, the celebrants eat bratwurst, and the importer is left to eat a loss—or what would in this case be a reduced profit.

What will he do, as Karl Malden asks reproachfully in his TV commercials for American Express Travellers Checks, what *will* he do? The solution lies, not in buying travellers checks, but in going long eight DM contracts for three months' forward delivery. But, as we all discover sooner or later in life, there is no such thing as a free lunch—nor free sausage, nor free forward marks, for that matter. As we learned during our earlier discourse on forward rates, forward Deutsche marks are nearly always quoted at a premium over spot, at least over the past decade. Let's assume that at the time of our sausage fable 3-month $/DM is 0.6310. By buying forward at that rate, the sausage importer manages to fix his dollar price at $631,000, not at $625,000, and $6,000 of his projected $50,000 profit has already been expended to buy protection—not insurance—against the risk of further exchange rate loss. But rates haven't moved yet and the importer is already dipping into profits he hasn't yet received. Is such protection worth the cost, he asks himself?

The cost in this case is the amount of the forward premium to the time of the contract's maturity. It might, under different circumstances involving another currency, turn out to be the forward discount. Like the forward premium or discount itself, the cost of a hedge can be expressed in annualized percentage terms. In the case of the bratwurst hedge, $6,000 as against $625,000 works out to be slightly less than 1 percent for the three months the hedge is in force, or about 4 percent on an annualized basis. The formula for computing the cost of hedging through the purchase or sale of futures contracts is therefore a familiar one. It is, in fact, the formula with which in Chapter 8 we equated a particular forward premium or discount with the prevailing interest rate differential.[2]

$$\frac{\text{Forward rate} - \text{Spot rate}}{\text{Spot rate}} \times \frac{12}{\text{Months to maturity}} \times 100$$

$$= \text{Hedging cost (or benefit)}$$

---

[2] Page 155, Footnote 6.

Thus, the bratwurst hedge:

$$\frac{0.6310 - 0.6250}{0.6250} \times \frac{12}{3} \times 100 = 3.84\%$$

The matter of maturity also requires some explanation. In addition to being of standard size, exchange traded futures contracts have uniform maturity dates. Contract maturities will in most cases not be a perfect match for the exposure to be hedged, but will usually fall on the next closest contract delivery date.[3] Since such futures positions are in almost every instance liquidated by an offsetting sale or purchase, rather than being settled through the exchange's delivery procedure, the absence of an exact maturity match-up is not usually a significant handicap.

Translation hedging

Hedging translation exposure in the futures market is in most respects similar to covering transaction risk there. Assume that the Canadian subsidiary of a U.S. parent shows in its balance sheet a net asset position amounting to 10 million Canadian dollars. To cover this long exposure upon translation of the subsidiary's Canadian dollar position into its December 31 consolidated balance sheet, the parent firm might sell 100 December CD contracts, each with a contract value of CD 100,000. Thereupon, any loss incurred by the group as a consequence of a depreciation in the Canadian dollar against its U.S. counterpart would be offset by an approximately equivalent profit on the short 100 December CD futures position.

But here, again, the cost of hedging must be taken into account. Contrary to the premium on the forward Deutsche marks purchased in the example cited earlier, the parent company is in this instance selling Canadian dollar futures contracts quoted at a discount to spot. The difference in this case between spot and six-month forward Canadian dollars (assume that we're contemplating the situation in late June) represents the cost to the U.S. parent of placing the short hedge. Given the forward rate structure indicated in Table 13–1, the parent company would be selling December CD at a 80-point discount from spot (0.8800 − 0.8720) or on the CD 10 million net exposure, a six-month cost of $80,000.

The primary difference between hedging translation risk and transaction risk is that in the former case, there is no actual foreign exchange transaction at the balance sheet closing date, and therefore no delivery of currency. In the case of the Canadian subsidiary, the CD 10 million represents an existing investment in fixed plant, cash, accounts receivable, and other assets. The purpose of a hedge in this instance is to maintain the reported

---

[3]To counter the competitive challenge of a foreign currency futures market—the New York Futures Exchange—established in 1980 by the New York Stock Exchange, the IMM expanded its number of contract delivery months in a year from four to six.

Table 13-1
Canadian dollar forward
rate structure

$/CD spot	= 0.8800
$/CD 3-mos. (September)	= 0.8770
$/CD 6-mos. (December)	= 0.8720

value of these assets after they are consolidated into the group statement. As in the Deutsche mark transaction hedge, the hedging company has the option until the contract delivery date of buying spot Canadian dollars in satisfaction of its short futures position or, as is customarily the case, of cancelling the short position by buying back the 100 December CD contracts it sold six months earlier. In either event, should the spot $/CD rate have dropped from 0.8800 to 0.8200 or thereabouts, the resulting $600,000 unrealized loss in the consolidated balance sheet would have been offset by a comparable gain in the short futures position, less the $80,000 forward discount. The U.S. parent company might not regard a hedging cost of that magnitude as a bargain, but it would be hard to argue in those circumstances that spending $80,000 to save on balance $520,000 was not a prudent and, as it turned out, a correct decision. Needless to say, the story does not always have such a happy outcome. If, as readers should by this time have come to expect, the company's forecast went awry and the Canadian dollar scored a strong recovery for any of a number of possible reasons, pointed questions might be raised within the board of directors and elsewhere as to why the treasury department felt it necessary to fool around in the futures market. Alongside the maxim about there being no free lunch, there is chiseled in granite the one about success having a thousand parents and failure being an orphan.

A variation on the hedging theme is the use of forward swaps. In both the German sausage and the Canadian subsidiary examples, the problem was one of covering the consequences of any rate change between a present date and the future. Situations may arise where a company might wish to be covered between two future dates, say from three to six months from the present time. If, to continue with the Canadian dollar example, the parent company had bought September CD futures contracts and sold December, the net long exposure would have been hedged for the three-month period between those delivery months. The hedging cost in that instance would be the 50-point discount from September to December (0.8770–0.8720) or $50,000, as contrasted with the $80,000 hedging cost from June to December.

Other kinds of hedges

Futures contracts are not the only means available to cover foreign exchange exposure. Before settling upon any one technique, the corporate officers responsible for devising and implementing a hedging strategy should make themselves familiar with the several possibilities that are open to them. Only then are they in a position to select that method which promises to get the job done at the least apparent cost.

A collection of frequently used hedging techniques that don't involve futures contracts at all falls under the common heading of leads and lags. *Leading* is the practice of speeding up the conversion into, and payment of a commitment denominated in a foreign currency you believe is likely to appreciate, or of obtaining payment before the scheduled time of a currency which is liable to depreciate so as to be able to exchange it for your own before it does so. *Lagging* is simply the reverse tactic. You would try to defer making payment in a depreciation-prone currency or receiving payment in a strong currency to obtain the benefit of the lower cost or higher return in terms of your own currency if in fact the anticipated rate change comes to pass.

Again, there is no free lunch in the sense that each of these leading or lagging techniques has its own explicit or implicit cost. If your intent is to make early payment so as to avoid converting funds at a less favorable rate, you must presumably either borrow the domestic currency you plan to exchange or else withdraw funds already in your possession from an interest-bearing account. In either case, the effective cost of hedging against exchange rate appreciation is the difference between the interest rate level on the domestic currency that is to be converted and the obtainable yield after the funds are exchanged into the currency of payment on the presumption that the recipient of the funds will therewith compensate you for making early payment.

Leads and lags accomplished within multinational groups are known as *intercompany term adjustments*. Like payments to and from third parties (outside the group), funds are taken from one subsidiary and credited to the account of another before or later than such a transfer is nominally due. It is the responsibility of the parent corporation's headquarters treasury to determine whether its taking liquid funds from one of the subsidiaries and allotting them to another ahead of or behind schedule is to the advantage of the group's overall exposure. These premature or belated adjustments are a controversial issue, since some countries disallow them entirely because of their adverse balance-of-payments consequences, while others impose enough of an interest rate penalty on the deposit of leading intercompany payments to deprive the group of any economic benefit that may otherwise accrue from them.

A simpler means to the same end, because it is fraught with fewer regulatory obstacles, is *exposure netting*. Here, an effort is made to establish open positions in two or more currencies that are thought to counterbalance each other, and which therefore do not require any additional hedging action. A typical case of exposure netting would be one maintaining simultaneous long and short positions in two European snake currencies, where it's believed that a loss on one position will be covered automatically by a roughly equal profit in the other. A broader application of the same concept would be to carry simultaneous long *or* short positions in separate currencies that are held to be chronically strong and weak, respectively, so that, in theory at any rate, the company will be gaining profits in the strong currency at the same time that it is incurring losses on the weak one. The trouble with both of these netting approaches, and what makes them intrinsically speculative, is that what are thought to be constant relationships always seem to deviate from their norms at precisely the wrong time—if they did not, no one would notice—and companies that base their hedging strategies on the supposition that they will always hold true are liable to suffer substantial losses when they do not.

Management tactics

Leads and lags and exposure netting are essentially ad hoc measures intended to mitigate a company's current exchange exposure. Action of an anticipatory, and therefore of a more far-ranging nature may be taken with respect to a firm's pricing policies and its asset/liability management techniques. A subsidiary that operates in a country whose currency is believed likely to depreciate has the possibility of raising its product prices before that happens. Such a step will help to maintain the subsidiary's sales and possibly its profits at their pre-depreciation levels so far as the parent company is concerned. If there is a danger of the host government's imposing price controls to put a brake on rampant inflation, it is important that the subsidiary take whatever anticipatory measures it can to protect the exchange value of its cash flow before the controls are put into effect. The subsidiary also may have the option of raising its export prices denominated in other currencies if its domestic and international marketing position allows such a move.

Another alternative is for a company to change its currency of billing. An exporting firm typically would switch, if it had the option, from billing in a weak currency to doing so in a strong one. The primary drawback to this response is that once such a shift is made, it is not easily reversed. The company that made the change would find itself back in the same position if exchange rates turned around and the old billing currency strengthened while the new one weakened. A refinement of the technique is for the parent company to change its export billing from a weak to a strong currency as a means of transferring profits from one subsidiary to another. This, however, is one of the controversial practices of transfer pricing that has come under the critical scrutiny of local tax and customs officials. Because of the regulatory cloud, this particular approach cannot be recommended as a bona fide means of reducing exchange rate exposure.

Another technique, similar to leading and lagging, is for a multinational company to reduce, as far as possible, its assets, and to build up its liabilities in weak currencies. Here again, the unqualified use of such measures hinges upon the exchange control regulations in effect in the various countries that are involved, the attitude of local tax officials, and the cooperation of customers and creditors. More specialized, less frequently used techniques include taking foreign currency-denominated loans, discounting foreign currency receivables, maintaining authorized currency offset accounts, leasing, and utilizing, where available, government-sponsored exchange risk insurance.

Weighing the alternatives

Once the primary strategy has been set by the senior management of a multinational corporation, the job of the unit appointed to act as the headquarters hedge management team is to weigh the available alternatives— including, certainly, the purchase and sale of futures contracts—and to determine the method best suited to covering the type, amount, and currency of exposure in question. The primary grounds for the decision are cost, effectiveness, and exchange control regulations affecting particular hedging techniques in certain countries.

Consider, then, the case of a U.S. parent corporation with, for the sake of simplicity, a single subsidiary situated in Germany. The latter's balance sheet, drawn up in domestic and foreign currency equivalents of one million Deutsche marks, is summarized in Table 13–2. The subsidiary has translation exposure in its British pound and French franc accounts receivable and in its Swiss franc accounts payable.

Table 13–2
German subsidiary balance sheet, Deutsche mark million equivalents

	DM	£	FF		DM	SF
Cash	45			Accounts payable	30	30
Accounts receivable	30	45	15	Other	15	
Inventory	30			Current liabilities	75	
Current assets	165					
Fixed assets	270			Long-term debt	210	
				Equity	150	
Total assets	435			Total liabilities	435	

The parent's and subsidiary's consolidated Deutsche mark exposure under the FASB 8-mandated temporal accounting method therefore comes to:[4]

	Plus		Minus
Cash	45	Accounts payable	60
Accounts receivable	90	Other current	15
		Long-term debt	210
	135		285

[4]Chapter 12, p. 233.

Net short-term exposure in Deutsche marks has been reduced to DM 150 million, a decided improvement from the parent company's point of view. From this point, the hedge-management team's function is to:

1. Determine the potential risk attending each nondollar currency in which the group maintains an asset or liability position—Deutsche marks, British pounds, French francs, and Swiss francs.
2. Decide which of these risks require covering.
3. Select among those methods described above the most effective hedging technique, taking into account the costs and legal constraints of each.

In that the exposure of the British pound, French franc, and Swiss franc positions is assessed as being minimal, it is decided that they do not require covering. The size of the Deutsche mark position is not expected to change materially over the course of the current accounting period. The hedge-management team, supported by advice from the firm's outside foreign exchange consultants, forecasts a possible 10 percent appreciation in the mark during the period. If that forecast is realized, the group will incur a translation loss if long-term debt is included of DM 15 million or, at the current spot $/DM rate, approximately $9 million computed as follows:

$/DM = 0.6200   DM 150 million = $ 93   million
$/DM = 0.6820(+10%) DM 150 million = $102.3 million
                    Translation loss = ($ 9.3 million)

The hedge team concludes that exposure of that magnitude should not go unhedged, because a loss of that amount, if charged against current income, would have a materially adverse effect on the parent company's per-share earnings. The problem then becomes one of selecting the method that will hedge the indicated exposure at the least cost.

With an objective of reducing the group's net Deutsche mark liabilities, two possibilities as indicated above would be for the parent company to accelerate its scheduled payments to Germany, or to permit its subsidiary there to lag in its payments back to the United States. The net cost to the group of this lead-lag approach consists of the difference between the interest income on the transferred funds had they remained on deposit in the United States, and the comparable deposit yield in Germany. As has been noted, the use of these techniques is to a considerable extent limited by exchange control regulations in a number of countries.

Given enough time, the subsidiary may find other means by which it can add to the asset side of its balance sheet. It may be in a strong enough marketing position to prevail upon its export and local customers to hasten payment on its accounts receivables. Changing the currency of billing would not be appropriate, since there have been no major currencies, with the possible exception of the Swiss franc, that have been consistently stronger than the Deutsche mark. Finally, there is the alternative of buying DM futures contracts. The situation is similar to that of the dramatic sausage import example described earlier in the chapter, except that the stakes have risen from DM 1 million to DM 150 million.

Table 13-3 summarizes the options available to the hedge management group and the estimated cost of each.

Table 13-3
Hedging alternatives and estimated costs, German subsidiary example

Method	Cost basis	Estimated cost (annual)
Leading-lagging	Borrowing cost to U.S. parent for X months less interest yield on Deutsche marks	4.2%
Asset buildup	Loss of yield on investments denominated in other currencies	5.6%
Premature settlement of German subsidiary's accounts receivable	Financing cost	8.8%
Borrowing dollars	Domestic or Eurodollar borrowing cost less yield on Deutschemark deposit	4.4%
Purchase of Deutsche mark futures	Forward premium	2.8%
Remaining entirely uncovered	X-month appreciation of spot DM	?

Some companies use the team approach in managing their foreign exchange exposure, with personnel representing the treasury, controller, tax, and possibly the firm's marketing departments sharing the decision-making role. Other companies delegate the responsibility to one individual who evaluates, selects, and initiates the appropriate hedging actions under the supervision of the firm's chief financial officer. Policies also vary with regard to the execution of the designated strategy. Authority is sometimes delegated to the local subsidiary managers to issue instructions to banks that must in some countries be licensed to deal in foreign exchange. Local exchange control regulations often require this decentralized approach. Otherwise, the responsibility for both decision making and execution are best centralized at the headquarters level. The latter approach, with its global perspective, is usually better suited to dealing with exchange exposure—particularly of the translation variety—on a multicurrency basis, as contrasted with what is a more limited country-by-country approach.

What does hedging cost?

Returning to the focus of our discussion, namely the use of futures contracts to hedge exchange rate exposure, the question is frequently raised whether the forward premium or discount on such contracts is the true measure of hedging cost. Using the formula on page 248, we determined in the German sausage example that the 60-point premium between the spot $/DM rate of 0.6250 and the three-month forward rate of 0.6310 represented a hedging cost on a DM 1 million transaction of $6,000, or 3.84% on an annualized basis.

Now, to muddy the waters still further, the notion has been advanced that this method of computing the cost of forward cover is incorrect and misleading. If that is so, it is necessary to discard the cost comparisons made in Table 13–3 and start afresh. According to this dissenting opinion, so to speak, the true cost of hedging under such circumstances is the difference between the futures contract price (i.e., the forward rate) and the prevailing spot rate at the time the contract matures. In the case of the imported sausage example, that would make the cost of the hedge not $6,000 but the difference between 0.6310 and whatever spot $/DM happened to be when payment for the sausages was due three months later. If, for the sake of argument, spot $/DM was 0.6500 at that time, there would, under this method of computation, not have been a hedging cost at all, but rather a benefit of $19,000 because that is the dollar amount the importer would have saved by covering his short Deutsche mark position. If, however, spot $/DM had declined to 0.5800 during the same period, there would have been an after-the-fact hedging cost of $51,000, or the difference between the importer's hedged rate on DM 1 million and the rate at which he could have bought marks in the spot market at settlement date.

Pursuing this line of reasoning one step further, Table 13–4 recapitulates what would have been the comparable costs of hedging in the forward exchange market between 1974 and 1977 using the alternate methods of calculation described earlier.[5] The simulated results were obtained under the assumption of repeatedly rolling over three-month interbank forward contracts—that is, buying a new contract upon the expiration of a maturing one. Column A of the table lists the average spot three-month appreciation (depreciation in parentheses) of five major currencies during the 1974–1977 period in terms of U.S. dollars. Column B represents the conventional calculation of the hedging cost for each currency as the annualized percentage value of the forward premium or discount.

The figures in column C are the differences between those in columns A and B. They represent the computation of hedging costs by the use of the eventual spot rate.

---

[5]Source: *The Management of Foreign Exchange Risk* (London: Euromoney Publications Limited, 1978).

Table 13–4
Hedging cost calculations on rollover of three-month contracts

	(A) Avg. change in spot rate	(B) Three-month forward premium/(discount)	(C) Profit (loss) on forward coverage
British pound	(2.47%)	(1.59%)	.88%
French franc	(0.17)	(0.41)	(0.24)
Swiss franc	1.60	0.94	(0.66)
Deutsche mark	.80	0.57	(0.23)
Japanese yen	.32	(0.67)	(0.99)

According to the figures in Table 13–4, a corporate hedger would have paid an average of 1.59 percent under the premium/discount cost concept to hedge a series of three-month exposures in British pounds between 1974 and 1977, and 0.51 percent to hedge Deutsche mark positions during the same period. But, as is indicated in column C, the average cost of hedging pounds during that period was, according to the ex post facto calculation, a gain of .88 percent while there was a true cost of .23 percent to hedge Deutsche mark positions. The difference between the two methods of calculating hedging costs is even more striking in the case of the Swiss franc, where buying three-month forward contracts would have entailed a hedging cost, after taking the average appreciation of that currency into account of nearly twice that indicated by the premium/discount method.

Other considerations

So where does all of this leave us? It is, of course, of more than passing interest what the relative results of hedging and not hedging might have been in a given situation. But the final spot rate method of determining cost assumes the benefit of hindsight, which is not at all realistic for our purposes. The after-the-fact method is of no direct help to management in determining whether to hedge and by what means. Even as a point of historical reference, given the varying degrees of risk aversion at different companies, it is not certain whether a known cost, as is provided by the premium/discount method, is directly comparable to that of what amounts to a speculative open position. One would surmise intuitively that it does not.

A more realistic alternative would be to compare the forward premium or discount with the expected spot rate at the time the open transaction causing the exposure was slated to be consumated. Using such a projection as a point of comparison, a sale of futures contracts would be indicated if the forecast was for a spot rate lower than the one suggested by the forward discount, or conversely, buying futures when the forecast was for a higher spot rate than the forward premium gave reason to expect. And that, ladies and gentlemen, brings us full circle back to our discussion in Chapter 9—whether and to what extent the forward rate is an accurate predictor of the future spot rate.[6] If our conclusion there, that the bias is a minor one, is to be believed, everyone, with the possible exception of the statistical nit-pickers, should be satisfied that the forward rate, whether at a discount or premium, is as good a forecast as we are likely to get. Seen in those terms, there is no cost of forward cover in the long run—nor any benefit for that matter—and the spot and futures markets simply become an average alternate means of establishing the same rate of exchange. Neither has an inherent cost advantage over the other when viewed over a large number of transactions.

If the foregoing argument is correct—and it is only an argument—there is nothing left but to dismantle the futures and interbank forward markets, or else accept them for being what their critics have long maintained they are, just another form of gambling. But differing opinions are what make markets and horse races, and the question of whether to hedge or not to hedge is no exception. While covering exchange rate risk in the forward market may not be the unalloyed blessing that its most fervent advocates—many of whom, unsurprisingly, have a vested interest in that market—would have us believe it is, neither is it simply a disguised form of speculation. As is usually the case in such debates, the truth lies in some middle ground. If there were not a legitimate need to cover, there would not be so many otherwise astute people doing it. It is, in any event, difficult to put a finite value on obtaining a measure of certainty in what is otherwise an uncertain world of continually and rapidly changing currency relationships.

A futures hedge is just what the definition says it is: a temporary substitute—not a replacement—for an intended spot currency transaction. As such, it allows greater flexibility to a company in establishing rates at which it converts currencies. Confining itself to the spot market limits a firm to one or at most two days in which to make a required exchange, often at rates which are from its standpoint unfavorable. Its use of the futures market affords a company wider latitude in selecting the time to make an exchange, and therefore increases the opportunities to obtain a more attractive rate. Moreover, with the enhanced volatility of both spot and forward exchange rates, periods have frequently occurred during which a spot rate varied by a margin greater than the premium or discount to the related forward rate. Under such unsettled conditions, the futures market provides a hedge manager with an added dimension in selecting a rate that is to his liking.

Though the forward rate may be no better nor worse a prognosticator of future spot rates than any other prophet, there is a decided, if not always

---

[6]Pages 166–68.

quantifiable value in stabilizing a company's cash flow for the purposes, for example, of planning, pricing, budgeting, and declaring dividends. Despite our earlier hairsplitting—or was it nitpicking?—about the true definition of insurance, and whether currency hedging fits that definition— we stand by our claim that it does not—there is in fact an element of insurance, in the broader sense, that corporate planning is likely to be more effective when the value of present and projected assets, liabilities, and cash flows is known.

Chapter 14

International money management

WE HAVE REFERRED REPEATEDLY throughout this book to the speculators whose aggressive buying and selling force exchange rates to soar and then plummet, often with no apparent reason. But we haven't been very explicit about who these marketplace swashbucklers in reality are. There are, of course, the self-proclaimed speculators who trade currency futures on the International Monetary Market and on other organized exchanges. They have, to be sure, increased in numbers and presumably in market impact since the founding of the IMM in 1972. But it is unlikely that even with their growing influence futures traders can by themselves precipitate major shifts in the rates of exchange between leading currencies.

With regard to the banks, we noted in Chapter 11 that interbank market traders are often compelled by circumstances not of their own making to assume exposed long or short positions in a particular currency. However, the limits imposed by bank management on the amount and length of time open positions are permitted prevent these traders from doing much more than respond to, and perhaps reinforce, prevailing market trends.

The only other possible villains remaining, then, are the multinational corporations. They certainly have the financial clout to affect exchange rates and, with their subsidiary companies and bank accounts scattered around the globe, they are in a position to shift massive volumes of funds quickly and unobtrusively out of one currency and into another. It is a plausible argument that they are the heavies who have caused the increasingly erratic behavior in exchange rates since the inception of the currency float, and it is an argument that is often made. It portrays an image of the multinational treasurer unleashing huge outpourings of funds across national borders, or at least from one Eurocurrency deposit to another, at the slightest provocation—the release of an economic indicator, a revised exchange rate forecast, the rumor of a new election—and thereby creating havoc in the foreign exchange markets.

The corporate treasurers, in turn, protest that they are the victims of the same type of muckraking that conjured up the "gnomes of Zurich",[1] and that far from causing currency upheavals by moving their companies' millions around at the drop of a hat, they're as confounded by exchange rate volatility as anyone else. The safety and liquidity of the funds in their charge are their paramount considerations, and the business of shifting money about to pick up a slightly higher interest rate is greatly exaggerated. To hear them tell it, the treasurers would like nothing better than for the exchange markets to settle down and let them go about their customary business of projecting sales and earnings and planning bond issues without having to give undue weight to foreign exchange considerations.

Methodology and objectives

To separate fact from fiction, and, in so doing, to gain a closer insight into the practice of hedging foreign exchange exposure, it is necessary to delve more deeply into the methodology and objectives of international money management. That latter term itself requires a closer definition. The initial and most basic part of the process involves the expeditious transfer of funds to minimize the loss of interest yield while they are in the banking system pipeline. These transfers include intercompany payments across national boundaries, netted out insofar as is possible, and receipts from and payments to third parties. What amounts to the rationalization of collections and disbursements comes under the heading of *international cash management.* The next level, *international financial management,* entails the formulation of short-term financing programs, investment decisions, and, our specific area of interest, foreign exchange exposure strategies. *International money management,* then, is the collective term embracing all of these functions. It is a system of procedures to achieve the

---

[1] The deprecatory term given to Swiss bankers by British politicians in search of someone—other than themselves, of course—on which to place the blame for the weakness in the pound prior to its 1967 devaluation.

efficient control over, and productive use of, the financial assets of a multinational corporation.

Money, whatever form and currency it is in, is never idle. Unless it is hoarded (i.e., kept in a mattress or a safety deposit box), it is always earning interest for someone, somewhere. A company is therefore losing income while its funds are moving through the banking system, making it imperative that transfers be effected as quickly as possible. The process is often delayed in the case of international transfers by the fact that currencies, whatever their remitting points or their destinations, are ultimately transferred on the books of banks within their countries of origin. A payment in dollars by a company in the United Kingdom to one in France, for example, at some point has to be recorded by a paying and a receiving bank in the U.S. A Japanese-yen transaction between two banks, each in Zurich, is settled by their respective correspondent banks in Tokyo. The banks involved have little incentive to speed up this settlement process. Quite to the contrary, interest earned on float—funds in transit from payer to payee—is an important source of income for banks that handle such intercurrency transfers.

The traditional international transfer instrument is the mail payment order. An international transfer by airmail can take up to 8 to 10 business days when two or more banks are involved. A cable transfer is much faster, but it costs more. Other payment instruments include bank drafts, checks, and trade bills. When payment is tied to the extension of bank credit, then time drafts, trade acceptances, and letters of credit are the principal documents used to advise the paying bank of the conditions under which the recipient's account in it is to be credited with the designated funds.

When there is an exchange of currencies involved in a transfer of funds, the standard procedure is for the bank account of the remitting company to be debited by the appropriate amount two days before its equivalent in another currency is credited by a correspondent bank to the account of the payee company. If one bank is handling both sides of the transfer, it may elect to waive the two so-called value days during which it would otherwise earn interest on the funds to be transferred, and perhaps waive cable charges as well, as an accommodation for customers with which the bank has a relationship other than as a funds transfer agent.

Having arrived at their destination, the transferred funds are usually kept on deposit by the recipient firm in one of five forms: (1) Eurodollar time deposits, (2) Eurodollar certificates of deposit, (3) other Eurocurrencies, (4) local currencies, (5) local money market instruments, including treasury bills and notes, bankers acceptances, and commercial paper. For U.S.-based multinationals, and for a number of other international companies as well, the Eurodollar time deposit is the most common form of investment, although certificates of deposit (CDs) have gained in popularity in recent years. The latter instruments are negotiable, and are issued for both short- and medium-term maturities. Most companies, however, prefer to keep their funds in CDs with maturities of less than one year. Other than a possible difference in yield, the only distinction between deposits maintained in the form of local currencies or in Eurocurrencies is that the former are held by a bank located in the country of currency issue, while the latter are held in some other national money center, which very often turns out to be London.

Though interest return is an important consideration in the investment of surplus funds, it generally ranks behind safety and liquidity on a corporate treasurer's list of priorities. As a rule, larger corporations are more influenced by comparative interest rate levels than are medium-sized and smaller firms because bigger companies already enjoy the protection that comes with diversification of deposits. Some U.S. companies consider a yield pickup of 25 basis points—one quarter of 1 percent—a sufficient incentive to switch funds from dollar accounts to Eurodollar deposits; but most require an improvement of 50 basis points or one half of 1 percent to induce them to shift their funds.

When a firm transfers funds into another currency for the sake of securing a higher interest return, it also assumes exchange rate risk. This is particularly true since high interest rates usually go hand in hand with a depreciating currency. Any nominal yield differential that is to be obtained between different currency deposits should therefore be evaluated after the cost of obtaining forward cover for the duration of the investment is taken into account. When the proposed currency of deposit is believed subject to appreciation, that, too, should be taken into account in measuring comparative yields. But it usually occurs in those cases when another currency is strong, that the interest rate level in that country is lower than in the country where the funds are already deposited.

When it comes to the point of weighing investment opportunities denominated in various currencies, it is time for the company to establish an exposure management policy. The reporting procedures outlined in the previous chapter, or some variation thereof, will enable the corporation to determine its net accounting and, more difficult to quantify, its economic exposure. The treasurer and other senior management members should by then have decided whether the company will follow a cautious policy and endeavor to avoid, as far as possible, all foreign exchange risks, or else assume a more aggressive stance by seeking higher yields on deposits and greater profits on sales denominated in foreign currencies. Whatever policy is decided upon, it should be coordinated with the overall financial program of the corporation. For example, if a subsidiary of the group needs to borrow short-term funds for working capital purposes, the parent company should consider in arriving at its financial decision how the group's exposure will be affected by its choice of currency in which the subsidiary will borrow. The company's production and marketing management should, as well as its financial management, have a say in the determination of exposure policy. If, for example, the cost of hedging the anticipated proceeds of an export sale is estimated at 1 percent, the decision whether or not to hedge may turn on the projected profit margin on that particular piece of export business.

Intercurrency transfers

Various methods or devices used by companies to rationalize the intercurrency transfer of funds between subsidiaries and third parties, and thereby to reduce exchange exposure, include: a dollar lockbox system; an authorized retained foreign currency hold account; bilateral and multilateral netting; an intermediary company, and an accumulation or pool account. The lockbox device can reduce the time required to credit a firm's bank account with the proceeds of its export sales by five days or more by giving the bank direct access to incoming payments. Retained foreign currency accounts are employed in countries where exchange controls are in effect, and allow firms with a legitimate business need for foreign exchange to avoid repeated exchanges into and out of the domestic currency as regulations would normally require. Instead of duplicating conversion costs, transfer fees, and possible hedging costs, affiliated companies of the same multinational group with two-way or multiple payments in the same currency may net out such payments and remit the remaining balances on a periodic basis. Exchange control authorities in most countries tolerate this sort of arrangement where it can be demonstrated that actual reciprocal sales, shipments, and invoicing are carried on between a domestic company and a related foreign affiliate. Similar arrangements involving dividends, fees, and royalties are not as readily accepted, because the opportunities for the unauthorized and unreported transfer of income from one tax jurisdiction to another are much greater than in the case of sales transactions.

A result similar to what is accomplished through netting may be obtained by means of an intermediary company or through the establishment of a pool or accumulation account. The purpose of both devices is to assemble the cash, short-term investments, and certain other balance sheet items of a number of subsidiaries and to treat them as if they were the assets of a single company. The ultimate object of such a pooling arrangement is to allow subsidiaries that are in a surplus position to finance those that lack liquidity. The subsidiaries taken as a group will incur lower interest costs when they borrow from one another, rather than from an outside lender, and should likewise derive a proportionately better return on their pooled investments.

Effect of flexible rates

The advent of flexible exchange rates, along with the attendant uncertainty, have induced more companies to finance subsidiaries' operations with their local currencies as one way of reducing exposure even when the cost of such financing is greater than what is obtainable in the parent company's domestic money market. The assumption is that exchange rate risk, if left uncovered, will prove to be the higher cost in the long run.

The principal response of companies to flexible exchange rates, in the management of their working capital, has been their increased reliance on the leading and lagging techniques described in the previous chapter. The precise applications vary according to the circumstances at hand. Some treasurers try to hold the cash balances of the foreign subsidiaries at a minimum, particularly when they consist of weak currencies. Others take the opposite approach, striving to keep as much of the group's excess cash as possible held by subsidiaries with strong currencies, rather than having the funds repatriated to the parent company.

There is also greater attention paid to the selection of currencies in which companies conduct their trade. They generally will seek to invoice foreign sales in their own currencies whenever possible. The ideal solution would be to buy raw materials with weak currencies and sell finished goods for strong ones, but international trade would come to a standstill if every company tried to accomplish that. Some companies have incorporated provisions into their sales contracts stipulating a periodic price revision to compensate them for any untoward movements in exchange rates during the term of the contract. Other companies have gone so far as to adjust their sales to particular countries in accordance with their views of probable exchange rate developments within those countries.

Where hedging against exchange rate change has led to higher costs on international transactions, the response of many companies has been to raise prices to preserve their profit margins. Companies also have become more inclined to initiate anticipatory price changes, especially in the case of product prices of subsidiaries in countries whose local currencies are expected to depreciate. Most corporate treasurers are of the opinion that flexible exchange rates, with the heightened volatility they entail, have increased the costs of doing business abroad. They cite in particular the widening of premiums and discounts on futures contracts commensurate with the increased risk of maintaining exposed positions. Many financial officers complain that volatile exchange rates obscure the actual prices with which they are dealing, which in turn makes it more difficult for them to measure and compare the performance of subsidiary companies.

Reluctant forecasters

In spite of their reservations about its worth, most multinational treasurers feel that they have little choice but to involve themselves with forecasting exchange rates. In addition to using outside advisors, many companies make their own monthly or quarterly forecasts. Treasurers' departments generally limit their forecasts to a time horizon of one year or, more frequently, six months. Forecasts extending beyond one year, if they are undertaken, are usually left to the company's economics research department. There tends to be greater confidence in the reliability of three-to-six-month forecasts, compared with those for a full year. Even at that, everyone agrees that whatever the horizon, exchange rates are enormously difficult to predict, and that a batting average of .500—coming tolerably close to the actual spot rate half the time—is as good as they're likely to achieve.

Some companies that have little confidence in their ability, or that of anyone else, to forecast exchange rate movements with consistent accuracy, may attempt either to hedge all of their foreign exchange exposure or else hedge none at all. Most companies, however, try to steer a middle course between those extremes. The latter group attempts to calculate when it is to a company's advantage to maintain its exposure, and when it may be more beneficial to increase or reduce exposure in a particular currency. Companies that take this flexible course are usually the ones that are accused of engaging in foreign exchange speculation.

The adoption of a policy of selective exposure management involves estimating the impact of likely exchange rate changes on a company's present exposure, its earnings, net worth, and the market value of its securities. It also entails a cost comparison of the various methods of changing exposure described in Chapter 13, immediately and at various future dates. As noted earlier, there should also be a determination of management's attitude toward risk, in particular the price it is willing to pay, namely the cost of hedging, to achieve a measure of certainty within a highly uncertain exchange rate environment.

Selecting risk-control strategies

This selective approach is incorporated within the broader framework of a company's international money management program through the adjustment of the currency mix of the group's liquid assets and liabilities. As with the company's choice of investments and the adaptation of its funds transfer, invoicing, and pricing policies, so, too, is there an exposure strategy that is consistent with the company's attitude toward exposure risk and the price it is willing to pay to control such risk.

As was noted, at one end of the spectrum is the strategy of absolute risk neutralization. The objective here is to eliminate exposure entirely by remaining fully hedged at all times. The supposition underlying this policy is that the company is best advised to tend to its own knitting, tire production, or what have you, and not become involved in the business of exchange rate forecasting or currency trading. As has also been noted, at the other extreme is the strategy of ignoring accounting exposure completely, since the risk of exposure is essentially equal to the cost of covering it, inasmuch as the premium or discount on forward contracts is as accurate a measure of the probable change in an exchange rate as the company believes it is likely to get. If this is the strategy—or nonstrategy—the company selects, its currency mix of assets and liabilities will be the random result of international transactions as they occur. The rationale here is that the currency gains and losses arising from such an unplanned approach will in the long run balance out.

A third alternative is that of maintaining a predominantly short net foreign currency exposure, based upon the supposition that interest rate and forward exchange differentials underestimate the exchange rate risk implicit in foreign currency-denominated investments. The company that adopts this strategy will attempt to finance its subsidiaries abroad with foreign currency borrowings, and in some instances its domestic operations as well, in the belief that the value of these borrowings in terms of its own currency will depreciate by an amount greater than the additional interest cost that may be incurred. A contrasting strategy is one of maintaining the greatest possible long net position in foreign currencies, in the view that interest rate and forward differentials are upward biased, making it a less-costly proposition over the long run for the firm to borrow its domestic currency for the purposes of financing foreign operations and of investing in foreign currency-denominated investments.

Each of the strategies outlined above is nonjudgmental in the sense that it doesn't involve any attempt to predict the extent and timing of exchange rate changes, nor does it entail any reaction by the firm to the release of new information concerning balance of payments, inflation rates, monetary policy, and the like. A somewhat different approach, which requires more flexibility and discretion, is to select one or the other of these strategies as being the most appropriate for one currency, say a short net position for the Canadian dollar, and another, perhaps the net long strategy, for a persistently strong currency, such as the Swiss franc. Once a strategy is applied to a particular currency, the company will continue to match them until something occurs to prompt a reappraisal of the situation.

More complex strategies

There are more complex strategies that require greater discretion concerning current and future changes in the currency mix of the company's assets and liabilities, its response to changes in exchange rates and interest rate differentials, and to revisions of forecasts regarding such changes.

In each instance the basic decision comes down to whether the corporation should maintain net long or short positions in the several currencies in which it conducts its business, and when and how such positions should be covered. As with the more-or-less automatic strategies, the possible effects of each should be assessed for the current accounting period (period 1) as well as for a number of succeeding (N) periods. The single-period case is one in which the company has a net long or short position in a particular currency on the first day of period I, and must estimate the effects of possible rate changes in that currency on the closing date of the period. Any decision to hedge or not hedge in the light of that estimate is made with the assumption that the exposed position will be liquidated by a scheduled transaction on the closing day of period I. The N-period situations allow greater latitude inasmuch as there are a number of opportunities for the firm to adjust its exposure. There may in fact be periods during which it appears necessary to cover, and those in which a fully or partially exposed position seems desirable. In the event that futures contracts are considered to be the best available means of hedging a specific exposure, there remains the question of what contract maturities to select, which in turn would determine the number of times a forward position would be rolled over in securing coverage over an extended period. At issue is the amount of forward premium or discount to various maturities, which determines the transaction cost each time a contract is rolled over. In deciding upon contract maturities, therefore—four 6-month contracts, for example, rather than one 24-month contract—the company is weighing current against estimated future hedging costs. Here again, there arises the opportunity to adjust strategies to conform with changing market conditions. It is conceivable that a firm would tolerate a long net exposure in a depreciating currency when, according to its forecasts, the likelihood of a further significant decline is low. But when a revised forecast indicates a greater possibility of depreciation in that currency, the company would be inclined to shift to a short position, in a sense speculating on the basis of its forecast.

To hedge or not

It is in this regard that a company's proclivity to tolerate or to avoid exchange rate exposure will influence its hedge-or-not-to-hedge decisions. Thus, two firms may reach contrary decisions even though their estimates of hedging costs in a given situation are essentially the same, just as firms with the same degree of risk-aversion may arrive at opposite decisions because they differ in their estimates of the costs of increasing or decreasing exposure.

Figure 14–1 provides a graphic means of expressing these choices. The hedging cost, as measured by the forward premium or discount on a particular currency, is plotted in annual percentage terms along the vertical axis of the chart, while the anticipated change in the relevant exchange rate, also expressed in percentages, is plotted along the horizontal axis. The locus of the points that form the diagonal line X–X, which intersects the two axes at a 45-degree angle, mark the exchange rates at which the forward premium and the expected change in the exchange rate are equal.

By referring to such a diagram, a hedge manager may determine the estimated cost or benefit to the firm of altering its exposure in that currency. All points on the chart above and to the left of the 45-degree line represent rates at which the forward premium is greater than the expected appreciation in the spot rate for that currency. The reverse—expected appreciation greater than the forward premium—holds for all points below and to the right of line X–X.

For Figure 14–1 to provide sufficient data from which to make an informed hedge-no-hedge decision, there must be included some graphic representation of the firm's attitude toward exchange risk. Will the company tolerate a 50-point variation in a particular rate without much concern, but feel decidedly uncomfortable in the face of a 500-point swing? Such a determination can be indicated by the width of the band encompassing the 45-degree line. A company that will accept rate variations between X'–X', for example, is more risk-disposed than one that is tolerant of rate swings within the wider X'–X' band. The more risk-disposed the company, the narrower the band along the 45-degree line will be.

Within such a schematic framework, a company can define its own risk parameters by creating a band that represents its particular tolerances, say 2 percent or 5 percent, beyond which the company would deem it worthwhile to maintain an exposed position in a certain currency. If the premium (discount) exceeded the expected appreciation (depreciation), according to the chart, by an amount greater than the area described by the band, the

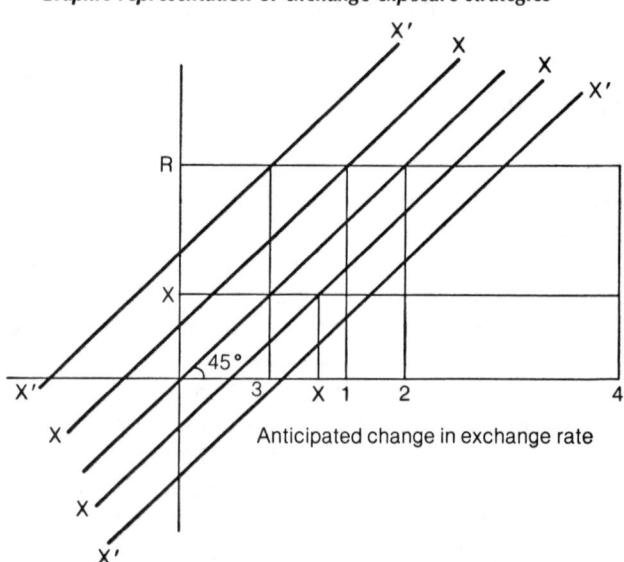

Figure 14–1
Graphic representation of exchange exposure strategies

Anticipated change in exchange rate

Source: Adapted from Robert Z. Aliber, *Exchange Risk and Corporate International Finance* (London: The Macmillan Press Ltd., 1978), p. 124.

company would be disposed toward maintaining or assuming a long position in that currency. If, however, the relationship were so reversed that the expected appreciation (depreciation) exceeded the forward premium (discount), the company might be inclined to maintain a short exposure.

Figures similar to 14–1 can be created for each period in an N-period model. To draw such a series of charts, forward premiums and discounts must be estimated along with the future spot rate. It is possible in such a case that different risk tolerance/aversion bands will be used in successive charts in the series on the grounds that uncertainty increases as the time horizon is extended.

Other hedge models have been advanced that incorporate a variety of decision rules. A typical example proposes that hedge decisions be made on the basis of the predicted change in the spot rate, the resulting loss that would be incurred on an exposed position, the estimated error of the rate forecast, and the risk propensity of the firm. To illustrate, if the probable exposure loss is projected at 10 percent, the estimated forecast error at 20 percent, and the company's risk factor is put at 15 percent, a company using this model would be disposed to hedge when the forward premium or discount is less than the product of (0.10 × 1.20 × 1.15), or 1.38 percent.

The introduction of forecast error to the decision model renders the foregoing analysis subject to adjustment to the extent that a company might assume a hedged position even when the forward premium exceeds the predicted variation in the spot rate. As a general rule, the larger and more frequent is the incidence of forecast error, the greater will be the company's disposition to hedge. Another viewpoint is that the element of forecast error is already reflected in the company's risk tolerance/aversion, and that accounting for it separately accords it undue weight.

The real test of any model is its performance record. It is possible to conduct simulations in which a particular model's track record is compared with historical data. A shortcoming of such simulations is that it's difficult if not impossible to duplicate the precise circumstances surrounding a particular exposure problem after the fact.

Tax considerations

Additional factors that need to be taken into account in the selection and implementation of an exposure strategy are the tax consequences of an exposed position and of the hedging technique used to cover it. The schedule of corporate income taxes to which a firm is subject will affect the calculation of costs and benefits in exposure management, the means by which the company seeks to alter exposure and the countries within which, given the option, it elects to realize exchange related gains and losses. A decline in corporate income attributable to changes in exchange rates, or to measures undertaken to alter a company's exposure, serve to reduce its taxable income. Additional income from those sources are generally taxed at the same rates that apply to ordinary income. Foreign exchange related gains or losses affect a company's taxable income only when they are realized. Gains incurred on futures or forward contracts are treated as ordinary income, even though their maturity exceeds the minimum holding period for capital gains treatment at a lower tax rate.

The income of a foreign subsidiary is fully taxed in the country in which it is earned. Dividends paid by subsidiaries to U.S.-based parent companies are taxed when they are repatriated. The parent company in turn obtains a credit against its tax liability in the United States for the corporate income tax it has paid abroad.

The tax rates that apply to a company's ordinary income, and to the profits and losses that arise from its foreign exchange transactions, therefore determine that company's potential tax liability on its exchange exposure—and influence management's attitude concerning that exposure. The higher the tax rate to which a company is subject, the less effect on corporate income that exchange rate changes will have on an after-tax basis. For example, a corporate income tax rate of 50 percent reduces the effect of an exchange related gain or loss by half on an after-tax basis.

The results of a company's exposure strategy may be materially altered if the tax rate on profits that accrue on futures contracts differs from the rate that applies to ordinary income. Translation losses are a case in point, since they are not usually realized and are therefore not deductible from taxable income, whereas gains that are realized on a futures hedge initiated to offset that exposure are taxed as ordinary income. If the firm's applicable tax rate is 50 percent, such a situation would normally lead to "double hedging," or the purchase or sale of futures contracts amounting to twice the value of the exposed position. The practice of double hedging may entail unnecessary costs, inasmuch as the diminution of a company's net worth as a consequence of translation losses is more apparent than real.

If, instead of buying or selling futures contracts, the company moves to change its exposure through leading or lagging payments, the effective change in its income is the sum of net interest payments and foreign exchange related gains or losses. Interest payments, in the case of the former, constitute a tax-deductible expense.

Tax considerations are sometimes decisive, therefore, in determining a company's choice between forward cover and leading or lagging as the preferred means of altering exposure. If, as was discussed at some length in Chapter 13,[2] interest rate parity applies, there should be no before-tax cost difference between the alternate techniques. In that event, the method with the after-tax cost advantage would normally be selected. Taxes would not be the deciding factor, however, if the tax rate on futures gains were equal to the company's marginal income tax rate.

---

[2] Pages 256–58.

It is sometimes possible for a company to reduce its tax liabilities and either to increase its after-tax income, or else to reduce the number of futures contracts needed to secure the desired coverage, by apportioning exchange related gains and losses among subsidiaries located in countries with different tax rates. The controlling question in this regard is whether profits incurred on futures contracts are best treated from the parent company's perspective as foreign or domestic income and, conversely, whether futures losses are best treated as charges against foreign or domestic income. Generally, the effective tax rate on foreign income from a subsidiary may be lower than the corporate income tax rate for a U.S.-based parent company if the foreign tax rate is lower than the U.S. rate and if the foreign income is not repatriated in the year in which it is earned.

Hedging translation exposure

As noted earlier in the chapter, translation exposure can be a source of misunderstanding because, while it may lead to a reported loss, it will not become a tax-deductible loss since it is never realized. If a company nevertheless elects to hedge a position involving translation exposure, and the sale of futures contracts is the technique that has been selected, the customary procedure is to sell the number of contracts whose value most closely approximates the amount of exposure and which mature at or about the balance sheet closing date. At the closing date, the requisite currency is purchased in the spot market to meet the delivery obligation of the short futures position, or else the short position is closed out through the offsetting purchase of equivalent contracts.

The hedging company is attempting through the sale of an appropriate number of contracts to accrue a gain on the short futures position, which should approximate any translation loss that may occur during the accounting period as a result of exchange rate movement. The proper number of contracts to be sold can be determined by the following formula:

$$\frac{\text{Potential translation loss}}{\text{Forward rate} - \text{Expected future spot rate}} \div \text{Contract size} = \text{Number of futures contracts}$$

Dividing the potential translation loss from an exposed position in a particular currency by the difference between the forward rate (futures price) and the expected future spot rate give the amount of currency that must be sold forward to obtain full coverage. Dividing that amount in turn by the futures contract size provides the number of contracts that most nearly approximate in value the amount of potential translation loss.

We may prove the formula by calculating the number of IMM British pound contracts required to hedge a potential translation loss, given the following data:

Potential translation loss	$500,000
IMM British pound contract size	£ 25,000
One-year futures price	$2.30
Expected one-year future spot rate	$2.10

$$\frac{\$500,000}{2.30 - 2.10} \div £25,000 = 100 \text{ contracts}$$

Table 14–1 is the profit calculation on a futures hedge assumed on the basis of the information listed above and carried over the course of a one-year accounting period:

Table 14–1
British pound hedge profit calculation

1. Sell 100 one-year BP futures contracts (£25,000 contract size) at present delivery price	
100 × £25,000 × 2.30	$5,750,000
2. Buy back 100 BP futures contracts or spot pounds one year later at expected rate	
100 × £25,000 × 2.10	$5,250,000
Profit on futures hedge	$ 500,000

Thus, the translation loss caused by a depreciation of the British pound from $2.30 to $2.10 was offset by a profit on the short BP futures position of $500,000.

Futures hedge methodology

For a more detailed look at the methodology of a futures hedge, we return to what is by now our familiar example of the German subsidiary of a U.S.-based multinational corporation. The subsidiary has as of December 31, 1980, a short (liability) net exposure of DM 10 million, which for the purpose of our illustration remains unchanged throughout 1981. The $/DM translation rate on December 31, 1980 is 0.5640. The corporate income tax rate for the U.S.-based parent is 50 percent. The exposure management group within the parent company's treasury department forecasts at the beginning of 1981 a 10 percent to 15 percent appreciation in the Deutsche mark over the current year, and therefore buys 160 one-year forward contracts totalling DM 20 million for December 1981 delivery at a price of 0.5760.

The 1981 forecast was a good one, but it undershot the mark somewhat (pardon the pun, but we are in dire need of some levity at this point) as spot $/DM actually appreciated over the course of the year by some 17 percent. From January to December, the spot rate moved as follows:

$/DM	12/31/80	=	0.5640
$/DM	6/30/81	=	0.6250
$/DM	12/31/81	=	0.6610

	(1)	(2) First half, 1981	(3) Second half, 1981	(4) Cumulative, 1981
Balance sheet exposure:				
1. Date	12/31/80	6/30/81	12/31/81	
2. DM exposure	(10,000,000)	(10,000,000)	(10,000,000)	
3. $/DM exchange rates	0.5640	0.6250	0.6610	
4. $ Equivalents	(5,640,000)	(6,250,000)	(6,610,000)	
5. FX gain (loss) before tax		(610,000)	(360,000)	(970,000)
6. Tax (0 percent)		0	0	0
7. FX gain (loss) after tax, lines (5) + (6)		(610,000)	(360,000)	(970,000)
Futures contracts:				
8. Date		12/31/81	12/31/81	
9. Amount bought		20,000,000	20,000,000	
10. Number of contracts		160	160	
11. Spot $/DM		0.5640	0.6610	
12. $ value of contracts		11,280,000	13,220,000	
13. FX gain (loss) before tax		980,000	720,000	1,700,000
14. Tax (50 percent)		(490,000)	(360,000)	(850,000)
15. FX gain (loss) after tax		490,000	360,000	850,000
FASB 8 gain/loss:				
16. FX Gain (loss) reported (FASB 8), lines (5) + (13)		370,000	360,000	730,000
17. Increase (decrease) in net income (before premium), lines (6) + (14)		(120,000)	0	(120,000)
Income and cash impact:				
18. Premium to be amortized (spot $/DM − forward $/DM × no. of contracts)		(610,000)	(610,000)	(1,220,000)
19. Tax (50%)		305,000	305,000	610,000
20. Decrease in after-tax incomes, lines (17) + (18) + (19)		(425,000)	(305,000)	(730,000)
21. Total cash flow from futures contracts at maturity, lines (15) + (20)		65,000	55,000	120,000
22. Total increase (decrease) in net income, lines (17) + (20)		(545,000)	(305,000)	(850,000)
23. Total economic impact (implied cash flow), lines (7) + (21)		(545,000)	(305,000)	(850,000)

Source: Adapted from *The Management of Foreign Exchange Risk*, (London: Euromoney Publications Limited, 1978), p. 56.

The exposure data for the German subsidiary, as well as that for the long futures position carried by the U.S.-based parent company, are listed in Column 1 of Table 14–2. Columns 2 and 3 show the successive changes in the values of the two positions as the spot $/DM rate appreciates over the first and second halves of 1981. Column 4 lists the cumulative impact of the exchange rate change over the entire year.

The first seven lines in Table 14–2 define the balance sheet exposure of the German subsidiary in Deutsche marks, including the resulting translation loss. If the spot dollar/mark rate had in fact risen as indicated to 0.6250 by June 30, 1981, a foreign exchange loss of $610,000 would have flowed through to the group's consolidated income statement for the six-month period. As the mark continued to appreciate to 0.6610 during the second half of the year, the foreign exchange related charge against earnings increased to $970,000. This loss, according to line (6) does not comprise a credit or a deduction against corporate income taxes in Germany or the United States.

Lines (8) through (15) show the generation of the cumulative after-tax gain of $850,000 on the long futures position. The net foreign exchange loss of the hedged position is shown in lines (16) and (17) according to the accounting treatment stipulated by *FASB 8*. Line (16) shows the total reported *FASB 8* foreign exchange gain, the net difference between the translation loss on the subsidiary's DM 10 million short exposure and the pre-tax gain on the long futures position. The reported *FASB 8* foreign exchange loss net of the tax liability on the futures profit is entered on line (17). If the Deutsche mark exposure of the subsidiary company had been perfectly hedged, the entry on line (17) would have been zero. As it was, the parent company in the illustration incurred a net loss on the hedged position of $120,000.

FASB 8 controversy

As noted in Chapter 12, the accounting treatment of foreign exchange related gains and losses prescribed in *FASB 8* has provoked considerable controversy since that opinion was issued in 1975. The principal argument advanced in favor of the opinion is that it sets forth a standard method and format for foreign exchange accounting when before there had been no uniformity of practice observed by companies in the United States. Other supporting arguments have been that the temporal method is the most realistic of the accounting conventions described in Chapter 12, and that it in any case corresponds most closely to the reporting procedures observed by most companies before the publication of *FASB 8*.

The argument most frequently cited by those who would see *FASB 8* amended or, even better, repealed outright is that the variations in reported earnings, caused by charging foreign exchange losses against current income, distort a company's actual earnings record, upset the stockholders, and confuse security analysts.[3]

FASB 8 is also criticized for requiring that foreign currency-denominated inventories carried at cost be valued at their historic exchange rates, rather than at balance sheet closing rates. A number of corporate financial officers have pointed out that their companies' inventories turn over two to four times a year on average, and that they should therefore be treated as monetary assets and translated at current rates. Since *FASB 8* requires companies to charge translation losses against earnings on a quarterly reporting basis, more firms have been impelled to cover their translation exposure by the purchase or sale of futures contracts, as is illustrated in Table 14–2. This in turn gives rise to the complaint by some treasurers that *FASB 8* rules make it impossible for them to hedge both their accounting and economic exposure at the same time. Others have complained that the immediate recognition of foreign exchange related gains or losses on a company's long-term debt is misleading, and that the temporal method fails to underscore the important distinction between losses realized on foreign exchange transactions and translation losses which may never be realized. Some critics have proposed that the use of accounting reserves once again be allowed to amortize foreign exchange gains and losses over a number of years, and thereby smooth out exchange related variations in earnings. Another proposal has been to charge translation gains and losses directly to net worth on the balance sheet, leaving only transaction gains and losses to be passed through the income statement.

Heeding the growing criticism of *FASB 8*—it was, indeed, impossible to ignore the uproar—the Financial Accounting Standards Board agreed in 1980 to consider what changes, if any, should be made to correct its alleged faults. After holding public meetings and deliberating for most of the year, the board recommended that the regulations be so revised that first, certain adjustments arising from foreign exchange fluctuations be made directly to stockholder equity, rather than to a company's current earnings, and second, that all assets and liabilities be translated at the balance sheet closing rate. If and when the board's amendments were ratified, the proposed changes were slated to become effective with the fiscal years commencing on or after December 15, 1981.

Debating the merits

Corporate financial officers hold varying opinions concerning the relative difficulty of operating within a floating exchange rate environment, as con-

---

[3]Half in jest, but making their point abundantly clear, two security analysts in early 1980 offered in a research newsletter a $1,000 reward to anyone who could provide them with complete information regarding the effects of exchange rate fluctuations on the consolidated 1979 earnings of IBM.

trasted with the earlier fixed-rate system. The treasurer of a diversified producer of chemicals, pigments, and fabricated metal products complains that, "We have to put in a hell of a lot of time and effort to minimize our exposure worldwide," in the more than 20 currencies in which his company does business. He longs for a return to the days of fixed rates when "you could operate abroad in your chosen business without having to worry about being a currency expert, too."[4]

Other treasurers take the view that the recurring devaluations that were the primary means of exchange rate adjustment during the fixed-rate years created just as many problems then as floating rates do today. Such devaluations "came suddenly and in huge amounts and were merely a political recognition of a well-known economic fact," says Clyde A. MacFie, vice president, finance, of Ferro Corporation, a Cleveland-based steel producer.[5] Yet others maintain that there isn't any significant difference between the two exchange systems. If exchange rates move into imbalance in either case, claims Donald R. Hughes, executive vice president of Burlington Industries, Inc., a large textile manufacturer, "there's going to have to be an adjustment. And the real difference between fixed rates and floating rates is that floating gets you there a heck of a lot faster."[6]

Precisely because they do "get you there a heck of a lot faster," many companies have modified their international financing and cash management methods in response to the greater volatility of floating rates. During the days of fixed parities, the U.S. dollar value of French franc-denominated invoices was computed by the U.S. Tobacco Company the same day the invoices were received at its Greenwich, Connecticut, headquarters, and dollar checks in those amounts were routinely mailed to its French supplier. Significant dollar savings have been realized, according to domestic and international cash manager Anthony F. Apuzzo, since U.S. Tobacco revised its overseas payment procedure to take advantage of the 10-day payment period granted under the invoice terms. Monitoring the day-to-day changes in the dollar/franc exchange rate within that period, Apuzzo aims to make cable transfers to France on the date he deems the rate to be most favorable to the company, instead of mailing dollar checks as in the past.

Some companies try to persuade their foreign suppliers and customers to share their exchange rate risks. An American textile manufacturer prevailed upon a Swiss machinery company to absorb 10 percent of any potential exchange loss, for example, by accepting 10 percent of its payment in dollars and 90 percent in Swiss francs.

There remains a wide range of opinion among multinationals concerning the desirability of constantly being fully hedged against foreign exchange

---

[4]"Battered by the Floating of Currencies, Some Companies Long for Fixed Rates," *The Wall Street Journal*, December 1, 1977, p. 30.

[5]Ibid.

[6]Ibid.

risk. Some companies contend that being fully hedged at all times is the safest course, while others, who subscribe to the notion that the best defense is a good offense, pursue a more selective hedging strategy. Raymond P. Ruzek, director of finance at Emery Air Freight, believes that adjusting his company's worldwide receivables and payables with an eye toward exchange rate trends is a normal part of sound exposure management. Though conceding that there is in practice a fine line between selective hedging and speculation, Ruzek contends that the opportunities that arise to enhance Emery's dollar income stream justify his taking a more aggressive hedging stance than an always fully hedged policy would allow him.

On the whole, corporate financial managers who are concerned with foreign exchange exposure, while urging a revision of *FASB 8,* are reasonably confident that most bankers, brokers, security analysts, and financial journalists are familiar enough with the difficulties therein that they are not unduly disconcerted by large foreign exchange related losses. No one, it seems, ever worries about the opposite—exchange generated gains. However, Maurice Prendergast, treasurer of Intsel Corporation, a trading arm of the Paris-based multinational Pechiney Ugine Kuhlmann, believes that, although lip service is accorded the noneconomic nature of translation losses, the actual implications of such losses are in fact ill-understood by those investment professionals who evaluate a company's shares and are therefore in a position to influence their price.

Mr. Ruzek of Emery Air Freight believes that, as a practical matter, a foreign exchange hedge manager must make his decisions on two levels simultaneously, with one eye on the accounting effects of his hedge activity and the other on the "real dollar" or economic results of same.

Chapter 15

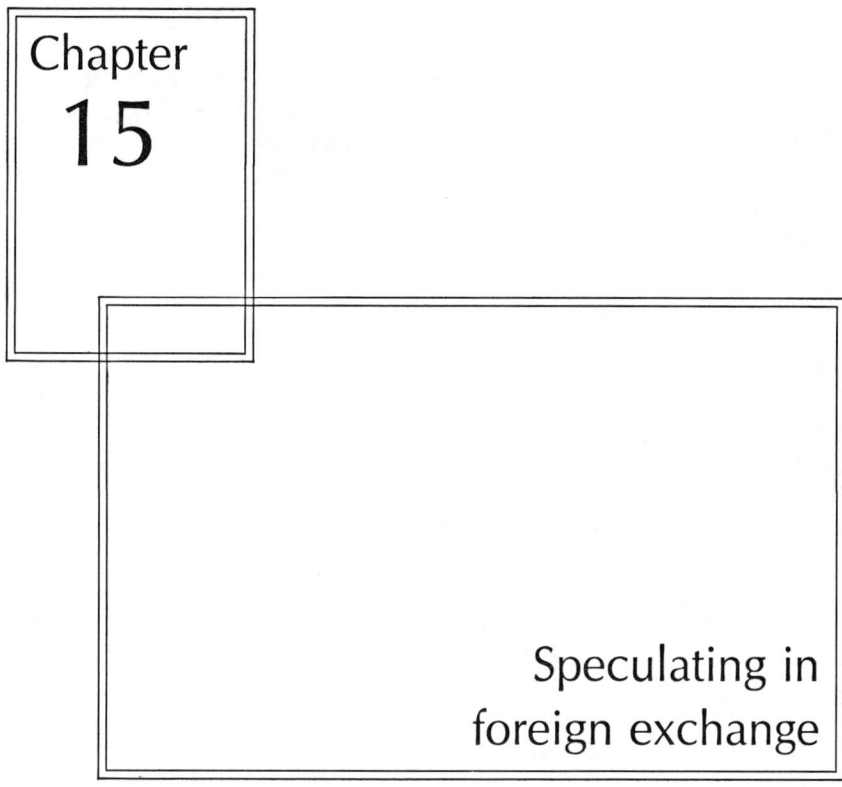

Speculating in foreign exchange

THIS CONCLUDING CHAPTER is dedicated to two wise men. The first is a Cabinet officer in a recent administration, who said of his pre-political profession: "My view about economists, being trained in the mysteries of that craft, is that there are those who don't know and there are those who don't know they don't know."[1]

The second is an unidentified foreign currency futures trader on the floor of the International Monetary Market, who said of his occupation: "My year in Vietnam as a fighter pilot was the best possible training I could have gotten for this job."[2]

Two wise men, indeed. The chapter might also have been dedicated to a third, a sadder but wiser man whom we must perforce call Mr. X. But more of him later.

The reader is no doubt weary of seeing the caveat repeated throughout this book that speculating in foreign exchange is a hazardous undertaking.

---

[1]Ray Marshall, U.S. Secretary of Labor 1977–1980, quoted in the *New York Post,* July 11, 1980.
[2]*The Wall Street Journal,* November 10, 1977.

I am tired of writing it. What is worse, I earn my living advising clients who do precisely that! There may be such a thing as being too admonitory, but brokers soon learn that the best customers are the ones who make money. Besides being difficult to deal with, the others drop by the wayside rather quickly.

So for the final time, speculating in foreign exchange futures is a high-risk game, quite possibly the riskiest one in town. Our favorite addage about there being no such thing as a free lunch is right on the money in that respect. If you hope to win big, you've got to be prepared to risk big. Otherwise, stay out of the game. But, having dutifully said that, if the professional traders, such as the ex-fighter pilot, the corporate treasurers with all the resources and information they have at their disposal, and the forecasters-for-hire with their fancy computer models pat themselves on the back if they're right 50 percent of the time—and "being right" is usually interpreted rather freely—how can the part-time amateur hope to compete without losing his or her shirt? The answer is: with a lot of hard work, discipline, and maybe more than a fair share of good luck. There is no accounting for the luck factor, but the other two are within the province of anyone who is determined enough.

The 1976 peso plunge

The 1976 experience with the Mexican peso is the most dramatic confirmation of the foregoing to have occurred in recent years. The peso is not regarded as a major currency in world foreign exchange markets, but due to the geographic proximity of Mexico to the United States and the close economic ties between the two countries, the dollar/peso exchange rate is an important one for investors and business people on both sides of the border. A major factor in the Mexican economy is the more than $750 million expended by North American tourists there annually. Mexico is in turn an important importer of goods from the United States. Multinational corporations based in the latter country have in the aggregate invested well over $3 billion in Mexico in support of their subsidiary companies domiciled there.

One of the cornerstones of the close economic—if not always diplomatic—relationship between the two countries has been the stable exchange rate between their currencies. Since 1954, and after other countries abandoned fixed-dollar parities, the peso was maintained at its official parity of 12.50 to the dollar, or $0.08. By mid-1976, however, the economic equilibrium that allowed such exchange rate stability was beset by the same worldwide inflationary pressures that had disrupted long-standing economic relationships elsewhere. The Mexican consumer price index rose 22 percent in 1974, an advance that only moderated to 16 percent during the following recession year. The inflation rate accelerated again in 1976, amid a growing flight of private capital out of the country, and amid spreading rumors that wage and price controls were about to be imposed.

One proposed means of alleviating the country's economic troubles was to abandon the 12.50-to-1 parity and allow the peso to float against the dollar as other currencies had done several years earlier. In such an event the peso would almost certainly decline, and the arguments advanced in favor of such a de facto devaluation were the conventional ones of boosting exports, including tourism, and discouraging imports. Such a measure, it was hoped, would improve the country's balance-of-payments position, check the flight of capital, and, in time, dampen inflation.

During the first half of 1976, Mexican officials tried to ignore the growing rumors of devaluation, and when that was no longer possible, denied them out of hand. In April, the country's finance minister stated publicly that there was no need to float or devalue the peso. Self-styled financial consultants who made their livings inducing American investors to buy Mexican bonds or deposit their funds in high interest-yielding peso accounts derided the rumors as the underhanded attempts of American banks and brokerage firms to halt the flow of investment dollars into Mexican financial institutions. The chief financial officer of a large U.S. multinational later claimed that the company's New York bankers insisted throughout the year that there would be no peso devaluation. "Why were we caught with so many pesos?" he asked a newspaper reporter rhetorically. "Because we were completely suckered, that's why."[3]

In his annual September 1 State of the Union address to Congress, the President of Mexico dropped the bombshell that the country's central bank would after 22 years no longer attempt to hold the peso at any predetermined level vis-à-vis the dollar, announcing, in effect, that the peso would henceforth be allowed to float. The finance minister later added that the float was intended as a temporary measure to halt the flight of capital from the country and to aid Mexico's stricken tourist industry. He stated that the government would probably reestablish an official parity with the dollar at a later date, but did not give any indication of when, or at what exchange rate, that might be done.

The day the president spoke was a bank holiday in Mexico, but the foreign exchange market in New York reacted predictably to the news. As one U.S. investor—who only the week before exchanged $80,000 at the eight-cent parity for deposit in a "guaranteed" 12 percent yielding peso account—bitterly observed, "the damned thing floated all right, just like a rock!" By the close of trading in New York, the peso had plummeted from 8 cents to between 6.4 and 6.9 cents without any indication at what rate the Bank of Mexico would intervene to support the peso the following day. Traders were shocked when the bank opened for business in the morning

---

[3]H. J. Maidenberg, "Peso Devaluation's Impact on Earnings," *New York Times*, October 5, 1976, p. 70.

and officials announced that it was ready to buy U.S. dollars at a rate of 20.40 pesos and sell them for 20.60 pesos, putting the peso at about 4.9 cents for an overnight devaluation of approximately 40 percent from the rate which had held for 22 years.

Little wonder that the U.S. investor who had opened a peso account a week earlier was embittered. His savings of $80,000, if they were to be converted back into dollars, would come to less than $50,000. The total value of such deposits in peso-denominated accounts, estimated before the devaluation at between $6 billion and $8 billion, were now worth in dollars 40 percent less. The same applied to the more than $3 billion U.S. corporations had invested in their Mexican subsidiaries.

The Mexican government and its creditors attempted to put the best possible face on the devaluation. Business persons and bankers in Mexico were reported to be enthusiastically in favor of the measure, hailing it as a courageous act on the part of the government. American bankers professed to be optimistic about the prospects for economic recovery, now that the necessary step had been taken. A European banker was less sanguine: "We knew this measure was bound to come, but we've been continuing to lend. And the large American banks—Citibank, Chase, and Bank of America—are in so deep here that they'll continue to lend."[4]

Everyone agreed, however, that the devaluation would lead to naught unless the government was able to contain its expected inflationary impact. Once again, all the right statements were made for the record. But actions speak louder. During the night of September 1–2, the price of a General Electric refrigerator on sale in Puerto de Liverpool, a leading Mexico City department store, was raised from 6,995 pesos to 8,300 pesos. That was but one example of the rush to lift prices which threatened to negate the intended positive effects of the devaluation.

The saga of Mr. X

So much for the big picture. What we are immediately concerned with is how the events of September 1–2 affected trading in Mexican peso futures contracts at the International Monetary Market. For an answer to that, we herewith recount the sorry tale of Mr. X. We cannot reveal his true identity, because when Mr. X agreed to be interviewed by *The Wall Street Journal* concerning his experience during that period, he did so with the stipulation that his name not be used. After all, he pointed out to *The Journal* reporter, "My name isn't a household word. I'm not Howard Hughes." In a less whimsical vein, he insisted upon anonymity to preserve what might have

---

[4]"Devaluation of 25% in Peso Is Expected to Bring Benefits to Mexican Economy," *New York Times*, September 2, 1976, p. 1.

been left of his business reputation. "How could anyone trust me as a financial consultant," he reasoned, "if they knew I can't take care of my own finances?" So, too, shall we respect Mr. X's request that he remain anonymous and proceed with the story in his own words:[5]

"A couple years ago I got sick and was lying in bed with nothing to do. I started playing with a calculator and figured out how I could make money on the peso. It turned out to be a very expensive illness."

Having accumulated a stake of $750,000 in earlier futures trading forays, Mr. X, by this time in partnership with his son, decided during the summer of 1976 that the time was right to plunge heavily on the long side of the peso. Placing orders through five different brokerage firms—any single firm would probably not have allowed such a large number of contracts in one trading account—father and son accumulated within a brief period 90 September 1976 IMM Mexican peso contracts. Each contract specified the delivery in mid-September of one million Mexican pesos worth, at the eight-cent parity rate, about $80,000. Mr. X had therefore committed himself and his son to accept delivery in September of 90 million pesos, or what was then the equivalent of $7.2 million. To do so, the Xs were required to post margin with the five brokers totaling $720,000, or substantially their entire trading capital.

When a friend telephoned on September 1 to tell him the bad news that the Mexican government was allowing the peso to float against the dollar and other currencies, Mr. X said that he "turned ice cold." He considered informing X, Jr., but decided against it. "Why should both of us go through a sleepless night?" he inquired of his interviewer.

What followed is a matter of record. Although the peso dropped in the spot market from eight to five cents in one sickening plunge on September 1–2, the daily price-fluctuation limit on the futures exchange drew the agony out over five trading sessions. The September IMM peso contract settled at .07990 on August 31, the eve of the president's speech. On the following day, with the news of the float public knowledge, peso futures were "down the limit." The September contract nominally settled at .07915, off the permissible 75-point daily price limit, although no trading took place during the course of that day's session. Nor was there any trading during either of the two days following, with contracts marked down an additional 75 points each day. Neither Mr. X nor any other unfortunate longs could have gotten out of their devastating positions during this period for love or money. There were no buyers at those prices, with spot pesos already down to .4900. The price anomaly was the result of the exchange's daily fluctuation limits. The rules called for expanded limits after three consec-

---

[5]Richard E. Rustin and Shirley A. Jackewicz, "No Mariachi Music, Please. Mr. X Isn't in a Fiesta Mood. Losses on Peso Futures Put N.Y. Speculator in Hole with Five Big Brokers." *The Wall Street Journal,* January 6, 1977. Permission granted by Dow Jones & Company to reproduce quotations.

utive limit moves, so that on September 7, the Tuesday following Labor Day in the United States, the September contract was allowed to fall 150 points, bringing it down to .07577. Finally, on September 8, with the daily limits dispensed with according to the rules, futures prices came into line with spot rates, the September contract plummeting an unprecedented 2687 points to settle at .04890.

During the course of that week the aggregate value of Mr. X's long 90-contract position sank proportionately by nearly $3 million—yes, million—on an investment or initial margin deposit of $720,000. As the contract price fell the limit each day, and Mr. X and his son were unable to meet the maintenance margin calls from the five brokerage firms where their accounts were being carried, the firms were committed to liquidating the contracts held in each account when trading resumed on September 8. After seizing collateral totaling $900,000 that remained in various accounts, the brokers were left with unsatisfied claims of $2 million or so, although at that point no one was worrying about a few thousand dollars either way.

Mr. X admitted that he had chosen to disregard the persistent rumors of an imminent devaluation of the peso. "I thought that if they were forced to do something, the worst they would do would be to impose external currency controls, limiting the amount of pesos anyone could take out of the country. Then, in mid-August, I saw a full-page newspaper ad by the Mexican government saying that everything was okay. I believed it. Looking back, that ad should have been my first warning signal," Mr. X said simply.

During the week following the devaluation, Mr. X confessed, "I really had problems with myself. I thought that I was an idiot and that I had lost my self-respect. But then I realized I had to go on living. I knew I had the resources to pay the debt eventually. This was the toughest loss I've ever suffered. But I'm tough, too. I'm not trying to chisel the brokers and I'm not going out the window. I lost the money, but I have nobody to blame but myself."

The rest of Mr. X's story involves his efforts to negotiate a settlement with the brokerage firms that were left holding the bag. Even with a $2 million uncollected—and quite possibly uncollectible—debt on their hands, the brokers admitted to a grudging respect for the way in which Mr. X was handling the situation. "If it were anyone else," said one, "we'd have sued a month ago." Treading very cautiously lest their actions push Mr. X into bankruptcy and eliminate any chance they might have of collecting on the debt, another of the brokerage representatives remarked sourly that, "If there is a moral to this story, it is that if you are going to lose in the market, you want to lose big."

As to Mr. X and his son, looking back on the unhappy episode, "We put in our own quote machine two weeks before the disaster. Now it sits there idly. We don't look at it because it's a reminder of unpleasant things."

The trading plan

The moral of Mr. X's story is, of course, not that it pays to lose big, but that greed untempered by a reasonable measure of fear is a prescription for, as he termed it, disaster. Greed, to be frank about it, is the motive underlying all speculation. But unless a speculator takes the precautionary steps necessary to restrain his impulse to make a killing, he is almost certain to suffer a fate similar to that of Mr. X, even if not on the same spectacular scale. The way to avoid such a catastrophe is to prepare, in writing, a formal trading plan before the first order is entered with a broker, and to follow that plan every step of the way. Failing that, a would-be trader may as well spare himself a lot of time and trouble by donating his money to a worthy charity. Then, he'll at least feel the satisfaction that comes from aiding one's fellow man.

A speculative trading plan is normally composed of two parts, the trader's budgetary guidelines and his decision rules. The former define the total amount it has been decided to commit to futures trading, and the portion of that total which might be allotted as margin for a particular trade. Having made these budget determinations, it is the decision rules which stipulate how the earmarked funds may best be deployed to obtain more profits than losses. That, remember, is the objective—to compile a good batting average rather than swinging for the fences each time you come to the plate.

The key question in framing your budget guidelines is not how much money do you want to make—we all want to make millions—but how much can you afford to lose? If Mr. X had in reality been Howard Hughes, he couldn't be faulted for dabbling in Mexican peso futures to the tune of a few million dollars. But he was not. To say that he, as non-Hughes, plunged into the market vastly over his head and had good cause for wishing to conceal his folly from his clients is understating the case.

An individual's capacity to speculate in currency futures or in anything else is a function of a person's total net worth and level of income, and of his or her penchant for risk-taking in general. There is no hard and fast rule concerning the proper percentage of an individual's net worth one should or shouldn't devote to financial speculation. That depends for the most part on one's personal circumstances—his or her family responsibilities and the like—as well as the relative attraction in terms of value of alternate commitments. Though it's an entirely arbitrary figure, a speculative limit of 10 percent of one's total net worth seems to have a common sense ring to it. That appears to be a substantial enough amount with which to assume sizable market positions, but one whose loss normally would not be a devastating one.

The next step in containing market risk within acceptable limits is to divide the total allotted trading capital into a distinct number of units. The idea is the simple one of not putting all your eggs—or pesos—into one basket. Mr. X went for broke in putting everything he had into pesos, and that is precisely what happened to him. Not only is it necessary to diversify the risk, but it's equally important to hold some portion of one's trading capital back as a strategic reserve to cushion the impact of such unforeseeable circumstances as the peso devaluation.

If, for example, $50,000 is the amount earmarked for currency futures trading, that figure might in turn be divided into 10 $5,000 units. Of these 10 units, 4 or 40 percent of the allotted trading capital, might be kept in reserve, leaving $30,000 for immediate commitments, or when suitable opportunities presented themselves. Which contracts, and how many of each, should be bought or sold with the six active units will depend in each case on the initial margin requirements set by the exchanges and brokerage firms. If the initial margin on Dutch guilder contracts is $2,500 per contract, for example, one trading unit may be used to buy or sell one contract, with the remaining $2,500 again held in reserve to meet any maintenance margin calls that may be incurred. Novice traders, during their period of apprenticeship in the market, should limit themselves to single-contract positions until they've gained sufficient experience with each of the various currency contracts to feel comfortable with larger positions.

The decision rules represent a trader's conscious and constant efforts to impose self-discipline, without which the market is in control of the trader, instead of the other way around, as it should be. The reason that most traders walk away from the futures market in disgust after losing money faster than they ever thought possible was because they allowed their emotions to govern their actions rather than their reason. The purpose of a trading plan's decision rules is to prevent a trader from falling victim to self-destructive impulses.

Planning with prices

The supposedly sacrosanct first rule of futures trading, which seems to have been stated and restated in every book written on the subject, is that a trader must without fail cut his or her losses short and let the profits run. If we introduce this cardinal rule with something less than the reverence it would appear to deserve, it is only because repeating it yet one more time is like quoting the Seventh Commandment inside what is known in sophisticated circles as a "Swing Club." In short, the rule about cutting losses short is honored primarily in its breach, which is precisely why most new traders climb out of the pit bloodied and vowing never to return.

Before initiating *any* position, whether it be a long or a short one, a trader should decide upon three prices which will define the tactics for that particular position: (1) the entry price at which the contract is intended to be bought or sold, (2) the loss limit price, at which a stop order would customarily be placed to prevent a loss from going beyond a predetermined amount, and (3) the price objective at which a trader plans to take a profit should the market move in the direction he or she anticipates. Some traders recommend entering a limit order at the latter price, while others maintain that it is preferable to keep one's options open. In either case, it is essential that a trader have a target price in mind—and have a good reason for changing it as market action unfolds. A commonly observed rule of thumb is that a profit objective should be three times or greater than the loss limit to warrant taking on any position.

To illustrate, if a decision is made to buy a British pound contract at 2.3000, with a sell stop order entered at 2.2500 to limit the prospective loss to $1,250, a trader should have a reasonable expectation of liquidating the contract at around 2.4500 for a gain of about $3,750. If this three-to-one profit/loss ratio is not realistic, the trader would do well, according to this decision rule, to bide his or her time and perhaps seek out another opportunity.

By this means of selecting in advance prices to meet any foreseeable contingency, a trader can to a great extent avoid having to make decisions under the pressure of adverse market behavior—in the heat of battle as it were—which is precisely the time at which anyone's judgment is most suspect. Another advantage to be gained from this approach is that it helps a trader to resist being carried along with popular sentiment, which invariably turns bullish as prices advance and bearish when they decline. The obvious lesson to be drawn from the fact that there are more traders who lose money on balance than those who make money is that it pays to go against the crowd. Like most market maxims, however, that bit of wisdom is far easier to preach than to practice.

When it comes to closing out a position at a loss, the rule is: the sooner the better. A long position that has declined—or a short one that has advanced—far enough to incur a maintenance margin call, has usually been allowed to go too far. If it has come to that point, the proper response almost always is to liquidate the position then and there, rather than depositing additional margin in the hope of buying time until a market reversal saves the day. This latter reaction usually falls in the category of wishful thinking.

It should be immaterial to a trader whether he or she assumes a long or short position as long as the position satisfies all of the trader's decision rules. Traders whose experience was gained in the stock market are almost always predisposed to be long, an attitude which will seriously reduce their chances for success if carried over into futures trading. Futures traders should also be more impatient than stock market investors. The higher degree of risk which the former assume requires their securing a higher rate of return, which is in turn a function of the speed with which positions are turned over, as well as the amount of profit on each transaction. Some successful traders go so far as automatically liquidating a position if it has not begun to show a profit after three trading sessions, on the grounds that the initial transaction was ill-timed. Should a trader, by faithfully following the decision rules, manage to increase the trading capital, he or she should resist the common urge to become a "big-time operator" by accumulating large positions, as Mr. X did, and continue to adhere to what has proven to be a successful trading plan.

Technical analysis

The two methods of evaluating currency values and of predicting exchange rate movements, which were discussed in Chapter 10, fundamental and technical, are essentially the same means by which a futures trader arrives at buy/sell decisions. But the emphasis in this instance is usually put on the technical approach, in that the time in which a typical futures transaction is completed is so brief, on average a matter of weeks.

An in-depth analysis of a particular currency may be important to a corporate hedge manager, say, but it is not a speculator's immediate concern. To be sure, when the news comes over the Dow Jones News Service or Reuters International Banking Wire that the prior month's trade balance in the United Kingdom was thus-and-so, the futures trader should know without hesitation whether that specific news item is bullish or bearish for British pound contracts. But in that regard, a glance at the price ticker or quote machine will tell the trader immediately all he or she needs to know as the "locals" who trade on the exchange floor leap to act on the news.

Of greater importance to the futures trader than, say, knowing the Bank of England's intervention policy, is being on the right side of the market, long when exchange rates are climbing, and short when they're dropping. That much is obvious, and sounds quite simple. But once again, judging from the lackluster performance—or worse—of most traders, there must be more to it than at first meets the eye.

Price trends can be tricky things, as the chart of the September 1980 IMM British pound contract in Figure 15-1 bears out. From January 28, 1980, the contract rose over the course of seven trading sessions from 2.2200 to 2.2820, after which it declined over the following eight days to 2.2450. The decline back to 2.2450 retraced about two thirds of the previous advance. With this sort of roller coaster price behavior, how does a trader know whether he or she is dealing with an uptrend or a downtrend and, therefore, whether to think in terms of going long or short? The answer in this instance is that the trader doesn't, at least not yet. It is only after the September 1980 British pound contract has reversed its direction again and then fails to surpass the earlier high settlement price of 2.2820 that the trader has the first intimation that the basic, or major, trend has turned downward. That intimation is reinforced when the subsequent pullback reaches 2.2000 by March 4, and, in so doing, penetrates the former 2.2200 low. Following the next rally to 2.2400, the trader can take a pencil and straight edge and draw a descending line between the two rally tops at 2.2700 and 2.2400. This line defines a major trendline and indicates the position a trader should maintain—in this case a short one, since the trend is down—until ample evidence is seen on his or her chart that the trend has reversed itself yet again. The contract price will continue to rise and fall, but as long as each successive rally, which we may now identify as a minor contrary trend, fails to rise over the trendline, the major downtrend is considered to be intact, and to be on the right side of the market means to be short. In the September 1980 British pound illustration, the downtrend carried to 2.1400, after which a two-day spurt back up to 2.1900 on April 7 and 8 was a decisive signal that a major trend reversal had taken place.

The reverse is true of a major uptrend. Each succeeding rally is interrupted, as a rule, by a minor retraction of several days' duration, after which the price ascent resumes to a new high level. In the case of an uptrend, the trendline is traced through the lows of each minor correction. As long as none of these dips penetrates the trendline, the uptrend remains intact, and the trader should maintain a long position.

Putting a plan into action

A major uptrend line is also referred to as a *support line*, since that is where, as long as the uptrend remains intact, minor downtrends will come to a halt. Likewise, it is known in the case of a major downtrend as a *resistance line*, because that is where the minor rallies tend to run out of steam.

With regard to the downtrend depicted in Figure 15–1, the picture is clear enough after the fact. Unfortunately, the trader on the spot doesn't have the benefit of hindsight. As seen from the trader's perspective, at what point on the chart would he or she have been justified on the basis of trend analysis in taking a short position? Certainly not at 2.2800, even though that is about the highest price on the chart, because the trader has no way of knowing at that point whether the major trend is up or down. Acting at 2.2700 would also have been premature since, short of confirmation, the downtrend is at that point merely a possibility. It's only after the September 1980 pound contract fails to recover to 2.2800 and resumes its decline that the trader may assume with some conviction that a major downtrend is underway, and thereupon move to establish a short position.

But at what specific price should the trader do it? At 2.2500? At 2.2200, or 2.2000? The longer the trader waits before acting—if a downtrend is indeed in progress—the lower the price for selling the contract. And the more the trader delays, the more likely he or she is to sell just before the market reverses into a minor uptrend. If the trader goes short at 2.2000 and his or her decision rules indicate entering a buy stop order

Figure 15-1

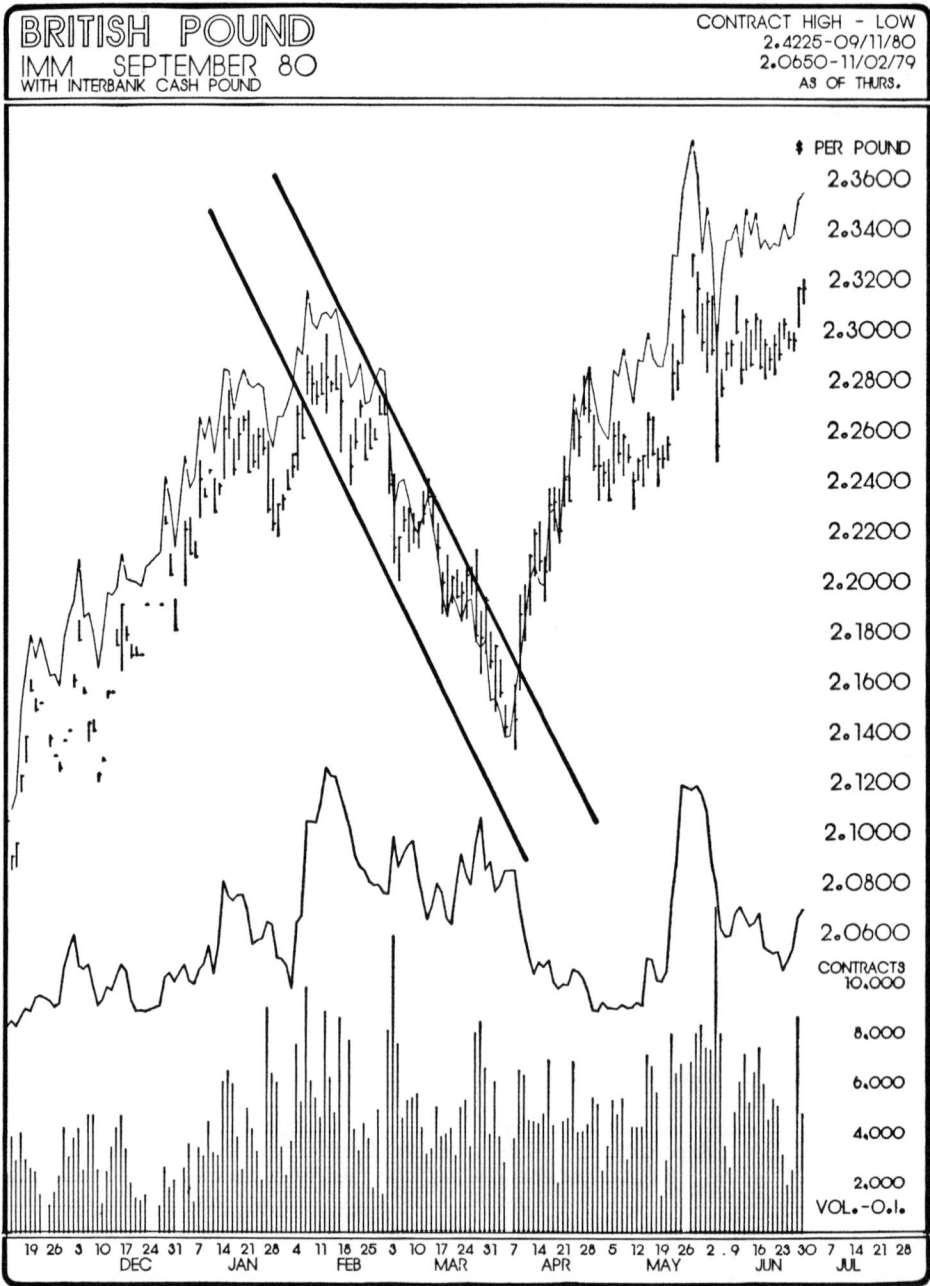

Source: *Financial Futures* (Chicago: Data Lab Publications, June 1980), p. 42. Reprinted by permission.

200 points above the entry level, he or she would be stopped out on the rally to 2.2400. The alternative would be to await a minor rally to the

resistance line and attempt to sell there. The trader might in fact place a limit order with his or her broker to sell the September 1980 pound contract at or just beneath the major downtrend line, at 2.2350, say, and at the same time instruct the broker to place a contingent buy stop order 200 points above the trader's projected entry point, or 2.2550. If in the event that he or she succeeds in going short at 2.2350 and the contract price continues to climb to the point where the buy stop order is activated at 2.2550, it will by that time be evident that major resistance has been penetrated, signaling a reversal of the major trend and indicating that it is time to be long rather than short.

By the same line of reasoning, the best point at which to establish a long position is at the uptrend support line, with a sell stop placed a predetermined number of points below the line. The continuation of a minor correction through and appreciably below the support line would signal a reversal of the major uptrend and alert the trader and his or her broker that they might be well advised to liquidate the long position then and there instead of waiting to be "stopped out" at the designated price.

Futures traders who adhere to decision rules based upon such trend analysis quickly find that their moves to go long or short are proven to be wrong about as often as they are right. Even so, by endeavoring to identify and then to trade with the major trend, they only need a .500 "batting average" to come away from the game as winners. That, ladies and gentlemen, is the secret—if there is such a thing—to successful trading.

If the trader is proven correct in establishing a long or short position at the initial point of entry and the market moves in his favor, he or she should move the protective stop, in either instance, below or above the market price, up or down to the next plateau indicated by the trendline. The purpose is to lock-in some of the profits that have accrued, but keeping the winning position in place as long as the trend remains intact.

On the basis of the foregoing, it is possible to add the following decision rules to the trading plan:[6]

1. Do not initiate or maintain a position that is contrary to the major and minor trends. Liquidate the existing position and, if budget considerations allow, consider assuming an opposite one—long to short or vice versa—as soon as there is confirmation of a major trend reversal.
2. A major trend almost always persists longer than most traders expect. Do not liquidate a winning position while the trend remains intact. Move the stop order in the appropriate direction and await a reversal as above.
3. A minor trend seldom lasts for more than seven trading days. Attempt to buy on minor trend corrections to the support line or, in a major downtrend, sell on minor rallies to the resistance line.

---

[6]Stanley Kroll and Irwin Shishko, *The Commodity Futures Trading Guide* (New York: Harper & Row, 1973), pp. 224–36.

4. The penetration of major trendlines by minor contrary trends are the most critical signals of a major trend reversal. It is at such points that a position should be initiated or reversed.
5. Trend reversals or resistance to major trends are most likely to occur at previous high and low prices or where the contract has in the past fluctuated within a narrow range for some time.

Spreading approaches

An alternate approach to futures trading, which is thought to entail less risk than outright long or short positions, but which is nevertheless regarded as speculative, is the technique known as *spreading*. Somewhat similar to the interbank-futures market arbitrage described in Chapter 11, this technique involves the simultaneous purchase and sale of different maturities of the same currency contract, or in some cases concurrent long and short positions in different currencies.

Intermonth spreading is the purchase and sale for different delivery dates of the same currency contract traded on the same exchange. Its purpose is to profit from changes in forward premiums and discounts. If, for example, the forward premium (contract price difference) between a September contract and the following March delivery is expected to grow wider, the appropriate action would be to sell (short) the September contract and buy March. If the currency in question were instead quoted at a forward discount, the procedure would be reversed, namely, buying September and selling March.

If, to revert to our earlier discussion of interest rate differentials between national money markets, the differential between the United States and Germany were expected to grow wider in favor of the United States, the forward premium on the dollar/mark exchange rate would expand accordingly. A spread position would therefore be in order, one involving the sale of a nearby contract and the purchase of a distant one. A narrowing of the interest differential, though, would entail a narrowing of the $/DM forward premium as well. In that case, the indicated spread positions would be long the near month and short the deferred one. If the expectation of a narrower forward premium were then realized, the nearby contract would appreciate by a greater amount than the distant one, or the distant would decline by more, depending upon the overall price trend for that particular currency, thereby creating a net profit for the spread trader.

An *intercurrency spread* consists, as noted earlier, of concurrent long and short positions in different currency contracts. For the two positions to be regarded as a bona fide spread, however, there must be what is believed to be a consistent relationship between the currencies involved. Going short Dutch guilders and long French francs would qualify as a spread because the two currencies are part of the European Monetary System—the expanded snake—and the respective governments have undertaken to hold the rates at a defined relationship to the dollar and therefore to each other. As we have noted before, however, these relationships have a history of coming apart when they are least expected to do so, thereby investing intercurrency spreads with a higher degree of risk than the intermonth variety, inasmuch as the interest rate changes, which are the basis of the latter, are less abrupt in nature.   France, for example, may suddenly decide to leave the snake, as it has done in the past, making the spread position described above as volatile as an outright open position.   It would, in fact, subject the spread trader to severe losses, because the franc would most likely drop sharply versus the guilder, an outcome directly opposite to what would have been anticipated if that particular spread position had in fact been initiated.

An *intermarket spread* involves opposite positions in the same or similar contracts traded on different futures exchanges.   This type of spread is also similar in concept to the interbank futures arbitrage.   But there is the important difference that contracts purchased on one exchange, such as the IMM in Chicago, cannot be used to satisfy a short position on another market, such as the New York Futures Exchange.   Moreover, there is sometimes a disparity in delivery dates on contracts for the same currencies traded on the two exchanges, which makes it impossible to take delivery on a contract in one market and immediately deliver the currency involved to satisfy a short obligation on another exchange.

The big question is whether an old dog of a stock market investor should try to learn the new tricks needed to play the currency futures game.   The answer is that he probably shouldn't—unless he can live with a split personality, which allows him to do with a (minor) portion of his investment capital what his stock market training has taught him assiduously to avoid with the bulk of his funds.   We would venture to say that most investors whose philosophy is to buy a good quality stock or bond and put it away would find it difficult to adapt to the very different rules by which the futures game is played.   But for those of us who have a little of Mr. X in our makeups, the thrills and chills—and occasionally the profits—probably cannot be matched elsewhere.

Appendix A

Bibliography

Author's note

There is an extensive literature dealing with foreign exchange and related aspects of international economics and finance. Books on commodity futures trading also are plentiful. Few sources, if any, combine the two fields in treating foreign exchange futures trading as a distinct topic, however, an information gap which prompted the writing of this book.

The earlier volume, *Interest Rate Futures,* contains a bibliography of books on the money and futures markets. The ensuing list includes, in my estimation, the most important books on foreign exchange currently in print.

Aliber, Robert Z. *The International Market for Foreign Exchange.* New York: Frederick A. Praeger, 1969.

───────. *The International Money Game.* New York: Basic Books, 1973.

Angell, James W. *The Theory of International Prices.* New York: Augustus M. Kelley, 1965.

Black, Stanley W. *Floating Exchange Rates and National Economic Policy.* New Haven: Yale University Press, 1977.

Canterberry, E. Ray. *Foreign Exchange, Capital Flows, and Monetary Policy.* Princeton Studies in International Finance no. 15, 1965.

Clarke, William M., and George Pulay. *The World's Money: How It Works.* New York: Frederick A. Praeger, 1971.

Coninx, Raymond. *Foreign Exchange Today.* New York: John Wiley & Sons, 1978.

Crump, Norman. *The ABC of the Foreign Exchanges.* New York: Macmillan, 1963.

Dreyer, Jacob S., Gottfried Haberler, and Thomas D. Willett (ed.). *Exchange Rate Flexibility.* Washington, D.C.: American Enterprise Institute, 1978.

Eckes, Alfred E. *A Search for Solvency.* Austin: University of Texas Press, 1975.

Einzig, Paul. *A Dynamic Theory of Forward Exchange.* London: Macmillan, 1961.

—————. *The Euro-bond Market.* New York: St. Martin's Press, 1975.

—————. *The Euro-dollar System.* New York: St. Martin's Press, 1974.

—————. *The Exchange Clearing System.* London: Macmillan, 1935.

—————. *Exchange Control.* London: Macmillan, 1934.

—————. *Finance and Politics.* London: Macmillan, 1932.

—————. *Foreign Balances.* London: Macmillan, 1938.

—————. *The History of Foreign Exchange.* New York: St. Martin's Press, 1967.

—————. *A Textbook on Foreign Exchange.* New York: St. Martin's Press, 1966.

Evans, Thomas G. *The Currency Carousel: A New Era in Monetary Affairs.* Princeton, N.J.: Dow Jones Books, 1977.

Evitt, H. E. *A Manual of Foreign Exchange.* London: Sir Isaac Pitman & Sons, 1965.

Fatemi, Nasrollah S. *The Dollar Crisis.* New York: Fairleigh Dickinson University Press, 1964.

Federal Reserve Bank of Boston. *Managed Exchange Rate Flexibility: The Recent Experience.* Conference Series No. 20, 1978.

Glahe, Fred R. *An Empirical Study of the Foreign Exchange Market: Test of a Theory.* Princeton Studies in International Finance No. 20, 1967.

Haberler, Gottfried. *Money in the International Economy.* Cambridge, Mass.: Harvard University Press, 1965.

Halm, George N. *A Guide to International Monetary Reform.* Lexington, Mass.: Lexington Books, 1975.

Heller, H. Robert. *International Monetary Economics.* Englewood Cliffs, N.J.: Prentice-Hall, 1974.

Holbik, Karel (ed.). *Monetary Policy in Twelve Industrial Countries.* Boston: Federal Reserve Bank of Boston, 1973.

Holgate, H. C. F. *Exchange Arithmetic.* London: Sir Isaac Pitman & Sons, 1961.

Isard, Peter. *Exchange Rate Determination: A Survey of Popular Views and Recent Markets.* Princeton, N.J.: Princeton University Press, 1978.

Kubarych, Roger. *Foreign Exchange Markets in the United States.* New York: Federal Reserve Bank of New York, 1978.

Krause, Lawrence B. *Recent International Monetary Crises: Causes and Cures and Fixed and Gliding Exchange Rates.* Washington, D.C.: Brookings Institution, 1971.

Merns, Stephen. *Decision Making on Exchange Rates.* Washington, D.C.: Brookings Institution, 1970.

Ohlin, Bertil. *Interregional and International Trade.* Cambridge, Mass.: Harvard University Press, 1967.

Prindl, Andreas. *Foreign Exchange Risk.* New York: John Wiley & Sons, 1976.

Quinn, Brian Scott. *The New Euromarkets.* New York: John Wiley & Sons, 1975.

Riehl, Heinz. *Foreign Exchange Markets; A Guide to Foreign Currency Operations.* New York: McGraw-Hill, 1979.

Rolfe, Sidney E. and James Burtle. *The Great Wheel: The World Monetary System, A Reinterpretation.* New York: New York Times Book Co., 1973.

Scammell, W. M. *International Monetary Policy.* New York: St. Martin's Press, 1961.

Solomon, Robert. *The International Monetary System, 1945–1976: An Insider's View.* New York: Harper & Row, 1977.

Stein, Jerome L. *The Nature and Efficiency of the Foreign Exchange Market.* Princeton, N.J.: Princeton University Press, 1962.

Wasserman, Max J., Andreas Prindl, and Charles C. Townsend, Jr. *International Money Management.* New York: American Management Association, 1972.

Yeager, Leland B. *The International Monetary Mechanism.* New York: Holt, Rinehart & Winston, 1968.

──────. *International Monetary Relations: Theory, History and Policy,* New York: Harper & Row, 1966.

Appendix B

Foreign exchange calculations

1. *Formula to compute purchasing power parity (PPP) exchange rates*

$$\frac{\text{Index number of prices in one country}}{\text{Index number of prices in another country}} \times \begin{array}{c}\text{Rate of exchange}\\\text{in base period}\\\text{between the}\\\text{two countries}\end{array} = \begin{array}{c}\text{Purchasing power}\\\text{parity rate}\end{array}$$

Example

Assume prices for the same product in countries A and B are both 20 in the base period when two units of country A's currency are equal in terms of dollars to one unit of country B's currency.

If, during a subsequent period, the product price in A increases by 50 percent while the comparable price in country B remains unchanged, the

---

Source: Max Wasserman, Andreas Prindl, and Charles Townsend, Jr., *International Money Management* (New York: American Management Association, 1972), p. 48.

new purchasing power parity rate between the two countries would then be $3 instead of $2, as follows:

$$\frac{30}{20} \times \$2 = \$3$$

A primary drawback of the purchasing power parity approach to exchange rate analysis lies in the difficulty of selecting the most suitable price index. Among the possible choices, there is no all-inclusive index which, through the application of the formula cited above, produces the "correct" exchange rate.

Another limitation of the PPP theory and resulting formula is that the exchange rate produced by the calculation applies only to those goods and services that move between the two countries involved. Moreover, the theory does not take into account exchange rate changes brought about by capital flows and interest rate fluctuations, except for the effect of the latter on general price levels.

Nor does the PPP theory explain exchange rate fluctuations due to underlying economic and technological changes, apart from their effects on the particular price indices selected as the units of comparison.

2. Formula to compute the effect of a change in the balance of payments (BP) on an exchange rate

The *balance of payments* is defined as the difference between the quantity of a country's currency demanded and supplied in international foreign exchange markets.

If the quantity of, say, Deutsche marks demanded exceeds the quantity of Deutsche marks supplied, there is a balance-of-payments surplus. If the supply of Deutsche marks is greater than the demand for them, there is a BP deficit, so that:

$$BP = Q_{DM}^D - Q_{DM}^S$$

Changes in BP$^{(d)}$ can be further expressed in terms of changes in the exchange rate d$/DM, so that:

$$\frac{dBP}{d\$/DM} = \frac{dQ_{DM}^D}{d\$/DM} - \frac{dQ_{DM}^S}{d\$/DM}$$

Example

Assume that the quantity of DM demanded increases by 5 percent while the quantity of DM supplied remains unchanged. In that case, the DM BP

Source: H. Robert Heller, *International Monetary Economics* (Englewood Cliffs, N.J.: Prentice-Hall, 1974), p. 28.

surplus increases by 5 percent, causing an equivalent increase in the $/DM exchange rate, hence:

$$\frac{DM\ 3\ billion}{.0250} = \frac{DM\ 63\ billion}{.50 + .0250} - \frac{DM\ 55\ billion}{.50 + .0250}$$

A DM 3 billion increase in a DM BP surplus will accordingly spur an increase in $/DM in the example from .5000 to .5250.

3. Formula to compute implied interest rate/forward rate parity

The future value (forward rate) of a currency is equal to its present value (spot rate) plus the interest to be earned on assets denominated in that currency over a stated period. (Conversely, by discounting that interest rate one can convert the currency's future monetary value to its present equivalent).

To illustrate, if the annual interest rate in Germany is labeled I_{Ger}, the value of Deutsche marks one year in the future ($DM_{1\ yr}$) is equal to their present value (DM_{Spot}) plus the accrued interest, i.e.:

$$DM_{1\ yr.} = DM_{Spot} (1 + I_{Ger})$$

The future value of the dollar is likewise determined by the interest rate prevailing in the U.S., i.e.:

$$\$_{1\ yr.} = \$_{Spot} (1 + I_{U.S.})$$

Dividing the second equation by the first produces the following equation:

$$\$/DM_{1\ yr.} = \$/DM_{Spot} \frac{(1 + I_{U.S.})}{(1 + I_{Ger})}$$

Example

If $I_{U.S.}$ is 12 percent and I_{Ger} is 8 percent and $\$/DM_{Spot}$ is 0.5000, the one-year forward rate would be:

$$\$/DM_{1\ yr.} = 0.5000 \frac{(1.12)}{(1.08)}$$

$$\$/DM_{1\ yr.} = 0.5185$$

Under the same conditions, the 3-month forward rate is:

$$\$/DM_{3\text{-mo.}} = 0.5000 \left(\frac{1.12}{1.08} \div 4\right)$$

$$\$/DM_{3\text{-mo.}} = 0.5046$$

Source: M. Kreine, *International Economics*, p. 37.

Thus, the present exchange rate is equal to its future (foward) counterpart when each currency is translated into its future value by the relevant interest rate.

4. *Formula to compute annualized percentage cost, or gain, of hedging foreign exchange exposure through the use of forward contracts*

$$\frac{\text{Forward rate} - \text{Spot rate}}{\text{Spot rate}} = \frac{360}{T} \times 100 = \text{Percent per annum}$$

where T is the number of days remaining to the maturity of the forward contract employed to hedge the corporation's exchange exposure.

If the exposed position calls for the sale of a forward contract priced at a discount to the spot rate, the above calculation will produce a negative figure that should be regarded as a hedging cost, while a forward premium under the same circumstances will produce a positive figure that is an incidental benefit.

A contrary position involving the purchase of a forward contract is construed as a cost when the forward rate is quoted at a premium, and as a gain when it is quoted at a discount.

Examples

a. Buying three-month forward Deutsche marks at .4624 to hedge a short position when the spot rate is .4577

$$\frac{.4624 - .4577}{.4577} \times \frac{360}{90} \times 100 = 4.10 \text{ percent per annum}$$

b. Selling six-month forward Canadian dollars at .8347 to hedge a long position when the spot rate is .8378

$$\frac{.8347 - .8378}{.8378} \times \frac{360}{180} \times 100 = 0.74 \text{ percent per annum}$$

5. *Formula to compute equilibrium in the foreign exchange and international money markets (ignoring transaction costs)*

$$\frac{I_d - I_a}{1 + I_a} = \frac{R_f - R_s}{R_s}$$

where

Source: Wasserman, Prindl, and Townsend, *International Money Management*, p. 120.

I = interest rates
R = exchange rates
d = domestic
a = abroad
f = forward
s = spot

Example

$$\frac{.12 - .09}{1.09} = \frac{.5260 - .5120}{.5120}$$

$$.027 = .027$$

When the equilibrium condition indicated above is reached, there will continue to be arbitrage transactions carried out to the extent necessary to maintain equality of interest rate and forward exchange differentials. If the arbitrage were to cease completely, differentials would reappear and the markets would return to a state of disequilibrium.

In keeping with Calculation 3, when the term structure of interest rates in two countries is known, it is possible to compute the forward premium or discount from present spot rates at which equilibrium would exist and further arbitrage transactions would not be profitable.

6. *Calculating foreign exchange translation and transaction gains or losses*

Exposure definitions:

Currency exposure and *translation exposure* are the exposure of an entity in any currency, including that entity's own currency. *Transaction exposure* is the exposure of an entity in any other currency than its own.

Foreign exchange gain (loss) formulas:

Currency gain (loss) = Currency exposure times the exchange rate change of the exposed currency.

Transaction gain (loss) = Transaction exposure times the exchange rate change of the exposed entity's currency.

Translation gain (loss) = Translation exposure times the exchange rate change of the exposed currency less the exchange rate change of the exposed entity's currency.

Source: Heller, *International Monetary Economics*, p. 46.

Example:

The German subsidiary of a multinational corporation has a pound sterling receivable equal to $100 when the Deutsche mark is revalued by 5 percent while the British pound is devalued by 10 percent.

$$\text{Translation gain (loss)} = \$100 \times .05 = \$5$$
$$\text{Transaction gain (loss)} = \$100 \times (-.10 - .05) = \$(15)$$
$$\text{Currency gain (loss)} = \$100 \times -.10 = \$(10)$$

Source: Euromoney Publications, *The Management of Foreign Exchange Risk*, p. 26.

Appendix C

Calendar and sources of statistical information pertaining to foreign exchange

UNITED STATES (monthly reports)

Reserves: Weekly New York (usually late Thursday or Friday afternoon).
Balance of trade: Usually on or close to 27th day.
Retail sales: First part of second or third week (when available).
Consumer price index: Usually 22d day or close to it.
Personal income: Usually third Tuesday or Wednesday.
Leading Indicators: Usually the 27th day or close to it
Real spendable earnings: Usually third Thursday or Friday
Reserve assets: Usually fourth Tuesday or Wednesday.
Unemployment: Usually first Friday.
Wholesale price index: Latter part of second week.
Budget: Usually fourth Tuesday or Wednesday.
Industrial production index: Usually 15th day.
Factory and durable goods orders: Several times each month at different times.
Money supply: Weekly on Thursday.

Source: Chicago Mercantile Exchange—International Monetary Market, *Understanding Futures in Foreign Exchange.*

Quarterly reports (available any time):
Gross national product
Productivity.
Balance of payments.

UNITED KINGDOM (monthly reports)

Reserves: First Monday or Tuesday of month (unless month starts midweek, in which case it would be first few days of month)
Retail sales index: First or second Monday.
Industrial production index: Third Friday.
Retail price index: Usually third Friday (sometimes fourth).
Balance of trade: Usually Monday or Tuesday of fourth week.
Unemployment: Usually Thursday of fourth week.
Base wage rate index/average earnings: Third Wednesday.
Import/export volume index: Thursday of fourth week (not always available).
Money supply: five-week banking period: Usually third week.
Quarterly reports (available any time):
Balance of payments.
Invisible earnings.
Consumer expenditure.
Gross domestic product.

WEST GERMANY (monthly reports)

Reserves: Released weekly midweek or last part of week.
Balance of payments: First part of first week (usually one or two days following the release of trade figures).
Balance of trade: First part of first week.
Cost of living index: Middle of third week.
Import/export price index: Usually first part of last week.
Industrial turnover: Usually first few days.
Unemployment: Usually sixth calendar day.
Wholesale price index: Usually fourth Tuesday (sometimes Monday).
Industrial production index: Latter part of third week when available.
Producer price index: Usually 20th day (unless that day is on a weekend).

SWITZERLAND (monthly reports)

Reserves: Weekly midweek or latter part of week.
Balance of trade: Usually on 17th or 19th day.
Consumer price index: Usually on the eighth or ninth day.
Wholesale price index: Usually second Friday (when available).
Retail price index: Usually second Friday (when available).
Money supply: First week.
Quarterly report (released any time):
Industrial production index

CANADA (information available usually late in afternoon)

Industrial production index: End of third week to first part of fourth week.
Balance of trade: End of third week to first of fourth week.

Reserves: Usually first Monday.
Unemployment: Second Tuesday.
Money supply: Weekly on Thursday.
Wholesale price index: Usually beginning of second week.
Quarterly report (available any time):
  Gross national product.

MEXICO (does not provide current information.)

JAPAN (monthly reports)

Balance of payments and trade: Usually on or close to 15th day.
Consumer price index: First part of first week (when available).
Industrial production index: First part of the last week (when available).
Reserves: Usually last day (sometimes first week of new month).
Wholesale price index: Usually on or close to 20th day.
Money supply: First week.
Annual reports (released any time):
  External assets.
  Gross national product

THE NETHERLANDS

(Does not report on regular basis and information usually is from several months past when it does come out.)
Unemployment: End of first week or second week.
Balance of trade: Monthly any time.
Wholesale price index: End of first week to end of second week.
Cost of living index: End of first week to middle of second week.
Reserves: Weekly on Tuesday.
Quarterly report:
  Balance of Payments

FRANCE

Weekly reserves: Thursday.
Retail price index: Last Thursday or Friday at month's end.
Industrial production index: Third to fourth week.
Money supply: First week in new month.
Unemployment: Fourth week.
Import price index: Third week.
Monthly reserves: Beginning of second week.
Balance of trade: End of second week to beginning of third week.

PERIODICALS, NEWSPAPERS, AND PAMPHLETS

The Wall Street Journal (Midwest edition).   200 W. Monroe St., Chicago, IL 60606. (D, M–F)
Journal of Commerce.   99 Wall St., New York, NY 10005. (D, M–F)
The Money Manager.   The Bond Buyer, One State St. Plz., New York, NY 10004. (W)

International News Letter. Federal Reserve Bank of Chicago, Chicago, IL. (W)
Monetary Trends. Federal Reserve Bank of St. Louis, St. Louis, MO. (M)
National Economic Trends. Federal Reserve Bank of St. Louis, St. Louis, MO. (M)
The Times of London. U.S. Address: 201 E. 43rd St., New York, NY 10017. (D)
The Economist. U.S. Address: 527 Madison Ave., Room 1414, New York, NY 10022. (W)
Euromoney. Euromoney Publications, Ltd., 14 Finsbury Circus, London EC2, England. (B)
The New York Times. 229 W. 43rd St., New York, NY 10036. (D)
Financial Times of Canada. 1885 Leslie Street, Don Mills, Ont. M3B 3J4, Canada. (W)
International Money Markets and Foreign Exchange Rates. Harris Trust and Savings Bank, 111 West Monroe St., Chicago, IL 60690. (W)
London Financial Times. 75 Rockefeller Plz., New York, NY 10020. (D)

Index

A

Above-the-line transactions, 94, 98
Accounting; see Bookkeeping methods
Accumulation account, 265
An Act to Provide for Obtaining Accurate Statements of Foreign Commerce of the United States, 91
Adjustable exchange parities (adjustable pegs), 20–21, 23, 40
Adjustment process of balance of payments, 97–102
Aliber, Robert Z., 270
Alpha, 213
American Institute of Certified Public Accountants, Committee on Accounting Procedures, 230
Amex Bank Limited, 188, 195–98
Apple Computer, Inc., 203, 205
Apuzzo, Anthony, F., 278
Arbitrage, 55–56, 59, 62, 64, 216–17
   banks, 217–19
Arbitrageurs, 209, 219
Argentarii, 5
Asset/liability management, 252
Atari, 203
Authorized retained foreign currency hold accounts, 265

B

Balance on current account, 94
Balance on goods and services, 94
Balance of payments, 7–8
   adjustment process, 97–102
   definition, 90, 300
   elasticity of exchange rates, 98–100
   equilibrium, 98
   forward rate structure of currency, 101–2
   history of, 90–91
   liquidity, 100–102
   U.S. statements, 92–95, 97
Balance of trade, 91, 102
Bancor, 19–20, 28
Bank (currency par value range), 21
Bank of Canada, 160
Bank of England, 29, 43, 45, 161, 174–75
   forward market, 101
Bank of Italy, 22
Bank of Japan, 43, 147

Bank draft, 263
Banker, 6
Banking, 91
Barter, 5–6
Basic balance, 94
"Bear raids," 29
Belgium
   currency devaluation, 26
   inflation indicators, 131
   inflation rate, 123–24
Below-the-line accounts, 95–96, 98
Beneficial disequilibrium, 26
Beta, 213
Bid (buying price), 53, 63, 210
Bilateral netting, 265
Bills of exchange, 6
Bi/Metrics, 195–98
Bookkeeping methods, 228–31, 235, 240
Bretton Woods conference, 13, 36, 42, 70, 101, 145, 158, 212
   Articles of Agreement, 20
   forecasting, 181–82
   inflation transmission process, 128
   issues, 18–20
   maintenance of exchange market, 161
   monetary reserves, 98
   United States renounces agreement, 32
British pound, 12, 68, 137, 153, 174–77, 197, 241
   currency contract specifications, 72
   devaluation, 130
   floated, 132
   forecasting exchange rates, 194
   hedge profit calculation, 274
   IMF par values in U.S. dollars, 21
   IMM currency futures, 220
   New York interbank forward market arbitrage, 220
   price trend illustration, 290–92
   rumors affecting exchange rates, 175
Brokerage commissions, 73
Brokerage firms, 78–79
Brown Brothers, Harriman, 188, 192, 196–98
Bullion Committee, 118
Bundesbank, 161
Butter and Egg Board, 48
Buying price (bid), 53, 63, 210

309

C

Calendar and sources of statistical information pertaining to foreign exchange, 305–8
Canada
  annual inflation rate, 123–24
  calendar and sources of statistical information, 306
  financial statistics, 108–11
  imports, exports, and reserves versus exchange rates, 106
  multicountry model of exchange rates, 144
Canadian dollar, 72, 74, 104–5, 160, 194–95, 241
  floated, 130
  forecasting exchange rate, 194
  hedging example, 249–50
  IMF par values in U.S. dollars, 21
  IMM currency futures, 220
  New York interbank forward market arbitrage, 220
Cash market, 48 n
Central banks
  intervention in exchange rates, 157–62
  strategies, 158–60
  techniques, 160
Certificates of deposit (CDs), 263–64
Charting approach to exchange rate forecasting, 184, 186
  value of, 200, 203
Chase Econometrics, 188, 196–98
Chase Manhattan Bank, 188, 196–97
Chemical Bank, 188, 196–98
Chicago Board of Trade, 48
Chicago Mercantile Exchange (CME), 48–49, 69–70, 192 n, 212
"Chinese walls," 187
Churchill, Winston, 12
Citibank of New York, 52–54, 187–88, 192, 195–98
Class A clearing member firm, 218
Class B arbitrage, 216–17, 223
  banks, 217
Class B clearing member firm, 218–19
Clean float, 38, 57, 129
"Cleared" market, 57
Clearing corporation, 72, 78
Closing rate method of bookkeeping, 228–29
CME; see Chicago Mercantile Exchange
CMT Tradecenter Corporation, 205
Cohen, Laurie, 217 n
Committee of 20, 44
Commodity Exchange, Inc. (Comex), 70 n
Commodity futures contracts, 47–48
Commodity Futures Trading Commission, 71
Commodity Systems, Inc., 205
Common Market; see European Economic Community

Computers, 203, 205
Comtrend, 205
Constitution of the United States, currency clause, 3, 8
Consumer price index, 133
ContiCurrency, 189
Continental Illinois Bank, 78
Contract points, 74, 79–80, 84, 216 n
Control Data Corporation, 205
Converging of spot and futures rates, 84
Convertibility of currency, 23, 27
Cost-of-living escalator provisions, 126
Cost-push inflation, 119–20
Cotton futures, 48
Covered interest arbitrage, 62, 154
Covering, 243
Crawling pegs, 45
Cross rates, 56
Currencies
  appreciation, 22
  convertibility, 23, 27
  depreciation, 16, 22
  devaluation, 22–23, 25–26
  fluctuations affecting business, 13–16
  parity rate, 21
Currency of billing, change in, 252
Currency futures market, 49, 69–81
  delivery mechanism, 78
  development of, 211–12
  exchange differences from interbank, 70
  foreign currency futures, 50
  margin requirements, 76–78
  prices, 74–76
  rates, 74
  relationship with interbank market, 209
  statistical comparison with interbank rates, 214, 220–21
  stock and bond market compared, 71
Currency price, 19, 25
Currency speculation, 38
Current accounting period (Period 1), 268–69
Current/noncurrent method of bookkeeping, 229
Cybernet time-sharing system, 205

D

De Gaulle, Charles, 27
Delivery financing risk, 218
Delivery risk, 217–18
Demand-pull inflation, 119–20, 128
Denis, Jack, Jr., 213 n
Denmark, 41
  annual inflation rate, 123–24
  inflation indicators, 131
Depreciation of currency, 22
Derivative gold standard, 23
Deutsche mark, 30, 35, 56–57, 74, 241
  currency contract specifications, 72
  floated, 130, 132–33
  forecasting exchange rates, 194, 198

hedging example, 246–49, 253–55
IMF par values in U.S. dollars, 21
IMM currency futures, 221
New York interbank forward market arbitrage, 221–22
rumors affecting exchange rate, 177–78
trend analysis of price movement, 200–203
use in international commercial payments, 67
Devaluation, 22–23, 25–26, 39
Digital Equipment Corporation, 203
Dirty float; see Managed float
Discount, 60, 83–86
Discount forward rate, 60
Discount futures contract, 85
Disequilibrium
beneficial, 26
fundamental, 22, 25
temporary, 25
Dollar, U.S., 21
asymetrical, 24
devaluation, 34–35, 132
glut, 26–27
inflation, 127
shortage, 26
use in international commercial payments, 67
Dollar convertibility, 30
abrogation, 32–34
Dollar lockbox system, 265
Dollar/mark exchange rate, 57, 61
Dornbusch, Rudiger, 142 n
Double hedging, 272
Dow Jones Banking Report, 107
Dow Jones News Service, 205, 290
Dufey, Gunter, 166 n, 168 n
Dutch guilder, 22, 72, 74
floated, 130, 133
IMM par value in U.S. dollars, 21
Dyna line, 193–94

E

Econometric approach to exchange rate forecasting, 183, 194, 199
Econometric modeling, 140–42, 203–5
monetarist approach, 204
monetary theory, 141–42
multicountry model, 144
portfolio balance model, 142
Economic risk, 227
monitoring, 237–39
The Economist, 308
Edwards, R. D., 200 n
Efficient market, theory of, 183, 185, 212
Elasticity of exchange rates, 98–100
Emery Air Freight, 279
Employment, 120
inflation, 120–21
England; see Great Britain
Entry price, 288

Equilibrium dollar/mark exchange, 57
Equilibrium exchange rates, 57, 302–3
supply-demand forces determining, 57–58
Equity, 77
Eurocurrency loans and deposits, 164
Eurocurrency Management Corporation (EMCOR), 193–94
Eurocurrency market, 164
loans and deposits, 164–65
significance, 165
Eurodollar, 164–65, 169, 171–72
Eurodollar certificate of deposit, 263
Eurodollar market, 29, 164
Eurodollar time deposit, 263–64
Eurofinance, 189, 193, 198
Euromarks, 164–65, 169, 171–72
Euromoney, 30
European American Bank, 189, 195–98
European Economic Community (Common Market), 40, 177
European Monetary System (EMS), 177–78, 294
European snake, 40–44, 295
Euroyen, 164
Evans, Thomas G., 39 n
Exchange parity, 20–22
Exchange rate, 7–8, 14, 52
attitudes and conventions affecting, 178–79
elasticity, 98–100
expectations affecting, 142, 163, 165–66, 169–71
floating; see Floating exchange rates
forecasting; see Exchange rate forecasting
government policy; see Government intervention in foreign exchange rates
inflation effects, 125–27
interest rate, 149–56
monetarist approach to, 140–42
risk, 46, 62
rumors affecting, 174
speculation, 65–66
three rates, 156–57
two-tier structure, 27
volatility, 45, 89–90
Exchange rate determination, general theory of, 165
Exchange rate forecasting
Bretton Woods system, 181–82
econometric approach, 183, 186, 193
independent consulting firms, 187
international banks, 186–93
judgmental approach, 184, 186, 195
multinational corporations, 266
performance records, 194–200
securities or commodities firms, 186–87, 193
technical (charting) approach, 184, 186
Expectations of traders, 163, 165
Export/import firm

hedging risks, 245
information requirements, 236
Exports, 7–8, 18, 89
Exposure netting, 251–52

F

FASB 8, 232–34, 276–77, 279
Federal Reserve Bank of New York, 160–61
Federal Reserve System, 31, 160
Ferro Corporation, 278
Figlewski, Stephen, 185 n
Figlewski model, 199
Financial Accounting Standards Board (FASB), *Statement No. 8*, 232–34, 276–77, 279
Financial Times of Canada, 308
Fixed bands, 20
Fixed exchange rate, 13, 16, 39
Fixed parities, 35–38, 42, 128
"Flat" execution of orders, 210
Floating (flexible) exchange rates, 13, 16, 28, 35–38, 150, 156
  currency speculation, 38–39
  difficulties for corporate financial officers, 277
  effects on international money management, 265–66
  financing subsidiaries, 265–66
  forward markets, 64
  inflation transmission, 128–29
Forecasting; see exchange rate forecasting
Foreign currency contract specifications, 72
Foreign currency futures, 50
  contracts on IMM, 71–73
Foreign exchange
  definition, 4, 52
  development of, 5–7
  rates; see Exchange rate
  theories of, 7–8
Foreign exchange calculations, 299–304
  balance of payments change affecting exchange rates, 300–301
  equilibrium in foreign exchange and international money markets, 302–3
  foreign exchange translation and transaction gains or losses, 503–4
  hedging forward exchange exposure through forward contracts, 302
  implied interest rate/forward rate parity, 301
  purchasing power parity exchange rates, 299
Foreign exchange market, 69
  attitudes and conventions, 178
  competitive, 54–55
  financial risk, 46
  forward market, 58–61
  futures; see Currency futures market
  government participation, 101

  interest rates, 61–63
  speculation, 45
  spot market; see Spot market
Foreign exchange risk, 225
  flexible rates, 265–66
  hedging, 243–52
  management tactics, 252–53, 265–66
  pricing policies, 252
  reporting system, 236–37
Foreign Exchange Service, 192
Foreign exchange trader, 54, 178–79
  expectations; see Trader expectations
Foreign trader multiplier, 122
Forex, 197–98
Forward covered interest rate parity, 155–56
Forward covering, 225
Forward discount, 101–2
Forward exchange contract, 47–48, 52
Forward exchange rates, 10, 58–61
  major currencies, 132
  margin quoting, 63–65
  prediction of future spot rate, 258–59
  premium and discount, 60–61
  pricing, 67–68
  six-month rate, 64
  speculation impact, 65–67
  supply-and-demand schedules, 65
  trader expectations, 166–67
Forward market, 58–61
  government intervention, 101, 159
  interest rate differentials, 65–65
  term structure, 64–65
Forward premium, 101–2
Forward price hedging, 48
Forward rate parity, 301
Forward swaps, 250
France, 12–13
  annual inflation rate, 123–24
  calendar and sources of statistical information, 307
  currency devaluation, 27
  joint economic float, 41
Frankfurter Allegemeine, 112
Franklin National Bank, 71
Freedman, Charles, 149 n
Friedman, Milton, 49
French franc, 12, 72, 241
  devaluation, 130
  IMF par values in U.S. dollars, 21
Full employment Act of 1946, 119–20
Fundamental disequilibrium, 22, 25
Future value of a currency, 301
Futures contract
  limited life, 73
  price, 70
  specification, 72
Futures contract hedge, 246
Futures market; see Currency futures market

Futures market in agricultural commodities, 47–48
FXS services, 194

G

General Agreement on Tariffs and Trade (GATT), 20
Geographic arbitrage, 59
German subsidiary balance sheet, 229–32
  closing rate bookkeeping method, 228–29
  futures hedge, 274–76
  monetary/nonmonetary bookkeeping methods, 228, 230–31, 235, 240
  working capital bookkeeping method, 229–30
German/U.S. trade model, 62, 199
Germany
  calendar and sources of statistical information, 306
  central bank intervention in exchange rates, 161
  currency devaluation, 26
  currency inflation, 40
  dollar dumping, 35
  imports, exports, and reserves versus exchange rates, 104
  inflation, 11–12, 123–24, 234–36
  interest rates affecting exchange rates, 150–52
  joint currency float, 43
  money supply growth, 143–44
  multicountry model of exchange rates, 144, 147
Giddy, Jan H., 166 n, 168 n
"Gnomes of Zurich," 29, 262
Gold, 5–6, 9, 92
Gold and the Dollar Crisis, 27
Gold exchange standard, 11, 20, 23
Gold parities, 9, 13
Gold points, 9
Gold pool, 28
Gold standard, 8–13
  Bretton Woods conference, 19–20
  pure, 23
Goldsmiths, 5
Goodman, Stephen H., 195 n
Government-to-government grants, 94
Government intervention in foreign exchange rates, 8, 139–62
  central banks, 157–62
  interest rates, 149–56
  monetary policy, 143–49
  strategies of intervention, 158–60
  techniques of intervention, 160–61
Graham, Frank, 40 n
Grain market, 48
Great Britain, 12, 19, 23, 41, 43–44, 90–91, 103–4, 120, 175–76

annual inflation rate, 123–24
calendar and sources of statistical information, 306
indicators of inflation, 131
interest rate versus dollar-pound exchange rate, 153
money supply growth, 143
Great Depression, 11
Great Society social program, 28–29
Gresham's law, 9
Grossman, Sanford J., 185 n
Guest workers, 134

H

Harris Bank, 189, 196–98
Hedge management team, 253
Hedging, 62, 65, 68–69, 302
  choice of market, 212
  costs, 256–57
  definition, 243–44
  double, 272
  forward covering, 225
  futures contract, 246, 269
  futures methodology, 258, 274–76
  international money management, 262, 266–67, 269–71
  monetary/nonmonetary method of accounting, 235
  tax considerations, 272
  transaction risk, 249
  translation risk, 249, 273–76
Heller, H. Robert, 58, 122, 300 n, 303
Henley Centre for Forecasting, 196–98
Herman, Tom, 233 n
Hernándes-Catá, Ernesto, 146 n, 147 n, 148 n
Herstatt Bank, 71 n
Hewlett-Packard, 203
Historic (monetary/nonmonetary) method of bookkeeping, 228, 230–31, 235, 240
Holland; see Netherlands
"Hot money," 25, 104
Hughes, Donald R., 278

I

IFC, 190
IMF; see International Monetary Fund
IMF band, 22
IMM; see International Monetary Market
Implied interest rates, 61–62, 301
Import/export firms, 45, 89
Imports, 7, 18
Income translation, 232–34
Indirect parities, 56
Inflation, 117, 133–36
  currency value, 36
  economic growth versus inflation control, 120
  exchange rate affected, 118, 125–27
  floating exchange rate, 37, 39–40

indicators, 131
nature of, 119
transmittal from one country to another, 127–29
worldwide index, 133
Initial margin, 70, 76–77
An Inquiry Into the Principles of Political Economy, 91
Institute of Chartered Accountants (Great Britain), Accounting Standards Steering Committee, 233–34
Interactive Data Corporation, 205
Interagency Committee on Balance-of-Payments Statistics, 96
Interbank forward market, 48, 69, 70
differences from futures exchange, 70–71
relationship with currency futures exchange, 209
statistical comparison with IMM rate, 213–14, 220–21
Intercompany account of a multinational group, 235
Intercompany term adjustments, 251
Intercurrency spread, 294
Intercurrency transfers, 265
Interest Equalization Tax, 28–29
Interest rate
differentials as help in forecasting, 185–86
Eurocurrency, 165
exchange rates, 149–50
foreign exchange, 62–63
forward rates, 63
monetary policy, effect on, 143
parity, 62–63
related to currency value, 264
Interest rate arbitrage, 216
Interest rate differential, 83–84
Interest Rate futures, 296
Interest rate parity, 61–62, 154–56, 168
Eurocurrency, 165
German and U.S. money markets, 63
Intermarket spread, 295
Intermediary company, 265
Intermonth spread, 294
International Bank for Reconstruction and Development (World Bank), 20
International banking, 91–92
International cash management, 262
International Financial Management (IFM), 192
International financial management, 261
flexible exchange rates, effect of, 265
forecasting, 266–67
hedging decisions, 269–76
intercurrency transfers, 265
methodology and objectives, 262–65
risk-control strategies, 267–69
speculation, 261
tax considerations, 271–73

International Financial Statistics, 106
International Monetary Fund (IMF), 20, 42
central bank intervention policies, monitoring of, 162
Committee of 20, 44
par values in U.S. dollars, 21
International Monetary Market (IMM), 48–50, 70, 212, 295
foreign currency contract specifications, 72
Mexican peso futures contracts, 284
speculators, 261
International monetary system, 8
International Money Management, 192
International Money Markets and Foreign Exchange Rates, 308
International News Letter, 308
International Telephone and Telegraph Corporation, 233
International transmission accounts, 90
Intervention band, 21–22, 158
Intsel Corporation, 279
Inventory, 231
Invoicing for foreign transactions, 67–68
Ireland, inflation rate, 123–24, 131
Italy, 22–23, 35
inflation indicators, 131
inflation rate, 123–24
joint economic float, 41, 44
lira, 21–22, 35, 44, 241

J

Jackewicz, Shirley A., 285 n
Jamaica meeting of IFM Committee of 20, 44
Japan, 31
calendar and sources of statistical information, 307
inflation, 123–24, 131, 135
interest rates affecting exchange rates, 152
money supply growth, 143–44
multicountry model of exchange rates, 144, 147
oil imports, 42–43
Japanese yen, 72, 74, 153, 241
IMF par values in U.S. dollars, 21
IMM currency futures, 220
New York interbank forward market arbitrage, 220
Johnson, Lyndon B., 28
Joint currency float, 40, 128, 177
Journal of Commerce, 307
Judgmental approach to exchange rate forecasting, 184, 194, 199

K

K percent rules, 184, 200
Kennedy, John F., 28
Keynes, John Maynard, 12, 19–20, 149, 163
Keynesian economic theory, 122, 136

"Kitchen sink" approach to exchange rate forecasting, 187, 191
Kreinen, M., 301
Kroll, Stanley, 293 n

L

Laffer, Arthur, 39, 41
Laffer-Mundell theoretical model, 39
Lag, 215–216, 251–52, 254, 272
Leads, 215–16, 252, 254, 272
Leaning against the wind, 158, 173
Letter of credit, 263
Letter-of-credit risk, 218
Levi Strauss and Company, 4, 16, 46, 61–62, 165, 168
Levich, Richard M., 185 n
Limit orders, 80
Limping gold standard, 10
Liquidity, 100
  definition, 101
  Lira, 21–22, 35, 44, 241
London Financial Times, 308
Long net position in foreign currency, 268
Long position, 53–54
Loosigian, Allan, 47 n, 79 n, 120 n, 141 n, 200 n
Loss limit price, 288

M

MacFie, Clyde A., 278
Magee, John, 200 n
Maidenberg, H. J., 283 n
Mail payment order, 263
Maintenance margin, 77
Managed float, 38, 43, 58, 129, 156
Manufacturing/service corporation, 236
Margin, 63, 70
  future trades, 73
  requirements, 76–78
Margin variation loan risk, 218
Marine Midland bank, 190, 198
Market efficiency, 183, 185, 212
Market order, 79–80
Market risk, 227
Marking to market, 77, 211
Marshall, Ray, 281 n
Marshall, Plan, 26, 94
Melamed, Leo, 48–50
Merchant banker, 6
Mexican peso, 72, 74
  IMF par value in U.S. dollars, 21
  speculation incident, 282–86
Mexico
  currency, 282
  peso speculation, 282–86
Momentum studies, 194
Monetarist economy theory, 122, 136, 143
  exchange rate determination, 140–42
  forecasting, 184
Monetary expansion as cause of inflation, 40

Monetary/nonmonetary (historic) method of accounting, 228, 230–31, 235, 240
Monetary reserves, 98
Monetary Trends, 308
Money, 3, 263
  international role as medium of exchange, 4–5 paper, 6
  values compared between countries, 3
The Money Manager, 307
Money market instruments, 263
Money-supply growth, 143–44
Moneychanger, 5
Morgan Guaranty Trust Company, 190, 192
Multicountry model (MCM) of exchange rates and monetary growth, 144–49
Multilateral netting, 265
Multinational corporations, 29, 45
  accounting reserves, 232
  economic risk, 234-35
  foreign exchange risk, 46–48
  hedging, 245–46
  reporting system, 236, 238–42
  typical exposure, 245–46
Mundell, Robert, 39, 41

N

National Economic Trends, 308
National Institute of Economic and Social Research, 137
Net liquidity balance, 96
Netherlands, 22
  annual inflation rate, 123–24
  calendar and sources of statistical information, 307
  inflation indicators, 131
New York Futures Exchange, 249 n, 295
New York Times, 14 n, 112, 308
Norway, inflation, 123–24, 131
N periods (accounting periods), 269, 271

O

OECD; see Organization for Economic Cooperation and Development
Offer (selling price), 53, 63, 210
Office of Foreign Direct Investment, 29
Official reserve transactions balance, 96
OPEC (Organization of Petroleum Exporting Countries), 42
Open stop order, 81–82
Organization for Economic Cooperation and Development (OECD), 43
  annual inflation rate, 123–24
  inflation transmission, 127–36
Organization of Petroleum Exporting Countries (OPEC), 42
Outtrade, 219

P

Paine Webber Mitchell Hutchins, 196–98
Paper gains, 77
Paper money, 5–6

Par of produce, 118
Patterson, Little and Desmartin, 190, 198
Pechiney Ugine Kuhlmann, 279
Period 1 (accounting period), 268
Personal Computer Commodity Analysis Group, 205
Phillips, A. M., 120
Phillips curve, 121–22
Pool account, 265
Portfolio balance model, 142, 159
Position risk, 218
Pound sterling standard, 10
Powers, Mark J., 49
Prakken, Joel L., 127 n
Predex Corporation, 191, 193, 195–96, 198, 205
Premium forward rates, 60, 83–86
Premium futures contract, 85
Prendergast, Maurice, 279
Price correlation, 212
Price objectives of trader, 289
Pricing foreign transaction, 67–68
  forward rate affecting, 67–68
Pricing policies in foreign exchange exposure, 252
Prindl, A. R., 238 n, 299 n
Productivity, 121
Progressive dynamics of a currency, 193
Purchasing power parity theory, 8, 36, 118, 126, 140–41
Pure gold standard, 23–24

R

Reserve currency, 23, 28
Reserves, 101-5
Residents, 90
Resistance line, 291
Reuters International Banking Wire, 290
Reuters International News Service, 107
Revaluation, 22–23
Risk in foreign exchange; see foreign exchange risk
Rolling over, 73 n
Roman Empire, 5–6
Roosevelt, Franklin D., 13
Rothschild, N. M., and Sons, 191
Round turn, 73
Rueff, Jacques, 27
Rueff plan, 27
Rumors affecting exchange rates, 174–78
Rustin, Richard E., 285 n
Ruzek, Raymond P., 279

S

Selling price (offer), 53, 63, 210
Shishko, Irwin, 293 n
Shook, Edgar, 49 n
Short net forward currency exposure, 268
Short position, 53–54
Short-term capital flows, 96

Silver, 5–6, 9, 91–92
Simon, William, 44
Six-month forward rate, 64
Smithsonian agreement, 34–39, 70, 132, 212
Spatial arbitrage, 55–56, 216
Speculation, 29, 38–39, 45, 48, 258
  currency, 38
  impact on foreign exchange rates, 65–67
  Mexican peso, 282–86
  multinational corporations, 261–62
  price planning, 288–90
  technical analysis, 290
  trading plan, 287–88, 293–94
Speculative runs, theory of, 184
Spot exchange rate, 166–67
Spot market, 48, 52, 55, 59
  central bank intervention, 159
  interest rate differential, 64–65
  rates, 60, 68
  supply and demand schedule, 64
  theory, 56–58
Spreads, 179, 214, 294–95
Statement of international transactions, 90
Steuart, Sir James, 91
Stiglitz, Joseph E., 185 n
Stock market, 71–74
Stock Market Software, 205
Stop order, 80–81
  straight or limits, 81
Subsidiary
  balance sheet, 229–31
  economic risk, 234–35
  German company, balance sheet, 253–55
  hedging by parent company, 245–46
  income consolidation, 232
  pricing policies in exchange exposure, 252
  risk assumed in borrowing, 264–65
  taxation, 272
Supply and demand
  elasticity, 98
  equilibrium exchange rate, 57–58
Support line, 291
Swaps, 59–60, 63
  forward, 250
Sweden
  annual inflation rate, 123–24
  currency devaluation, 26
  inflation indicators, 131
Swiss franc, 67, 72, 133
  IMF par values in U.S. dollars, 21
  IMM currency futures, 221
  New York interbank forward market arbitrage, 221–22
Switzerland, 29, 35, 41–42
  calendar and sources of statistical information, 306
  "hot capital" inflows affecting exchange rates, 104

imports, exports, and reserves versus exchange rate, 105
interest rates affecting exchange rates, 151–52
monetary growth, 143–44

T

Tandy Corporation, 203
Taxation
 exposure strategy affected by, 271
 profits and losses from foreign exchange transactions, 272
 subsidiary income, 272
Technical approach to exchange rate forecasting, 184, 186, 199
Technical-momentum studies, 194, 199–200
Technicians, 184
Term structure of forward rates, 68
Tew, Brian, 41
Time draft, 263
Time horizon for predictions, 240
 extended, 240
 spot rate evaluation, 241
Times of London, 308
Townsend, Charles J., 299 n
Trade acceptances, 263
Trade bills, 263
Trade deficit, 7
Trade surplus, 7
Trader expectations, 163–79
 simulation, 169–71
Traders' accounts, 78–79
Trading banks, 52, 54
Transaction risk, 226–28, 303-4
 bookkeeping treatment, 228-32
 definition, 303
 hedging strategy, 245–46, 249–50
Transfer pricing, 252
Translation of income, 232–34
Translation risk, 226, 228, 303-4
 bookkeeping treatment, 228-32
 definition, 303
 hedging strategy, 244–46, 249–50, 273–76
Treasury Department, U.S., 31, 91
Treaty of Versailles, 11
Triangular arbitrage, 55–56
Triffin, Robert, 27, 35
Trilateral arbitrage, 216
Two-tier market, 28

U

U.K.; *see* Great Britain
Unbiased forward theorem, 174
United Nations, 17
United States, 91
 calendar and sources of statistical information, 305–6
 conversion from debtor to creditor nation, 92
 imports, exports, and reserves versus exchange rates, 107
 inflation, 133–34
 interest rates affecting exchange rate, 154, 156
 international balance of payments, 97
 money supply growth, 143–44
 multicountry model of exchange rates, 144, 146
U.S. Department of Commerce, 96
U.S. Tobacco Company 278
U.S. Treasury Department 31, 91
 intervention in exchange rate determination, 160
Usury laws, 6

V

Value date, 53
Value days, 263
Versailles, Treaty of, 11
Vietnam War, 28, 134

W

Wage-price inflationary spiral, 119
Wages, 126
Waldner and Company, 191, 193
Wall Street Journal, 14 n, 44, 74, 112, 173, 284, 307
Wanniski, Jude, 39 n
Wasserman, Max, 299 n
Wheatley, John, 118
White plan, 19–20
Willett, O. O., 40 n
Working capital method of bookkeeping, 228–30
World Bank (International Bank for Reconstruction and Development), 20
World War I, 92
World War II, 119
Worldwide inflation index, 133